CONTENTS

INTRODUCTION **1**
The Dantes Subject Standardized Tests 1
A List of Dantes Subject Standardized Tests 3
Overview of Tests Covered in this Book 4
Preparing for a DSST 6
Test-Taking Skills 8

BUSINESS MATHEMATICS **13**
Pretest 13
    Pretest Answers 17
General Overview 19
    Number Sense 19
    Algebra 20
    Business Applications 26
    Financial Mathematics 32
    Sample Questions 35
    Practice Set 36
    Practice Set Answers 38
Posttest 39
    Posttest Answers 50

ETHICS IN AMERICA **55**
Pretest 55
    Pretest Answers 59
General Overview 61
    Ethical Traditions 61
    Ethical Issues 72
    Ethical Decision Making 76
    Sample Questions 78
    Practice Set 79
    Practice Set Answers 81
Posttest 82
    Posttest Answers 93
    Case Study #1 97
    Case Study #2 99
    Case Study Answers 101

CONTENTS

HUMAN RESOURCE MANAGEMENT

Pretest 103

    Pretest Answers 108

General Overview 110

    Introduction 110

    General Employment Issues 110

    Job Analysis 113

    Training and Development 113

    Performance Appraisals 115

    Motivation, Communication, and Leadership 117

    Compensation 117

    Security Issues 121

    Legal Issues 122

    Labor Relations 124

    Current Issues and Trends 126

    Sample Questions 128

    Practice Set 129

    Practice Set Answers 131

Posttest 132

    Posttest Answers 143

INTRODUCTION TO BUSINESS 149

Pretest 149

    Pretest Answers 153

General Overview 154

    Economic Issues Affecting Business 154

    International Business 156

    Government and Business 157

    Forms of Business Ownership 158

    Small Business, Entrepreneurship, and Franchises 159

    The Management Process 160

    Human Resource Management 162

    Production and Operations Management 164

    Marketing Management 164

    Financial Management 167

    Risk Management and Insurance 169

    Management Information Systems and Accounting 169

    Sample Questions 171

    Practice Set 172

    Practice Set Answers 174

Posttest 175

    Posttest Answers 185

dsst
Dantes Subject Standardized Tests

Get College Credit!

dsst

The Offic[ial] [...] [G]uide

Business M[...] [...]ng
Human Res[...] [...]s
Organizational Beh[...] [...]pervision

THOMSON

PETERSON'S

Australia • Canada • Mexico • Singapore • Spain • United Kingdom • United States

About The Chauncey Group International

Founded in 1996, The Chauncey Group International is a subsidiary of Educational Testing Service (ETS®). The Chauncey Group and ETS share over 25 years of experience in designing, developing, and administering occupational certification and professional assessment programs. We have helped our customers define the competencies required for a variety of types of work and measure those competencies effectively and fairly. We are recognized as an industry leader in designing state-of-the-art assessment systems that meet professional testing standards. The Chauncey Group administers certification and licensure programs in 82 countries throughout the world. The Chauncey Group is headquartered in Princeton, New Jersey with offices in Washington, D.C., and Paris.

About Thomson Peterson's

About The Thomson Corporation and Peterson's

Thomson Peterson's (www.petersons.com) is a leading provider of education information and advice, with books and online resources focusing on education search, test preparation, and financial aid. Its Web site offers searchable databases and interactive tools for contacting educational institutions, online practice tests and instruction, and planning tools for securing financial aid. Thomson Peterson's serves 110 million education consumers annually.

About the Chauncey ● Peterson's Partnership

The Chauncey Group International/Peterson's alliance is a model agreement for producing quality products and services to help people achieve their goals. With Peterson's print production capabilities, focus on the Internet, and distribution channels, The Chauncey Group can bring greater awareness of the opportunity for people to obtain college credit for what they have learned in non-traditional ways. By jointly publishing a guide with the same company that administers the test, Peterson's can give its customers a superior product that is the only "official" DSST preparation resource.

Visit www.Chauncey.com (click on "continuing education/distance learning").

For more information, contact Peterson's, 2000 Lenox Drive, Lawrenceville, NJ 08648; 800-338-3282; or find us on the World Wide Web at www.petersons.com/about.

CONTENTS

ORGANIZATIONAL BEHAVIOR **189**

   Pretest 189

      Pretest Answers 193

   General Overview 195

      Overview 195

      Individual Processes and Characteristics 196

      Interpersonal and Group Processes and

          Characteristics 202

      Organizational Processes and Characteristics 208

      Change and Development 212

      Sample Questions 214

      Practice Set 215

      Practice Set Answers 217

   Posttest 218

      Posttest Answers 228

PERSONAL FINANCE **233**

   Pretest 233

      Pretest Answers 237

   General Overview 238

      Overview 238

      Credit and Debt 240

      Major Purchases 244

      Taxes 246

      Insurance 248

      Investments 250

      Estate Planning 254

      Sample Questions 256

      Practice Set 257

      Practice Set Answers 259

   Posttest 260

      Posttest Answers 270

PRINCIPLES OF FINANCIAL ACCOUNTING **275**

   Pretest 275

      Pretest Answers 279

   General Overview 281

      General Concepts and Principles 281

      Types of Accounts 282

      The Accounting Equation 283

      Transaction Analysis 284

      The Accounting Cycle 285

CONTENTS

Adjusting Entries 286
Merchandising Transactions. 288
Internal Control and Cash 288
Current Assets. 290
Plant Assets 293
Current and Long-Term Liabilities 294
Capital Stock, Retained Earnings, and Dividends 296
Financial Statements. 296
Sample Questions 299
Practice Set. 300
Practice Set Answers. 302
Posttest 303
Posttest Answers 316

PRINCIPLES OF SUPERVISION 321
Pretest. 321
Pretest Answers 325
General Overview 327
The Supervisor's Roles and Responsibilities 327
Management Functions 330
Other Topics of Concern to Supervisors 342
Sample Questions 345
Practice Set. 346
Practice Set Answers. 348
Posttest 349
Posttest Answers 361

DANTES SUBJECT STANDARDIZED TESTS 367
Fact Sheets/Study Guides. 367
Business Mathematics. 368
Ethics in America. 372
Human Resource Management 377
Introduction to Business 381
Organizational Behavior 384
Personal Finance 389
Principles of Financial Accounting 393
Principles of Supervision 397

Introduction

THE DANTES SUBJECT STANDARDIZED TESTS

Many adults have acquired the knowledge taught in college-level courses through reading, independent self-study, correspondence courses, on-the-job experience, or just through living. To earn college credit for knowledge acquired by nontraditional means, you can take one or more DANTES Subject Standardized Tests (DSSTs).

WHAT ARE THE DSSTs?

The DSSTs are examinations offered by The Chauncey Group International, a subsidiary of Educational Testing Service. DSSTs are used by colleges and universities and the U.S. Department of Defense. More than 1,400 colleges and universities nationwide use scores on the DSSTs to award credit for more than thirty-five courses in business, the humanities, social science, mathematics, physical science, and applied technology. A complete list of DSSTs appears on page 3.

The DSSTs are similar to the final exams given in many college courses. Most of the DSSTs consist entirely of questions in multiple-choice format. Some of the tests have other types of questions, such as yes/no questions or essays. To pass the public speaking exam, you have to give a speech as well as take a multiple-choice test.

THE BENEFITS OF TAKING DSSTs

Low-cost college credit is the main benefit of taking DSSTs. Passing a DSST exam is a convenient, relatively fast, and inexpensive way of earning college credit. Earning credit through DSSTs can help you

- gain admission to a college program,
- shorten the amount of time it takes to get a degree, or
- fill in any gaps in your course requirements.

Using the DSSTs to earn college credit is particularly attractive for people who don't want to take time off the job to take college courses. The money you save on tuition for lower-level courses can be spent on enrollment in upper-level courses.

The Cost of Taking DSSTs

The fee to take a DSST is $35 per exam plus any administrative costs incurred by the administering institution. The DSSTs are administered year-round by colleges and universities throughout the United States and overseas.

Further Information

The Chauncey Group International posts a great deal of information about the DSSTs on its Web site. You can find information about each test, the DSST (*DANTES Subject Standardized Test*) *Candidate Bulletin*, a directory of colleges that administer and accept DSST results, and technical data on the methods used for scoring the exams on the Web site. You can

- check the Chauncey Group Web site at www.chauncey.com/dantes.html
- e-mail dantes@chauncey.com or
- call 877-471-9860 for more information.

Military personnel on active duty can get further information about the exams from the DANTES Web site at www.voled.doded.mil/dantes/exam or by e-mailing exams@voled.doded.mil.

A LIST OF DANTES SUBJECT STANDARDIZED TESTS

In the following table, you will find all the courses for which a DANTES Subject Standardized Test is offered. The exams for which preparation material is included in this book are *italicized*. You can obtain Fact Sheets for any of the exams at the Chauncey Group International web site, www.chauncey.com/dantes-fact.html.

Course	Credit Hours*	Minimum Score†
Applied Technology		
Technical Writing	3B	46
Business		
Principles of Finance	3BU	46
Principles of Financial Accounting	3B	49
Human Resource Management	3B	46
Organizational Behavior	3B	48
Principles of Supervision	3B	46
Business Law II	3BU	52
Introduction to Computing	3B	47
Introduction to Business	3B	46
Money and Banking	3BU	48
Personal Finance	3B	46
Management Information Systems	3BU	46
Business Mathematics	3B	48
Humanities		
Ethics in America	3B	46
Introduction to World Religions	3B	49
Principles of Public Speaking	3B	47‡
Mathematics		
Fundamentals of College Algebra	3B	47
Principles of Statistics	3B	48
Physical Science		
Astronomy	3B	48
Here's to Your Health	3B	48
Environment and Humanity: The Race to Save the Planet	3B	46
Principles of Physical Science I	3B	47
Physical Geology	3B	46
Social Science		
Art of the Western World	3B	48
Contemporary Western Europe: 1946-1990	3B	48
An Introduction to the Modern Middle East	3B	44
Human/Cultural Geography	3B	48
Rise and Fall of the Soviet Union	3BU	45
A History of the Vietnam War	3B	49
The Civil War and Reconstruction	3BU	47
Foundations of Education	3B	46
Lifespan Developmental Psychology	3B	46
General Anthropology	3B	47
Drug and Alcohol Abuse	3BU	49
Introduction to Law Enforcement	3B	45
Criminal Justice	3B	49
Fundamentals of Counseling	3B	45

* B = Baccalaureate program; BU = Baccalaureate program upper division.

† These are scaled, not raw scores, with a scale from 20 to 80. The minimum credit-awarding score is equal to the mean score of students in the norming sample who received a grade of C in the course. Some schools may require a higher score.

‡ In addition to a minimum score of 47 on the multiple-choice test, an examinee must also receive a passing grade on the speech.

OVERVIEW OF TESTS COVERED IN THIS BOOK

BUSINESS COURSES

Principles of Financial Accounting

This exam tests knowledge of accounting principles, the accounting equation, transaction analysis, and financial statements. It contains 73 multiple-choice items, and the American Council on Education recommends that credit be awarded for a minimum scaled score of 49. Since about 40 percent of the questions require that you solve specific accounting problems, your knowledge of accounting needs to be fairly detailed.

Human Resource Management

This exam covers the basic management, employment, and legal issues relating to human resource management (personnel management). It consists of 99–100 multiple-choice items, depending on the form taken; credit is recommended for students who achieve a scaled score of 46. The emphasis is on basic terms, facts, and concepts.

Organizational Behavior

This exam covers the field of organizational behavior, including its history and research approaches; the role that individuals and groups play in organizations; and organizations as a whole. Its multiple-choice questions focus on basic facts, terms, principles, and concepts. Credit is recommended for a scaled score of 48.

Principles of Supervision

This exam tests knowledge of the supervisor's role in an organization, including the supervisor's responsibility to carry out the five basic management functions. It contains 85–86 multiple-choice items, depending on the form taken, and credit is recommended for those who achieve a scaled score of 46. More than half of the questions test knowledge of concepts and principles.

Introduction to Business

This test covers the introductory business course, which includes types of economic systems, types of business ownership, and basic business functions like production and marketing. It contains 100 multiple-choice items, and credit is recommended for a scaled score of 46. Most of the questions focus on basic facts, terms, principles, and concepts.

Personal Finance

This exam tests knowledge of basic financial matters relevant to individuals and households: financial goals and budgets, credit, consumer information, housing, taxes, insurance, investments, and retirement. It contains 98 items, and credit is recommended for a scaled score of 46. About one fifth of the items involve specific personal finance problems; the remainder focus on terms, facts, concepts, and principles.

Business Mathematics

This exam covers basic algebra, statistics, and business applications of mathematics. It contains 54–59 multiple-choice items, depending on the form taken, and credit is recommended for a scaled score of 48. Many of the items involve solving math problems.

HUMANITIES
Ethics in America

This exam tests knowledge of the Western ethical tradition and the ability to apply moral reasoning to specific situations. Unlike the other exams covered in this book, the Ethics in America exam includes yes/no questions and an essay question in addition to multiple-choice items. It contains 110–111 multiple-choice items, depending on the form taken, and an optional essay. The essay question requires you to analyze a moral problem, propose alternate solutions backed up by moral reasoning, and come to a conclusion about the right course of action. Credit is recommended for a scaled score of 46 on the multiple-choice section. The essay is not scored by the Chauncey Group but is forwarded to your college or university for grading.

Course	Credit Hours*	Minimum Score†	See Pages
Business			
Business Mathematics	3B	48	13–54
Human Resource Management	3B	46	103–147
Introduction to Business	3B	46	149–188
Organizational Behavior	3B	48	189–231
Personal Finance	3B	46	233–273
Principles of Financial Accounting	3B	49	275–320
Principles of Supervision	3B	46	321–365
Humanities			
Ethics in America	3B	46	55–101

* B = Baccalaureate program; BU = Baccalaureate program upper division.

† These are scaled, not raw scores, with a scale from 20 to 80. The minimum credit-awarding score is equal to the mean score of students in the norming sample who received a grade of C in the course. Some schools may require a higher score.

PREPARING FOR A DSST

There are a number of things you can do to ensure success in taking a DSST and receiving credit.

CHECKING WITH YOUR SCHOOL

Before you register for an exam or start any other preparations, you should check with your college or university to make sure that it recognizes the DSST program and awards credit for passing scores.

If you have already enrolled, your academic adviser can help you find out any relevant information. If you are applying, or just thinking of applying, check with the admissions office for help.

GETTING THE EXAM FACT SHEET

The Chauncey Group International publishes a Fact Sheet for each exam. The Fact Sheet describes the exam and its scoring, outlines the course content that will be tested, provides a list of references for studying, and gives a sample of test items and answers for practice.

Fact Sheets for the eight courses covered here are included in the book. Fact Sheets for other courses may be downloaded at no cost from the Chauncey Group International Web site at www.chauncey.com/dantes-fact.html. If you would prefer, you can e-mail Chauncey at dantes@chauncey.com or call 609-720-6740 for more information.

ASSESSING YOUR READINESS

If you are taking one of the eight exams covered in this book, take the pretest to assess your readiness for taking an exam in the subject. Then use the course summary to refresh your memory about the course contents, and take the remaining practice test and the posttest to thoroughly familiarize yourself with the types of items that will be on the exam.

If you are taking one of the exams that is not covered in this book, use the Fact Sheet as your resource. Review the course outline and take the sample test in the Fact Sheet.

If, after assessing how well you did, you feel you can pass the exam without further preparation, good luck! However, most people will need to do at least some studying.

OBTAINING STUDY MATERIALS

Each Fact Sheet contains a list of textbooks or other resource materials that can be used to study for an exam. For most courses, any standard college-level text in the subject is appropriate. Just check that the text's table of contents covers most of the course content as outlined on the Fact Sheet. You can check with your school to see which text it uses for a particular course and buy a copy at the school bookstore or pick up texts on the subject at the library.

You can also use trade books (books published for the general reader, not specifically for students) to prepare for your exam. However, if the course is one that does have texts written for it, you should use a text rather than a trade book to prepare. Texts are written specifically to teach, and their presentation is generally very clear: important concepts and terms are highlighted, and all the appropriate topics are covered in a logical and methodical way.

STUDYING

It hardly needs to be said that you can improve your score on a DSST exam by studying. These are tests of knowledge, so the more you know the better you will do.

Studying Over a Period of Time

Since the DSSTs are primarily objective tests of recall, it is best to set up a study schedule that allows you to read or skim the course material over several weeks, in one- or two-hour sessions. This will give you time to absorb a lot of information gradually and fix it in your long-term memory.

Doing Practice Problems

If you are taking an exam, such as mathematics or accounting, that will require you to solve problems, you should do practice problems. Most texts have answers in the back so you can check your work. Finally, if there are important formulas, memorize them.

Cramming

Cramming is not an effective way to learn or remember the content of an entire course, so avoid it if you can. However, if you must cram, you should be realistic about how much you can absorb in such a short amount of time. It is impossible to read an entire text in an evening, so you will have to be selective; read the chapter outlines and the end-of-chapter summaries. Study the key terms, which are usually boldfaced and often displayed in the margins of a chapter or collected at the end of the chapter. Then, if you have more time, you can go back and skim the entire text.

TEST-TAKING SKILLS
PREPARING YOURSELF MENTALLY

Thorough preparation is the best antidote for test anxiety. If you have done the practice test(s) and studied the text or other resource material, you will have an excellent idea of what will be covered on the test. In addition, you will be familiar with the types of questions, the directions, and so on. This knowledge should do a lot to alleviate test-related stress.

PREPARING YOURSELF PHYSICALLY

There's a lot you can do to prepare for taking the exam:

- Get a good night's sleep the night before the test.
- Don't drink too many caffeinated beverages that morning. They will only leave you feeling jumpy.
- Dress in layers so you will be prepared for a range of room temperatures.
- Check that you have everything you will need to take the exam: pencils, pens, scratch paper, watch, admission ticket, and proper identification.
- Leave yourself extra time to get to the testing site. It's better to get there 15 to 20 minutes early than just in time or even late.

TAKING THE EXAM
General Strategies

Here are some general test-taking strategies that may help improve your score.

- **Skim the test first.** Before you start answering any questions, quickly look over the entire exam. Note the types and number of items.
- **Read the directions carefully.** Be sure you know exactly what you are expected to do. Must you answer all the questions, or do you have a choice (as in responding to one essay question out of several)? If the test has more than one section, note the relative weight of each section in terms of the score. Be sure you understand how you are expected to mark the answer sheet.

- **Pace yourself**. Figure out how fast you'll have to work. For example, if the exam has 50 items and you have 90 minutes to complete it, you can spend almost 2 minutes per item. Remember to allocate your time according to the value of the questions. So, for example, if an essay is worth one third of the score, don't leave it for the last 5 minutes. If you finish early, don't leave—use the extra time to look over the exam.

- **Don't get bogged down.** If you find you are stuck on a particular item, don't dwell on it. Instead, put a mark beside it and move on. After you have answered all the "easy" questions, you can go back to the ones you have marked and try them again. Just make sure you skip that item on the answer sheet, too, otherwise your answer sheet will be wrong from that item on.

- **Guess.** You are not penalized for wrong answers to multiple choice and other nonessay items on the DSSTs. So guess—don't leave the answer blank.

- **Relax.** If you start to get nervous, stop for a moment. Take a few deep breaths and relax.

- **Check the exam.** If you have time, go over the exam, making sure the answers are clearly marked. Redo any calculations you made to check their accuracy. However, don't be too quick to change your answers. Often the first answer you choose is the correct one.

Strategies for Multiple-Choice Items

Here are some suggestions for answering multiple-choice questions.

- **Read the question carefully.** Don't make the mistake of concluding that you know what a question is asking after reading just a few words. Read the entire question carefully, making sure you understand it.

- **Answer the question before reading the options.** After reading the question, does an answer pop into your head even before you read the choices? If so, that answer is probably correct. Look for it when you read the options.

- **Eliminate any wrong answers.** You have a one in four chance of picking the correct answer to multiple-choice items. Sometimes you can immediately eliminate one or more of the choices as wrong, increasing the odds of picking the right answer to one out of three or one out of two.

- **Guess when you draw a blank.** If you haven't a single clue about the answer to a question, you can use some "insider" tips on guessing the answer:

  - If one option is longer than the others, it is often correct.
  - If the words *always* or *never* are in an option, it is probably incorrect.
  - If the options consist of a range of numbers, a number in the middle is often the right answer.
  - If two quantities are very close, one of them is probably right.

Strategies for Essay Questions

Essay questions test not only your recall of facts and concepts, but also your ability to select, interpret, and/or apply them. Because essays are fairly complex, there is no one right answer to an essay question. Here are some suggestions for improving your ability to write an essay:

- **Read the directions.** Make sure you know how many essay questions you will need to respond to. You are usually given a choice. Also be sure to allocate your time properly; if an essay question is worth one quarter of the test score, you should plan on spending about one quarter of your time on it.

- **Read the essay questions carefully.** Before you choose the question you will answer, read them all carefully. Once you've chosen your question, make sure you thoroughly understand it. Sometimes a question is presented in several parts, each of which you must address.

- **Think before you write.** Your essay will make more sense if you think about what you want to say before you begin writing. You may find it easier to organize your thoughts if you jot down a list of key points or outline your response. Be sure you have covered all the points asked for in the question.

- **Write your answer.** Write your response in well-developed paragraphs. Each paragraph should have a topic sentence that states the main idea and explanations, examples, or descriptions that support the topic sentence. Don't wander off the topic, and don't pad your answer with irrelevant material.

- **Check your grammar and spelling.** Make every effort to use correct grammar and spelling. Mistakes in grammar and spelling create a poor impression on the person scoring the essay, even if you have written an otherwise excellent answer.

- **Check that you have answered the question.** After you are done, reread the question to make sure you have addressed all the issues you are asked to cover.

Business Mathematics

PRETEST

1. Which of the following is closest to the value of the square root of 56?

    (A) 8.1
    (B) 7.5
    (C) 7.0
    (D) 6.8

2. $\left(\dfrac{9}{31}\right)(45)\left(\dfrac{1}{3}\right) =$

    (A) 4.05
    (B) 4.20
    (C) 4.35
    (D) 4.50

3. $\left(\dfrac{4}{7} + \dfrac{2}{6}\right)(4.3) =$

    (A) 1.98
    (B) 3.89
    (C) 5.11
    (D) 6.13

4. In the number forty-six thousand five hundred and twenty-three, which digit appears in the thousands place?

    (A) 46
    (B) 6
    (C) 5
    (D) 4

5. Monthly Budget for XYZ Corporation:

    | Rent | $ 4,000 |
    | Salary | $ 8,000 |
    | Inventory | $32,000 |

    Given the information above, which most closely represents the percent of the XYZ Corporation's monthly budget that is salary expense?

    (A) 0.18%
    (B) 8%
    (C) 18%
    (D) 28%

6. $2 + \dfrac{4}{6} - (11.3 + 7) =$

(A) 20.97

(B) 15.63

(C) −1.63

(D) −15.63

7. Six sevenths divided by one half is equal to

(A) Both (A) and (B) are correct.

(B) $\dfrac{12}{7}$

(C) $\dfrac{3}{7}$

(D) $\dfrac{6}{14}$

8. If $\left(\dfrac{1}{4}\right)x + 32 = 6x$, then $x =$

(A) 5.0

(B) 5.12

(C) 5.56

(D) 6.65

9. Which of the following is the slope of the line that passes through the points (1,6) and (−2,37)?

(A) −10.33

(B) −.097

(C) .097

(D) 10.33

10. If $f(x) = x^2 - 14x + 93$, then f(8) =

(A) −3

(B) 8

(C) 45

(D) 85

11. A class consists of 25 students. If 20 percent of the class received an A on the test, how many students did NOT receive an A?

(A) 5

(B) 15

(C) 18

(D) 20

12. If $y = z + 3x + 12$ and $y = 4x - z + 11$, then when $x = 4$, $y =$

(A) 22.5

(B) 24.0

(C) 24.5

(D) 27.0

13. If $15x - 6 = 3$, then $x =$

   (A) 0.8

   (B) 0.6

   (C) 0.4

   (D) 0.2

14. If $A + B = 12$, $B + C = 8$, and $A + C = 4$, then $A =$

   (A) 1

   (B) 2

   (C) 3

   (D) 4

15. If $\left(\dfrac{1}{4}\right)x + \dfrac{3}{8} = \dfrac{1}{2}$, then $x =$

   (A) $\dfrac{1}{2}$

   (B) $\dfrac{1}{4}$

   (C) $\dfrac{1}{6}$

   (D) $\dfrac{1}{8}$

16. If $f(x) = [(-3)\char`\^x]\left(\dfrac{x}{4}\right)$, then $f(-2) =$

   (A) 4.5

   (B) $\dfrac{1}{18}$

   (C) $-\dfrac{1}{18}$

   (D) -4.5

17. A grocery store sells apples for 30 cents per pound and oranges for 40 cents per pound. A customer purchases 2 pounds of apples and 3 pounds of oranges. Which of the following amounts does the purchase total?

   (A) $1.80

   (B) $1.95

   (C) $2.25

   (D) $3.20

18. Which of the following is the largest solution to the quadratic function $2x^2 - 7x - 3 = 0$

    (A) $\dfrac{1}{2}$

    (B) 1

    (C) 3

    (D) 5

19. In the month of July, XYZ Corporation had $1,500 total sales. If all merchandise is sold after a 30 percent markup on cost, which of the following is most near the cost of inventory sold in July?

    (A) $450

    (B) $1,150

    (C) $1,500

    (D) $1,950

20. Twenty-four percent of Terry's monthly budget is allotted to rent and 53 percent is allotted to food. If Terry spends $300 per month on rent, how much money does Terry have allotted to food?

    (A) $159.30

    (B) $527.85

    (C) $600.00

    (D) $662.50

PRETEST ANSWERS

1. **The correct answer is (B).** The square root of 56 is approximately 7.5.

2. **The correct answer is (C).** $\left(\dfrac{9}{31}\right)(45)\left(\dfrac{1}{3}\right) = 4.35$

3. **The correct answer is (B).** $\left(\dfrac{4}{7} + \dfrac{2}{6}\right)(4.3) = 3.89$

4. **The correct answer is (B).** The number 6 is in the thousands place ($4\underline{6},523$).

5. **The correct answer is (C).** $\dfrac{8,000}{44,000} = .1818 = $ approx. 18%

6. **The correct answer is (D).** $2.666667 - 18.3 = $ approx. -15.63

7. **The correct answer is (B).** $\dfrac{6}{7} \div \dfrac{1}{2} = \dfrac{6}{7} \times \dfrac{2}{1} = \dfrac{12}{7}.$

8. **The correct answer is (C).**

    $$5.75\, x = 32$$
    $$x = 5.56$$

9. **The correct answer is (A).**

    $$m = \frac{\text{(change in } y)}{\text{(change in } x)} = \frac{(37 - 6)}{(-2 - 1)} = \frac{-31}{3} = -10.33$$

10. **The correct answer is (C).** $f(8) = 64 - 14(8) + 93 = 45$

11. **The correct answer is (D).**

    $$1 - 0.2 = 0.8$$
    $$0.8(25) = 20$$

12. **The correct answer is (C).**

    $$2y = z + 3x + 12 + 4x - z + 11$$
    $$2y = 7x + 23$$
    $$y = \left(\frac{7}{2}\right)x + \left(\frac{23}{2}\right)$$

    recall:

    $$x = 4$$
    $$y = 25.5$$

13. **The correct answer is (B).**

    $$15x - 6 = 3$$
    $$15x = 9$$
    $$x = 0.6$$

14. **The correct answer is (D).**

$$A + B = 4; B + C = 8; A + B = 12$$
$$A + B + 2C = 12$$
$$12 + 2C = 12$$
$$C = 0$$
$$A + C = 4$$
$$A = 4$$

15. **The correct answer is (A).**

$$\frac{x}{4} = \frac{1}{2} - \frac{3}{8}$$
$$\frac{x}{4} = \frac{1}{8}$$
$$x = \frac{1}{2}$$

16. **The correct answer is (C).**

$$F(-2) = [(-3)^\wedge(-2)]\left(-\frac{2}{4}\right) = -\frac{1}{18}$$

17. **The correct answer is (A).** $.3(2) + .4(3) = 1.8$

18. **The correct answer is (C).** The quadratic equation is

$$\frac{-b \pm \sqrt{(b^2 - 4ac)}}{2a}$$
$$\frac{(7 \pm 5)}{4}$$
$$\frac{1}{2} \text{ and } 3$$
$$3 > \frac{1}{2}$$
$$3$$

19. **The correct answer is (B).**

$$0.3x + x = 1,500$$
$$1.3x = 1,500$$
$$x = \text{approx. } 1,150$$

20. **The correct answer is (D).** $\left(\frac{53}{24}\right)(300) = 662.50$

GENERAL OVERVIEW

NUMBER SENSE
PLACE VALUE

The **decimal system** of numbers uses ten digits—0, 1, 2, 3, 4, 5, 6, 7, 8, and 9—to represent all numbers. The value assigned to a digit in a particular number depends on its position in the number, called its **place value**. Numbers to the left of the decimal point are whole numbers, and numbers to the right of the decimal point represent parts of a whole (amounts less than 1).

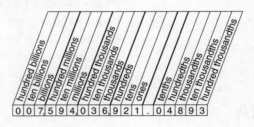

PERCENTS

A percent represents a part of a whole, just like fractions and decimals. Percents are hundredths, or parts of a hundred. One percent means "1 of 100 equal parts," or 1/100, or .01. It is written 1%.

Problems using percents have three main quantities:

- **Base**—The whole or total amount, the amount to which something is being compared
- **Rate**—The percent
- **Portion**—The result of multiplying the base and the rate

THE PERCENT FORMULA

The basic percent formula is

Portion (P) = Base (B) $\times$ Rate (R)

So, for example, to find the amount of sales tax (portion) owed on a $5,000 used car (base) if the sales tax was 5% (rate), the formula would be used as follows:

Portion = $5,000 $\times$ 5% *or*

Portion = $5,000 $\times$ .05

Portion = $250, the amount of sales tax

Is the Answer Reasonable?

It is easy to make errors when math problems are solved or arithmetic is performed, even when using a calculator.

One type of error is to misinterpret a word problem, and thus come up with the wrong answer. When a word problem is solved, the answer should be checked against the problem to see if it makes sense. If it does not, one possible source of error is that the wrong **operation** was used: division instead of multiplication or addition instead of subtraction. The problem can be redone using the opposite operation to see if the resulting answer makes more sense.

Another type of error is arithmetic—making a calculation mistake when adding, subtracting, multiplying, dividing, or making a data entry mistake when using a calculator. To check an answer when doing a calculation, the approximate answer can be estimated, or guessed, by rounding the numbers and performing the operation on them. If the estimate is close to the answer, the answer is probably correct. Another way to check an answer when using a calculator is to perform the calculation twice.

ALGEBRA

An **equation** is a mathematical statement indicating that two expressions are equal. For example, in the equation

$$x + 7 = 10$$

the expressions $x + 7$ and 10 are equal. The letter x is called a **variable**, a letter that represents a number.

Solving an Equation

Since the two expressions of an equation are equal, as long as both sides of an equation are changed in the same way, the resulting expressions will still be equal. There are two basic rules for solving an equation:

- **Addition rule**—The same number may be added or subtracted on both sides of the equation.
- **Multiplication rule**—The same number, other than zero, may be multiplied or divided on both sides of the equation.

Thus, to solve the equation $x + 7 = 10$, the number 7 can be subtracted from each side:

$$x + 7 = 10$$
$$x + 7 - 7 = 10 - 7$$
$$x = 3$$

Linear Equations

A **linear equation,** like the one shown above, is one in which the variables are raised to the first power (x^1), even though that is not stated. The basic form is

$$ax + by = c$$

where a, b, and c are real numbers and a and b cannot both equal zero. Equations are *not* linear if they contain a term with exponents other than one (x^2) or a term involving the product of two variables (xy). A linear equation with two variables, when graphed, is a straight line. To graph a linear equation, two pairs of values for x and y that satisfy the equation must first be found. These points are plotted on a graph, and a line is drawn connecting them. All points on the line represent solutions to the equation. Thus, a single linear equation has an infinite number of solutions.

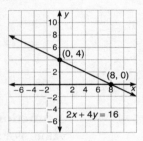

A set of two or more linear equations that are to be considered together is called a system of **simultaneous linear equations**. To solve a system of linear equations, the solution that satisfies all the equations is found. In a system of two linear equations with two variables, the solution is a number pair. One way to find the solution is to graph each equation on the same graph. The point where the two lines intersect is the solution.

Inequalities

An **inequality** expresses the condition that two quantities are not equal. The symbols $>$ (greater than) and $<$ (less than) are used:

$$19 > 7 \quad \text{``9 is greater than 7''}$$
$$x < 31 \quad \text{``the value of } x \text{ is less than 31''}$$
$$1 < y < 5 \quad \text{``the value of } y \text{ is greater than 1 and less than 5''}$$

Quadratic Equations

A **quadratic equation** is an equation that, when written in its simplest form, contains a variable to the second power (x^2). It may also contain the variable to the first power (x) and/or a constant (a real number). The basic form is

$$ax^2 + bx + c = 0$$

where a, b, and c represent real numbers, and a cannot equal 0. When a quadratic equation is graphed, the solution is a parabola, a smooth cup-shaped curve.

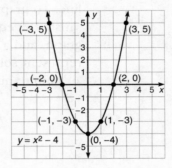

Functions

A **function** is a rule that assigns to each input value one output value. For example, in the equation $y = x^2 - 2x + 1$, if selected values of x are input, the equation yields corresponding values of y as outputs:

If $x = 1$ $y = (1)^2 - 2(1) + 1 = 0$

If $x = -4$ $y = (-4)^2 - 2(-4) + 1 = 25$

If $x = 10$ $y = (10)^2 - 2(10) + 1 = 81$

The **domain** of a function is the set of all possible input values, and the **range** is the set of all possible output values. A functional relationship is shown by the equation

$$y = (x)$$

which means that y is a function of x. In other words, the value of y depends upon the value of x.

STATISTICS

Statistics are numeric data that describe events in government, business, economics, and any other field in which data can be quantified.

Measures of Central Tendency

When a set of raw data must be analyzed, one way to make sense of the data is to find a **measure of central tendency**. There are three basic measures of central tendency: the mean, the median, and the mode; and another measure, the weighted mean.

Mean

The **mean** is the sum of the values divided by the number of values; it is also commonly known as the average. For example, suppose Marge Byers, a consultant, worked on seven client projects last year, valued at $4,500, $10,000, $2,700, $17,725, $1,300, $12,000, and $5,150. The mean value of one of Byers's projects is

$$\frac{\$4,500 + \$10,000 + \$2,700 + \$17,725 + \$1,300 + \$12,000 + \$5,150}{7}$$

or $53,375 (the sum of all the projects) divided by 7 (the number of projects). The mean value is $7,625.

Weighted Mean

The **weighted mean**, or **weighted average**, is used when some of the items in a data set occur more than once. Each value is then calculated by multiplying it by the number of times it occurs. A student's grade point average is a weighted mean.

Course	No. of Credits	Grade	Grade × No. of Credits
Business math	3	A (= 4)	4 × 3 = 12
Marketing	3	B (= 3)	3 × 3 = 9
Accounting	4	C (= 2)	2 × 4 = 8
Computer science	4	C (= 2)	2 × 4 = 8
Totals	14		37

In this case, the weighted sum is 37, which is divided by the number of credits, 14. The student's grade point average, to the nearest tenth, is 2.6. Note that if the mean had been calculated, the student's average would have been 2.8 (the sum of the grades divided by 4).

Median

The **median** divides a group of numbers in half. Half the numbers are at or above the median, and half are at or below the median. The first step in finding the median is to arrange the group of numbers in numeric order, smallest first. For example, the list of numbers 12, 14, 17, 8, 7, 5, and 9 would be written as

5, 7, 8, 9, 12, 14, 17

If there is an odd number of numbers, the number of numbers is divided by 2. The next higher whole number is the median. So in the example above, 7 numbers is divided by 2, giving 3.5. Rounding up to the next whole number gives 4. Therefore the fourth number, 9, is the median.

If there is an even number of numbers, divide by 2. The mean of that number and the next higher number is the median.

Mode

The **mode** is the number that occurs most often in a data set. For example, in one calendar year ten employees retire. Their ages are

65, 62, 61, 70, 66, 65, 67, 67, 69, 67

The mode of the retirees' ages is 67, the age that appears most often.

Percentiles

A **percentile** is an indication of the relative position of a single score in a group of scores. For example, suppose a student took the Scholastic Aptitude Test (SAT) and scored 1100. If 88 percent of her peers scored 1100 or lower, her percentile rank would be 88. That also means that 12 percent of her peers did better than she did, scoring above 1100.

The percentile scale, based on percents, has 100 units. Some points on the scale have special names. The first quartile is the 25th percentile, the second quartile (also equal to the median) is the 50th percentile, and the third quartile is the 75th percentile.

Frequency Distributions and Graphs

Numeric data is often displayed visually for ease of comprehension and greater impact. There are several types of visual displays:

- A **frequency distribution table** shows how many times various numbers occur; for example, the number of weeks that a particular number of widgets was produced during the course of a year.

No. of Widgets Produced	Frequency (No. of Weeks)
5,000–6,000	10
6,001–7,000	19
7,001–8,000	15
8,001–9,000	8

- A **bar graph** shows frequency data by means of the heights of the bars.

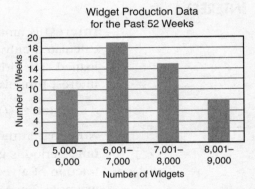

- A **line graph** shows trends over time; for example, widget sales over the last five years.

- A **circle graph** shows parts of a whole; for example, the portion of total sales that widget sales represent.

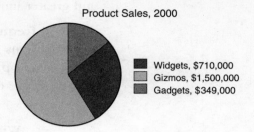

Product Sales, 2000

■ Widgets, $710,000
□ Gizmos, $1,500,000
▨ Gadgets, $349,000

Visual displays of information can sometimes misrepresent data. This may occur through omission of data, by focusing only on a portion of the data, or by emphasizing unimportant data at the expense of important data.

BUSINESS APPLICATIONS
SIMPLE INTEREST

Interest is money paid for the use of money. **Simple interest** is calculated only on the **principal**, or original amount borrowed or loaned. The principal plus interest is the **maturity value**. The simple interest formula is

Interest (*I*) = Principal (*P*) × Rate (*R*) × Time (*T*)

Note that in this formula, time is assumed to be in years. Thus, if a time period is given in months or days, it must be converted to a fraction of a year before being used in the formula as *T*. Suppose, for example, Jim Medeiros borrows $40,000 to buy equipment. He pays 8% annual interest for 6 months, when he must repay the principal plus interest (the maturity value).

$$I = 40,000 \ (P) \times .08 \ (R) \times \frac{6}{12} \ (T)$$

I = $1,600

MV = $40,000 (*P*) + $1,600 (*I*) = $41,600

Compound interest is discussed on page 000.

PROMISSORY NOTES

A lender usually requires a borrower to sign a **promissory note**, which states that the borrower will repay a certain sum at a fixed time in the future. The note may also state the interest rate.

The total amount due at the end of the loan is the maturity value—the sum of the face value and interest. When the issuer deducts the loan interest in advance, the note is a **simple discount note**, also called a **noninterest-bearing note**.

DISCOUNTING A NOTE

When the issuer of a promissory note needs cash, it can sell the note in advance of its maturity to a bank. The bank charges for this service, taking a **bank discount**. The amount the issuer actually receives is the **proceeds** of the note.

INSTALLMENT PURCHASES

In an **installment purchase**, the buyer makes a down payment and pays off the balance plus a **finance charge**, which includes interest, in regular periodic payments.

Finance charge = Total of all monthly payments − Amount financed

The finance charge is often expressed as an **annual percentage rate (APR)**, the true effective annual interest charge. The APR can be calculated by formulas or by using APR tables.

The **U.S. rule** states that any partial loan payment covers any interest that has accrued. The remainder of the payment reduces the loan principal. A variation of the U.S. Rule is the **Rule of 78**, which charges a larger portion of the finance charges to the earlier payments. These rules are applied in calculating the rebate amount of the finance charge and the payoff when the loan is repaid before it is due. (See page 240 for more on installment loans.)

DISCOUNTS AND CREDIT TERMS

Trade Discount

A **trade discount** is the amount a retailer receives off the list price when buying from a manufacturer or wholesaler:

Trade discount amount = List price x Trade discount rate

Cash Discount

Sellers may also offer a **cash discount**, a reduction from the invoice price if buyers pay the invoice within a specified amount of time, called the **discount period**, usually 30, 60, or 90 days. For example, the cash discount may be 2/10, n/30, which means that the buyer can take 2% off the invoice if it is paid within 10 days; otherwise the net amount is due between day 11 and day 30.

Cash discounts are not taken on freight, returned goods, sales tax, etc. The most common freight terms are **FOB shipping point** (the buyer pays the freight) and **FOB destination** (the seller pays the freight).

MARKUPS AND MARKDOWNS

A seller arrives at the selling price of his goods by adding a markup to the cost of the goods. The **markup** represents the amount needed to cover operating expenses and make a profit. Manufacturers and wholesalers generally calculate markup based on the cost. Retailers usually compute markup based on selling price. Whether cost or selling price is the basis, the same markup formula is used:

Selling price = Cost + Markup

Markdowns are reductions from the original selling price. They may be caused by the perishability of goods, style changes, seasonal changes, and so on.

$$\text{Markdown percent} = \frac{\text{Markdown amount}}{\text{Original selling price}}$$

BREAK-EVEN ANALYSIS

Goods that are marked down may result in a reduced net profit, breaking even, an operating loss, or a gross or absolute loss. The **breakeven point** is the point at which the reduced price just covers cost plus operating expenses.

Breakeven point = Cost + Operating expenses

Operating loss = Breakeven point − Reduced selling price

Absolute loss = Cost − Reduced selling price

INVENTORY
Valuation Methods

At the end of each accounting period, a company's inventory of raw materials and/or goods must be valued. To do this, a company must know the cost of its ending inventory and the cost of goods sold. There are four common methods.

- In the **specific identification method**, (1) the cost of goods available for sale is calculated, (2) the cost of ending inventory is calculated, and (3) the cost of good sold is calculated (Step 1 − Step 2).

- In the **weighted-average method**, (1) the average unit cost is calculated, (2) the cost of ending inventory is calculated, and (3) the cost of goods sold is calculated.
- In the **first-in, first-out (FIFO) method**, the first goods that are made or bought are assumed to be the first goods sold. In FIFO, (1) units and their costs to be included in ending inventory are listed; (2) the cost of ending inventory is calculated; and (3) the cost of goods sold is calculated.
- The **last-in, first-out (LIFO) method** is similar to FIFO, except the last goods made or bought are assumed to be the first goods sold.

Stock Turnover

Stock turnover can be calculated using retail or cost values:

$$\text{Turnover at retail} = \frac{\text{Retail sales}}{\text{Average inventory at retail}}$$

$$\text{Turnover at cost} = \frac{\text{Cost of goods sold}}{\text{Average inventory at cost}}$$

TAXES
Sales Tax

Many cities, counties, and states charge **sales tax** on the purchase of certain goods and services. When computing sales tax, sellers first subtract trade discounts and cash discounts from the original selling price. The tax is calculated on that amount. Costs of shipping and handling are not taxed.

PROPERTY TAX

All property owners pay **property tax** on the **assessed value** of their property. The tax is calculated according to the following formula:

Total property tax due = Tax rate × Total assessed value due

Depreciation

In accounting, **depreciation** is the amount of an asset's value that is considered an expense of doing business each year. There are three key factors: the original **cost** of the asset, the **estimated useful life** in years, and the **residual value** (salvage or trade-in value). There are several methods for calculating depreciation.

In the **straight-line method,**

$$\text{Annual depreciation expense} = \frac{\text{Cost} - \text{Residual value}}{\text{Estimated useful life in years}}$$

In the **units of activity method,**

$$\text{Depreciation per unit} = \frac{\text{Cost} - \text{Residual value}}{\text{Estimated units of useful life production}}$$

$$\text{Annual depreciation expense} = \text{Unit depreciation} \times \text{Units produced}$$

In the **sum-of-the-years'-digits method**, the depreciation rate is based on a fraction in which the numerator is the years of remaining life and the denominator is the sum of the individual years of total life.

$$\text{Annual depreciation expense} =$$

$$(\text{Cost} - \text{Residual value}) \times \frac{\text{Remaining life}}{\text{Sum of the Year's digits}}$$

In the **declining balance method**, the annual depreciation expense declines over the life of the asset because book value, rather than cost, is used.

Payroll

Employees are usually paid weekly, biweekly, semimonthly, or monthly. The calculation of **gross pay** for an employee paid an hourly wage is

$$\text{Gross pay} = \text{Hours of work} \times \text{Rate per hour}$$

When an hourly employee works more than 40 hours a week, the hours over 40 are paid at 1½ times the regular rate. For employees paid on a piecework basis, the formula is

$$\text{Gross pay} = \text{Number of units produced} \times \text{Rate per unit}$$

The gross pay of employees paid on a commission basis is calculated by multiplying the gross sales by the commission rate, which may vary at different sales levels. Some salespeople are paid a salary plus commission.

Companies deduct amounts from gross pay to arrive at **net pay**. Examples of deductions include Federal Insurance Contribution Act (FICA) payments (social security and Medicare); federal, state, and local income taxes; insurance; union dues; and pension contributions.

FINANCIAL STATEMENTS

Companies prepare financial statements at the end of each accounting period. There are three main financial statements.

- An **income statement** shows revenues, expenses, and resulting net income or net loss for the period of time.
- The **owner's equity statement** shows changes in the owner's equity for the period of time.
- The **balance sheet** shows the assets, liabilities, and owner's equity of the business on a specific date.

Financial Analysis

The financial statements of a company are used by the company's managers to assess performance and plan for the future. They are also used by investors to judge the company's performance as an investment. There are several basic tools of financial statement analysis.

Horizontal Analysis

Horizontal analysis, also called trend analysis, is the comparison of data over a period of time to see what the amount and percentage of increase or decrease has been. For example, horizontal analysis can be used to determine whether sales increased, decreased, or remained stagnant over a five-year period.

Vertical Analysis

Vertical analysis, also called common size analysis, expresses items in a financial statement in terms of percentages of a base amount. For example, cost of goods sold can be expressed as a percentage of net sales. This makes possible the comparison of companies of differing sizes.

Ratio Analysis

Ratios express mathematical relationships between two amounts as a percentage, a rate, or a proportion. Liquidity ratios measure the short-term ability of a company to pay its current liabilities. Profitability ratios measure the income or operating success of a company over a period of time. Solvency ratios measure a company's ability to survive. There are many of these ratios, the best known of which are the **current ratio**, which is current assets divided by current liabilities; the **profitability ratio**, which is net income divided by net sales; **earnings per share**, which is net income divided by the weighted average of common shares outstanding; and the **price-earnings ratio**, the market price per share of stock divided by earnings per share.

FINANCIAL MATHEMATICS
COMPOUND INTEREST (FUTURE VALUE)

As you recall, simple interest is calculated only on the principal. In **compound interest**, the interest is calculated periodically and added to the principal. For each period, the interest is calculated on the adjusted principal—the principal plus the interest of the previous period. For example, if $1 is deposited in a savings account with 8% interest compounded annually, at the end of the first year it is worth $1.08; at the end of the second year, $1.17; at the end of the third year, $1.26; and at the end of the fourth year, $1.36. (If that same $1 had been deposited in an account paying 8% simple interest, at the end of the fourth year the account balance would have been $1.32.) With compounding, an amount held today, the **present value**, will yield a greater amount in the future, or its **future value.**

Compound interest can be calculated by using the formulas

$$M = P(1 + i)^n$$
$$I = M - P$$

where M is the compound amount (future value), P is the principal (present value), i is the interest rate per period, n is the number of periods, and I is the total interest amount. A compound interest table can be used instead of formulas. Note that interest may be compounded annually, semiannually, quarterly, monthly, or daily. The more frequently it is compounded, the higher the effective interest rate.

PRESENT VALUE

Sometimes it is necessary to know what an amount in the future is worth today. For example, if a grandfather wanted to have $60,000 saved for his granddaughter to attend State University in sixteen years, how much would he need to put away now, given 8% interest compounded annually? The answer is the present value, or $17,513.

To calculate the present value P of the future amount M at compound interest rate of i per period for n periods, use the formula

$$P = \frac{M}{(1 + i)^n}$$

A present value table can be used instead of the formula.

ANNUITIES

A series of equal payments made at regular time periods is called an **annuity**. The **value of an annuity** is the value of a series of payments plus interest. Pension installment payments, social security payments, and home mortgages are all annuities. There are two basic types of annuities:

- **Contingent annuities** have no fixed number of payments; for example, paying a monthly pension until death.
- **Annuities certain** have a specific stated number of payments.

These two types of annuities can be further broken down into:

- **Ordinary annuities** in which regular payments are made at the end of each period. Therefore no interest is calculated on the amount deposited at the end of a period, only on the balance carried forward from previous periods.
- **Annuities due** in which regular payments are made at the beginning of each period. Interest is calculated on the current payment as well as the accumulated balance. If all else is equal, an annuity due has a higher final value than an ordinary annuity.

Present Value of an Annuity

The amount of money that must be invested today to generate a stream of payments for a given number of years in the future is the **present value of an annuity**. To find present value, the interest rate, number of periods, and the payment amount must be known; then a present value of an annuity table is needed to look up the table factor. The formula is

Present Value =

Payment $\times$ Factor from Present Value of an Annuity Table

SINKING FUNDS

A sinking fund sets aside regular periodic payments of a particular amount of money. Compound interest accumulates until a specific sum is reached at a predetermined future date. To determine the amount of the regular periodic payments needed to reach a certain sum, use the formula

Sinking fund payment =

Future value × Factor from Sinking Fund Table

Note that saving for a college education could be done using a sinking fund rather than investing a lump sum as discussed above. So to accumulate $60,000 for a granddaughter's education in sixteen years, given an 8 percent interest rate, $1,980 would have to be invested per year for sixteen years, a total investment of $31,680.

AMORTIZATION

A loan is **amortized** if both principal and interest are paid off in a series of equal periodic payments. This type of loan is called an installment loan (see page 240). Installment loans are typically used to finance the purchase of cars, boats, and home improvements.

The periodic payment that will pay off, or amortize, a loan can be found using the fomula

Payment = Loan Amount × Factor from Amortization Table

SAMPLE QUESTIONS

1. A seller who marks down merchandise below cost is
   (A) taking an absolute loss
   (B) taking an operating loss
   (C) breaking even
   (D) taking a reduced net profit

The correct answer is (A). When merchandise is marked down below the seller's cost, the seller takes an absolute loss. An operating loss means that the seller recovers the cost of the goods plus some operating expenses. Breaking even is the point at which cost plus operating expenses are covered. A reduced net profit allows the seller to recoup cost, operating expenses, and some profit.

2. A system of two simultaneous linear equations with two variables is graphed, and the lines intersect at (3, 1). Which of the following statements is true?
   (A) The ordered pair (3, 1) is one of an infinite number of solutions to the system of two simultaneous equations.
   (B) The ordered pair (3, 1) is the only solution to the system of two simultaneous equations.
   (C) All solutions to the simultaneous linear equations have values for x that are 3 or greater and values for y that are 1 or greater.
   (D) The lines representing each of the equations are cup-shaped curves called parabolas.

The correct answer is (B). The solution to a system of equations is the solution that satisfies each equation in the system. A system of two linear equations with two variables has only *one* solution—the point at which the lines intersect. A linear equation, when graphed, is a straight line, so choice (D) can be eliminated right away.

3. Mark Towney is paid a weekly base salary of $150 plus a piecework rate of $1 per unit for each unit over 450 that he produces each week. Last week he made 950 units. What was Towney's gross pay?
   (A) $150
   (B) $450
   (C) $600
   (D) $650

The correct answer is (D). Each week Towney earns $150 regardless of his output. To earn more, he must produce more than 450 units in a week. The week that he made 950 units, he produced 500 units over quota, for which he was paid $1 each. Therefore the base salary, $150, plus the piecework payment, $500, equals gross pay of $650.

PRACTICE SET

1. Benson's buys its stoves from a wholesaler. One model is $800 with a 40% trade discount, FOB destination. How much does Benson's pay for each stove?

   (A) $320 plus FOB destination
   (B) $320
   (C) $480 plus FOB destination
   (D) $480

2. If a set of data contained one very large or very small number, which of the following would be the best indicator of its central tendency?

   (A) Mean
   (B) Weighted mean
   (C) Median
   (D) Percentile

3. Why does an annuity due have a higher future value than an ordinary annuity with the same payment, number of periods, and interest rate?

   (A) In an annuity due, interest is compounded daily.
   (B) In an annuity due, money is invested at the beginning of each period.
   (C) In an annuity due, money is invested at a lower effective interest rate.
   (D) In an annuity due, the payments are made at irregular intervals.

4. A fraction is converted to a decimal by

   (A) multiplying the numerator by the denominator
   (B) dividing the numerator by the denominator
   (C) placing a decimal point between the numerator and the denominator
   (D) multiplying the numerator and denominator by 10

5. Carole Van Buren borrowed $12,000 to make a tuition payment to her son's college. The loan must be repaid at the end of 7 months with 7.5% interest. How much must Van Buren pay at the end of the 7 months?

   (A) $12,900
   (B) $12,525
   (C) $12,400
   (D) $12,075

6. The estimated value of an asset after it is fully depreciated is called the

   (A) replacement cost
   (B) variable value
   (C) residual value
   (D) net value

7. Town and Country Real Estate has monthly expenses as follows: salaries expense, $5,400; utilities expense $480, rent expense $2,000; commissions expense $12,500; and other expense, $340. What is the best way to visually depict the month's total expenses?

   (A) Frequency distribution table
   (B) Double bar graph
   (C) Line graph
   (D) Circle graph

8. Which of the following is a method of valuing inventory?

   (A) Weighted-average method
   (B) Double-declining-balance method
   (C) Sum-of-the-years'-digits method
   (D) Straight-line method

9. A collection agency charges a $25 fee for each account plus 20% of the amount collected. What is the total charge for collecting $5,000 on one account and $1,500 on another?

   (A) $1,300
   (B) $1,325
   (C) $1,350
   (D) $1,375

10. A landscaper has a truck loaded with 20 cubic yards of pine bark mulch. At his first client's yard, he unloads 2 1/2 cubic yards; at the second, 5 3/4 cubic yards; and at the third, 7 1/4 cubic yards. At the fourth client's yard, he finds that he is 1 1/2 cubic yards short. How much mulch does the fourth client's yard need?

    (A) 4 1/2 cubic yards
    (B) 5 cubic yards
    (C) 5 1/2 cubic yards
    (D) 6 cubic yards

PRACTICE SET ANSWERS

1. **The correct answer is (D).** To find the discount, multiply $800 by .4 to yield a $320 discount. Subtract the discount from the list price ($800 – $320) to get the price that Benson's pays, $480. Benson's does not pay freight charges because FOB destination is paid by the seller.

2. **The correct answer is (C).** The median is the best measure of central tendency to use when a data set contains one or two extreme numbers because it indicates the midpoint of the data set. Both the mean and the weighted mean would be skewed by the presence of a very large or very small number. A percentile is not a measure of central tendency; it measures relative performance.

3. **The correct answer is (B).** Because money is invested at the beginning of a period in an annuity due, interest is calculated on the period. In an ordinary annuity, money is invested at the end of the period, so no interest on that amount accrues for the period.

4. **The correct answer is (B).** To convert a fraction to a decimal, the numerator must be divided by the denominator. For example, $\frac{1}{2}$ equals 1.0 divided by 2, or .5.

5. **The correct answer is (B).** Annual interest on $12,000 is $900 (12,000 × .075). One month's interest is therefore $\frac{1}{12}$ of $900, or $75. Since the term of the loan is seven months, the total interest is 7 × $75, or $525. Added to the principal of $12,000, the total payment is $12,525.

6. **The correct answer is (C).** The value of a fully depreciated asset is its residual value, sometimes called the salvage value.

7. **The correct answer is (D).** A circle graph is appropriate when the relationships of the parts to the whole is being shown.

8. **The correct answer is (A).** This is the only inventory valuation method among the options; the other options are all depreciation methods.

9. **The correct answer is (C).** To calculate the answer, multiply $5,000 by 20% to yield $1,000; multiply $1,500 by 20% to yield $300. Then add: $1,000 + $300 + $25 (one fee) + $25 (second fee) = $1,350.

10. **The correct answer is (D).** First add the mulch the landscaper unloaded at the first three stops by converting the fractions to the least common denominator: $2\frac{2}{4} + 5\frac{3}{4} + 7\frac{1}{4} = 14\frac{6}{4}$, or $15\frac{2}{4}$, or $15\frac{1}{2}$ cubic yards of mulch. That means when he got to the fourth client's yard, he had $20 - 15\frac{1}{2}$ cubic yards of mulch left in the truck, or $4\frac{1}{2}$ cubic yards. Since he is short $1\frac{1}{2}$ cubic yards, the fourth client needs $4\frac{1}{2} + 1\frac{1}{2}$ cubic yards, or 6 cubic yards of mulch.

POSTTEST

1. Which of the following is the y-intercept of the line with slope $= -2$ and x-intercept $= 2$?

   (A) -2
   (B) 0
   (C) 4
   (D) 8

2. 77, 81, 85, 89, 93, 79, 81, 86, 87

   Which of the following is the median of the set of numbers shown above?

   (A) 81
   (B) 85
   (C) 89
   (D) 93

3. 5, 6, 6, 7, 9, 15

   Which of the following is the mean of the set of numbers shown above?

   (A) 6
   (B) 6.5
   (C) 7
   (D) 8

Use the following table for questions 4 and 5.

Barber Corporation Sales for
August, 1999

Value	Frequency
$1,000	1
$ 300	5
$ 150	2
$ 75	8

4. Which of the following amounts to the weighted mean of Barber Corporation's sales?

   (A) $183.50
   (B) $212.50
   (C) $275.75
   (D) $381.25

5. Which of the following sales value represents the mode?

   (A) 1,000
   (B) 300
   (C) 150
   (D) 75

6. 1, 9, 17, 38, 37, 32

   Which of the following is the median of the set of numbers shown above?

   (A) 24
   (B) 27
   (C) 37
   (D) 38

7. The average score of 4 students on a statistics examination was 76 percent. Which of the following sets of scores is consistent with this finding?

   (A) 46%, 83%, 72%, 100%
   (B) 50%, 82%, 89%, 83%
   (C) 73%, 76%, 76%, 77%
   (D) 74%, 75%, 76%, 77%

8. Widgets, Inc. sells 14 widgets for $30 each in July. In August, Widgets sells 12 widgets for $35 each. Which of the following is the average selling price in July and August?

   (A) $30.00
   (B) $32.30
   (C) $35.00
   (D) $37.30

9. 17, 23, 31, 47, 47, 52

   Which of the following is the 25th percentile (1st quartile) of the set of numbers shown above?

   (A) 23
   (B) 25
   (C) 39
   (D) 47

10. The 50th percentile is also known as the

    (A) mode
    (B) mean
    (C) median
    (D) quartile

11. If XYZ Corporation produces stoppers for $2.50 a piece and sells them for $10 a piece, which of the following is the percent markup on cost?

    (A) 7.50%
    (B) 300%
    (C) 400%
    (D) 750%

12. If ABC Company sells lamps for $50 a piece and has a percent markup on the selling price of 24 percent, which of the following is ABC's cost of producing one lamp?

   (A) $38
   (B) $47
   (C) $50
   (D) $62

13. Which of the following is the markdown percent on a television set marked down from $600 to $425?

   (A) 17.5%
   (B) 29.0%
   (C) 41.0%
   (D) 70.0%

14. An employee earns $32 per hour worked and worked 38 hours last week. If the employee's tax rate is 25 percent, which of the following is the employee's gross pay earned last week?

   (A) $304
   (B) $912
   (C) $1,216
   (D) $1,680

15. An employee earns both salary, at an hourly rate of $20, and commission, at a rate of 5 percent of net sales made. Last month, the employee made $8,000 in net sales in 120 hours and took a draw of $700. Which of the following is the employee's gross pay for last month?

   (A) $2,100
   (B) $2,800
   (C) $3,500
   (D) $5,700

16. Which of the following methods does the federal government use to calculate interest?

   (A) Exact time, exact interest
   (B) Exact time, ordinary interest
   (C) Ordinary time, exact interest
   (D) Ordinary time, ordinary interest

17. An individual makes a $10,000 loan with 8 percent interest. Considering the United States rule for partial loan payments, which of the following is the adjusted balance on the loan after a $500 payment at the end of 30 days?

   (A) $66.66
   (B) $433.33
   (C) $9,733.33
   (D) $9,566.66

18. If a customer uses an installment purchase plan to purchase an item priced at $400, and the purchase plan allows a down payment of 20 percent of the market price and 15 equal monthly payments of $25, which of the following is the total installment price?

(A) $400
(B) $450
(C) $455
(D) $480

19. Lenders are required to inform borrowers of the true APR on an installment loan in order to allow borrowers to

(A) compare the cost of loans
(B) compute monthly payments in advance
(C) calculate the length of the loan
(D) compute fees charged by the lender

20. Which of the following is the original (list) price of a dish-washer that has a net price of $500 when given a discount series of 20, 10, and 5 percent?

(A) $342
(B) $563
(C) $657
(D) $731

21. Which of the following is the net cash price of a water heater sold at $700 5/10, 3/10, N/60 that is paid in full 24 days after purchase?

(A) $645
(B) $665
(C) $679
(D) $700

22. Which of the following systems of inventory valuation is used when a firm evaluates its inventory by counting all merchandise in stock?

(A) Periodic inventory
(B) Perpetual inventory
(C) Inventory count
(D) Real inventory

23. Which of the following inventory valuation systems should be used for tax purposes in a period of inflation?

(A) FIFO
(B) LIFO
(C) Average cost method
(D) Specific identification method

24. Which of the following is the banker's discount on a $35,000 loan at 12 percent for 30 days?

(A) $345
(B) $350
(C) $1,160
(D) $4,200

25. A machine with a useful life of 900,000 units produced is purchased on January 1, year 1 for $70,000. The machine will have a salvage value of $2,000. Which of the following is the book value at December 31, year 1 if 62,000 units were produced in year 1?

(A) $4,684
(B) $46,840
(C) $64,715
(D) $65,315

26. Using the double declining balance method of depreciation, which of the following is the book value of a one-year-old computer that was purchased new for $6,000 and has a useful life of 4 years and a salvage value of $500?

(A) $1,500
(B) $2,700
(C) $3,000
(D) $4,500

27. Trucker's Hauling Company buys a new truck for $45,000. The truck has a useful life of 8 years and a salvage value of $2,000. Using the "sum of the years' digits" method of depreciation, which of the following is the depreciation expense for the third year of the truck's useful life?

(A) $7,166
(B) $7,500
(C) $9,555
(D) $10,000

28. Which of the following amounts is the property tax for real estate with an assessed value of $175,000 if the property tax rate is $1.35 per $100 of assessed value?

(A) $1,296.00
(B) $1,350.00
(C) $2,160.75
(D) $2,362.50

29. If the total cost of a television marked as $600 is $642, which of the following is the rate of sales tax?

(A) 0.07
(B) 0.7
(C) 1.07
(D) 42.0

30. State sales tax can be categorized as which of the following?

   (A) Progressive
   (B) Regressive
   (C) Marginal
   (D) Excise

31. A firm has a gross income of $725,000. If this firm had net sales of $900,000, and the firm's tax rate is 25 percent, which of the following is the firm's profit margin?

   (A) .201
   (B) .250
   (C) .604
   (D) .675

32. A firm's price-to-earnings (P/E) ratio is calculated by dividing market price per share by which of the following?

   (A) Net income
   (B) Earnings per share
   (C) Net sales
   (D) Number of shares of common stock

33. The current ratio and acid-test (quick) ratio differ in that the

   (A) acid-test ratio does not include inventory
   (B) current ratio is a measure of liquidity
   (C) denominator of the acid-test ratio is current liabilities
   (D) acid-test ratio is a measure of debt

34. The following are figures for MegaCorp for the year 1.

Beginning Inventory	$24,000
Inventory Purchases	$19,000
Ending Inventory	$20,000

   Which of the following is MegaCorp's inventory turnover for year 1?

   (A) 0.91
   (B) 0.95
   (C) 1.05
   (D) 1.15

35. The Timmond Corporation, as of December 31, year 1, had assets worth $20 million and liabilities of $15 million. If, in year 1, Timmond had a net income of $7 million, which of the following is the company's return on equity for year 1?

   (A) 0.35
   (B) 0.46
   (C) 0.71
   (D) 1.40

36. DEF, Inc. had a gross income of $65,000 in year 1. If DEF had net sales totaling $89,000, and the company's tax rate is 15 percent, which of the following is DEF's return on sales for year 1?

(A) 11%
(B) 62%
(C) 73%
(D) 86%

37. Spiffy Cleaners, Inc. had 37,000 outstanding shares of common stock when the company declared and paid dividends of $0.20 per share in year 1. Their net income for year 1 was $740,000, and their net sales totaled $1,250,000. Which of the following is Spiffy Cleaners' dividend payout ratio for year 1?

(A) 0%
(B) 0.6%
(C) 1.0%
(D) 5.0%

38. The market price of one share of the 24,000 outstanding shares of common stock of Bristles Toothbrushes, Inc. is $20. Bristles has decided to pay $90,000 in dividends in year 1 from its net income of $2,125,000. Which of the following is the dividend yield? (Assume that there is no preferred stock.)

(A) 3.75%
(B) 4.23%
(C) 14.06%
(D) 18.75%

39. A company's price-to-earnings (P/E) ratio does NOT represent which of the following?

(A) The amount consumers are willing to pay for each dollar of earnings
(B) The relationship between market value and current earnings
(C) The company's growth potential
(D) The profit earned for each dollar invested in the company

40. Which of the following most closely estimates the weight of 300 boxes, if each box weighs 20 grams?

(A) 9 kilograms
(B) 12 pounds
(C) 13 pounds
(D) 15 liters

41. One quart of milk costs $2.50 at a local grocery store. A customer wishes to purchase 4 gallons. If there is a 7 percent sales tax on milk, which of the following is the customer's total cost?

   (A) $2.80
   (B) $10.70
   (C) $40.00
   (D) $42.80

42. Which of the following firms is likely to have a high dividend payout ratio?

   (A) New software development firm
   (B) Pharmaceutical firm
   (C) Established merchandise retailer
   (D) Partnership with a high profit margin

43. Which of the following best describes an annuity?

   (A) A high interest loan
   (B) An interest bearing account
   (C) A method of installment purchasing
   (D) A series of equal payments

44. Which of the following amounts is the value of a 4-year ordinary annuity that pays 10 percent annual interest when annual deposits are $800?

   (A) $1,064.80
   (B) $3,200.00
   (C) $3,712.80
   (D) $4,084.08

45. Which of the following best describes the difference between an ordinary annuity and an annuity due?

   (A) Deposits are made at the end of each investment period in an ordinary annuity.
   (B) In an ordinary annuity, an investor earns interest, while in an annuity due, an investor pays interest accrued and owed.
   (C) Interest is paid for the first period in an ordinary annuity.
   (D) Annuity dues have much higher interest rates than ordinary annuities.

46. Terry has a 3-year annuity due that pays 12 percent interest when annual deposits total $400. Which of the following is the value of Terry's annuity?

   (A) $14.51
   (B) $1,200.00
   (C) $1,344.60
   (D) $1,511.73

47. Which of the following is the value of a 4-year annuity due that pays 12 percent interest when semi-annual deposits of $2,000 each are made?

(A) $17,794.90
(B) $17,920.00
(C) $19,535.64
(D) $20,982.58

48. Which of the following concepts can best be described as the amount of money an investor needs to invest to receive a stream of payments in the future?

(A) The present value of an ordinary annuity
(B) The future value of an ordinary annuity
(C) A future annuity payment structure
(D) Bookkeeping

49. Chris wants to receive a $20,000 annuity in 9 years. Interest on the annuity is 12 percent annually, and Chris will make withdrawals at the end of each year. Which of the following amounts does Chris need to invest today to receive this payment stream?

(A) $102,620
(B) $106,564
(C) $113,004
(D) $180,000

50. An investor is planning an annuity to pay for a child's college tuition with 6 percent annual interest and withdrawals made at the end of the period. The child will attend college in six years, and tuition costs are estimated at $35,000 per year. Which of the following amounts should be invested today in order to have the annuity exactly cover the estimated tuition expense?

(A) $85,500
(B) $96,253
(C) $121,278
(D) $140,000

51. Which of the following amounts will an individual need to invest in a 10 percent annuity today to receive $400 semi-annual payments for the next three years?

(A) $994.76
(B) $1,564.00
(C) $1,723.25
(D) $2,030.00

52. An individual invested $7,000 in an annuity. At the end of 4 years, the value of the annuity is $8,263. Which of the following is the interest amount on the annuity?

   (A) $315.75
   (B) $631.50
   (C) $1,263.00
   (D) $7,000.00

53. Terry owes Chris $10,000, payable in 4 years. If the market interest rate were 10 percent, which of the following is the minimum amount Terry would need to invest today in order to pay off Chris in full at the end of 4 years?

   (A) $6,830
   (B) $7,120
   (C) $8,425
   (D) $9,150

54. Which of the following is the interest rate of an annuity with a 10 percent APR that compounds quarterly?

   (A) 40.0%
   (B) 10.0%
   (C) 5.0%
   (D) 2.5%

55. Amortization is similar to depreciation and depletion EXCEPT that it deals with

   (A) annuities only
   (B) natural resources
   (C) physical assets
   (D) intangible assets

56. Which of the following is depicted by an amortization schedule?

   (A) The portion of each payment that is principal reduction
   (B) The amount of interest expense remaining
   (C) The future value of an investment
   (D) The present value of an interest expense

57. If the inflation rate is 2 percent, which of the following amounts is the decline in purchasing power of one dollar between today and one year from today?

   (A) $0.98
   (B) $0.80
   (C) $0.20
   (D) $0.02

58. Which of the following amounts must be invested today if an investor wants to receive a $14,000 annuity semiannually for 3 years, and the annual interest rate is 8 percent? (All withdrawals are to be made at the end of the investing period.)

(A) $36,079.40
(B) $52,624.40
(C) $73,389.40
(D) $92,862.40

59. An individual wants to withdraw at the end of each year $5,000 per year from a 3-year annuity with interest of 10 percent annually. Which of the following is the total interest amount the individual will earn over the 3 years?

(A) $500.00
(B) $2,565.50
(C) $12,434.50
(D) $15,000.00

60. An investor wants to receive a $2,000 annuity in 5 years that has a 6 percent interest rate and wants to make withdrawals at the end of the earning period. Which of the following amounts is the interest earned in the third year?

(A) $120.00
(B) $320.76
(C) $505.50
(D) $5,666.87

POSTTEST ANSWERS

1. **The correct answer is (C).** This line passes through (2,0) at the x-intercept. Therefore, the y-intercept lies -2 units in the x-direction. Slope is -2, so -2 units in the x-direction corresponds to 4 units in the y-direction. Four units in the y direction from 0 is 4.

2. **The correct answer is (B).** The numbers must be put in order; the middle number (the median) is 85.

3. **The correct answer is (D).** $\dfrac{(5 + 6 + 6 + 7 + 9 + 15)}{6} = 8$

4. **The correct answer is (B).**
$$\frac{[1000(1) + 300(5) + 150(2) + 75(8)]}{(1 + 5 + 2 + 8)} = 212.50$$

5. **The correct answer is (D).** The mode is the most frequently occurring submission. In this case, the mode is 75.

6. **The correct answer is (B).** When the numbers are put in order, the middle lies between 17 and 37.
$$\frac{(17+37)}{2} = 27$$

7. **The correct answer is (B).**
$$\frac{(50+82+89+83)}{4} = 76$$

8. **The correct answer is (B).** $\dfrac{[30(14) + 35(12)]}{26} = 32.3$

9. **The correct answer is (A).** The first quartile is the median of all numbers that fall to the left of the median. In this case, the first quartile is 23.

10. **The correct answer is (C).** The terms "50th percentile" and "median" are synonymous.

11. **The correct answer is (B).**
$$\frac{(10 - 2.5)}{2.5} = 3$$
$$3(100\%) = 300\%$$

12. **The correct answer is (A).** Cost = $50(1 - .24) = 38$

13. **The correct answer is (B).** Markdown % $= \dfrac{(600 - 425)}{600} = 29\%$

14. **The correct answer is (C).** Gross pay = (hrs worked)(hrly rate) = $32(38) = 1,216$

15. **The correct answer is (A).** $05(8,000) + 20(120) - 700 = 2,100$

16. **The correct answer is (A).** The federal government uses the exact time, exact interest method to calculate interest.

17. **The correct answer is (D).**

$$I = 10,000(.08)\left(\frac{30}{360}\right) = 66.66$$

$$500 - 66.66 = 433.33$$
$$10,000 - 433.33 = 9,566.66$$

18. **The correct answer is (C).** $2(400) + 15(25) = \$455$

19. **The correct answer is (A).** Lenders are required to inform borrowers of the true APR on an installment loan in order to allow borrowers to compare the cost of loans.

20. **The correct answer is (D).**

$$\frac{500}{[.95(.9)(.8)]} = \text{approximately } 731$$

21. **The correct answer is (C).**

$$700 (.03) = 21$$
$$700 - 21 = 679$$

22. **The correct answer is (A).** Periodic inventory systems include those in which a firm evaluates its inventory by counting all of the merchandise in stock.

23. **The correct answer is (B).** In periods of inflation, the cost of inventory most recently purchased will be the highest. LIFO systems value inventory sold at the price of inventory most recently purchased. Over-valuing inventory will result in an understated gross income and, therefore, less taxable income.

24. **The correct answer is (B).**

$$\text{Banker's discount} = 35,000(.12)\left(\frac{30}{360}\right) = 350$$

25. **The correct answer is (D).**

$$\frac{(700,000 - 2,000)}{900,000} = .0755$$

$$.0755(62,000) = 4,684.44$$
$$70,000 - 4,684.44 = \text{approximately } 65,315$$

26. **The correct answer is (C).**

$$\frac{4}{100} = .25$$

$$.25(2) = .5$$
$$.5(6,000) = 3,000$$
$$6,000 - 3,000 = 3,000$$

27. **The correct answer is (A).** $43,000\left(\frac{6}{36}\right) = 7,166$

28. The correct answer is (D).

$$\frac{175,000}{100} = 1,750$$

$$1,750(1.35) = 2,362.5$$

29. The correct answer is (A).

$$642 - 600 = 42$$

$$\frac{42}{600} = .07$$

30. The correct answer is (B). Regressive taxes charge either the same rate or higher to people with lower incomes than to those with higher incomes.

31. The correct answer is (C).

$$725,000(.75) = 543,750$$

$$\frac{543,750}{900,000} = .604$$

32. The correct answer is (B). P/E = (price per share)(# shares outstanding)/(net income), or price per share divided by EPS

33. The correct answer is (A). The current ratio and acid-test ratio differ in that the acid-test ratio does not include inventory.

34. The correct answer is (C). $\dfrac{(24,000 + 19,000 - 20,000)}{[.5(24,000+20,000)]} = 1.05$

35. The correct answer is (D). ROE = $\dfrac{7m}{(20m - 15m)} = 1.40$

36. The correct answer is (B). $\dfrac{.85(65,000)}{89,000} = 0.62$

37. The correct answer is (C). $\dfrac{.2(37,000)}{740,000} = .01$

38. The correct answer is (D). Dividend yield = 90,000/24,000/20 = .1875

39. The correct answer is (D). A company's price-to-earnings (P/E) ratio does NOT represent the profit earned for each dollar invested in the company.

40. The correct answer is (C).

$$300(20) = 6,000 \text{ grams}$$

$$\frac{6,000}{1,000} = 6 \text{ kilograms}$$

$$6\text{kg}\left(\frac{2.2 \text{ lbs}}{1\text{kg}}\right) = 13.2 \text{ lbs}$$

41. The correct answer is (D). (2.5)(16)(1.07) = 42.8

42. The correct answer is (C). Choice (D) is wrong, as partnerships have no stock. Choices (A) and (B) are both more likely to keep profits as retained earnings and re-invest them in the company than a merchandise retailer as they both have a research and development department.

43. **The correct answer is (B).** An annuity can be described as an interest bearing account.

44. **The correct answer is (C).** 800 + 800(1.1) + 880(1.1) + 968(1.1) = 3,712.8

45. **The correct answer is (A).** An ordinary annuity and an annuity due differ in that deposits are made at the end of each investment period in an ordinary annuity and at the beginning of the period with an annuity due.

46. **The correct answer is (D).**

$$400(1.12) = 448$$
$$448 + 400 = 848$$
$$848(1.12) = 949.76$$
$$949.76 + 400 = 1,349.76$$
$$1,349.76(1.12) = 1,511.73$$

47. **The correct answer is (D).**

$$2,000(1.06) = 2,120$$
$$4,120(1.06) = 4,367.2$$
$$6,367.2(1.06) = 6,749.2$$
$$8,749.2(1.06) = 9,274.2$$
$$11,274.2(1.06) = 11,950.6$$
$$13,950.6(1.06) = 14,787.6$$
$$16,787.6(1.06) = 17,794.9$$
$$19,794.9(1.06) = 20,982.58$$

48. **The correct answer is (A).** The present value of an ordinary annuity describes the amount of money one needs to invest to receive a stream of payments in the future.

49. **The correct answer is (B).** 5.3282 is the factor that can be found in a present value annuity table: 5.3282(20,000) = 106,564

50. **The correct answer is (A).** 3.4651 is the factor that can be found in the present value annuity table:

$$3.4651(35,000) = 121,278.5$$

.7050 can be found in the present value annuity table:

$$121,278.5(.7050) = 85,501.3$$

51. **The correct answer is (D).** 5.0757 can be found in the present value annuity table: 5.0757(400) = 2,029.88

52. **The correct answer is (C).** 8,263 − 7,000 = 1,263

53. **The correct answer is (A).** .6830 can be found in the present value annuity table: .6830(10,000) = 6,830

54. **The correct answer is (D).** 10%/4 = 2.5%

55. **The correct answer is (D).** Amortization, unlike depreciation and depletion, deals with intangible assets.

56. **The correct answer is (A).** An amortization schedule depicts the portion of each payment that goes toward principal reduction.

57. **The correct answer is (D).** $1(.02) = .02$

58. **The correct answer is (C).** 5.2421 can be found in the present value annuity table: $5.2421(14,000) = 73,389.4$

59. **The correct answer is (B).** 2.4869 can be found in the present value annuity table:

$$2.4869(5000) = 12,434.5$$
$$15,000 - 12,434.5 = 2,565.5$$

60. **The correct answer is (B).** 4.2124 can be found in the present value annuity table:

$$4.2124(2,000) = 8,424.8 = \text{initial payment}$$
$$8,424.8(1.06) = 8,930.28$$
$$8,930.28 - 2,000 = 6,930.28$$
$$6,930.28(1.06) = 7,346.11$$
$$7,346.11 - 2,000 = 5,346.11$$
$$5,346.11(.06) = 320.76$$

Ethics in America

PRETEST

1. Hobbes and Locke differed over whether

   (A) people are such that a state of war is inherent in a state of nature
   (B) a person may appeal to a state of nature in justifying a political system
   (C) there are governmental structures in a state of nature
   (D) a person could justify political anarchism by appeal to a state of nature

2. According to Aristotle, for an act to express a virtue, all of the following must be true EXCEPT that the actor must

   (A) know that the actor is performing the act
   (B) perform the act without attention to who benefits from it
   (C) perform the virtuous act for its own sake
   (D) perform the act out of a settled state of character

3. According to John Stuart Mill, pleasure is the only thing that is desirable for its own sake because pleasure is

   (A) the only sure thing in a complicated world
   (B) available on both the physical and the spiritual level
   (C) something that all people can experience
   (D) the only thing that is desired for its own sake

4. According to Aristotle, which of the following sets are the two main kinds of virtues?

   (A) Virtues in regard to self and virtues in regard to others
   (B) Perfect virtues and imperfect virtues
   (C) Virtues of intellect and virtues of character
   (D) Natural virtues and theological virtues

5. In the New Testament, the commandment to "love thy neighbor as thyself" is said to be

   (A) the "first commandment" of the Law
   (B) "like" the commandment to love God
   (C) "only for the meek"
   (D) a "parable of justice"

6. Aristotle defined virtue of character in part as "a state concerned with choice, lying in a mean relative to us." The "mean relative to us" is

   (A) what the individual feels is the intermediate in a given situation
   (B) what the society feels is the intermediate in a given situation
   (C) the arithmetical intermediate or average in a given situation
   (D) the intermediate called for by specific facts of a given situation

7. According to John Stuart Mill, "it is better to be Socrates dissatisfied than a pig satisfied" because Socrates

   (A) can obey the Moral Law, but the pig cannot
   (B) can experience pleasures of much greater quality than the pig
   (C) has the possibility of an afterlife, but the pig does not
   (D) has the potential for long-term pleasure, but the pig can only experience short-term pleasure

8. Rule-utilitarianism is similar to Kantian ethics in

   (A) locating rightness in the maxim or principle behind an action
   (B) using general happiness as the criterion of right action
   (C) viewing rightness as determined by something other than consequences
   (D) basing rightness ultimately on divine commandment

9. In the books of the law (Old Testament), the "covenant" is

   (A) a treaty between the ancient Israelites and the Canaanites, establishing a division of land and common ethical principles
   (B) the punishment meted out to Cain for killing Abel
   (C) the site where Moses received the Ten Commandments
   (D) a binding commitment of the Israelites to God to obey His laws in expectation of subsequent rewards

10. Both Plato and Aristotle believed that

   (A) justice is a principle that applies to societies and not to individuals
   (B) the just person is happier than the unjust person
   (C) the stronger person benefits from justice more than the weaker
   (D) justice is rewarded after death

11. For a Kantian, it is wrong to break promises because if a person breaks promises

   (A) everyone will break promises and no promises will be kept
   (B) the person violates a rule, which is conducive to the general happiness
   (C) the person acts on a principle, which cannot be willed to be universal without contradiction
   (D) the person will not, in the end, achieve the aim sought

12. Epicurus says people should not fear the gods because

   (A) the gods lack any influence on human life one way or the other
   (B) the gods are benevolent and look after the people
   (C) the people are created in the gods' image and so are a source of pleasure to the gods
   (D) there are no gods

13. The Stoics differed from the Epicureans in holding that

   (A) there is a universal brotherhood of human beings
   (B) reason is a valuable ethical tool
   (C) friendship is of value
   (D) justice is a desirable thing

14. Hobbes differed from Aquinas in holding that natural law

   (A) is a concept to be eliminated from ethical and political thought
   (B) is not based on divine law
   (C) derives its authority from the existing political system
   (D) provides the proper basis for determining which particular laws should be enacted

15. According to many advocates of feminist ethics, which of the following statements is true?

   (A) Caring about justice defines the moral life.
   (B) People ought to care most about the female human beings in their lives.
   (C) The principle of equal pay for equal work is a model for moral behavior.
   (D) Moral behavior often requires the perspective of a caregiver.

16. According to Aristotle, an act is involuntary if it is done from

   (A) ignorance of moral principles
   (B) ignorance of particular facts of the situation
   (C) a settled state of character
   (D) a desire for pleasure

17. To the thesis that "the good is what God wills," the question is sometimes raised: "(i) Does God will it because it is good, or (ii) is it good because God wills it?" The dilemma involved in that question is that

   (A) (i) contradicts God's omnipotence, while (ii) contradicts God's all-goodness
   (B) (i) contradicts God's all-goodness, while (ii) contradicts God's omnipotence
   (C) (i) contradicts God's omniscience, while (ii) limits God's freedom
   (D) there may not be a God

18. In the *Crito,* Socrates offered all of the following reasons why individuals should obey the law EXCEPT:

   (A) The law has provided benefits that obligate the individuals to obey the society's laws.
   (B) The law embodies, albeit imperfectly, the eternal Form of the Good.
   (C) Individuals ought to avoid doing wrong to their society even if it has wronged them.
   (D) Individuals commit to obeying society's laws by voluntarily remaining in the society.

19. The Christian doctrine of "original sin" involves each of the following ideas EXCEPT:

   (A) Adam's eating of the apple was a sin.
   (B) Sin can be inherited.
   (C) There is a tendency toward sin in all human beings today.
   (D) Sinful acts originate in people's relationship with other human beings.

20. Which of the following philosophers accepted Aristotle's list of "natural" virtues but added the theological virtues of faith, hope, and love (charity)?

   (A) Epictetus
   (B) Augustine
   (C) Aquinas
   (D) Hobbes

PRETEST ANSWERS

1. **The correct answer is (A).** Locke denied that war was inherent. Although he did acknowledge that there would be harmful individuals, he believed the creation of a state would protect other individuals against those who were harmful.

2. **The correct answer is (B).** Choices (A), (C), and (D) are stated in *Nicomachean Ethics* II.4. Aristotle takes benefit into account, e.g., in the virtue of generosity.

3. **The correct answer is (D).** This is stated explicitly (see Mill's *Utilitarianism*, Chapter IV).

4. **The correct answer is (C).** Aristotle divides virtue according as it pertains to action and feeling (virtues of character) or as it pertains to intellect (virtues of intellect).

5. **The correct answer is (B).** This is stated explicitly: "and a second is like unto it" (see *Gospel According to Matthew*, 22.39).

6. **The correct answer is (D).** The mean (analogized by Aristotle to the right amount of food for an ordinary person vs. a wrestler) is not a matter of feeling or a numerical average but of specific facts about actual needs in that situation.

7. **The correct answer is (B).** This is stated explicitly (see Mill's *Utilitarianism*, Chapter II).

8. **The correct answer is (A).** Rule-utilitarianism was created to incorporate just that Kantian perspective, while retaining the consequentialist orientation of traditional act-utilitarianism.

9. **The correct answer is (D).** Scholars appear to differ over the precise meaning of the word, but most accept that it means a commitment.

10. **The correct answer is (B).** This is the main thesis of Plato's *Republic* and is implicit in Aristotle's definition of happiness, partly in terms of virtue.

11. **The correct answer is (C).** This is Kant's example of just that—if the principle were made universal, no promises would be believed and so none could be broken.

12. **The correct answer is (A).** This is stated explicitly.

13. **The correct answer is (A).** Epicurus spoke of the desirability of gathering with friends, but only the Stoics spoke of a universal brotherhood of man.

14. **The correct answer is (B).** Hobbes based natural law on certain simple (alleged) facts of human nature, without reference to human nature.

15. **The correct answer is (D).** Care ethic and ethic of trust are, in feminist ethics, two "alternative visions" to the allegedly masculine justice ethic.

16. **The correct answer is (B).** Aristotle distinguishes acting from ignorance of moral principles, which is not excusable, and acting from ignorance of particular facts, which can be excusable, if the facts are not available to a person.

17. **The correct answer is (A).** If God wills it because it's good, goodness appears to be prior to God; if it's good because God wills it, then God's doing what's good is merely God doing what God wants, and is no moral achievement.

18. **The correct answer is (B).** Socrates in the *Crito* does not recognize an eternal Form of the Good as Plato does in the *Republic*.

19. **The correct answer is (D).** Sinful acts can originate in any situation, and are ultimately defined in terms of disobedience to God.

20. **The correct answer is (C).** This is stated explicitly in various writings.

GENERAL OVERVIEW

Philosophy is an activity in which the larger issues, such as the nature of reality, God, and art, are addressed and sound, rational reasons for holding particular views are developed. **Ethics**, also called moral philosophy, is the branch of philosophy that deals with good and evil, right and wrong, and the principles of morality. It seeks to answer two basic questions: How should we live? Why?

ETHICAL TRADITIONS

All cultures have views on ethics. This course focuses on the Western philosophical tradition, which underlies modern approaches to ethics in the United States.

THE ANCIENT GREEKS

Thucydides

Thucydides (460–400 B.C.) was the foremost historian of the ancient world. In his history of the Pelopennesian War between Athens and Sparta, he describes how Athenians dismissed all notions of right and justice in their plan to slaughter or enslave the people of the island of Melos, giving the rulers of Melos the choice of their fate. Although the Melians claim that justice is on their side, the Athenians declare that the strong prevail, the weak submit, and morality is irrelevant. This statement of **"might makes right"** is in contrast with the Greek ideal of the life of virtue, set forth by Socrates, Plato, Aristotle, and other Greek philosophers.

Socrates

According to Socrates (470–399 B.C.), a contemporary of Thucydides, people behave as they do because they are seeking happiness, the ultimate human good. To be happy, however, you must have a healthy, virtuous soul. If you know that a healthy soul is necessary for happiness, then you will understand how to choose virtuous actions that will make you happy.

Acting viciously makes the soul vicious, according to Socrates. Thus, it is far better to suffer an injustice than to inflict one. When you suffer an injustice, only your body is harmed, but when you inflict injustice, your soul is harmed. For example, when Socrates considered whether he should escape from jail, he did not focus on the question of whether or not he had been unjustly imprisoned. That question, in his view, concerned the well being of his body. Instead, he focused on the question of whether escaping, and thus violating the law, would be just, a question that concerns the well being of his soul.

Socrates also believed that people only desire what is good for them or what they *believe* is good. According to Socrates, no one acts contrary to what he or she perceives as good.

Thus, Socrates claimed that **virtue is knowledge**. If no one behaves contrary to what he or she believes is good, then it follows that no one acts viciously except out of ignorance. People who understand that happiness arises from a healthy soul, which results from acting virtuously, want to act ethically because they know it is good for them. Without knowledge, people are not in a position to recognize what is good for their soul and what is not. Thus, wrongdoers need to be taught what is virtuous; they do not need to be punished.

Socrates also believed in the **unity of virtues**. A person who knows that acting virtuously will be to his or her own good will act virtuously in all areas of life—personal, social, military, and religious.

Plato

A student of Socrates, Plato (ca. 428–347 B.C.) left a body of work, called dialogues, in which the main speaker is often Socrates. In the *Republic*, Plato goes beyond Socrates' idea that happiness requires a virtuous soul and asks why people should be virtuous. In the course of answering the question "Why be just?", Plato accepts that people often know what is good for them and yet fail to do it.

The *Republic* begins with Socrates asking, "What is justice?" Thrasymachus answers that justice is bad for the person doing the just act but good for someone else—the stronger, who would punish the person if he or she failed to act to benefit the stronger. People simply want to avoid the consequences imposed upon them by the stronger. Thus, people want the appearance of justice, not justice itself. To rebut this view, Socrates must show that justice is desired not simply for its appearance but for its own sake.

Socrates first describes the **ideal city**, composed of three classes of citizens: workers who provide goods and services, soldiers who protect the city from attack, and guardians who rule the city. According to Socrates, wisdom is the province of the guardians, courage belongs to the soldiers, and temperance applies to all classes. What is left that makes the city good is justice, the fact that each class of citizens performs its own task. Socrates then moves on to consider justice in the individual. An individual's soul, like the city, has three aspects: the appetite (pure desire), the reason (based on knowledge and logic), and the spirit (naturally allied to reason). Justice in the individual is each part of the soul performing its own task.

The ideal city degenerates in a series of stages until it is ruled by a tyrannical individual, one in whom appetites rule. The tyrannical city is the most unhappy city, just as the individual ruled by appetite is the most unhappy individual. In contrast, the individual in whom each part of the soul performs its own task is the happiest, most just individual. Thus, happiness is not the result of the appearance of justice but of the very nature of justice. Those who are just in this sense will reap numerous rewards and avoid punishment in the afterlife. Justice is therefore desirable for its own sake and for its consequences.

Aristotle

Aristotle (384–322 B.C.) left a large body of work, including views on moral theory, that has been enormously influential in many fields. Aristotle believed that to lead a good life, people have to fulfill their natural goals. In order to do this, they must develop a good character that is manifest in good actions. They must possess a set of virtues— inner dispositions to have the right emotions and to perform the right actions.

Humans share many capacities with animals—perception as well as the need for nutrition, for example—but what distinguishes humans from animals is the ability to reason. Our capacity to reason can be exercised in the pursuit of knowledge and in practical living (ethics). Humans should develop the virtues that lead to rational, practical action. These virtues enable us to respond with the right emotions and the right actions. To fail to respond is a defect, to over-respond is an excess. According to Aristotle, **virtue is a mean** between under- and over-responding. For example, courage is a virtue that is the mean between cowardice, or failure to respond, and recklessness, or over-responding. To determine the appropriate middle course in a given set of circumstances is the task of practical reason.

According to Aristotle, the **best human life** is the one devoted to actively using reason to understand the principles of science and philosophy without regard to applying them. This life is impossible unless one has first attained moral virtue. Aristotle also believed that moral virtue required early training and the support of good **laws**. Thus, the proper setting for the moral life is the good community, and those who are concerned with making people good should take an active part in the legislative life of the community.

THE BIBLICAL TRADITION

The Bible is not a work of philosophy as defined at the beginning of this chapter. However, it is the oldest and most familiar collection of ethical directives in the Western world. The Ten Commandments, the rest of the Jewish law, and the Christian way of life are deeply ingrained models of ethical behavior, even though the Bible gives little or no rational justification for them.

The Hebrew Bible

In the beginning of the first book of the Hebrew Bible, *Genesis*, Adam and Eve exist in a premoral state of innocence. When they disobey God's command not to eat off of the tree of knowledge of good and evil, Adam immediately understands his guilt and the justice of their punishment.

After Adam and Eve are expelled from the Garden of Eden, sin proliferates and people are powerless to behave properly until God offers a group of them a **covenant**, or contract. He selects Abraham to be the founder of a great and blessed nation, the Israelites; in return, Abraham and his descendants are to obey God. The story of the Israelites continues until Moses leads them out of slavery in Egypt and God renews the covenant on Mount Sinai, giving Moses laws for his people—the **Ten Commandments**. The Ten Commandments are general and abstract rules for good behavior, so God immediately supplements them with detailed, concrete, and fair **laws applying to specific situations**.

As soon as the Israelites cross the Jordan River into the Promised Land, they begin to break the laws. God punishes them with war, exile, and famine and rewards them from time to time with a good king who restores the nation. God also sends them **prophets**, men and women whose role is to remind the Israelites that they are the chosen people of God and therefore they must behave justly and care for one another. If they do not, God will punish them.

The Christian Bible

The books of the Christian Bible begin with the four **gospels**, which tell the story of Jesus's life, death, and resurrection. Jesus, a Jew brought up in the tradition of the law, emphasizes the internal spiritual aspect of keeping the laws and tells his followers to go beyond just keeping the law by leaving material concerns behind. He takes the ancient law of loving your neighbor as you love yourself and extends it to loving strangers and anyone in need. This idea is a foundation of the modern notion of respecting the rights and autonomy of all individuals.

Although Jesus performed his ministry primarily as a prophet among Jews, after his death his followers decided that their mission was to take his teachings to all nations. The most influential of the early followers of Jesus was Saul of Tarsus, a Jew who took the name Paul after his conversion. Paul founded Christian communities all over the Roman Empire and kept in touch with them through letters, many of which contain ethical instruction.

The Divine Command Theory

According to the Biblical tradition, God gives people laws that they must obey. People are free agents, so they can choose to obey or not to obey. According to the divine command theory of ethics, *morally right* means commanded by God, and *morally wrong* means forbidden by God. There are two interpretations of this theory, both of which lead to problems. (1) Conduct is right simply because God commands it; therefore nothing is inherently good or bad. (2) God commands right conduct because it is right; therefore there is a standard of good and evil independent of God's will. Both interpretations suggest that right and wrong cannot be interpreted in terms of God's will. Although this may seem to be an irreligious conclusion, many theologians agree with it. The dominant theory of ethics in the Christian tradition has not been the divine command theory; rather it has been natural law, which is discussed in the next section.

MORAL LAW

With the decline of the Greek city-states, the ideal city, or *polis*, that had been a central element of Plato and Aristotle's views on ethics no longer existed. Instead, philosophers were left with its underlying moral structure—the law. This development of moral philosophy started with the Greek Stoics.

Epictetus

Compared to the Athenian polis, the world of Epictetus (ca. 55 A.D.–135 A.D.) was disorderly, incorporating war, slavery, and oppression. Epictetus, one of the Stoics, sought to discover how to lead a virtuous, happy life in the midst of uncertainty. He decided that the key was "to do what was in accordance with nature." If people conform to whatever nature sends them, they make the best of things to their ability and take the rest as it comes.

Aquinas

In the *Summa Theologica* of Thomas Aquinas (1225–1274), the natural law tradition, the Biblical tradition, and the philosophical thinking of Aristotle are united. Aquinas, a Dominican monk born in Italy, believed that all things subject to God are ruled to some extent by God's eternal law. Humans, as rational beings, are subject to God's eternal law and have a share of God's eternal reason. The rational human participation in eternal reason is the **natural law**. Through our natural reason, we can discern good and evil. Thus, knowing the difference between right and wrong is not the province of religious people but a faculty of all people. It is our duty to think through the reasons for and against various courses of conduct and to choose the action that seems most reasonable. According to Aquinas, "Conscience is the dictate of reason . . . he who acts against his conscience always sins."

Aquinas indicated that several precepts arise from the foundation of natural law. First, humans have an inclination to good in accordance with the preservation of human life. Second, humans have in common with other animals certain specific inclinations, such as sexual intercourse and education of offspring. Third, humans have an inclination to good, according to the nature of reason, and want to know the truth about God and live in society with others.

Although people have a natural aptitude for virtue, it must be perfected by training. For some people, the training they receive from their families is sufficient. But others, who are more prone to vice, must be restrained from doing evil through force and fear, in the hope that eventually they may be trained to become virtuous. The means by which this force, fear, and retraining is accomplished is **human law**. Human law, if it is just, is derived from natural law, either as a conclusion from natural law premises (the natural law premise, "do harm to no man," leads to the human law conclusion, "one must not kill"); or by determination (the law of nature is that evil-doers should be punished, but the human law may determine many different ways to punish).

Hobbes

Thomas Hobbes (1588–1679) published a major work of political philosophy, *Leviathan*, about ten years after Puritan revolutionaries had overthrown and beheaded King Charles I of England. Until Hobbes, theories of the moral foundation of government had focused on the divine right of kings or on natural law, allowing a few to exercise the right to govern the many.

According to Hobbes, the laws of nature are rules of reason that indicate the best way to further our self-preservation. Thus, people avoid war and seek peace as a means to self-preservation. However, people are also led to war by their reason—also as a means for self-preservation. To resolve this contradiction, Hobbes proposes that all people should agree to lay down their right to do anything necessary to preserve themselves. To back up such an agreement, Hobbes proposes the establishment of a **sovereign power** to whom people cede their right to all things in return for enforcing the agreement—at best, an absolute monarch. The citizens' survival depends on accepting the authority of the monarch because revolution cannot be justified on the grounds of individual liberty.

Locke

John Locke (1632–1704), another Englishman, carries on from Hobbes, but he has a much more positive view of human nature. According to Locke, natural law obliges people to preserve not only themselves but others as well, as long as their own preservation is not threatened. People also can expect assistance from others in preserving themselves. Each rational being legislates the law of nature and executes it in practice, so each person must judge when the law has been broken and what reparation or punishment is needed. For Locke, the state of nature is a virtual natural government in which all take part in the legislative, executive, and judicial branches.

According to Locke, each person has a property in him- or herself, and nobody else has a right to that property. The idea of property extends to the fruits of a person's labor. Locke's notion of the **social contract** is that it exists to protect property—a person's body, freedom, and fruits of labor. And since under natural law physical property is most at risk, **civil law** is needed primarily to protect lands and industry. Thus, the fundamental rights of citizens are life, liberty, and property, and the role of the law is to protect those rights. Locke's writings profoundly influenced the development of democracy in the United States and throughout the world.

Jefferson

Thomas Jefferson (1743-1826), the author of the American Declaration of Independence, was greatly influenced by Locke's description of a society that protects the rights of individuals to live their own lives. Since liberties and the laws that protect them are equally extended to all citizens, the idea of justice is embedded in the political framework of the society—a society ruled by laws, not men. And since laws are to be made for the common good, concern for the welfare or happiness of citizens is institutionalized in the political system.

The intermingling of the ethical and the legal in the political theory that underlies Locke's writings as well as the Declaration of Independence makes ethical and legal issues intertwined in the American mind. The Declaration of Independence summarized the consequences of Locke's ideas for the political future of America: revolution is justified when a government becomes destructive of its citizens' rights to life, liberty, and the pursuit of happiness.

Kant

With German philosopher Immanuel Kant (1724-1804), the focus shifts from the ethical underpinnings of the state to the nature of morality. He is one of the few philosophers who believe that morality is a matter of following absolute rules.

Kant believed that much of human conduct is governed by the notion of "ought." For example, if you decide you want something, you recognize that a certain course of action will help you get what you want; therefore, you ought to follow that course of action. Kant called this type of situation a **hypothetical imperative**—what you ought to do depends on what you desire. If you renounce the desire, you can renounce the course of action.

In contrast, moral obligations do not depend on an individual's desires. Moral requirements are **categorical imperatives:** you should do something regardless of your personal wishes and desires. Kant believed that hypothetical imperatives are possible because people have desires, but categorical imperatives exist because people have reason. This is because categorical imperatives are derived from a principle that every rational being must accept, "Act only according to that maxim by which you can at the same time will that it should become a universal law." For example, you must give charity whether you desire to or not, because if you do not, others may not give charity to you when you need it.

Thus, acting as a moral agent means guiding your behavior by universal laws, moral rules that hold without exception in all circumstances. Moral agency also involves honoring the fundamental worth and **dignity** of people and treating them with respect. Thus, you cannot treat another human being as a **means** to an end, as you might treat an animal; human beings are **ends** in themselves. Moral agency also presupposes that people are rational, autonomous beings—that they can make or follow laws as necessary and recognize others as autonomous.

Royce

American Josiah Royce (1855-1916) approached ethical principles from the deontological perspective. He selects a principle that represents the highest duty and from which other duties originate and judges behavior on whether or not it is in accord with that highest duty. According to Royce, that highest duty is **loyalty**, or commitment in general to the idea of duty as well as commitment in particular to the duties and ideals specific to a particular person. Basic moral principles, such as autonomy, justice, and benevolence, are aspects of loyalty.

Rawls

John Rawls (1921-) is interested in how justice might be ensured in a society in which social institutions totally ignore its most disadvantaged members on the premise that the greater good of the greater number is served by abandoning the "underclass," a premise that he finds unjust. According to Rawls, the point at which the institutional practices of a society are determined is the point at which the state of nature is left behind and the civil state is formed. The original social contract becomes a model for a just society. A group of rational people, all of whom are equals who are bargaining for the best possible society without knowing whether they will be advantaged or disadvantaged, will have to establish a set of rules that are fair for all.

According to Rawls, such a group would choose two principles of justice: "First, each person is to have an equal right to the most extensive basic liberty compatible with a similar liberty for others. Second, social inequalities are to be arranged so that they are both (a) reasonably expected to be to everyone's advantage and (b) attached to positions and offices open to all."

King

Martin Luther King, Jr. (1929–1968) explained that the American civil rights movement was working for the cause of justice. He drew from the Biblical tradition, Aquinas, Hobbes, Locke, Jefferson, and Kant. For King, the obligation to do justice overrode the possibilities of violence and threats to order. In a letter from jail justifying the Birmingham boycott of 1963, King explained how he could simultaneously urge people to obey the law and break the law: "I agree with St. Augustine that 'an unjust law is no law at all.' A just law is a man-made code that squares with the moral law or the law of God. An unjust law is a code that is out of harmony with the moral law . . . Any law that degrades human personality is unjust. All segregation statutes are unjust because segregation distorts the soul and damages the personality."

CONSEQUENTIAL ETHICS

The hedonists of ancient Greece were the first philosophers of consequential ethics, in which the morality of an action is determined by its consequences. Their approach was later adapted by the Utilitarians Jeremy Bentham and John Stuart Mill.

Epicurus

An early hedonist, Epicurus (341 B.C.–270 B.C.) believed that it was possible to lead a calm and enjoyable life by carefully managing the appetites. **Pleasure** is the first good; it is the basis of every choice we make for or against something, and it is the standard by which we judge what is good. Epicurus understood pleasure to mean freedom from pain in the body and from trouble in the mind. Prudence, therefore, is the greatest virtue, for it enables us to live pleasantly, managing our desires.

Bentham

Jeremy Bentham's (1748–1832) moral philosophy is based on the **principle of utility**: "that principle which approves or disapproves of every action whatsoever, according to the tendency which it appears to have to augment or diminish the happiness of the party whose interest is in question; or what is the same thing in other words, to promote or to oppose that happiness." The principle of utility is not easy to apply, because it involves thinking before acting and figuring out the consequences of action for yourself, others, and even the community as a whole.

Bentham sets forth a method of **calculating the value of consequential pleasure or pain to an individual** according to its intensity, duration, certainty or uncertainty, propinquity or remoteness, fecundity, and purity. To calculate its value to a number of people, one must consider the factors previously listed and add a seventh factor: its extent, that is, the number of people who will be affected by the act. When the interests of a community are affected, a complex process of balancing pleasure and pain is followed.

Mill

John Stuart Mill (1806–1873) was the leading exponent of Utilitarian theory in the generation following Bentham. According to Mill, people long for a state of being in which they are as happy as possible, which he called the **greatest happiness principle**. The primary rule of morality is, therefore, to act in a manner that brings the greatest state of happiness to all those affected by our conduct. Thus, actions are judged to be right or wrong based solely on the virtue of their consequences. In assessing consequences, only happiness or unhappiness matters, and no one's happiness or unhappiness is more important than any other person's.

Mill believed that the state has limited authority to interfere with personal freedom as long as the individual's actions are not harming others. The inconvenience to society is bearable because the greater good of human freedom for all is being honored. In addition, he thought that when the state does interfere with purely personal conduct, it usually interferes wrongly.

FEMINIST ETHICS

A feminist critique of traditional moral philosophy arose in the 1980s on the basis that traditional ethics are ethics of principle based on a "male" way of thinking. Carol Gilligan, a psychologist, suggested that women's basic moral orientation was to care for others (personally, not humanity in general) and to attend to their needs. Their moral responses tend to seem diffuse and confused because they have an overriding concern with relationships rather than logical principles. According to Virginia Held, caring for other people's feelings and needs may be better indicators of what morality requires in specific situations than abstract rules of reason. This feminist approach to moral philosophy is called the **ethics of care**.

THE ETHICS OF VIRTUE

The philosophers who focused on the moral law asked, "What should we do?" Some modern philosophers have suggested a return to Aristotle's approach, asking, "What traits make a good person?"

A trait of character that is demonstrated by habitual action and that is deemed good for a person to have is called a **virtue.** Examples of virtues include benevolence, compassion, courage, fairness, honesty, moderation, self-confidence, self-discipline, tactfulness, and tolerance. Each virtue has its own distinctive characteristics and problems. For example, it can be argued that courage on behalf of an evil cause is wicked, not virtuous, behavior.

ETHICAL ISSUES

As we have seen, ethics deals with questions of right behavior that arise in all areas of life, including our relationships with family and friends, in government and law, in business, in science and medicine, and in our occupational roles. We touch on just a few issues here.

FAMILY AND FRIENDS

People do not treat their family and friends as they do strangers because they are bound to them by ties of kinship and affection. For example, according to some moral theories the idea of impartiality might suggest that parents should treat their children as they would the children of strangers, but that seems wrong; we expect parents to love and pay a great deal more attention to their own children than to others. Similarly, a judge is expected to be impartial when presiding over trials and sentencing criminals, but no one expects a judge to preside over the trial of her own son.

The special treatment afforded family is even codified in our laws: husbands and wives cannot be compelled to testify in court against one another. In relationships with family and friends, therefore, loyalty usually prevails over justice.

GOVERNMENT AND THE LAW

Questions of ethics arise in almost all aspects of government and law, from the law's intrinsic impartiality and fairness (justice) to the rightness of defending criminals to the idea of retribution, to name just a few.

JUSTICE

The most fundamental principle of **justice** is that people should be treated the same unless they differ in ways that are relevant to the situation at hand. This is the basic principle underlying equal employment opportunity legislation, which seeks to prevent discrimination in employment on the basis of gender, race, sex, religion, or national origin. In most employment situations, these characteristics are considered irrelevant to the ability to do a job and are not to be used to discriminate against an individual. For example, a woman should be paid the same wages if she is doing the same job as a man. However, there are situations in which one of the characteristics might be relevant. For example, an airline would be justified in discriminating against an elderly pilot on the grounds that age affects performance in that job.

There are different kinds of justice:

- **Distributive, or social, justice** refers to the extent to which our legal and social institutions ensure that benefits and burdens are distributed fairly among the members of society. When benefits and burdens are distributed unfairly, we assume that our institutions need to change. Slavery in the United States and apartheid in South Africa were both condemned as unjust because benefits and burdens were distributed unfairly on the basis of race.

- **Retributive justice** refers to the fairness of punishments. In general, punishment is considered fair if it accounts for the seriousness of the crime and the intent of the criminal and if it does not account for irrelevant criteria such as race. The disproportionate number of black men on death row suggests that injustice still exists in the criminal justice system of the United States.

- **Compensatory justice** refers to the extent to which people are fairly compensated for their injuries by those who have injured them. Smokers suing the tobacco companies are seeking compensatory justice.

BUSINESS

In a business that takes account of moral as well as economic issues, management assesses the effect of business decisions and actions on society as well as on the business. Three major areas of ethical concern are consumers (product safety, public health, product information, product choices, privacy, and the resolution of complaints), employees (equal employment opportunity, affirmative action, and retraining), and the environment (safety, pollution, and conservation).

In an organization with an ethical corporate culture, ethical guidelines are clearly stated and communicated to employees; managers are committed to ethical values, normal business practices reflect ethical values, and managers are trained to make ethically sound decisions. Ideally, businesses would regulate themselves behaving in an ethical and socially responsible manner. In reality, the government imposes regulations to help ensure that businesses operate in an ethical and socially responsible manner.

SCIENCE

There are many ethical issues in science today that involve both the content of experiments (such as embryonic stem cell research or genetic engineering) and the manner in which they are carried out. Two ethical issues that arise frequently are animal rights and informed consent.

ANIMAL RIGHTS

Natural law held that animals were intended for the use of humans. The social contract among rational beings excluded animals because they did not have the ability to reason, and Christian tradition said that animals lacked a "soul" and were not human. Thus, on most fronts of moral philosophy animals could be killed or made to suffer if there was a purpose for doing so. The first philosophers to challenge this view were the Utilitarians. According to Bentham, what matters is whether the animal is capable of happiness or suffering.

When animal rights activists protest animal experiments, they use the Utilitarian argument that animals are capable of suffering. Scientists counter with the argument that there is a compensating gain in happiness elsewhere—the possible future benefits to humans from animal experimentation.

INFORMED CONSENT

When humans are the subjects of experiments, the ethical duty of researchers is to minimize their exposure to physical or psychological risks. Research institutions and hospitals generally have review boards that make sure that each proposed study follows ethical guidelines. Researchers must ensure that participants understand what is or may be involved in the study by obtaining their informed consent before the study begins. Informed consent is premised on the rational capacity of humans to judge the risks and benefits of their actions. Subjects are permitted to withdraw from an experiment at any time. In addition, all information about participants must be kept confidential to protect their privacy.

HEALTH CARE

Scientific and technological advances have enabled medical professionals to treat disorders and prolong life. Along with these new abilities have come ethical issues. Some of these are life-and-death or quality-of-life issues for which there are no accepted moral codes as yet. For example, the care owed to a very premature infant is an area still being explored since our ability to intervene with these babies is so recent. Other ethical dilemmas have arisen in dealing with reproductive technology, organ transplant, keeping terminally ill patients alive on life support systems, and physician-assisted suicide. Ethical dilemmas involving health care are so serious that many hospitals and other health-care institutions seek the advice of ethicists in resolving these problems.

OCCUPATIONAL ETHICS

Many professional groups have codes of ethics that are guidelines for moral behavior. For example, lawyers, psychotherapists, doctors, counselors, and clergy are expected to keep information their clients share with them confidential. Doctors are also expected "to do no harm," which is part of the Hippocratic oath that they take upon entering medical practice. Some occupational ethics may not be articulated in a written code but exist nevertheless. For example, teachers are expected to treat their students impartially. Business people are expected to honor their agreements.

ETHICAL DECISION MAKING

When confronted by a serious ethical dilemma that they cannot resolve instinctively, people are sometimes at a loss as to how to proceed. In such cases, using a framework for ethical decision making can be helpful in clarifying the issues. The framework outlined here is adapted from one developed by Santa Clara University's Markkula Center for Applied Ethics.

RECOGNIZING A MORAL PROBLEM

The first step in any decision-making framework is to make sure the moral problem is thoroughly understood. What exactly is wrong that may result in harm to myself, others, animals, the environment, or society at large? Can the issue be resolved by recourse to the law or to the rules of an institution (a church or school, for example), or must a decision be made independent of these resources?

ESTABLISHING THE FACTS

The fact-finding activities are important because the decision will be made in part based upon an assessment of the facts that exist and the alternatives that are possible. So, for example, in deciding whether or not to intervene medically in a severely premature baby's condition, it is important to know exactly what the condition is and what the probable outcomes are—both of acting and not acting.

Questions to ask include "What are the relevant facts of the situation?" "What people and groups have a stake in the outcome?" "Do some have a greater stake than others?" "Are there people other than those directly involved who might have a stake in the outcome?"

"What are the alternatives for action?" Doing nothing is one alternative, but there may be several others. Involving the stakeholders in the search for alternatives can be helpful. Whose advice on the alternatives might be helpful?

EVALUATING THE ALTERNATIVES

Once it's clear what the alternatives are, each must be evaluated from a moral perspective. There are four major schools of moral philosophy today, Utilitarianism, Kantianism, social contract theory, and virtue theory. Each alternative can be evaluated from the perspective of each of these theories:

- Which alternative would do the most good and the least harm? (Utilitarianism)

- Which alternative takes into account the rights and dignity of everyone involved? Will everyone be treated fairly? (Kantianism)

- Which alternative would increase the common good of the group, company, community, society, etc.? (social contract theory)
- Which alternative would develop the virtues that we value as individuals, as a profession, or as a family? (virtue theory)
- **Making a Decision**
- After all the alternatives have been considered and reasons for and against each have been evaluated, a decision can be made as to which alternative is best in the circumstances.

ASSESSING THE DECISION

At some point in the future it will be possible to look back at the ethical issue and its resolution in order to evaluate the action that was taken. How did solving the problem affect each of the stakeholders? Were there unanticipated consequences? If you were again confronted with this problem, what would you do?

SAMPLE QUESTIONS

1. Which of the following people has a moral philosophy that is in accord with St. Augustine's statement that "an unjust law is no law at all"?
   - (A) Epicurus
   - (B) Jeremy Bentham
   - (C) Martin Luther King, Jr.
   - (D) Carol Gilligan

   The correct answer is (C). When he was jailed for breaking the law in Birmingham, Alabama, King wrote a letter to his critics explaining why breaking some laws was justifiable in the pursuit of civil rights. In this letter he quoted St. Augustine. Epicurus was a hedonist who advocated the attainment of pleasure through control of the appetites; Bentham's moral philosophy was based on the degree to which an action contributed to the increase or decrease of happiness. Gilligan is a psychologist who first objected to the male orientation of moral philosophy.

   Questions 2 and 3 are based on the following situation.

   Peter Valenti makes $25,000 a year and lives alone. Still, he gives no money to charity. Valenti's excuse is that charitable organizations waste money, and he does not want to give them his money to waste.

   Answer this question with yes *or* no. *Is each of the following a relevant moral argument for someone to make in trying to persuade Valenti to donate money to charity?*

2. Charity is a categorical imperative: you should give to charity regardless of your personal opinions.

   The correct answer is Yes. This is a Kantian moral argument. There are some actions that are moral duties, regardless of our personal wishes and opinions.

3. A yearly salary of $25,000 is more than enough for one person; Valenti can afford to give money to charity.

   The correct answer is No. The amount of Valenti's salary is not morally relevant; if he made half as much or twice as much, he should still give to charity.

PRACTICE SET

1. Which of the following thinkers believed that people should give up rights to the extent that others are also willing to give up rights in order to live in peace?

   (A) Aristotle
   (B) Epictetus
   (C) Hobbes
   (D) Kant

2. Under which of the following moral philosophies would telling a "white" lie in order to avoid hurting someone's feelings be most likely to be justified?

   (A) Kantianism
   (B) Ethic of care
   (C) Virtue philosophy
   (D) Hedonism

3. According to the Hebrew Bible, in return for God's protection and generosity, the people of Israel were expected to

   (A) convert others to their religion
   (B) go into exile in Babylon
   (C) give most of their wealth to the poor
   (D) obey God's laws

4. Which ancient Greek thinker drew a parallel between the structure of the ideal state and the structure of the soul?

   (A) Socrates
   (B) Thrasymachus
   (C) Aristotle
   (D) Thucydides

Directions: The following questions are based on a fictional situation and are in a different format than that of other questions in this test. Moral relevance and moral reasons are to be understood in terms of the theories presented in the course materials. Judge a consideration to be morally relevant if at least one of those views would allow its relevance.

Preceding each group of numbered phrases or statements is a question that can be answered "yes" or "no." Answer this question separately for each phrase or statement in the group. Do not assume that there are more "yes" answers or more "no" answers.

Questions 5-9 are based on the following situation.

Kevin McGiven, a microbiologist, has just finished his Ph.D. and has been offered a high-paying position in a nearby lab devoted to research on biological weapons. McGiven and his wife wish to stay in the region in order to raise their children near their families, and the position he has been offered is one of the few positions he could hope to find locally. McGiven's wife is urging him to accept it. However, McGiven is opposed to biological warfare since it is designed to harm large numbers of civilians.

Is the following a relevant fact or moral position that would lead McGiven to *accept* this position?

5. Whether someone else would take the job if he doesn't

6. His wife's opinion on what he should do

7. The salary the lab is offering

8. His opposition to biological weapons research

Is the following an appropriate action for McGiven to take if he follows the Utilitarian principle of taking the action that would do the most good?

9. Accept the position.

PRACTICE SET ANSWERS

1. **The correct answer is (C).** Hobbes thought that when men pursued all their rights and did whatever they could for their own self-preservation, this led to war; in order to avoid war, people had to compromise their rights and turn authority over to the government to enforce the compromise.

2. **The correct answer is (B).** This feminist approach to ethics emphasizes the importance of interpersonal relationships, and so a "white" lie might be justified by reasoning that the truth would inflict harm. Kantianism holds that lying is always wrong; virtue philosophy emphasizes traits of character; and hedonism is concerned with the pursuit of pleasure.

3. **The correct answer is (D).** These were the terms of the covenant between God and the Israelites: God would make them a blessed and prosperous nation, but in return they had to obey his laws. Conversion was never an important process in Judaism; the religion is based primarily on membership by birth in the group. The Babylonian exile was one of God's punishments for their unlawful behavior. Giving your wealth to the poor was one of Jesus's commands to those who were already living according to the law.

4. **The correct answer is (A).** In Plato's dialogue, the *Republic*, Socrates draws a parallel between the structure of the ideal state and the structure of the soul when attempting to describe justice.

5. **The correct answer is No.** The fact that someone else will be hired in his place should not influence his decision. He has to live with his actions, and as Socrates said, vicious behavior makes the soul vicious.

6. **The correct answer is No.** His wife is a stakeholder in all he does, so her opinion does count. However, he is a greater stakeholder in this decision than she is, so his thoughts have more weight.

7. **The correct answer is No.** The amount of money involved is irrelevant. The same issues would arise whatever the salary.

8. **The correct answer is Yes.** Since McGiven believes that biological weapons are capable of inflicting much suffering among thousands, perhaps millions of people, a Utilitarian approach would indicate he should not participate.

9. **The correct answer is No.** If you consider that this dilemma potentially has millions of stakeholders—the civilian targets of the biological weapons—then Utilitarian ethics would prevent McGiven from accepting. The small good that would benefit his wife and family does not outweigh the larger suffering.

POSTTEST

1. According to Plato, which of the following was the culminating virtue for the state?

    (A) Temperance
    (B) Community
    (C) Empathy
    (D) Justice

2. According to Aristotle, the human good is

    (A) happiness, which he defined as pleasure and the absence of pain
    (B) happiness, which he defined as an activity of the soul in accordance with virtue
    (C) quietude, which he defined as the absence of pain
    (D) a just society, which he defined as one with distribution according to merit

3. According to Rawls, social and economic inequalities are justified only if they

    (A) arise through the voluntary choices of the individuals involved
    (B) are slight in amount and widely distributed
    (C) tend in the long run to be eliminated
    (D) are reasonably expected to be to everyone's advantage

4. In Plato's writings, the thesis that justice is the interest of the stronger was advocated by

    (A) Socrates
    (B) Crito
    (C) Meletus
    (D) Thrasymachus

5. Locke justified a right to property by arguing that

(A) individuals have a right to their own persons, and thus a right to their labor and to whatever they have mixed with their labor

(B) individuals have an obligation to maximize the general happiness, and thus to create goods, and so they have the right to whatever is necessary to create goods

(C) economic gains are the result of God's will, and thus should be protected by the state

(D) collective ownership of the means of production is inefficient

6. Each of the following statements is part of Martin Luther King's justification of civil disobedience EXCEPT:

(A) Some laws are unjust.

(B) The law of man must be squared with the law of God.

(C) In seeking to arouse the conscience of the community, a person expresses respect for the law.

(D) Laws that are too strictly enforced violate citizens' rights.

7. Psychological egoism is the thesis that in everything a person does, that person

(A) should pursue own good

(B) should strengthen own psyche or ego

(C) in fact pursues own good

(D) in fact pursues the strengthening of own psyche or ego

8. Aristotle and Epicurus shared the same view on each of the following EXCEPT:

(A) Pleasure is a good.

(B) Active political involvement is unwise.

(C) Friendship is an important component of the good life.

(D) Prudence (practical wisdom) is necessary for happiness.

9. A deontological moral framework holds that right actions

(A) maximize the greatest balance of pleasure over pain

(B) are right in themselves and not because of their consequences

(C) are those that are in accordance with nature

(D) are those that are commanded by God

10. "Love not the world nor the things that are in the world. If any man loves the world, the love of the Father is not in him. For all that is in the world, the lust of the flesh, and the lust of the eyes, and the pride of life, is not of the Father, but is of the world. And the world passeth away, and the lust thereof: but he that doeth the will of God abideth forever."

This passage from the First Letter of John in the New Testament expresses or directly implies each of the following frequent teachings of Christian ethics EXCEPT:

(A) Love God above all.
(B) Ethical behavior is rewarded in Heaven.
(C) Love thy neighbor as thyself.
(D) Have humility before God.

11. John Stuart Mill held that "In the golden rule of Jesus of Nazareth, we read the complete spirit of the ethics of utility" because both teachings maintain that

(A) moral principles derive ultimately from God
(B) the general happiness should be a person's primary ethical concern
(C) a person should not give greater weight to own interests than to the interests of others
(D) the rights of individuals should be protected by the government

12. Plato defined a just society as one in which

(A) philosophers act only as teachers
(B) the members of each class play their proper role
(C) knowledgeable people are rewarded for good acts
(D) all members are able to achieve ultimate pleasure

13. Kant held that everyone has a duty to help others in need because

(A) no person can will a world where others would refuse helping that person in a time of need
(B) the general happiness is most surely maximized by helping others in need
(C) the moral individual is defined by the person's caring for others, especially in situations of need
(D) a person's moral character is developed by helping others in need

14. The value of a pleasure, according to hedonic calculus, is measured by each of the following EXCEPT its

(A) intensity
(B) duration
(C) source
(D) certainty

15. Mill is concerned about specifying motivations for acting on the principle of utility because

   (A) no philosopher before him advocated a principle of utility

   (B) a person does not automatically pursue pleasures of the highest quality

   (C) a person who acts on the principle of utility is likely to be perceived by fellow human beings as morally objectionable

   (D) the principle of utility requires pursuing the general happiness, while human beings inherently pursue their own happiness

16. Which of the following statements is an example of a categorical imperative?

   (A) "To have friends, do not tell lies."

   (B) "Obey the moral law, if you want to be moral."

   (C) "Keep to the right as you drive."

   (D) "If you wish to be happy, study philosophy."

17. Which of the following thinkers held charity (love) to be a virtue?

   (A) Plato

   (B) Augustine

   (C) Aristotle

   (D) Kant

18. Which of the following thinkers made the concept of an "original position" central to his theory of justice?

   (A) Plato

   (B) Aristotle

   (C) John Rawls

   (D) Martin Luther King, Jr.

19. Plato argued that people should pursue which of the following above all else?

   (A) Power

   (B) Material goods

   (C) Pleasure

   (D) Truth

20. All of the following thinkers viewed self-interest and morality as potentially or actually in conflict EXCEPT

   (A) Epicurus

   (B) Kant

   (C) Mill

   (D) Rawls

21. Which of the following thinkers advocated independence from external circumstances?

(A) Plato
(B) Aristotle
(C) Epictetus
(D) Mill

22. Which two of the following thinkers based their political theories on a social contract?

(A) Aristotle and Aquinas
(B) Epicurus and Epictetus
(C) Augustine and Mill
(D) Rousseau and Rawls

23. In determining how a person should act, a rule-utilitarian asks

(A) what are the good and bad consequences of the rules the person could follow
(B) what rules established by the person's society are applicable
(C) how useful a rule is for achieving the person's ends
(D) what rules have been commanded by God

24. Which of the following thinkers distinguished general justice from particular justice?

(A) Plato
(B) Aristotle
(C) Epicurus
(D) Epictetus

25. Which of the following thinkers declared virtue to be "second nature"?

(A) Aristotle
(B) Augustine
(C) Kant
(D) Rawls

26. The charge that it cannot provide a principled way of resolving conflicts of interest between people is often levied at

(A) utilitarianism
(B) ethical egoism
(C) deontological ethics
(D) natural law ethics

27. Which of the following philosophers declared that justice in the state is justice in the individual "writ large"?

(A) Plato
(B) Hobbes
(C) Kant
(D) Mill

28. Which of the following philosophers is an advocate of ethical hedonism?

(A) Aristotle
(B) Epictetus
(C) Kant
(D) Bentham

29. Advocates of feminist ethics typically hold all of the following beliefs EXCEPT:

(A) To say that "men are more sensitive to rational considerations and women are more concerned with emotional considerations" is to perpetuate a stereotype.
(B) Traditional ethical philosophy has tended to be male-biased in failing to give attention to the circumstances and sensitivities of women.
(C) Ethical systems that focus on rationality and justice, and exclude trust and community, tend to reflect a male bias.
(D) Moral principles can be justified by reference to objective considerations that make reference to feeling.

30. John Stuart Mill defends freedom of thought and expression on the grounds that

(A) each individual has an inalienable right to one's own person
(B) man is created in God's image
(C) the general happiness is best served by allowing it
(D) it is self-evident that individuals possess a right to thought and expression

31. If an individual has a right to a certain action, then

(A) others must ensure that action is successful
(B) others may not interfere with that action
(C) the individual must undertake that action
(D) the individual is morally justified in taking that action

32. The moral principle that an individual must treat persons always as ends and never as means is explicitly stated as a basic principle by

(A) Hobbes
(B) Locke
(C) Kant
(D) Mill

33. Hobbes bases his ethical theory in part on the

(A) natural tendency to self-preservation
(B) requirements of a good will
(C) Ten Commandments
(D) Moral Law

34. According to the writings of Paul, freedom of the Spirit is found in

(A) the afterlife
(B) the laws of the Church
(C) a righteous relationship with God
(D) regular prayer

35. According to Plato, the fundamental human virtues are

(A) wisdom, courage, temperance, and justice
(B) happiness, material goods, and security
(C) community, family, and goodness
(D) strength, intelligence, empathy, and honor

36. The "veil of ignorance" is a device Rawls uses to help individuals identify

(A) what they really desire, regardless of surface appearances
(B) basic human goods, for which they would wish without knowing their personal and social situations
(C) skeptical arguments that cast doubt on the objectivity of ethics
(D) which moral principles have been maintained by virtually all philosophers

37. Which of the following thinkers held philosophical study or contemplation to be central to the best human life?

(A) Aristotle
(B) Epictetus
(C) Kant
(D) Martin Luther King, Jr.

38. Which of the following thinkers held that revolution is justified if the state ignores or violates the individual rights of its citizens?

(A) Plato
(B) Epicurus
(C) Hobbes
(D) Jefferson

39. Which of the following philosophers believed that humans by nature are depraved, bound by original sin inherited from Adam's acts against God's edicts?

(A) Augustine
(B) St. Gregory
(C) Aquinas
(D) St. Benedict

40. The Quaker movement was based on the doctrine that
    (A) the revolt against formalism will lead to spiritual damnation
    (B) every man or woman is potentially God's spokesperson
    (C) only those individuals who are members of the Society of Friends will go to heaven
    (D) the traditional sacraments of the Church must be protected

41. The Universalist Church held that God's ultimate purpose was to
    (A) reward the good and punish the bad in everyone
    (B) convert everyone to Protestantism
    (C) save every member of the human race
    (D) care for the needy

42. Plato and Socrates maintained that human beings are social by nature and that proper human conduct must include principles regarding a person's relationships to others. This belief formed the basis of Western philosophical theories regarding the
    (A) definition of a righteous person
    (B) relationship between morality and community
    (C) nature of individual rights
    (D) differences between socialism and capitalism

43. Rousseau's social contract requires that
    (A) each citizen accepts the law individually
    (B) the group votes and the majority rules
    (C) a democratic process be initiated for public issues
    (D) the satisfaction of common interest overrule self-interest

44. Which of the following philosophers defined virtuous actions as those actions that members of society take that support harmony among the parts of the soul (appetite, spirit, and reason)?
    (A) Socrates
    (B) The Sophists
    (C) Plato
    (D) Aristotle

45. Aristotle's concept of corrective justice can best be defined as
    (A) taking the right action for the right reason
    (B) absolute harmony among all the parts of the soul
    (C) allowing nature to guide human beings in making moral decisions
    (D) making amends or equalizing harms for injuries done to individuals

46. The belief that "might makes right" and that justice is determined by those who have power was held by which of the following philosophers?

    (A) The Sophists
    (B) Socrates
    (C) Aristotle
    (D) Thucydides

47. According to Kant, the only thing good in itself is

    (A) happiness
    (B) a good will
    (C) helping others in need
    (D) perfect duty

48. "For men are good in but one way, but bad in many." Which of the following ethical theories is illustrated by this statement?

    (A) Plato's theory of forms
    (B) Classical Natural Law
    (C) Aristotle's doctrine of the mean
    (D) Aristotle's concept of happiness

49. Aristotle defined a voluntary action as one in which the cause of an act is derived from

    (A) external circumstances
    (B) a higher ideal
    (C) natural forces
    (D) the agent itself

50. When a judge imposes a penalty on a person because that person has inflicted injury on or defrauded another person, the judge is applying which of the following classical ethical principles?

    (A) A Socratic approach to social equality
    (B) A Utilitarian theory of moral goodness
    (C) A Hobbesian law of nature
    (D) An Aristotelian concept of equity as the proper ratio of benefits

51. Which of the following philosophers explained all human motivation in terms of "appetites" and "aversions"?

    (A) Aristotle
    (B) Hobbes
    (C) Plato
    (D) Aquinas

52. Rousseau's concept of the general will and the social contract supports which of the following theories of political authority?

    (A) Autocratic
    (B) Communistic
    (C) Democratic
    (D) Fascistic

53. The theory that any act or institution is good if it increases the happiness of all those likely to be affected by it is generally known as

    (A) libertarianism
    (B) individualism
    (C) objectivism
    (D) utilitarianism

54. The concept of "hedonic calculus," that the value of things can be measured in terms of the pleasure or happiness they promote, was advocated by

    (A) Bentham
    (B) Hume
    (C) Locke
    (D) Aquinas

55. Which of the following philosophers supported the idea that human beings act morally when they put aside their personal desires and adhere to the moral law as grasped by reason?

    (A) Hume
    (B) Kant
    (C) Plato
    (D) Rousseau

56. Thucydides held that, though justice is the right course, human beings often stray from it because they

    (A) do not believe there really is such a thing as justice
    (B) seek the pleasure of philosophical or historical investigation
    (C) fear the negative opinions of their fellow citizens
    (D) seek power in order to pursue personal or civic gain

57. Aristotle's belief about the role of law in human society can best be summarized by which of the following statements?

    (A) Laws are principles that naturally separate social classes.

    (B) Laws should be determined by those who naturally have power.

    (C) Laws should order the society rationally in accordance with justice.

    (D) Laws allow society to tame human irrationality.

58. Which of the following thinkers held that it is impossible for human beings to achieve knowledge or goodness without the illumination and grace of God?

    (A) Epicurus

    (B) Augustine

    (C) Aquinas

    (D) Kant

59. An individual who believes that it is wrong to punish an innocent person even if society would benefit from that punishment is most likely to be an advocate of which of the following types of ethical theory?

    (A) Deontological

    (B) Natural law

    (C) Consequentialist

    (D) Utilitarian

60. A consequentialist is often defined as a person who holds that

    (A) individuals may do whatever they wish as long as they accept the consequences

    (B) actions have consequences that are morally relevant

    (C) the rightness of an action is determined by the goodness of its consequences

    (D) the long-term consequences of right action include a happy afterlife

POSTTEST ANSWERS

1. **The correct answer is (D).** Justice allowed the other three parts to work together and produce a balanced constitution overall.

2. **The correct answer is (B).** This is stated explicitly (see Aristotle's *Nicomachean Ethics*, I.7).

3. **The correct answer is (D).** That is stated explicitly (see Rawls's *A Theory of Justice*).

4. **The correct answer is (D).** This occurs in *Republic*, Book I.

5. **The correct answer is (A).** Hobbes stated this explicitly.

6. **The correct answer is (D).** Choice (D) does not appear in King's justification for civil disobedience; the other choices (A), (B), and (C) do.

7. **The correct answer is (C).** This is a standard definition of psychological egoism.

8. **The correct answer is (B).** Aristotle holds that, if a person is a citizen of the state that person inhabits, active political involvement is a potential source of happiness.

9. **The correct answer is (B).** This is how the deontological framework is defined and contrasted with the consequentialist framework.

10. **The correct answer is (C).** There is no mention of others, while the rejection of pride entails the attitude of humility.

11. **The correct answer is (C).** This is stated explicitly (see Mill's *Utilitarianism*, Chapter II).

12. **The correct answer is (B).** Plato defined a just society as one in which the members of each class play their proper role.

13. **The correct answer is (A).** Kant's universalizability principle asks if there could be, or if a person could will, a world in which a certain maxim were universally followed; if the answer is "no," then a person has a duty not to follow that maxim.

14. **The correct answer is (C).** The source is important only insofar as it affects various dimensions of subsequent pleasures, as specified in the calculus.

15. **The correct answer is (D).** This is stated explicitly (see Mill's *Utilitarianism*, Chapter III).

16. **The correct answer is (C).** No conditions are stated on this imperative. The conditions stated in choices (A), (B), and (D) preclude those choices from being categorical imperatives.

17. **The correct answer is (B).** This is stated explicitly (see Augustine's *Enchiridion on Faith, Hope, and Love*).

18. **The correct answer is (C).** This is made clear in Chapter 3 of Rawls's *A Theory of Justice*.

19. **The correct answer is (D).** Plato believed truth to be the source of ultimate happiness.

20. **The correct answer is (A).** Epicurus is the only one of the four choices given to define morality (or ethics) in terms of self-interest.

21. **The correct answer is (C).** This is central to Epictetus's thought.

22. **The correct answer is (D).** Rousseau wrote a whole book on the subject, and Rawls declares himself in the footsteps of that tradition (see Rawls' *A Theory of Justice*).

23. **The correct answer is (A).** This is the standard definition within rule-utilitarianism.

24. **The correct answer is (B).** This is stated explicitly (see *Aristotle's Nicomachean Ethics*, I.A.10 and I.C.16).

25. **The correct answer is (A).** This is stated explicitly (see Aristotle's *Nicomachean Ethics*, II.1).

26. **The correct answer is (B).** This is a commonly stated objection to ethical egoism.

27. **The correct answer is (A).** This is stated explicitly (see Plato's *Republic*, Book II).

28. **The correct answer is (D).** Ethical hedonism is the view that the only thing good in itself is pleasure (and the absence of pain). Bentham advocates this viewpoint.

29. **The correct answer is (A).** Traditional "liberal feminists" have made this point, but it is denied or not taken up by writers in the "feminist ethics" tradition.

30. **The correct answer is (C).** This is stated explicitly in Mill's *On Liberty*.

31. **The correct answer is (B).** This is standard definition of an individual's right to a certain action.

32. **The correct answer is (C).** Though perhaps held by (some of) the other choices offered, only Kant actually states it.

33. **The correct answer is (A).** This is explicit in Hobbes' writings.

34. **The correct answer is (C).** According to the writings of Paul, freedom of the Spirit is found in a righteous relationship with God.

35. **The correct answer is (A).** According to Plato, the fundamental virtues are wisdom, courage, temperance, and justice.

36. **The correct answer is (B).** Under the "veil of ignorance," a person asks self what the person would wish if that person knew nothing about own particular talents, advantages, desires, etc.

37. **The correct answer is (A).** This is stated explicitly (see Aristotle's *Nicomachean Ethics,* X.7).

38. **The correct answer is (D).** This is a noticeable feature of the U.S. Declaration of Independence.

39. The correct answer is (A). Augustine believed that humans by their nature are depraved, bound by original sin inherited from Adam's acts against God's edicts.

40. The correct answer is (B). The Quaker movement was based on the doctrine that every man or woman is potentially God's spokesperson.

41. The correct answer is (C). The Universalist Church held that God's ultimate purpose was to save every member of the human race.

42. The correct answer is (B). The belief of Plato and Socrates, that human beings are social by nature and that proper human conduct can be defined only in terms of a person's relationships to others, formed the basis of Western philosophical theories regarding the relationship between morality and community.

43. The correct answer is (A). Rousseau's social contract requires that each citizen accepts the law individually.

44. The correct answer is (C). Plato defined virtuous actions as those actions that members of society take that support harmony among the parts of the soul (appetite, spirit, and reason).

45. The correct answer is (D). Aristotle's concept of corrective justice can best be defined as making amends or equalizing harms for injuries done to individuals.

46. The correct answer is (A). The Sophists held the belief that "might makes right" and that justice is determined by those who have power.

47. The correct answer is (B). Kant argues this explicitly at the beginning of the *Groundwork of the Metaphysics of Morals*.

48. The correct answer is (C). "For men are good in but one way, but bad in many" illustrates Aristotle's doctrine of the mean.

49. The correct answer is (D). Aristotle defined a voluntary action as one in which the cause of an act is derived from the agent itself.

50. The correct answer is (D). When a judge imposes a penalty on a person who has inflicted injury on or defrauded another person, the judge is applying an Aristotelian concept of equity as the proper ratio of benefits.

51. The correct answer is (B). Hobbes believed that human beings are characterized by appetites (attraction to motion) and aversions (repulsion from rest).

52. The correct answer is (C). Rousseau's concept of the general will and the social contract supports a democratic theory of political authority.

53. The correct answer is (D). Utilitarianism is the theory that any act or institution is good if it increases the happiness of all those likely to be affected by it.

54. The correct answer is (A). Bentham purported the concept of "hedonic calculus," that the value of things can be measured in terms of the pleasure or happiness they promote.

55. The correct answer is (B). Kant supported the idea that human beings act morally because their self-interests are driven by an adherence to moral reason.

56. The correct answer is (D). Thucydides held that, though justice is the right course, human beings often stray from it because they seek power in order to pursue personal or civic gain.

57. The correct answer is (C). That laws should order the society rationally in accordance with justice best summarizes Aristotle's belief about the role of laws in human society.

58. The correct answer is (B). Augustine held that knowledge could not be acquired by human beings without divine illumination and that goodness could not be acquired by human beings without the grace of God.

59. The correct answer is (A). A deontological ethical theory holds that the rightness of an act does not depend on the benefits that issue from the act.

60. The correct answer is (C). This is the standard definition, by which consequentialists are distinguished from deontologists.

CASE STUDY #1

Directions: The following questions are based on fictional situations and are in a different format from that of other questions in this test. A scenario is given, followed by a number of questions that can be answered "Yes" or "No." On the actual exam, the lettered space (A) on the answer sheet would be marked for "Yes" or lettered space (B) for "No." Each question shuld be considered separately.

FOR THIS SECTION, DO NOT MARK ANY ANSWERS IN SPACES (C) OR (D).

Questions 1–5 are based on the following situation.

Professor Harrison is an excellent teacher who enjoys teaching at Basehart University in Boston. Her students and courses are exactly the sort she enjoys teaching. She likes her colleagues at Basehart and enjoys living in a big city. Professor Harrison receives an offer of a permanent teaching position from Stanley College, a small college in a small, isolated country town. Stanley's students are of much lesser ability, and the range of courses Harrison could teach there is significantly less than at Basehart. The salary is lower, but quite livable, and the town and surrounding countryside are pretty, though Harrison would miss the big city. Stanley College—because of its isolated location, its limited budget, and the generally lower level of its students—has been unable to attract a good professor in Harrison's field. Working with the students at Stanley would be satisfying, but not as much as at Basehart. Basehart could easily replace Harrison with someone of her approximate talents. Stanley can find no one else. Professor Harrison reflects rationally on her desires, her values, and her obligations, and decides that, given the superior personal and professional benefits of remaining at Basehart, the right thing is for her to decline Stanley College's offer.

1. Does this situation dramatize the difference between psychological egoism and ethical egoism?

    (A) Yes
    (B) No
    (C)
    (D)

2. According to ethical egoism, did Harrison probably make the right choice?.

   (A) Yes
   (B) No
   (C)
   (D)

3. Is a Kantian likely to judge that Harrison's decision had moral worth?

   (A) Yes
   (B) No
   (C)
   (D)

4. Does Harrison's decision show clear evidence of her having a feminist ethics orientation?

   (A) Yes
   (B) No
   (C)
   (D)

5. If Harrison decided to accept the job offer from Stanley College, would her decision likely be an act of retributive justice?

   (A) Yes
   (B) No
   (C)
   (D)

CASE STUDY #2

Questions 6–8 are based on the following situation.

Mr. Samuels is a brilliant theoretical physicist on the verge of some major discoveries. His cardiologist, Dr. Rivera, a talented heart surgeon, finds that Mr. Samuels has a heart condition that if left uncorrected will severely limit his physical activity and his mental energy, but will not be life-threatening. Dr. Rivera explains that there is an experimental surgical procedure that could restore full physical activity. However, this procedure is risky, and there would be a 70 percent chance that Mr. Samuels would not survive the operation. Mr. Samuels agrees to the operation. Midway into the operation, Dr. Rivera realizes that the procedure cannot work. Mr. Samuels has a very different, very rare condition. Dr. Rivera can terminate the operation, leaving Mr. Samuels as he was before the surgery, but she realizes that there is another experimental procedure that can restore full activity, both physical and mental, with only a 40 percent chance that Mr. Samuels will not survive the operation. Dr. Rivera needs to decide whether to proceed.

6. Would the principle established in the Hippocratic oath, "Do no harm," allow Dr. Rivera to decide what the ethical course of action is?

    (A) Yes
    (B) No
    (C)
    (D)

7. Is the principle of informed consent ethically relevant to the surgeon's decision?

    (A) Yes
    (B) No
    (C)
    (D)

Dr. Rivera decides to perform the procedure. She can raise the probability that Mr. Samuels will survive the operation by using a rare immuno-suppressant drug, which the hospital has in very limited quantity. Unfortunately, the drug has already been promised to another patient, scheduled for surgery later that week. The surgeon reasons, however, that Mr. Samuels is much more likely to make important contributions to society than the other patient and decides to use the drug in Mr. Samuels's procedure.

8. Selecting from among the philosophers Locke, Kant, and Mill, is the principle Dr. Rivera employs to make this decision one that would be endorsed most fully by Mill?

(A) Yes
(B) No
(C)
(D)

CASE STUDY ANSWERS

1. **The correct answer is No.** The issue dramatized is not whether Professor Harrison, like all human beings, always *does* what she believes to be in her self-interest (which is what psychological egoism claims), but what she thinks is the *right* course of action. The issue dramatized is between ethical egoism (the thesis that a person *should* always act in what that person rationally judges to be in own self-interest) and some non-egoistic ethical system, whether altruistic or deontological.

2. **The correct answer is Yes.** Professor Harrison appears to have acted on what she judged to be in her rational self-interest.

3. **The correct answer is No.** For an action to have moral worth, according to Kant, it must be done from duty. Professor Harrison clearly gave important motivational weight to her personal preferences.

4. **The correct answer is No.** Issues of caring or trust are not involved, nor does Professor Harrison give more weight to feelings of sympathy or other emotional considerations than to impartial rational ones.

5. **The correct answer is No.** There is no evidence provided that Professor Harrison is giving Stanley College something the college deserves based on prior actions of the college, which is required for an act of retributive justice.

6. **The correct answer is No.** The harm possible in this new situation is no greater than that which was possible under the procedure that Mr. Samuels had agreed to, and the probability of success—of doing good—is significantly greater. So, the principle does not prohibit the new procedure, nor does it require it, since returning Mr. Samuels to his original condition involves no harm.

7. **The correct answer is Yes.** Informed consent is a basic principle of medical ethics. Mr. Samuels has consented to the originally planned procedure, but not explicitly to the substitute procedure. Dr. Rivera, or anyone evaluating the situation, will have to decide if consent to the former procedure constitutes consent to the latter, but in either case the principle of informed consent must be considered in this situation.

8. **The correct answer is Yes.** Dr. Rivera does not appeal to natural rights or the obligation to keep a contract, as Locke might. Nor does she appeal to a duty that derives from the principle that a person's maxims must be universalizable or to the need to treat others as ends and not as means, as Kant would. Rather, she appeals to the principle that a person should choose that course of action which produces overall greater utility, in this case the greater benefit to society of Mr. Samuels being in a healthy condition than the other patient. This is a utilitarian principle of the sort that Mill advocates, whether or not Mill would agree with Dr. Rivera's application of the principle in this case.

Human Resource Management

PRETEST

1. Frederick Taylor, an American mechanical engineer, invented the approach called scientific management, or industrial engineering, that was the foundation of the emergence of

   (A) union organizations and collective bargaining procedures
   (B) incentive systems used to motivate employees and reward performance
   (C) human relations and professional personnel training programs
   (D) standardized performance appraisal tools and guidelines

2. Which of the following is a constituency, or group, external to an organization but affected by the human resource department?

   (A) Board of directors
   (B) Executives
   (C) Stockholders
   (D) Employees

3. The department within most organizations responsible for organizing, structuring, and rewarding employees is called

   (A) employee relations
   (B) human resources
   (C) staffing
   (D) benefits

4. The process by which organizations forecast future staffing needs and design programs according to organizational plans and goals is known as

   (A) demand forecasting
   (B) internal analysis
   (C) strategic planning
   (D) human resource planning

5. Using future sales forecasts, estimates of future production, and other business factors combined with productivity ratios to predict the number of employees needed for a specific type of labor is an example of demand forecasting using

(A) an intuitive approach
(B) a judgmental method
(C) a mathematical method
(D) a direct approach

6. A large health-care provider with 20,000 employees in hospitals and nursing homes is examining whether or not to switch from centralized to decentralized recruiting as budgets become tighter. Which of the following would most likely occur if the company's current centralized recruiting system is maintained?

(A) There would be an inconsistent corporate identity projected to job candidates and the public.
(B) There would be an increase in overall recruiting expenses.
(C) There would be less accurate EEO/AA statistics maintained due to multiple record-keeping systems.
(D) There would be less competition between divisions and branch offices to recruit candidates from the same labor market.

7. Which of the following is the primary difference between internal recruiting for a nonexempt position and internal recruiting for an exempt position?

(A) The job posting and bidding process is rarely used for recruiting exempt positions.
(B) Nonexempt positions can only be filled by employees with the highest seniority.
(C) Favoritism and hoarding are generally not an issue affecting exempt position recruiting.
(D) Only exempt positions are subject to EEO/AA regulations.

8. Which of the following tools would be used LAST in an employee selection process?

(A) Tests
(B) Screening interview
(C) Physical examination
(D) Reference checks

9. Personal history, personal experience, and education, typically known as biodata, are often considered an effective means of predicting

(A) behavior and job performance
(B) emotional stability
(C) skill level
(D) job satisfaction

10. The main purpose of a new employee orientation program is to

(A) outline company rules and procedures and discuss corporate culture
(B) introduce employees to a specific job/department and inform them of the organization's values, principles, and goals
(C) determine the extent to which training programs have accomplished their stated goals
(D) present information on employee benefits and compensation systems

11. All of the following are advantages of promoting employees from within an organization EXCEPT:

(A) There is a higher degree of certainty about the candidate's suitability for a promotion because the person's abilities are already known.
(B) Promoting from within often motivates current employees to perform better.
(C) Training and orientation time is greatly reduced because the candidate is already familiar with the organization.
(D) A ripple effect is created when the promoted employee's old position must be filled.

12. Hiring an outside firm to perform an entire support function, such as maintenance, office services, or security, for an organization is commonly known as

(A) employee leasing
(B) outsourcing
(C) outplacement
(D) downsizing

13. Well-qualified job candidates are often more likely to

(A) leave a position after one year of employment
(B) use newspapers and agencies to identify job positions
(C) obtain a job through a word-of-mouth referral
(D) find reemployment through an outplacement firm

14. When an organization institutes a "hiring freeze" and then achieves workforce reduction through terminations and natural turnover, this process is called

(A) attrition
(B) job redeployment
(C) downsizing
(D) across-the-board reductions

15. Alternatives to reducing staff, such as hiring part-time employees, job sharing, and reduced work hours, all reduce labor costs and can help a company to AVOID

(A) actions requiring the renegotiation of union contracts
(B) declining cash flow, profitability, market share, and productivity
(C) recruiting in the open market for new employees after a short-term oversupply of labor
(D) lawsuits filed by former workers who argue that a layoff has made them unattractive to other employers

16. The federal law commonly known as the "Plant Closing Bill" requires employers with 100 or more full-time employees to

(A) offer reemployment to workers with greater seniority and demonstrated higher performance
(B) provide continuation of benefits to all employees during a temporary layoff
(C) provide counseling and outplacement assistance after 50 percent or more of a workforce is reduced
(D) give laid-off workers 60 days written notice of an anticipated mass layoff

17. Helping laid-off workers become reemployed through the use of outplacement programs can help an organization to reduce the costs of

(A) unemployment insurance benefits
(B) employee counseling
(C) early retirement
(D) restructuring

18. Identifying tasks, skills, abilities, and knowledge that will be needed to perform a job in the future is known as

(A) strategic job analysis
(B) job assessment
(C) traditional job analysis
(D) generic job analysis

19. The Critical Incidents Technique, the Department of Labor (DOL) Method, functional job analysis (FJA), and the Position Analysis Questionnaire (PAQ) are structured ways of collecting information about a specific

(A) task
(B) duty
(C) occupation
(D) job

20. Consultants and contract employees are more likely to seek which kinds of career paths within an organization?

(A) Spiral
(B) Transitory
(C) Broad banding
(D) Linear

PRETEST ANSWERS

1. **The correct answer is (B).** The field of scientific management or industrial engineering provided the early basis for incentive and reward systems instituted in the early twentieth century.

2. **The correct answer is (C).** The board of directors, executives, and employees are internal groups either directly or indirectly affected by human resource management. Stockholders are an external group affected by human resource decisions.

3. **The correct answer is (B).** The department within most organizations responsible for organizing, structuring, and rewarding employees is called human resources.

4. **The correct answer is (D).** Human resource planning is the process by which organizations forecast future staffing needs and design programs according to organizational plans and goals.

5. **The correct answer is (C).** Using real numbers and variables in prediction equations to estimate future labor needs is called demand forecasting using a mathematical method.

6. **The correct answer is (D).** Typically, when a company recruits job candidates through a central or corporate office, there is less duplication of effort and fewer attempts to recruit the same individuals by various branch offices or divisions.

7. **The correct answer is (A).** The posting and bidding process is rarely used as a method of internal recruiting for professional and managerial positions in the private sector.

8. **The correct answer is (C).** Job candidates are typically required to have a physical examination after completing all other parts of the job interview and selection process but before the date of hire.

9. **The correct answer is (A).** In studies, biodata have been shown to be one of the strongest predictors of future job behavior and performance.

10. **The correct answer is (B).** The most relevant and effective new employee orientation programs generally have an introduction to a specific job/department that is provided by a supervisor as well as several sessions of general orientation to the company that are provided by the human resource department.

11. **The correct answer is (D).** A disadvantage of promoting employees from within is that when one vacancy is filled internally, a second vacancy is created, i.e., the position of the person who was promoted to fill the first vacancy. If this vacancy is also filled internally, a ripple effect occurs.

12. **The correct answer is (B).** Hiring an outside firm to perform an entire support function is known as outsourcing or subcontracting.

13. **The correct answer is (C).** Research generally supports the theory that higher quality job candidates are usually located internally and through word-of-mouth referrals and that less desirable candidates are matched with jobs via traditional methods such as agencies and newspaper ads.

14. **The correct answer is (A).** Attrition is the organizational process of achieving workforce reductions through the natural process of terminations, retirements, and voluntary turnover.

15. **The correct answer is (C).** While alternatives to reducing staff have many secondary benefits, their greatest strategic advantage is the retention of current employees without the expense associated with re-staffing on the open market.

16. **The correct answer is (D).** The Worker Adjustment and Retraining Act (WARN) or "Plant Closing Bill" requires employers with 100 or more full-time employees to give laid-off workers 60 days written notice of an anticipated plant closing or other mass layoff.

17. **The correct answer is (A).** Among its other benefits, outplacement programs help employees find reemployment faster and thus reduce long-term unemployment insurance costs for most organizations.

18. **The correct answer is (A).** Strategic job analysis is the process of identifying tasks, skills, abilities, and knowledge that will be needed to perform a job in the future.

19. **The correct answer is (D).** The Critical Incidents Technique, the Department of Labor (DOL) Method, functional job analysis (FJA), and the Position Analysis Questionnaire (PAQ) are types of structured job analysis procedures used to collect information about specific jobs.

20. **The correct answer is (B).** Consultants, short-term employees, and independent contractors most often build a portfolio of experience gained from numerous positions with various employers rather than long-term positions at one organization.

GENERAL OVERVIEW

INTRODUCTION

Human resource management, also called **personnel management,** is the use of an organization's human resources to achieve its goals. Human resource managers function in a staff (advisory) capacity, working with other managers on human resource activities. In a large organization with a human resource department, the top human resource executive reports directly to the chief executive officer or a division head. Human resource middle managers, supervisors, and workers usually specialize in one of the main human resource activities. These include human resource planning, recruiting, and selecting; human resource development; compensation and benefits; safety and health; employee and labor relations; and human resource research.

Globalization, technological change, work force diversity, and a more service-oriented economy have enlarged the role played by human resource management. Today human resource managers work with other top managers to help formulate and execute an organization's strategies.

GENERAL EMPLOYMENT ISSUES

HUMAN RESOURCE PLANNING

Human resource planning is part of a firm's strategic planning process. Plans to expand into new lines of business or acquire another company influence the human resource needs of the organization. For example, decisions must be made regarding the types and number of positions to be added or eliminated. To predict the need for personnel, the demand for the product or service is projected; then the volume of production required to meet demand; and finally the number and type of personnel needed to achieve these production estimates.

A basic employment planning decision is whether to fill positions from inside or outside of the organization. Part of planning involves forecasting (1) overall personnel requirements, (2) the supply of inside candidates, and (3) the supply of outside candidates.

RECRUITMENT

The process of attracting a sufficient number of qualified applicants to apply for jobs within an organization is called **recruitment**. After identifying sources of potential employees, the human resource manager chooses the appropriate methods for internal and/or external recruitment. **Internal recruitment methods** include maintaining management and skill inventories of employees and job posting. **External recruitment methods** advertise in the appropriate media, including the Internet; use public or private employment agencies; canvas high schools and colleges; hold special events such as job fairs; offer internships; and use executive search firms for high-level managers.

Environmental factors can influence recruitment to a great degree. For example, the demand for workers with specific skills may greatly exceed the supply, making extraordinary recruitment efforts necessary. On the other hand, when there is high unemployment in the company's labor market, recruitment is simplified considerably.

SELECTION

In the **selection** process, the best candidate for a particular position is chosen from the pool of applicants. The first step in the selection process is an **initial screening**, often of resumes or letters of application, to eliminate candidates who are clearly unqualified for the job. Next, prospective employees may fill out an **employment application**.

Applicants who progress this far are interviewed. The **interview** is a directed conversation in which the interviewer and applicant give and get information. Interviews may be conducted in many ways. In a group interview, several applicants talk with one or more company representatives at the same time. In a board interview, one applicant is interviewed by several company representatives at once. In a stress interview, the company representative deliberately creates anxiety to see how the applicant reacts. A realistic job preview gives an applicant objective information about the job.

Selection tests are sometimes used to help assess an applicant's skills, abilities, and potential for success. Good tests are objective, standardized, have norms, are reliable (consistent in their results), and valid (the test measures what it is intended to measure). Tests can measure general cognitive abilities, psychomotor abilities, job knowledge, performance, vocational interests, personality, and drug tests.

Reference checks are used to confirm the accuracy of information gained in the selection process. In some cases, background checks are necessary.

Finally, one applicant is offered the position, often contingent on passing a physical examination.

ORIENTATION

Orientation is a procedure in which a new employee is educated about the company and the job. In a small firm, orientation may consist of introducing the employee to everyone. In a large firm, there may be a formal, lengthy orientation program, conducted by the human resource department, including a video presentation, a tour of the facility, and an employee handbook. The remainder of the job-specific orientation is then done by the employee's supervisor.

PROMOTIONS AND TRANSFERS

The human resource department helps set company policy on how promotions are handled. Some companies base promotion on an employee's seniority; others use competence as the basis for promotion; and still others use a combination of the two. If competence is the yardstick of promotion, then the company must establish how competence is measured. Competence in performing the tasks of the current job is fairly easy to determine, but promotion involves predicting future performance of higher level tasks. In most cases, future potential is extrapolated from present performance.

A **transfer** is a movement to another job, usually at the same grade level and salary. Employees sometimes seek transfers to get a better location, more interesting work, or better hours. Employers transfer employees in order to vacate an eliminated position or achieve a better fit between employee and job. Transfers have become increasingly common as organizations have flattened, with fewer levels of management in which to be promoted. Transfers can give employees more diverse work experience and opportunities for personal growth.

LAYOFFS, DOWNSIZING, AND OUTPLACEMENT

A **layoff** is a temporary or permanent termination of employment because there is not enough work to be done. In a unionized company, the layoff proceeds according to the terms of the labor contract, usually with the least senior employees going first. In other companies, layoffs may be decided on the basis of competence or internal politics. **Downsizing** involves the permanent shrinking of the organization in order to remain competitive. With downsizing, many employees lose their jobs.

Outplacement is a procedure used to help a terminated employee conduct a self-appraisal and execute a job search. Outplacement is conducted by a human resource department specialist or an outplacement firm.

JOB ANALYSIS

Job analysis is the procedure by which the duties of a specific position and the characteristics of the people who can fill the position are determined. Job analysis yields information used in generating **job descriptions** (what the job involves) and **job specifications** (what kind of people to hire for the job). Information collected in the course of a job analysis may include work activities; human behaviors; machines, tools, equipment, and supplies used; standards of performance; the context of the job—physical, social, and organizational; and human requirements, including knowledge, skills, and personal attributes. The information can be collected in a variety of ways: through interviews, questionnaires, observation, employee diaries/logs, and quantitative techniques.

A job analysis is the basis for several other human resource management activities, including recruitment and selection, compensation, performance appraisal, training, and ensuring that all the firm's activities are explicitly assigned. Thus, it plays a central role in complying with **equal employment opportunity laws** (see page 122). An employer must be able to prove that its employment screening tools, compensation policies, and performance appraisals are actually related to the job in question.

TRAINING AND DEVELOPMENT

Training gives new or current employees the knowledge and skills they need to perform on the job. In contrast, **employee and management development** focuses on long-term issues, preparing employees and managers for future jobs in the organization. **Retraining** refers to programs in which employees whose skills and knowledge are outmoded are trained for new positions in an organization or outside it.

TRAINING AND LEARNING

Since training involves learning on the part of the employee, suggestions based on learning theory can improve results.

One basic principle of learning is that it is easier to learn something if it is meaningful. To that end, trainees should be given an overall picture of the purpose of the training. The material should be broken into meaningful chunks, and familiar terms, examples, and concepts should be used. A second basic principle is that learning must be transferred from the training site to the work site. To accomplish this, the similarity between the training situation and the work situation should be maximized and lots of opportunity to practice should be given. Third, it is easier to learn if there is motivation to learn. Trainees should learn by doing, be praised for correct responses, and be allowed to pace themselves.

TRAINING PROGRAMS

There are many techniques for training employees, including the following:

- **On-the-job training**—A person learns a job by actually performing it. Every employee gets some on-the-job training.
- **Job instruction training**—This is a step-by-step method of teaching jobs that consist of a logical sequence of tasks.
- **Lectures**—Lectures are used when a lot of knowledge needs to be imparted to a group; for example, teaching the sales force the key features of new products.
- **Vestibule training**—This is a training method that uses simulation in an off-site location.
- **Programmed learning**—This is a system of teaching job skills in which information is presented, a question is asked, the employee responds, and then the employee is given feedback on her answers.
- **Computer-based training**—Employees use an interactive computer programs to increase knowledge or skills.

MANAGEMENT DEVELOPMENT PROGRAMS

Programs designed to improve current or future employee and managerial performance by teaching knowledge, changing attitudes, or increasing skills are called **employee** or **management development programs**. The aim of such programs is to maximize the future performance of the organization as a whole. Thus, a company's needs are first assessed, then its employees' performance is appraised, and finally development programs are implemented. Most employee development programs focus on management development.

There are several **on-the-job training methods** used for management development, including:

- **Job rotation**—Management trainees are moved from department to department to increase their understanding of the business as a whole.
- **Coaching/understudy approach**—The new manager works directly under the manager he is replacing.
- **Junior board**—Managers sit on a "board of directors," analyzing company problems and recommending solutions.
- **Action learning**—Managers work full-time analyzing and solving problems in other departments.

Off-the-job training is also used:

- **Case study method**—Managers are presented with case studies of organizational problems that they must solve.
- **Management games**—Teams of managers compete by making decisions about realistic but simulated companies.
- **Outside seminars**—Managers attend special conferences and seminars to learn new skills.
- **University-related programs**—Managers take courses and programs offered at colleges and universities.
- **Role playing**—Managers act out the parts of people in a realistic management situation.
- **Organizational development**—Employees and managers undergo a program designed to change attitudes, values, and beliefs so that they can improve the organization.

CAREER PLANNING AND DEVELOPMENT

A process through which an employee becomes aware of personal career-related attributes and the series of stages in a career is called **career planning and development**. Many companies have instituted programs to help employees manage their careers and to promote from within. In such companies, career-oriented performance appraisals help employees develop appropriate career plans. Career records and open job postings also provide opportunities for employees to advance.

PERFORMANCE APPRAISALS

Performance appraisals are periodic reviews of employee performance, usually conducted by the employee's supervisor with policy-making and advisory input from the human resource department. In some organizations, the human resource department simply provides advice and assistance; in others, it prepares detailed forms and procedures for use throughout the company. The human resource department trains supervisors to conduct appraisals. Finally, the department monitors the organization's appraisal system, ensuring that appraisals comply with equal employment opportunity laws.

PURPOSES OF PERFORMANCE APPRAISAL

Conducting performance appraisals accomplishes three basic purposes: providing information upon which salary and promotion decisions can be made, reviewing and correcting employee behavior, and providing an opportunity to discuss career planning and development.

PERFORMANCE APPRAISAL TECHNIQUES

Appraisals are conducted according to a predetermined format. There are several techniques used alone or in combination:

- **Graphic rating scale method**—Rating employees on a list of traits and/or duties according to a range of performance values, from unsatisfactory to outstanding.
- **Alternation ranking method**—Ranking employees from best to worst on a particular trait.
- **Paired comparison method**—Comparing each employee to every other employee in the group for each trait, which is a ranking method.
- **Forced distribution method**—Assigning employees to predetermined performance categories according to preset percentages, which is similar to grading on a curve.
- **Critical incident method**—Keeping a record of an employee's excellent or poor work-related behavior and reviewing it with the employee.
- **Narrative forms**—Rating performance in terms of standards accompanied by critical incident examples and an improvement plan.
- **Behaviorally anchored rating scales**—Evaluating performance by combining narrative critical incidents and quantified ratings.
- **Management by objectives**—Setting specific measurable goals with each employee and reviewing those goals periodically.

PROBLEMS

Appraisal problems can undermine the legal defensibility of an appraisal according to equal employment opportunity laws. Problems in the performance appraisal process can arise at any stage. For example, there may be problems with the **standards of performance** being used. They may be irrelevant to the job, subjective rather than objective and measurable, ambiguous, or unrealistic. In some cases there may be no articulated standards against which to judge performance.

The supervisor can create problems by skewing the performance ratings in several ways. For instance, the **halo effect** is a problem that occurs when a supervisor's rating on one trait biases the rating on other traits. It is a common problem when the employee is very friendly or unfriendly toward the supervisor. The **central tendency** is to rate toward the middle of a rating scale, making all employees average. Some supervisors are **strict** or **lenient** in rating all of the employees in the work unit. Finally, a supervisor's **bias** in matters such as gender, age, race, and ethnicity can affect appraisal ratings.

In their appraisal interviews with employees, supervisors can create problems by failing to give appropriate feedback in order to improve performance. They can destroy the effectiveness of the process by communicating negative attitudes.

Finally, failure to use the information gathered in the course of performance appraisals means that their purpose is partially negated.

MOTIVATION, COMMUNICATION, AND LEADERSHIP

Motivation is that which energizes, directs, and sustains human behavior. Employees can be motivated by a well-designed incentive system (see Compensation, below) or by the satisfactions built into their jobs. The human resource department plays a role in redesigning work through programs such as alternative work arrangements, quality circle programs, quality improvement programs, self-directed teams, and reengineering.

Communication is a key activity in a well-run organization, especially in ensuring fair treatment of employees. The human resource department in some companies runs programs that encourage two-way communication between management and employees: a confidential hotline that employees can use to communicate about problems and issues, periodic opinion surveys, and top-down communications to ensure that information is disseminated.

The human resource department is also involved in **leadership** identification and training. Through employee skills inventories and career planning programs, employees who show leadership potential are identified. Through employee and management development programs, leadership skills are developed.

COMPENSATION

Compensation refers to all forms of pay and rewards that workers get because of their employment. Compensation may take the form of direct financial payments, such as wages, salary, incentives, commissions, and bonuses, or indirect financial payments like vacation time and employer-paid insurance.

ESTABLISHING PAY RATES

There are several steps involved in establishing pay rates that compare equitably with rates for similar jobs in other organizations and rates of other jobs within the organization.

1. **Salary survey**—A survey is taken to determine the prevailing pay rates for a particular job, called a **benchmark job**. This can be done through informal communication, consulting with employment agencies, reviewing newspaper ads, or conducting a formal survey. Once the salaries of several benchmark jobs are known, salaries of other jobs in the organization can be pegged on those.

2. **Job evaluation**—Job evaluation is a systematic process of determining the worth of one job relative to another. The basic procedure is to compare the content of one job with that of another, in terms of **compensable factors** such as effort, responsibility, skills, and working conditions. Other compensable factors can be used; for example, a method popularized by one consulting firm uses know-how, problem-solving, and accountability.

   The simplest method is to rank jobs according to an overall factor such as difficulty. Another method is to categorize jobs into groups: groups with similar jobs are called **classes** and groups with jobs similar in difficulty but different otherwise are called **grades**. A third method, the **point method**, uses several compensable factors and then assigns a point value for each to each job.

3. **Pay grades**—Once a job evaluation has determined the relative worth of each job, the jobs can be grouped into pay grades. A pay grade consists of jobs of similar difficulty or importance.

4. **Pay rates**—To establish pay rates, a wage curve is drawn. A wage curve shows the pay rates currently being paid for jobs in each pay grade, relative to their points or other ranking. Once the rates are plotted, a line called the wage line is drawn through them. Rates along the line are the target pay rates.

5. **Rate ranges**—Most employers pay a range of rates for a particular job, not just one rate. The range may extend 15 percent above and below the wage line, for example.

Wage and Salary Administration

Wage and salary administration is the human resource function responsible for making compensation policy, implementing compensation systems, and keeping compensation records for an organization. Specialists in this area also ensure that the organization is in compliance with the many laws that apply to employee compensation.

Incentive Plans

Programs that link pay directly to performance are called **incentive plans**. Different types of incentive plans are used for different categories of employees. Typical incentive plans for operations employees include:

- **Piecework plan**—A system of paying employees for the number of items they process. In a straight piecework plan the employee is paid a certain amount per item. In a guaranteed piecework plan, the employee is paid the minimum wage and additional per-item compensation for production above a certain number of items per hour.

- **Standard hour plan**—A system in which employees are paid a base hourly rate and an additional percentage of the base rate for production above a certain standard per hour or per day.

- **Team or group incentive plan**—A plan in which production standards are set for a work group and incentives are paid out if the team exceeds the standard.

For managerial employees, incentive plans include:

- **Annual bonus**—A payment designed to motivate the short-term performance of executives and managers and tied to company profitability.

- **Stock options**—The right to purchase a specified number of shares of company stock at today's price some time in the future.

Incentive plans for sales people include:

- **Salary plan**—A fixed salary with occasional bonuses or prizes. Typically used when a salesperson's major activity is prospecting or servicing accounts.

- **Commission**—Payment in direct proportion to sales.

- **Combination plan**—A base salary plus an additional proportional incentive, such as a commission.

There are also incentive plans that apply to many employees or an entire organization:

- **Employee stock ownership (ESOP) plan**—A corporation contributes stock to an employee account held in trust; the employee gets the stock upon retirement or other separation.
- **Gainsharing plan**—A plan that engages employees in an effort to achieve improved productivity and to share the gains.
- **At-risk pay plan**—A plan that puts a percentage of an employee's pay at risk, subject to the company's meeting its financial objectives.

BENEFITS

Benefits are a form of financial compensation that employees receive indirectly. They are not tied to individual employee performance, but rather are available to employees as members of the organization. There are several major types of benefits:

- **Payment for time not worked**—This includes paid vacation, paid holidays, sick time, and severance pay.
- **Health and security benefits**—These include health insurance, dental insurance, disability protection, vision care, life insurance, retirement plans (including social security and pensions), and supplemental unemployment insurance.
- **Employee services**—Organizations provide services such as employee cafeterias, fitness centers, day-care centers, legal advice, credit unions, discounts on products and services, parking spaces, and tuition reimbursement.

Employees tend to prefer certain types of benefits depending on their age, marital status, and gender. As a result, many companies provide a **cafeteria approach** to benefits, allowing each employee to put together his or her own benefit plan, subject to a maximum cost and nonoptional inclusion of certain items.

NONFINANCIAL INCENTIVES

Although compensation is the major motivation for most employees, many employees also appreciate nonfinancial incentives for work performance. These may include flextime, a four-day workweek, job sharing, or telecommuting. They also include programs that give employees more control over their work, such as quality circles, total quality management programs, self-directed work teams, participative decision making, and reengineering work processes.

SECURITY ISSUES

EMPLOYEE SAFETY AND HEALTH

Accidents occur by chance, because of unsafe conditions or due to unsafe acts on the part of employees. Work-related factors also contribute to accidents, including the job itself, the work schedule, and the atmosphere of the workplace. Employers institute safety programs for moral, legal, and economic reasons. There are several approaches: to remove unsafe conditions, to hire and place people appropriately, to train, through propaganda, and through the commitment of top management to safety.

Employee health problems can adversely affect the workplace. Alcoholism, drug abuse, stress, and mental illness are particularly serious problems. Techniques for dealing with these include counseling, referrals to outside agencies, disciplining, and discharge.

DISCIPLINE

The process of correcting or punishing an employee for breaking a rule or violating a procedure is called **discipline**. In most large organizations, discipline is a formal procedure with rules and regulations, a system of progressive penalties, and an appeals process. Since arbitration may be a step in the process, especially in unionized workplaces, employers must ensure that discipline is well documented and fair.

DISMISSAL

There are four basic grounds for dismissal:

- **Unsatisfactory work performance**—A persistent failure to perform assigned tasks or to meet standards on the job. Excessive absenteeism, lack of punctuality, and a negative attitude toward fellow employees and the company are included under this category.

- **Misconduct**—Willful and deliberate breaking of the employer's rules, including stealing and insubordination.

- **Lack of qualifications**—An inability to do the job despite diligent effort. Dismissal is a last resort for these employees.

- **Changed requirements of the job**—An inability to do the job once it changes despite effort. Again, dismissal is a last resort.

LEGAL ISSUES

EQUAL EMPLOYMENT OPPORTUNITY

Congress passed the **Civil Rights Act of 1964, Title VII** of which bars employment discrimination because of race, color, religion, sex, or national origin. One provision of the act was to create the **Equal Employment Opportunity Commission**. It is empowered to conciliate discrimination complaints; if these fail, the Commission can go to court to enforce the law. Other laws and regulations that bar discrimination include the Equal Pay Act of 1963, the Age Discrimination in Employment Act of 1967, the Pregnancy Discrimination Act of 1978, the Americans with Disabilities Act of 1990, executive orders, federal guidelines on selection tools, Supreme Court cases, and state and local laws.

Until the late 1980s, most Supreme Court decisions regarding workplace discrimination came down on the side of women and minorities. However, in 1989 several Supreme Court decisions made it more difficult for employees to prevail in the courts. In response, Congress passed the **Civil Rights Act of 1991**. This returned the burden of proving that a job qualification was a **business necessity** or **bona fide occupational qualification** back to the employer. In addition, the act provides for compensatory and punitive damages and a jury trial.

Sexual harassment refers to harassment on the basis of sex that has the purpose or effect of substantially interfering with work performance or that creates a hostile environment. The harassment may take the form of quid pro quo (rejecting a sexual advance may have affected an employee's raises or promotions); a hostile environment created by a supervisor (consequences of harassment can be intangible, such as psychological stress); or a hostile environment created by coworkers or nonemployees.

AFFIRMATIVE ACTION

Affirmative action goes beyond equal employment opportunity by requiring that employers make an extra effort to hire and promote those who are in protected groups. Affirmative action includes specific actions in recruitment, hiring, promotions, and compensation that eliminate the present effects of past discrimination.

Two basic strategies underlie affirmative action plans. The first is the **good faith effort strategy**, in which the employer changes practices that in the past contributed to excluding or underusing members of protected groups. The assumption underlying this approach is that if the obstacles to hiring and advancement are removed, the result will be that more women and minorities will succeed. The second is the **quota approach**, in which the employer mandates affirmative action results by setting numeric hiring and promotion goals. This approach has been challenged by members of unprotected groups, such as white males, on the basis of **reverse discrimination**.

COMPENSATION

There are many laws that regulate what an employer must pay in terms of minimum wages, overtime, and benefits. These include:

- **Fair Labor Standards Act of 1938 (amended)**—This act contains provisions regarding minimum wage, overtime pay, equal pay, recordkeeping, and child labor protection. It covers most employees.

- **Equal Pay Act of 1963**—This act requires equal pay for women doing the same work as men.

- **Employee Retirement Income Security Act of 1974 (ERISA)**—A law that provides government protection of pensions for employees of companies with pension plans. It regulates vesting and portability rights.

- **Unemployment insurance or compensation acts**—These are state laws that provide weekly benefits if a person is unable to work through no fault of his own.

- **Worker's compensation laws**—These are state laws that provide income and medical benefits to workers injured on the job.

SAFETY AND HEALTH

In 1970 Congress passed the Occupational Safety and Health Act, the purpose of which was to ensure the health and safety of workers on the job. Under the provisions of the act, the **Occupational Safety and Health Administration (OSHA)** was established as part of the Department of Labor. The purpose of OSHA is to administer the provisions of the act and to set and enforce safety and health standards.

OSHA standards are very comprehensive and detailed. In addition to specifying physical conditions such as the dimensions of a guardrail, OSHA requires that employers establish hazard communication programs to inform employees about dangerous chemicals. OSHA standards are enforced through inspections and citations.

OSHA requires that all employers with more than 11 employees keep detailed records of occupational injuries and illnesses. Injuries requiring medical attention and illnesses must be reported. If a workplace accident results in the death of an employee or the hospitalization of 5 or more employees, all employers, even those with fewer than 11 employees, must report the incident.

OTHER LEGISLATION

- **The Family and Medical Leave Act of 1993** provides for up to twelve weeks of unpaid leave for an employee's own serious illness, the birth or adoption of a child, or the care of a seriously ill child, spouse, or parent. This law applies only to private employers with 50 or more employees.

- **Comprehensive Omnibus Budget Reconciliation Act (COBRA)**—This law requires that private employers offer continued health benefits to terminated or retired employees for a period of time, usually eighteen months.

LABOR RELATIONS

LABOR UNIONS

Approximately 16 percent of U.S. workers belong to **labor unions,** organizations of workers that bargain collectively for a labor contract with an employer. In general, the weekly earnings of unionized workers are higher than those of nonunionized workers, and they receive significantly more benefits.

There are several ways in which a union can organize the employees of a work unit:

- **Closed shop**—The company can hire only union members; this was outlawed in 1947 but still exists in a few industries.

- **Union shop**—The company can hire nonunion workers, but they must join the union and pay dues within a specified period of time.

- **Agency shop**—Both union and nonunion employees must pay union dues since what the union does benefits all workers.

- **Open shop**—Both union and nonunion employees work, but only union employees must pay dues.

The **American Federation of Labor and Congress of Industrial Organizations (AFL-CIO)** is a voluntary federation of about 100 national and international labor unions. Workers belong to a local union, which is a chapter in a national union that may belong to the AFL-CIO. Although the AFL-CIO has limited power to act, it has a great deal of political power as the representative of labor.

LABOR LAW

Several laws affect union activity and labor-management relations, including:

- **Norris-LaGuardia Act of 1932**—Guaranteed each employee the right to bargain collectively.
- **National Labor Relations (Wagner) Act of 1935**—Banned certain unfair labor practices and provided secret ballots and majority rule in elections determining whether or not a firm's employees would join a union.
- **Taft-Hartley Act of 1947**—Prohibited certain unfair labor practices on the part of unions and listed the rights of employees as union members. The act allows the president to intervene in national emergency strikes.
- **Landrum-Griffin Act of 1959**—Protects union members from wrongdoing on the part of union leaders.

COLLECTIVE BARGAINING

Collective bargaining is the process through which a labor contract is negotiated between management and the labor union. Bargaining must be conducted in **good faith**, meaning that both sides are communicating, negotiating, and matching proposals with counter-proposals in an effort to arrive at an agreement. Items on which agreement must be reached may be mandatory (such as wages and hours of employment); permissible (pension benefits, employment of strikebreakers); or illegal (closed shop, discriminatory treatment).

Collective bargaining usually goes through several stages. First, both sides present their demands; they are typically far apart on many items. In the second stage, both sides back off a little from their initial positions and trade off some demands for others. The third stage is the formation of subcommittees to work out alternatives. Next, an informal settlement is reached and each group goes back to its constituents to consult. Last, a formal agreement is written and signed.

When collective bargaining reaches an impasse, it is sometimes resolved through a mediator or arbitrator. A **mediator** is a neutral third party who helps the two parties reach an agreement. An **arbitrator** usually has the power to determine and dictate the terms of the settlement. If labor decides to withdraw from the negotiations, a **strike** is called.

GRIEVANCES

Under the terms of a labor contract, a **grievance** is any factor involving wages, hours, or conditions of employment that an employee complains about. Most contracts have a very specific grievance procedure. Grievance procedures that are designed by the human resource department are used for nonunion employees.

CURRENT ISSUES AND TRENDS

COMPARABLE WORTH

Equal pay legislation mandates that women must be paid equal wages for doing equal work. The concept of **comparable worth** is that women should be paid equal wages for doing work comparable to work done by men. Comparable worth court cases are usually based on a company's use of points in a job evaluation system. If two dissimilar jobs, such as a clerk-typist and a junior engineer, have the same number of points, this implies they should be paid at the same rate even though market rates for engineers (usually male) are higher than for clerk-typists (usually female).

EMPLOYEE PARTICIPATION GROUPS

Plans designed to increase worker motivation, involvement, and commitment to the organization, such as quality circles and total quality management, are often viewed by unions as attempts to deflect worker loyalty from the union to management. Research indicates that most employee participation groups are not the threat that labor unions fear them to be. In general, labor-management conflict can be reduced when union representatives participate in the programs.

ALTERNATIVE WORK ARRANGEMENTS

Alternative work arrangements allow employees some flexibility in setting up their work schedules.

- **Flextime** is a plan in which the employer sets up core hours around midday during which all employees are expected to work, and then allows workers to set their own starting and ending times.
- A **four-day workweek** allows workers to work four 10-hour days instead of five 8-hour days.
- **Job sharing** allows two or more people to share a single job.
- **Telecommuting** allows workers to work from home.
- **Flexyears** allow workers to choose how many hours they want to work each month for the next year.

SAMPLE QUESTIONS

1. A method of rating employees on a list of traits and/or duties according to a range of performance values is called the

    (A) forced distribution method
    (B) alternation ranking method
    (C) graphic rating scale method
    (D) paired comparison method

    The correct answer is (C). The graphic rating scale method is one of the simplest methods of appraising performance. For each trait or duty, the supervisor must rate the employee based on a scale (for example, from unsatisfactory to outstanding).

2. Which of the following statements summarizes the underlying assumption of financial incentive plans?

    (A) Employees are compensated simply because they are members of the organization.
    (B) Compensation should be pegged to an employee's seniority rather than competence.
    (C) The more control an employee has over his work, the greater his job satisfaction.
    (D) People work more productively if their productivity is rewarded.

    The correct answer is (D). Financial incentive plans link pay to performance, so they are a way to boost productivity. Choice (A) describes benefits, choice (B) describes compensation in many unionized work units, and choice (C) describes the intrinsic rewards of work.

3. When Miguel Ortega was let go because his corporation downsized, he was able to continue his family's health insurance coverage for eighteen months by taking over the premium payments. What law guaranteed him this right?

    (A) OSHA
    (B) COBRA
    (C) ERISA
    (D) EEO

    The correct answer is (B). The Comprehensive Omnibus Budget Reconciliation Act is the law that ensures employees continuity in their health insurance coverage.

PRACTICE SET

1. Which of the following is a provision of the Age Discrimination in Employment Act (amended)?

   (A) Designating the use of seniority in promotion decisions for employers with fewer than 50 employees
   (B) Prohibiting employers from requiring retirement at any particular age
   (C) Setting aside the minimum wage requirements for workers over age 70
   (D) Extending unemployment compensation for an additional six weeks for workers over age 40

2. What is the underlying cause of salary compression?

   (A) Out-of-date job evaluations
   (B) Pegging pay rates to market rates
   (C) Inflation
   (D) Collective bargaining

3. Which of the following results when a U.S. union forms an alliance with its counterpart overseas?

   (A) Wages fall both in the United States and in the foreign nation.
   (B) Wages rise overseas but fall in the United States.
   (C) The union is fined by the National Labor Relations Board.
   (D) Companies are discouraged from moving U.S. jobs overseas.

4. If those who do well on an employment screening test also do well on the job, that shows that the test has

   (A) criterion validity
   (B) content validity
   (C) reliability
   (D) internal consistency

5. When Marisa Kam started work at EmTech, her supervisor showed her how to perform several tasks, taking her over each of them step by step. Which training method was Kam's supervisor using?

   (A) Vestibule training
   (B) Lecture
   (C) Programmed learning
   (D) Job instruction training

6. Which of the following is the major drawback of the 10-hour, four-day work schedule?

   (A) Employee fatigue
   (B) Increased cost of employee pay
   (C) Lack of supervision
   (D) Complex record keeping

7. Which of the following would NOT be a bona fide occupational qualification for a truck driver?
   (A) Driver's license
   (B) Age
   (C) Vision
   (D) Gender

8. How can effective selection and placement help reduce the number of unsafe acts committed by employees?
   (A) By redesigning jobs to be safer
   (B) By reducing the number of accident-prone employees
   (C) By ensuring employee commitment to safety practices
   (D) By using safety propaganda during the employment process

9. Irina Belski is rating the performance of Thea Benz, one of her favorite employees. Which of the following rating problems should she be particularly on guard against?
   (A) Halo effect
   (B) Central tendency
   (C) Strictness
   (D) Age bias

10. The procedure by which the duties of a specific position and the characteristics of the people who can fill the position are determined is called
    (A) grade description
    (B) broadbanding
    (C) job analysis
    (D) job evaluation

PRACTICE SET ANSWERS

1. **The correct answer is (B).** The Age Discrimination in Employment Act originally prohibited employers from discriminating against workers aged 40 to 65. In 1987 it was amended to prohibit a mandatory retirement age.

2. **The correct answer is (C).** Salary compression is the situation in which long-term employees' salaries are lower than those of people just starting at a company. This can arise when the rate of inflation outpaces normal pay increases.

3. **The correct answer is (D).** By helping foreign unions raise workers' standard of living abroad, the U.S. union makes the cost difference between U.S. workers and foreign workers decrease, thus discouraging the shipment of jobs abroad.

4. **The correct answer is (A).** A selection test has criterion validity when it can be shown that test scores predict job performance. Content validity exists when the test is a fair sample of the content of the job.

5. **The correct answer is (D).** Job instruction training involves breaking each job into tasks, and each task into steps, so as to teach the employee in a thorough, systematic manner.

6. **The correct answer is (A).** One reason for the current standard 7- or 8-hour workday is that longer days cause fatigue, which decreases productivity.

7. **The correct answer is (D).** Gender does not affect the ability to drive a truck, but the other three options do.

8. **The correct answer is (B).** By identifying a basic trait that might be related to increased accidents on a specific job, human resource personnel devise tests for the trait. For example, tests of emotional stability have been used to screen out accident-prone taxi drivers.

9. **The correct answer is (A).** With the halo effect, a positive rating on one trait is likely to influence ratings on other traits, resulting in a rating that is better than it should be. It generally happens when a supervisor either likes or dislikes the employee.

10. **The correct answer is (C).** This procedure is called job analysis; it forms the basis for job descriptions and job specifications.

POSTTEST

1. Outplacement, self-assessment tools, and skill development are all used by human resource managers to provide which of the following types of support to employees?

   (A) Career planning
   (B) Mentoring
   (C) Incentives and bonuses
   (D) Retirement planning

2. A large multinational corporation has an ongoing need to orient new hires to its policies, procedures, strategy, and culture. Orientation materials are needed in seven different languages and must be available off-the-shelf to various worldwide branches. Which of the following would be the most appropriate and effective training method for this type of need?

   (A) Computer-based training
   (B) Live instruction, a videotape, and a Leader's manual
   (C) An off-site workshop
   (D) Simulation and role playing

3. A human resources specialist must gather information for needs assessment purposes concerning the training of several hundred current employees. The best method of collecting the information in this circumstance is by

   (A) observation
   (B) telephone
   (C) questionnaires
   (D) critical incidents files

4. In today's global economy, management development programs are fundamentally driven by

   (A) M.B.A. programs
   (B) financial pressures
   (C) market forces
   (D) corporate culture and strategic focus

5. A trainer is delivering a management training program to employees in several different units worldwide. In choosing the content and method for the program, the trainer should

   (A) consider cultural assumptions and practices that might affect learner understanding
   (B) conduct interviews with all learners prior to delivery
   (C) group supervisors and managers separately in order to encourage free discussion
   (D) present concrete examples of all theories and concepts using an inductive approach

6. A training program that utilizes classroom time and that is followed by an on-the-job application and a presentation of project results is called

   (A) adult learning
   (B) action learning
   (C) transfer of skills
   (D) simulation

7. A software design company must train several new marketing representatives in the product promotion and support process. In this situation, the trainer should use which learning approach?

   (A) Whole
   (B) Massed
   (C) Part
   (D) Overlearning

8. An administrative use of a performance appraisal would be

   (A) human resource planning
   (B) identifying individual training needs
   (C) determining company-wide training needs
   (D) making layoff decisions

9. A disadvantage of forced distribution appraisal systems is that employees are

   (A) often discouraged rather than motivated to improve by low numerical ratings
   (B) rewarded for displaying only behavior consistent with corporate culture
   (C) given no opportunity to respond and offer feedback
   (D) rated according to criteria that may not be job-related or valid

10. A results-based performance appraisal system measures

   (A) the extent to which an employee exhibits predefined behaviors on-the-job
   (B) the "bottom line" associated with an employee's work
   (C) personality traits such as decision-making ability and communication skills
   (D) actual tasks and overall completion rates

11. A developmental use of a performance appraisal would be

   (A) decision making about merit raises
   (B) human resource planning
   (C) identification of individual training needs
   (D) evaluation of organizational goal achievement

12. Performance appraisal data are often used by organizations to

   (A) help employees become involved in organizational planning
   (B) supply required information to government agencies according to federal mandates
   (C) determine the nature of employee benefit plans
   (D) design jobs and systems to accomplish organizational goals

13. A performance appraisal system may be viewed as discriminatory from a legal point of view if

   (A) the rating criteria is not based on a thorough job analysis
   (B) a high percentage of employees are rated unfavorably
   (C) a behavior-based approach is used exclusively
   (D) an employee is rated according to production speed

14. Communication ability, company loyalty, and cooperativeness would be personal characteristics measured in which of the following types of employee appraisal systems?

   (A) Behavior-based
   (B) Trait-based
   (C) Results-based
   (D) Procedure-based

15. One reason that trait-based appraisal systems are considered unreliable is that

   (A) they do not include all traits that contribute to job performance
   (B) they are in conflict with most popular organizational theories
   (C) employee behavior often varies depending upon the situation and environmental factors
   (D) personality traits are not under an individual's control according to researchers

16. A performance appraisal system that allows the employee to conduct a self-appraisal and discuss appropriate actions and goals with a manager is

   (A) an autocratic model
   (B) traditional
   (C) a rating scale
   (D) involvement-oriented

17. Behavior modification techniques attempt to change behaviors by manipulating the consequences of the behaviors, but they do NOT

   (A) address the underlying motivation of the employee
   (B) reward undesirable performance immediately
   (C) discourage the use of negative reinforcement
   (D) allow for situational and environmental differences

18. A corporation that uses teams of workers to provide information about layoffs to factory employees, along with direct mailings to employees' homes, is trying to maintain

   (A) visibility within its industry
   (B) communication with employees
   (C) a positive attitude
   (D) a minimum level of performance

19. An organization that supports participative leadership would most likely have a management development program that encourages managers to

   (A) use behavior modification techniques to reward performance
   (B) allow employees to train themselves and be self-motivating
   (C) inform employees about issues affecting their jobs and encourage them to express their ideas
   (D) emphasize negative consequences over positive reinforcement

20. The point method, which divides a job into elements and compares each element to a specifically constructed scale, can be described as a

   (A) qualitative approach to job evaluation
   (B) quantitative job design technique
   (C) qualitative job design technique
   (D) quantitative approach to job evaluation

21. The requirements, or aspects, of a job that are used by an organization as the basis for paying employees are called

   (A) compensable factors
   (B) incentives
   (C) economic motivators
   (D) job grades

22. A technique of bypassing the job evaluation process in which compensation is based on a survey of salaries paid by competitors is known as

(A) internal equity
(B) ranking to market
(C) factor comparison
(D) skill-based pay

23. The dean of a university chooses to use a limited budget primarily to attract and recruit new faculty members. The result is that inexperienced new assistant professors are hired at $40,000 per year, whereas the university's current assistant professors, who have two to three years of experience, are paid $37,000 per year. This situation is an example of

(A) inflation
(B) a lag approach
(C) wage compression
(D) merit pay

24. The typical criteria for setting the pay of individuals within a wage grade include

(A) knowledge, intelligence, and productivity
(B) equity, fairness, and comparable worth
(C) decision making, leadership, and accountability
(D) seniority, merit, and skill

25. Which of the following would NOT be a reason why employees doing the same job in an organization might receive different compensation?

(A) Factor comparison
(B) Wage compression
(C) Seniority
(D) Skill-based pay

26. One of the purposes of an individual incentive system is to

(A) replace previous job grading and classification systems
(B) motivate employees to devise strategies for improving their own performance
(C) improve overall group performance
(D) reinforce the self-directed team method

27. Gain sharing, lump-sum bonuses, profit sharing, and earned time off are all examples of

(A) job characteristics
(B) wage variables
(C) incentive systems
(D) cost-saving measures

28. When a company links compensation to organizational performance, the company is trying to ensure that individual employee objectives are consistent with

(A) federal laws and regulations
(B) a focus on quality
(C) overall market conditions
(D) the goals of the organization

29. Which of the following pension plans depends on a formula for retirement benefits that includes length of service and average earnings in the final years of employment?

(A) Defined benefit
(B) Capital accumulation
(C) Undefined benefit
(D) Early retirement

30. When an employee may be covered both by the employee's own health insurance plan and by a working spouse's benefits, the employers must be concerned with

(A) coinsurance
(B) coordinating benefits
(C) a preferred provider
(D) partial coverage

31. Which of the following may be a concern to XYZ Corp., which has 35 employees and is studying the feasibility of containing its health insurance costs by switching from Blue Cross/Blue Shield to self-insurance?

(A) A benefits-cost consultant may be needed to perform a complete analysis.
(B) Employees currently receiving medical treatments may be affected.
(C) Because the base number of employees may not be large enough to spread the risk, XYZ Corp. may not achieve significant savings.
(D) Federal laws prohibit such changes in health-care coverage for employers with less than 50 employees.

32. Company exercise facilities, tuition reimbursement, on-site childcare, and legal counseling may all be described as

(A) cost containment measures
(B) pay-for-performance
(C) nonfinancial compensation
(D) employee ownership

33. Total compensation is the combination of salary or wages and which of the following?

(A) Job satisfaction
(B) Perks
(C) Insurance
(D) Benefits

34. A job outline that give details about potential dangers involved in each step of a job task, causes of the danger, and remedies to reduce or remove the danger is called

(A) a hazard analysis
(B) a safety procedure
(C) an OSHA standard regulation
(D) safety training

35. An effective disciplinary process would NOT

(A) focus on a specific behavior to clarify the offense
(B) include public reprimand to deter other employees from inappropriate behavior
(C) be administered by a trusted individual
(D) be in proportion to the nature of the undesirable behavior

36. Unsatisfactory work performance can best be monitored and improved through the use of which of the following employee-involvement appraisal methods?

(A) Forced distribution
(B) Graphic rating scale
(C) Critical-incident
(D) Management by objectives

37. Social Security/Medicare is designed to protect employees and their dependents by providing

(A) retirement income, disability income, and health-care and survivor benefits
(B) insurance programs, pension benefits, and hospital/major medical coverage
(C) workers' compensation, unemployment compensation, and health-care coverage
(D) unemployment compensation, disability coverage, and catastrophic illness coverage

38. At the present time, Social Security/Medicare benefits are provided from

(A) a combination of state and federal government funds
(B) employee earnings and employer payments
(C) income taxes
(D) taxes paid by senior citizens

39. One of the controversial issues surrounding the future of Social Security/Medicare is increasing
    - (A) the workforce
    - (B) employer contributions
    - (C) the retirement age
    - (D) the costs of pharmaceuticals

40. Which of the following types of employees are subject to the provisions of the Fair Labor Standards Act (FLSA)?
    - (A) Exempt
    - (B) Minority
    - (C) All employees
    - (D) Nonexempt

41. Minimum wage provisions do NOT apply to
    - (A) exempt employees
    - (B) nonexempt employees
    - (C) supervisors
    - (D) employees under the age of 18

42. The overtime provisions of the Fair Labor Standards Act (FLSA) require
    - (A) payment of overtime after 35 hours worked per week
    - (B) payment of 1½ the regular hourly rate of work after 40 hours worked per week
    - (C) employers to pay overtime to exempt employees
    - (D) regular monthly inspections of company payroll records

43. Testing procedures used to hire employees should be validated using techniques consistent with
    - (A) the Fair Labor Standards Act
    - (B) Supreme Court rulings
    - (C) EEOC Uniform Guidelines
    - (D) the *McDonnell Douglas* vs. *Green* decision

44. An Equal Employment Opportunity regulation that provides job security to employees who must be absent from work under certain personal circumstances is called
    - (A) the Fair Labor Standards Act
    - (B) ERISA
    - (C) OSHA
    - (D) the Family and Medical Leave Act

45. The federal regulation that prevents organizations from giving men and women different job titles and compensating them with different wages, even though they perform essentially the same work, is known as the

(A) Equal Pay Act
(B) Fair Labor Standards Act
(C) Civil Rights Act
(D) Fair Pay Act

46. The Pension Benefit Guaranty Corp. (PBGC), which protects employee pensions in the event of a company bankruptcy, was created as a result of

(A) OSHA legislation
(B) ERISA legislation
(C) the Fair Labor Standards Act
(D) Equal Employment Opportunity legislation

47. The right to receive pension benefits contributed by the company on the employee's behalf, even if the employee leaves the company before retirement, is known as

(A) guaranteed benefits
(B) compensation for service
(C) vesting
(D) stakeholding

48. The Occupational Safety and Health Administration (OSHA) focuses its standards and regulations on

(A) minimal training requirements only
(B) equipment inspections only
(C) government contractors and their employment procedures
(D) on-the-job inquiries, hazardous substances, and diseases related to the workplace

49. The National Labor Relations Board plays a role in which of the following employment issues?

(A) Minimum wage standards
(B) Union-management relations
(C) Antidiscrimination policies
(D) Sexual harassment cases

50. Which of the following industries typically has very low union membership?

(A) Financial services
(B) Construction
(C) Public utilities
(D) Education

51. Labor-management joint committees in nonunionized companies have been criticized as

    (A) anti-Semitic
    (B) discriminatory
    (C) an unfair labor practice
    (D) biased toward management

52. To resolve union disputes and provide a mechanism for handling strikes that create a national emergency, which of the following federal agencies was created?

    (A) National Labor Relations Board
    (B) Occupational Safety and Hazards Administration
    (C) Department of Labor
    (D) Federal Mediation and Conciliation Service

53. The Federal Labor Relations Authority (FLRA) is responsible for overseeing and investigating unfair labor practices in

    (A) the federal public sector
    (B) the private sector
    (C) publicly owned companies
    (D) privately owned companies

54. The process in which different employers combine to negotiate a common agreement with a union is called

    (A) a unilateral approach
    (B) multiemployer bargaining
    (C) collective negotiating
    (D) structured bargaining

55. Wages, overtime, grievance procedures, and safety conditions are all considered to be which of the following types of issues in the collective bargaining process?

    (A) Permissive
    (B) Structured
    (C) Mandatory
    (D) Private sector

56. The mutual obligation between an employer and a union to bargain toward the settlement of a collective-bargaining contract is called

    (A) contract ratification
    (B) petition agreement
    (C) fairness
    (D) good faith

57. An employer's decision to reassign union employee work to outside firms or to employees that work outside of the union is known as

(A) subcontracting
(B) an impasse
(C) a strike
(D) bad faith

58. Female clerical workers are suing their employer. They claim that their jobs are equivalent to those of male physical plant workers in terms of job evaluation points, yet the male workers are paid at a higher rate. The female workers' claim involves which of the following issues?

(A) Wage compression
(B) Comparable worth
(C) Alternative compensation
(D) Pay secrecy

59. Quality circles, management by objectives, employee surveys, task forces, and job evaluation committees are all examples of

(A) collective bargaining
(B) decentralized management
(C) employee participation
(D) self-directed work teams

60. Possession of narcotics at work is generally considered a justifiable reason for immediate

(A) suspension
(B) probation
(C) termination
(D) counseling

POSTTEST ANSWERS

1. **The correct answer is (A).** Outplacement, self-assessment tools, and computer-aided training are all career planning and development tools commonly used by human resource managers.

2. **The correct answer is (B).** Although large organizations need standardized materials that can be handed off for orienting large numbers of new hires, cultural diversity and multilingual situations are best handled by a live instructor who can present a consistent corporate message.

3. **The correct answer is (C).** When a large number of employees are involved in a potential training situation or when they are dispersed geographically, a questionnaire on needs assessment is most often distributed and the responses are reviewed.

4. **The correct answer is (D).** Today's multinational corporations are increasingly developing upper-management personnel through the use of customized internal programs rather than traditional university-based M.B.A. programs. Management development is driven more by the need to maintain strategic focus than simply by short-term profitability.

5. **The correct answer is (A).** Especially in the case of management training, the content of a training program may be inappropriate or unsuccessful in a certain country or culture due to local practices and assumptions. Careful research is important prior to choosing the content and method for a program.

6. **The correct answer is (B).** Action learning is the training method that utilizes classroom time and that is followed by an on-the-job application and a presentation of project results.

7. **The correct answer is (C).** If a task is complex, comprised of many different parts, it should (in most cases) be broken down into components that can be taught and practiced as separate elements.

8. **The correct answer is (D).** Making layoff decisions is an administrative function. Layoffs are generally decided on the basis of performance appraisal information and other factors.

9. **The correct answer is (A).** Forced distribution appraisal systems, which rate employees according to very fine numerical categories, have been criticized for their negative rather than positive affect on employee performance.

10. **The correct answer is (B).** A results-based performance appraisal system measures the "bottom line" associated with an employee's work.

11. **The correct answer is (C).** Performance appraisals can be used to encourage employee development by determining the training needs of individual employees.

12. **The correct answer is (D).** Performance appraisal data are often used by organizations to design jobs and systems to accomplish organizational goals.

13. **The correct answer is (A).** A performance appraisal system may be viewed as discriminatory from a legal point of view if the rating content is not based on a thorough job analysis.

14. **The correct answer is (B).** A trait-based appraisal system typically assesses the personality or personal characteristics of employees, such as the ability to make decisions, loyalty to the company, communication skills, or level of initiative.

15. **The correct answer is (C).** One reason that trait-based appraisal systems are considered unreliable is that employee behavior is strongly influenced by situational and environmental factors.

16. **The correct answer is (D).** An involvement-oriented performance appraisal is based more on the employee's self-review than a manager's assessment alone.

17. **The correct answer is (A).** Behavior modification techniques do not address the underlying motivation of the employee.

18. **The correct answer is (B).** Maintaining communication with employees plays a significant role in the success of layoff procedures.

19. **The correct answer is (C).** An organization that supports participative leadership typically informs employees about issues affecting their jobs and encourages them to express their ideas.

20. **The correct answer is (D).** The point method, which divides a job into elements and compares each element to a specifically constructed scale, is a quantitative approach to job evaluation.

21. **The correct answer is (A).** Compensable factors are the requirements, or aspects, of a job that are used by an organization as the basis for paying employees.

22. **The correct answer is (B).** Ranking to market is a technique of bypassing the job evaluation process in which compensation is based on a survey of salaries paid by competitors.

23. **The correct answer is (C).** Wage compression results when wages for new hires are higher than the wages of employees already on the payroll.

24. **The correct answer is (D).** The typical criteria for setting the pay of individuals within a wage grade include seniority, merit, and skill.

25. **The correct answer is (A).** Choices (B), (C), and (D) reflect rationales for compensation differences among employees doing the same job in an organization. Factor comparison is a method of quantifying a variety of differences among dissimilar jobs.

26. **The correct answer is (B).** One of the purposes of an individual incentive system is to motivate employees to devise strategies for improving their own performance.

27. **The correct answer is (C).** Gain sharing, lump-sum bonuses, profit sharing, and earned time off are all examples of incentive systems used to motivate and reward employee performance.

28. **The correct answer is (D).** By linking employee compensation to organizational performance, a company encourages employees to perform their jobs in a manner that also leads to good organizational performance.

29. **The correct answer is (A).** In a defined benefit pension plan, benefits depend on a formula that includes length of service and average earnings in the final years of employment.

30. **The correct answer is (B).** When an employee may be covered both by the employee's own employer's health insurance plan and by a working spouse's benefits, the employers must be concerned with coordinating benefits.

31. **The correct answer is (C).** Self-insurance, in which an employer sets aside funds to pay medical claims in lieu of insurance coverage, can result in savings if the base number of employees is large enough to spread the risk.

32. **The correct answer is (C).** Company exercise facilities, tuition reimbursement, on-site child care, and legal counseling can all be described as nonfinancial compensation.

33. **The correct answer is (D).** Total compensation is the combination of salary or wages and benefits.

34. **The correct answer is (A).** A hazard analysis is a job outline that gives details about potential dangers involved in each step of a job task, causes of the danger, and remedies to reduce or remove the danger.

35. **The correct answer is (B).** Public reprimand is not part of an effective disciplinary process.

36. **The correct answer is (D).** Management by Objectives (MBO) is considered the most effective method of monitoring and improving employee performance using an employee-involvement approach.

37. **The correct answer is (A).** Social Security/Medicare is designed to protect employees and their dependents by providing retirement income, disability income, and health-care and survivor benefits.

38. **The correct answer is (B).** At the present time, the Social Security/ Medicare benefits are provided from a combination of employee earnings and employer payments.

39. **The correct answer is (C).** Increasing the age at which individuals retire and begin to collect benefits is one of the controversial issues surrounding the future of Social Security/Medicare.

40. **The correct answer is (D).** Nonexempt employees, i.e., those who are paid an hourly wage and are eligible for overtime pay, are subject to the provisions of the Fair Labor Standards Act (FLSA).

41. **The correct answer is (A).** Exempt employees are not subject to minimum wage provisions.

42. **The correct answer is (B).** The overtime provisions of the Fair Labor Standards Act (FLSA) require payment of 1½ the regular hourly rate of work over 40 hours per week.

43. The correct answer is (C). Testing procedures used to hire employees should be validated using techniques consistent with EEOC Uniform Guidelines.

44. The correct answer is (D). The Family and Medical Leave Act (FMLA) is an Equal Employment Opportunity regulation that provides job security to employees who must take a leave of absence from work due to personal, medical, or other family-related circumstances.

45. The correct answer is (A). The Equal Pay Act is a federal regulation that prevents organizations from giving men and women different job titles and compensating them with different wages, even though they perform essentially the same work.

46. The correct answer is (B). The Pension Benefit Guaranty Corp. (PBGC), which protects employee pensions in the event of a company bankruptcy, was created as a result of ERISA legislation.

47. The correct answer is (C). Vesting is the right of an employee to receive pension benefits contributed by the company on the employee's behalf even if the employee leaves the company before retirement.

48. The correct answer is (D). The Occupational Safety and Health Administration (OSHA) focuses its standards and regulations on on-the-job inquiries, hazardous substances, and occupational diseases.

49. The correct answer is (B). Union-management relations in the United States are governed by the executive branch of the federal government through the National Labor Relations Board.

50. The correct answer is (A). Financial services is an industry in which union membership is typically very low.

51. The correct answer is (C). In a nonunionized workplace, it has been suggested that labor-management joint committees might be a violation of Section 8(a)(2) of the NLRA, which makes it illegal for an employer to dominate or interfere with the formation of a labor organization or contribute financial or other support to it.

52. The correct answer is (D). The Federal Mediation and Conciliation Service was created to resolve union disputes and provide a mechanism for handling strikes that create a national emergency.

53. The correct answer is (A). The Federal Labor Relations Authority (FLRA) is responsible for overseeing and investigating unfair labor practices in the federal public sector.

54. The correct answer is (B). Multiemployer bargaining is the process in which different employers combine to negotiate a common agreement with a union.

55. The correct answer is (C). Mandatory issues in the collective bargaining process are material and significant to the employment relationship, such as wages, overtime, grievance procedures, and safety conditions.

56. The correct answer is (D). The obligation between an employer and a union to bargain toward the settlement of a collective-bargaining contract is called good faith.

57. **The correct answer is (A).** Subcontracting is an employer's decision to reassign union employee work to outside firms or to employees that work outside of the union.

58. **The correct answer is (B).** Comparable worth is based on the idea that traditionally female-dominated jobs are underpaid relative to traditionally male-dominated jobs that require the same level of skill and make an equally valuable contribution to the employer.

59. **The correct answer is (C).** Quality circles, management by objectives (MBO), employee surveys, task forces, and job evaluation committees are all examples of employee participation.

60. **The correct answer is (C).** Possession of a narcotics at work is generally considered a justifiable reason for immediate termination or dismissal.

Introduction to Business

PRETEST

1. Which of the following best describes the term "free enterprise"?

   • (A) A system in which individuals decide what and how to produce goods
   (B) A study of how goods are produced and distributed
   (C) Motivating factors for starting a business
   (D) Individuals who buy goods for their personal use

2. Which of the following distinguishes a capitalistic economy from a command economy?

   (A) In a command economy, the individual consumer plays a major role in planning the economy.
   • (B) In a capitalistic economy, buyers and sellers can enter the market as they choose.
   (C) In a capitalistic economy, goods and services are rationed by the federal government.
   (D) In a command economy, competition is encouraged.

3. Which of the following terms best describes a person who invests his time, effort, and money to start a business?

   (A) Communist
   (B) Middleman
   • (C) Entrepreneur
   (D) Consumer

4. In the United States, monopolies are

   • (A) heavily regulated by the federal government
   (B) per se illegal
   (C) unregulated by the government
   (D) immediately broken up by the government

5. Which of the following describes an individual's level of satisfaction in terms of goods?

   (A) Consumer price index (CPI)
   (B) Business cycle
   (C) Entrepreneurship
   • (D) Standard of living

6. Which of the following is the term for periods of time when the purchasing power of the dollar is in decline?

   (A) Recession
   (B) Inflation
   (C) Depression
   (D) Business cycle

7. Which of the following is NOT a factor of production?

   (A) Productivity
   (B) Capital
   (C) Entrepreneurship
   (D) Labor

8. In a socialistic society, which of the following describes the place of key industries?

   (A) Owned and regulated privately
   (B) Owned privately, but regulated by the government
   (C) Owned by the government
   (D) Owned by the government, which distributes goods produced directly by consumers

9. Which of the following acts as an incentive for business owners to produce?

   (A) Profit
   (B) Customer satisfaction
   (C) Specialization
   (D) Factors of production

10. Which of the following best describes the process of selling goods to foreign nations?

    (A) Importing
    (B) Exporting
    (C) International business
    (D) Balance of trade

11. A small island nation produces $2 million worth of goods in 1999. Of this $2 million of goods, the nation exports $600,000. In the same year, the nation imports $900,000 worth of goods. Which of the following is this nation's trade deficit?

    (A) $300,000
    (B) $900,000
    (C) $1,100,000
    (D) $1,400,000

12. The country of Naterra produces baskets more efficiently than it can produce any other product. However, there are other nations that can produce baskets more efficiently than Naterra. With respect to its basket production, which of the following best describes Naterra's situation?

    (A) It has a comparative advantage.
    (B) It has an absolute advantage.
    (C) It has a trade deficit.
    (D) It has a favorable balance of trade.

13. Which of the following best describes the purpose of the North American Free Trade Agreement (NAFTA)?

    (A) Reducing tariffs between the United States, Canada, and Mexico
    (B) Eliminating tariffs between the United States, Canada, and Mexico
    (C) Allowing for free movement of goods throughout the United States and Europe
    (D) Assisting in financing American firms' exports

14. The United States does not trade with Cuba. For this reason, the United States can be said to have established which of the following with Cuba?

    (A) An import quota
    (B) A joint venture
    (C) An embargo
    (D) An absolute advantage

15. Which of the following types of businesses is considered to be a separate legal entity from its owners?

    (A) Sole proprietorship
    (B) Corporation
    (C) Partnership
    (D) Limited partnership

16. Which of the following represents the greatest risk for individuals who want to start their own companies?

    (A) Unlimited liability
    (B) Double taxation
    (C) Cost of formation
    (D) Lack of control

17. Two large merchandising chains that specialize in electronics merge to form a new company. The new company is the result of which of the following types of mergers?

    (A) Conglomerate
    (B) Vertical
    (C) Horizontal
    (D) Cooperative

18. Private corporations and open corporations differ mainly in that

   (A) open corporations sell stock on the market

   (B) private corporations have a special tax status

   (C) open corporations are subject to double taxation

   (D) private corporations' owners have unlimited liability

19. Which of the following is NOT included in a firm's articles of partnership?

   (A) Each partner's duties

   (B) The dissolution of the partnership

   (C) Protocol for settling managerial disagreements

   (D) The number of shares of stock to be issued

20. The privileges of holding shares of stock in a corporation do NOT include which of the following?

   (A) Appointing corporate officers

   (B) Receiving dividends

   (C) Having limited liability

   (D) Electing management

PRETEST ANSWERS

1. **The correct answer is (A).** Free enterprise can be described as a system in which individuals decide what and how to produce goods.

2. **The correct answer is (B).** Buyers and sellers can enter the market as they choose in a capitalistic economy.

3. **The correct answer is (C).** A person who invests his time, effort, and money to start a business is an entrepreneur.

4. **The correct answer is (A).** The government in the United States heavily regulates monopolies.

5. **The correct answer is (D).** The standard of living is an individual's level of satisfaction in terms of goods.

6. **The correct answer is (B).** The purchasing power of the dollar is in decline during periods of inflation.

7. **The correct answer is (A).** The factors of production are land, labor, capital, and entrepreneurship.

8. **The correct answer is (C).** In a socialistic society, key industries are owned by the government.

9. **The correct answer is (A).** Profit is an incentive for business owners to produce.

10. **The correct answer is (B).** Selling goods to foreign nations is referred to as exporting.

11. **The correct answer is (A).** Trade deficit = imports − exports = 900,000 − 600,000 = 300,000.

12. **The correct answer is (A).** Comparative advantages occur when one nation can produce one product more efficiently than any other product.

13. **The correct answer is (B).** NAFTA was implemented with the purpose of eliminating all tariffs between the United States, Canada, and Mexico.

14. **The correct answer is (C).** An embargo is a situation in which one nation refuses to trade with another.

15. **The correct answer is (B).** A corporation is, legally, considered an entity separate from its owners.

16. **The correct answer is (A).** The greatest worry for a sole proprietor is the individual's unlimited liability.

17. **The correct answer is (C).** A horizontal merger includes firms that produce the same product.

18. **The correct answer is (A).** Open corporations sell stock on the market; private corporations do not.

19. **The correct answer is (D).** Corporations issue stock; partnerships do not.

20. **The correct answer is (D).** Shareholders do not take part in the employee hiring process.

GENERAL OVERVIEW

ECONOMIC ISSUES AFFECTING BUSINESS

A **business** is an organization of individuals that, for a profit, produces and sells goods and services that satisfy a society's needs. **Profits** are the rewards earned by businesses after all the expenses of doing business have been subtracted from revenue, or income. In contrast, the primary purpose of **nonprofit organizations,** such as museums and universities, is something other than to make profits for their owners.

PRIVATE ENTERPRISE SYSTEM

U.S. businesses operate as part of the **private enterprise system**, or **capitalism**, an economic system in which businesses must match and improve on the offerings of their competitors in order to succeed. The key characteristic of a private enterprise system is **competition**, the battle among businesses for consumer acceptance. Over time, businesses that satisfy consumers will succeed, and those that do not will fail. **Entrepreneurs** are key figures in private enterprise systems. They take the risk of exploiting an opportunity to make a profit by forming a new business or revitalizing an old one.

In the private enterprise system, there are four **factors of production**, or inputs, that businesses need in order to operate successfully. These include natural resources, human resources, capital, and entrepreneurship. Each business uses a unique mix of the four factors.

In order for the private enterprise system to succeed, people must have certain **rights**. These include the right to own private property, to keep their profits, and to choose their employment and purchases. In addition, people have the right to make rules concerning fair competition.

Competition takes different forms in different industries. **Pure competition** is characterized by many businesses of similar size that sell similar products, so no one firm can influence prices (farms). In **monopolistic competition**, businesses differentiate their products and have some influence over prices (department stores). An **oligopoly** is a situation in which there are few companies, and the price of entering the industry is high (automobiles, aircraft manufacture). In a **monopoly**, there are no direct competitors and the industry is regulated by the government (some utilities).

OTHER ECONOMIC SYSTEMS

Communism

In a communist system, all property is owned by the people in common, and a strong central government directs production. The government is the employer as well as the provider of goods, so there is little choice on the part of workers and consumers. **Karl Marx**, whose theories form the basis of communism, thought that each person should contribute to society according to his or her abilities and should be rewarded according to his or her needs. In an ideal communist society, there would be no economic classes. During the twentieth century, until the breakup of the Soviet Union and the loosening of its hold on Eastern Europe, many nations had a communist system. Today only a few, such as Cuba, remain.

Socialism

Socialism is similar to communism in that the government owns key industriesùthose considered vital to the welfare of the nation, such as utilities, energy, health care, and transportation. Private ownership is permitted in less important sectors. Israel is a socialist nation, although it is moving in the direction of **privatization** for many enterprises.

Mixed Economies

Many nations have mixed economies that combine public and private ownership to different degrees. Great Britain, the Netherlands, and Chile are a few examples.

Today's Challenges

The environment of business today includes several major influences:

- **Globalization**—Increasingly, businesses operate internationally, whether through exporting or importing goods or establishing production and/or marketing facilities overseas.
- **Strategic alliances**—Businesses often form alliances with other businesses in order to improve their competitiveness in a market or when they enter new markets.
- **Quality**—Commitment to quality is an important factor in business in order to attract new customers and retain old ones.
- **Technology**—The pace of technological development means a constant research and development effort to bring new products to the market place and to use technology to the greatest benefit in operations.

- **Outsourcing**—Companies often subcontract internal operations to an outside vendor in order to save money. Examples of outsourced operations include payroll, warehousing, delivery, and data processing.
- **Employee empowerment**—A growing emphasis on the importance of human resources has meant increased employee control over decision making, more teamwork, and a flatter organization.

INTERNATIONAL BUSINESS

There are three major aspects to international business: (1) **exporting**, or selling U.S. goods and services abroad; (2) **importing**, or buying raw materials, products, and services from businesses in foreign nations; and (3) **foreign production**, making goods and supplying services in a foreign nation for sale there or elsewhere.

LEVELS OF INTERNATIONAL INVOLVEMENT

The most common form of international business is exporting. A company may have an export manager on staff or may rely on an exporting firm for expertise. With **foreign licensing**, a company allows foreign firms to produce and/or distribute its products or services in a particular region abroad. Because there is little capital investment, this is a low-cost way to enter foreign markets. With **overseas marketing**, a company opens a sales office in a foreign nation and manages foreign sales itself. The highest level of international involvement is foreign production, when a company both produces and markets its products overseas. This is sometimes done by means of a joint venture with a local company. Businesses with significant international operations are called **multinational corporations**.

OBSTACLES TO INTERNATIONAL BUSINESS

Doing business internationally can be very difficult, and problems often arise in several key areas. **Cultural misunderstandings** result from a firm's ignorance of key factors such as language, customs, education, social values, religious values, and consumer behavior. **Physical barriers** such as distance, time zone differentials, poor terrain and roads, and lack of infrastructure pose problems for people seeking to do business overseas.

Tariffs (tax on imported products) and **trade restrictions** such as import quotas impede a firm's ability to trade freely. An **embargo** is a complete restriction on trade of certain products and/or with certain nations. Nations can also restrict trade through currency exchange controls, requiring that foreign businesses buy and sell only through the country's central bank or another designated agency. Although tariffs and trade restrictions continue to affect international business, the trend in recent years has shifted toward relaxing restrictions. The General Agreement on Tariffs and Trade (GATT) is an international agreement that has reduced tariffs and restrictions.

MULTINATIONAL ECONOMIC ORGANIZATIONS

Several multinational economic organizations have been established since World War II to facilitate trade among members, including:

- **North American Free Trade Agreement (NAFTA)**—This agreement established a free trade zone consisting of the United States, Canada, and Mexico.
- **European Union**—This is a common market of twelve nations working together to reduce trade barriers. It has adopted a common currency, the euro, to facilitate trade.

GOVERNMENT AND BUSINESS

Some government activity benefits and supports the interests of business. For example, the U.S. Census Bureau collects and makes available huge amounts of demographic information that businesses use in marketing. Other agencies provide information and assistance to businesses. The government also funds much of the basic research that leads to new product development. It is a major consumer of products and services sold by American businesses.

REGULATIONS REGARDING COMPETITION

Some federal laws protect competition, including:

- **Sherman Antitrust Act (1890)**—Prohibits any contract or agreement entered into for the purpose of restraining trade. This includes price fixing, market allocation, and boycotts in restraint of trade.
- **Clayton Act (1914)**—Prohibits five practices: price discrimination, the tying agreement, the binding contract, the interlocking directorate, and the community of interests.
- **Federal Trade Commission Act (1914)**—Created the Federal Trade Commission (FTC), which investigates illegal trade practices and enforces antitrust laws.

OTHER REGULATIONS

Many government agencies have regulatory power over specific aspects of business. A few of these include:

- **Environmental Protection Agency**—Regulates pollution
- **Equal Employment Opportunity Commission**—Regulates discrimination in employment practices
- **Federal Communications Commission**—Regulates broadcast, telephone, and telegraph communication
- **Interstate Commerce Commission**—Regulates railroads, bus lines, trucking, pipelines, and waterways

FORMS OF BUSINESS OWNERSHIP

SOLE PROPRIETORSHIP

A **sole proprietorship** is a business owned and operated by one person. It is the oldest and simplest form of ownership. About two thirds of the businesses in the United States are sole proprietorships.

Sole proprietorships are easy to start and easy to dissolve. All the profits from the business belong to the owner. Since decision making is done by just one person, it is easy to change the business's operations. Sometimes there are tax advantages, because the income of the business is taxed as the personal income of the owner. On the other hand, the owner has unlimited liability for all debts. He or she has a limited ability to borrow and limited skills and knowledge. In the event of the owner's death, the business dissolves.

PARTNERSHIP

A **partnership** is an association of two or more people to act as co-owners of a business for profit. About one tenth of U.S. businesses are partnerships. There are many types of partners, including (1) a **general partner**, who assumes full or shared responsibility for the operation of the business; and (2) a **limited partner**, who contributes capital to a business but does not take part in managing it.

Partnerships are easy to form; there are multiple sources of capital, all profits belong to the partnership, there are several sources of business skills and knowledge, and the partners have a strong personal interest in the business. Disadvantages include unlimited liability for general partners, the lack of continuity in cases of death, the potential for serious disagreements among partners, and difficulty in withdrawing the partner's investment from the firm.

CORPORATION

A **corporation** is an artificial person created by law, with most of the legal rights of a person. The corporation is owned by people called shareholders, or stockholders, in the form of shares of stock. A **close corporation** is owned by a few people and is not openly traded on a stock market; an **open corporation** is one whose stock is traded openly and can be bought by anyone. About one fifth of U.S. businesses are corporations; they earn about nine tenths of sales.

One of the main advantages of a corporation is that it is a separate legal entity with limited liability on the part of the owners. Other advantages include easy transfer of ownership through the sale of stock, ease of raising capital, perpetual life of the business, and specialized management. Disadvantages include difficulty and expense of formation, much government regulation, double taxation of income, and lack of secrecy.

SMALL BUSINESS, ENTREPRENEURSHIP, AND FRANCHISES

According to the Small Business Administration, a **small business** is "one which is independently owned and operated for profit and is not dominant in its field." The size of a small business can vary considerably, depending on the industry. Certain industries are suitable for small businesses because they do not require a huge outlay of capital: retailing, wholesaling, transportation, services, financial services, agriculture, construction, mining, and some manufacturing.

Small businesses are usually operated by the entrepreneurs who started and own them. Most entrepreneurs are between the ages of 25 and 44, and they have acquired the knowledge and management ability to run a successful business, often by working for another firm. These small businesses promote technical innovation, provide employment, and compete with larger firms in certain niches.

More than 70 percent of new businesses fail within the first five years, usually because of problems with capital, management, and/or planning. Entrepreneurs often lack the capital to run a business during the sometimes lengthy startup phase when there are no profits. Many start with a good idea but lack the management skills needed to run a business. Sometimes success and overexpansion tax the capacity of the business to function effectively.

A **franchise** is a license to operate an individually owned business as if it were part of a chain. The **franchiser** provides the business name, management skills, business methods and procedures, training, and any required materials. The **franchisee** provides capital and labor and operates the business abiding by the terms of the franchise agreement. Oil company service stations, new car dealers, soft drink bottlers, and fast food outlets are usually franchises.

THE MANAGEMENT PROCESS

MANAGING THE ORGANIZATION

Before a business can operate effectively, it must have an articulated purpose and a plan for achieving that purpose. To these ends, the top managers of a company formulate a **mission statement**, a written explanation of a company's aims. The mission statement may include information about goods, services, and markets as well as less tangible matters, such as beliefs, values, and attitudes. Top managers also set forth objectives, goals that the company should accomplish in specific areas such as sales and customer service.

MANAGEMENT FUNCTIONS

The basic management functions include five broad processes:

- **Planning** is the process of establishing guidelines for achieving objectives. The outcome of the planning process is a plan, a road map for achieving goals.

- **Organizing** is a natural outgrowth of planning. At its most fundamental level, organizing involves a division of labor and an allocation of resources. For instance, there are thousands of tasks that need to be done in order to accomplish an organization's objectives.

- **Staffing** begins with the organization's structure—the kinds of jobs and workers that are needed to meet the organization's objectives.

- **Directing** involves using human relations skills, technical skills, and administrative skills to guide the activities of employees.

- **Controlling** ensures that plans are being carried out and objectives are being reached.

MANAGERIAL DECISION MAKING

Decision making is the process of examining alternative solutions to a problem and choosing one of them. Managers are required to make decisions about complex problems in a variety of situations. To do this effectively, they use a systematic approach involving four steps:

1. Identify and define the problem or opportunity.

2. Come up with alternative solutions or approaches.

3. Select the most effective and practical alternative.

4. Implement the decision.

HUMAN RELATIONS

Human relations are an important aspect of management. To succeed, managers must be able to motivate, lead, and effectively communicate with people.

- **Motivation** is that which energizes, directs, and sustains human behavior. Employees can be motivated by monetary rewards and by the satisfactions built into their jobs.

- **Leadership** is the ability to get others to do what the manager wants them to do without coercion. Typically, a good leader can adjust his or her leadership style to match the leader's abilities, the situation at hand, and the people involved.

- **Communication** is a key activity in a well-run organization, especially in ensuring that objectives are met and employees are satisfied. Two-way communication between management and employees as well as top-down communication ensures that information is disseminated throughout an organization.

SOCIAL RESPONSIBILITY, BUSINESS ETHICS, AND REGULATION

In a business that values **social responsibility**, management assesses the effect of business decisions and actions on society as well as on the business. Three major areas of social concern are consumers (product safety, public health, product information, product choices, and the resolution of complaints), employees (equal employment opportunity, affirmative action, and retraining), and the environment (safety, pollution, conservation).

Business ethics is the application of moral standards to business situations. In an organization with an ethical corporate culture, ethical guidelines are clearly stated and communicated to employees, managers are committed to ethical values, normal business practices reflect ethical values, and managers are trained to make ethically sound decisions.

Ideally, businesses would regulate themselves, behaving in an ethical and socially responsible manner. In reality, the government must impose regulations to help ensure that businesses operate in an ethical and socially responsible manner. Regulation exists in the areas of maintaining fair competition, specific business practices, consumer protection, environmental protection, employment practices, etc.

HUMAN RESOURCE MANAGEMENT

Human resource management consists of the activities required to acquire, maintain, and develop the human resources of an organization. In very small organizations, the owner or manager performs all the human resource management functions. In large organizations, a human resource department is responsible for these activities. Human resource management can be divided into three main areas: acquiring human resources, maintaining human resources, and developing human resources.

HUMAN RESOURCE ACQUISITION

Acquiring the appropriate people to staff an organization has several basic steps. These include:

- **Planning**—From the company's strategic plan, human resource managers can forecast the future staffing needs of the organization and come up with a plan to meet them.

- **Job analysis**—Through job analysis, the organization determines the elements and requirements of each job and comes up with job descriptions and job specifications (the skills and qualities needed to perform a job).

- **Recruitment, selection, and orientation**—The human resource staff finds appropriate candidates, evaluates and chooses the best candidates, and introduces them to the organization and the job.

HUMAN RESOURCE MAINTENANCE

The chief activity involved in maintaining a firm's human resources is to reward employee effort through compensation (monetary payment) and benefits (services or expenses paid by the company).

The **compensation system** of a firm must be positioned relative to the pay levels of competing firms in the industry. Within the organization, the relative wages for all positions must be determined. Finally, the specific payment that an individual worker receives must be decided upon. Compensation may take many forms, including wages, salary, commissions, bonuses, and profit sharing.

Benefits are a form of compensation that employees receive indirectly. There are several major types of benefits, including payment for time not worked (vacations, sick days), health and security benefits (insurance, retirement plans), and employee services (cafeterias, tuition reimbursement).

HUMAN RESOURCE DEVELOPMENT

Training and development are both aimed at improving employees' knowledge and skills. **Training** generally involves teaching employees the skills they need to do their present jobs; **development** generally prepares employees to take on additional responsibility in the future.

Another function of human resource development is **performance appraisal**, a periodic evaluation of employees' work-related behavior. Conducting performance appraisals accomplishes three basic purposes: providing information upon which salary and promotion decisions are made, reviewing and correcting employee behavior, and providing an opportunity to discuss career development.

LABOR RELATIONS

About one sixth of U.S. workers belong to **labor unions,** organizations of workers that bargain collectively for a labor contract with an employer. The **American Federation of Labor and Congress of Industrial Organizations (AFL-CIO)** is a voluntary federation of about 100 national and international labor unions. Workers belong to a local union, which is a chapter in the national union, which in turn may belong to the AFL-CIO.

Collective bargaining is the process through which a labor contract is negotiated between management and the labor union. Bargaining must be conducted in **good faith**, meaning that both sides are communicating, negotiating, and matching proposals with counterproposals in an effort to arrive at agreement. Items on which agreement must be reached may be mandatory (such as wages and hours of employment), permissible (pension benefits, employment of strikebreakers), or illegal (closed shop, discriminatory treatment).

PRODUCTION AND OPERATIONS MANAGEMENT

Production is the application of resources like raw materials and people to convert materials into finished goods or services. **Production and operations management** is the management of this process.

Production and operations management often begins with the **research and development (R&D)** effort. The result may be a completely new product or an alteration of an existing product.

Next, operations planning involves the design of both the product and the manufacturing processes. Then, through operational planning, managers determine how to use facilities and resources to produce enough to meet customer demand.

Finally, operations control involves several major functions: purchasing, inventory control, scheduling, and quality control.

MARKETING MANAGEMENT

According to the American Marketing Association, **marketing** is "the process of planning and executing the conception, pricing, promotion, and distributions of ideas, goods, and services to create exchanges that satisfy individual and organizational objectives." The **marketing concept** is an approach to business in which the entire organization, from product development to accounting to sales, is involved with satisfying customers' needs while achieving the organization's goals.

A **market strategy** is a plan that enables an organization to make the best use of its resources in order to meet its objectives. It typically consists of the selection and analysis of a target market and the development of an appropriate marketing mix (a combination of product, price, distribution, and promotion).

TARGET MARKETS

A **target market** is a group of customers and potential customers for whom a firm develops and maintains an appropriate market mix. There are two basic approaches to selecting a target market.

TOTAL MARKET APPROACH

In the **total market approach**, also called the undifferentiated approach, a company designs a single marketing mix for a product or service and directs it at the entire market. The company assumes that individual customers who buy the product have similar needs, and therefore they will all be satisfied with one marketing mix. Examples of products that are often marketed this way are staple foods, such as salt or flour, and certain types of produce.

MARKET SEGMENTATION APPROACH

In the **market segmentation approach**, a company focuses on a market segment, a group of individuals or organizations within a market who share one or more common characteristics. The company develops and directs its marketing mix for a product or service at one or more segments rather than the entire market.

To market successfully, a company must segment a market based on characteristics that actually relate to differences in people's need for a product or service. Common bases of market segmentation include product-related characteristics (end use, brand loyalty), demographic characteristics (age, sex, income), psychographic characteristics (personality traits, lifestyles), and geographic characteristics (region, climate, urban).

MARKETING MIX

The **marketing mix** consists of four elements in combination: product, price, distribution, and promotion.

PRODUCT

A **product** may be an idea, service, or manufactured item. Products are classified according to their ultimate use, the two main types being consumer products and industrial products. A **product line** is a group of similar products marketed by a firm. The company's **product mix** is all the products it markets.

Each product goes through a series of four stages—introduction, growth, maturity, and decline—which together form the product's life cycle. As a product moves through the life cycle its profitability increases, peaks, and then declines. Companies must continually introduce new products in order to replace the declining products.

PRICE

In an ideal world, product prices would be set by the laws of supply and demand. However, sellers do exert some control over the prices of their products, primarily through product differentiation. When setting a price, a company must decide whether it will compete on the basis of having a low price or on the basis of some other characteristic. It also must take into account whether or not price is an important consideration in the target market. Prices are generally set based on a combination of costs, demands, and the competition's prices.

DISTRIBUTION

A **marketing channel** is a chain of marketers that moves a product from its producer to its ultimate user. For consumer products, the marketing channel may go from producer to consumer; producer to retailer to consumer; producer to wholesaler to retailer to consumer; or producer to agent to wholesaler to retailer to consumer. For industrial products, the major marketing channels are producer to user and producer to middleman to user. **Wholesalers** are intermediaries who buy products from producers or other intermediaries and sell them to industrial users, retailers, or other wholesalers. Wholesalers generally provide product-related services to both producers and other intermediaries.

One of the responsibilities of the organizations in the marketing channel is the **physical distribution** of goods. Physical distribution includes inventory management, warehousing, order processing, materials handling, and transportation.

PROMOTION

Promotion is communication with two main purposes: (1) to expedite sales directly by conveying information about a product, idea, or service to a particular market segment; and (2) to expedite sales indirectly, by maintaining good relationships with the various groups in the company's environment.

There are several promotional methods that a company can use to communicate:

- **Advertising**—Paid message communicated to a selected audience through the media
- **Personal selling**—A one-to-one personal communication designed to inform customers and persuade them to purchase the company's products
- **Sales promotion**—Activities or materials that offer incentives to consumers or salespeople to buy a product
- **Publicity**—An unpaid message, usually in the form of a news story, about a product or company
- The **promotion mix** for a particular product is the combination of promotional methods put together for that product.

FINANCIAL MANAGEMENT

MONEY

Money is anything used to purchase goods or services. Money (1) functions as a means of exchange, (2) serves as a yardstick of value, and (3) represents a store of value.

In the United States, there are three measures of the supply of money in the economy:

- **M_1 supply**—Currency and demand deposits (amounts on deposit in a checking account)
- **M_2 supply**—The M_1 supply plus certain securities and small-denomination time deposits
- **M_3 supply**—The M_1 and M_2 supplies plus large time deposits of $100,000 or more

The **Federal Reserve System** (the Fed) is the U.S. agency that regulates the supply of money and the banking industry. The Fed controls the money supply by (1) controlling the **bank reserve requirement**, the percentage of deposits a bank must have on hand; and by (2) setting the **discount rate**, the interest rate it charges member banks on loans. When the discount rate is lowered, the money supply increases, decreasing key interest rates and stimulating the economy. When the discount rate is raised, the money supply decreases, increasing interest rates and slowing the economy.

BANKS AND OTHER FINANCIAL INSTITUTIONS

There are several types of banks:

- **Commercial bank**—A profit-making institution that accepts deposits, makes loans, and provides related services
- **State bank**—A commercial bank chartered by an individual state
- **National bank**—A commercial bank chartered by the federal government

In addition, there are other types of financial institutions:

- **Thrift institutions**—Institutions, such as **savings and loan associations** and **savings banks**, that offer banking services (home mortgages, savings accounts, loans, and time deposits, etc.)
- **Credit unions**—Member-owned financial cooperatives that pay interest to depositors, make short-term loans, and offer mortgages
- **Non-deposit institutions**—Insurance companies, pension funds, and consumer and commercial finance companies that offer various types of financial services

FINANCIAL STRATEGIES

Financial management consists of all the activities related to obtaining and using money. Money is needed to start a business and keep it going. In a successful business, the income from sales is enough to keep the business operating. However, sales income does not flow evenly, so temporary funding of operations may be necessary. In addition, money may be needed to finance the purchase of a plant, equipment or to expand into new markets. Thus, businesses have several sources of financing: sales revenue, equity capital (from the sale of stock), debt capital, and proceeds from the sale of assets. Once money is obtained, the firm's financial managers are responsible for monitoring its effective use and its repayment.

Short-term financing is money that will be used for a period of a year or less and then repaid. Sources of unsecured short-term financing (no collateral) include promissory notes issued to suppliers, unsecured bank loans, commercial paper, trade credit, and commercial drafts. Sources of secured short-term financing include loans secured by inventory or accounts receivable and the sale of receivables to factors.

Long-term financing is money that will be used for more than one year, as in a business startup or expansion or for the purchase of assets. Sources of long-term debt financing are the sale of corporate bonds with maturities of up to forty years and long-term loans such as mortgages.

SECURITIES MARKETS

Securities, or stocks, may be bought in either the primary or secondary markets. In the **primary market**, investors purchase financial securities (common stock or preferred stock) from the issuer of those securities, using the services of an investment bank (a company that assists corporations in raising funds) or another representative. The **secondary market** involves buying and selling securities through a securities exchange or over-the-counter market. The New York Stock Exchange and American Stock Exchange are the largest U.S. securities exchanges. The **over-the-counter market** is a network of stockbrokers who deal in securities that are not traded in exchanges. The National Association of Securities Dealers Automated Quotation (NASDAQ) is a large nationwide over-the-counter market. Both individual and institutional investors buy securities. Institutional investors include mutual funds, pension funds, insurance companies, and commercial banks.

Bonds are another type of financial instrument. Bondholders are creditors, rather than owners, of a corporation or government agency.

The **Securities and Exchange Commission** regulates the stock exchanges and over-the-counter market.

RISK MANAGEMENT AND INSURANCE

A **risk** is the chance that an injury or loss will occur. Some risks are **speculative risks**; they accompany the possibility of earning a profit. Marketing a new widget involves speculative risk because the widget may fail in the marketplace. Other risks are **pure risks**; they involve only the possibility of loss with no potential for gain. Damages caused by weather or accidents are pure risks. **Risk management** is the evaluation of risks faced by an organization and the minimization of their costs. There are several **strategies for risk reduction**: avoiding the risk (never ride in a car), reducing the risk (wear a seat belt), assuming the risk (drive anyway), and shifting the risk (buy auto insurance).

An insurance company assumes financial responsibility, for a fee called a premium, for all or part of a risk. In general, pure risks are insurable and speculative risks are not. In the event of a loss, the insured person or organization cannot collect more than the dollar amount of the loss from the insurer, a concept known as the **principle of indemnity**.

Property and casualty insurance protects the insured against losses of property and losses due to accidents. Businesses may buy fire insurance; burglary, robbery, and theft insurance; fidelity bonds (which protect against theft, forgery, or embezzlement by employees); motor vehicle insurance; business liability insurance, including public liability insurance and product liability insurance; marine or transportation insurance; and business interruption insurance.

MANAGEMENT INFORMATION SYSTEMS AND ACCOUNTING

A **management information system (MIS)** is an organized method of providing useful and timely information for managerial decision making. The information comes both from internal operations and the external environment. Large organizations generally place responsibility for MIS and computer operations under the chief information officer (CIO).

Functions of the MIS include collecting reliable internal and external data; storing and updating data; processing data into a useful form; and presenting information, usually in the form of reports. The basic element of an MIS is the organization's **database**, a centralized, integrated collection of data resources. Computer networks connect the organization's computers internally, and the Internet links the organization to the outside world. While both of these developments have greatly improved access to and use of information, they have also introduced new risks, including computer crime, hacking, and viruses.

Accounting is the process of systematically collecting, analyzing, and reporting the financial information of a firm. Accounting information is used by the organization's management as well as creditors, suppliers, investors, and government agencies. The accounting process is based on the basic **accounting equation**: Assets = Liabilities + Owner's Equity. Double-entry bookkeeping keeps the accounting equation of a firm in balance.

The **accounting cycle** has several basic steps:

1. Source documents are analyzed to determine which accounts, and therefore which parts of the accounting equation, are affected by a transaction.

2. Each transaction is recorded chronologically in a journal.

3. Each journal entry is posted to two or more appropriate ledger accounts.

4. At the end of each accounting period, the balances in the accounts are tallied and checked to ensure that the accounting equation balances.

5. Financial statements, including the income statement, owner's equity statement, and balance sheet are prepared.

SAMPLE QUESTIONS

1. The federal agency that investigates illegal trade practices and enforces antitrust laws is the

   (A) National Labor Relations Board
   (B) Securities and Exchange Commission
   (C) Federal Trade Commission
   (D) Interstate Commerce Commission

   The correct answer is (C). The Federal Trade Commission was established in 1914 to investigate illegal trade practices and enforce antitrust laws. The National Labor Relations Boards oversees management–employee relations and unions; the Securities and Exchange Commission regulates the securities exchanges and over-the-counter markets; and the Interstate Commerce Commission regulates interstate transportation such as railroads, waterways, and pipelines.

2. All of the following rights are necessary for the private enterprise system to succeed EXCEPT the right to

   (A) own property
   (B) keep earned profits
   (C) choose employment and purchases
   (D) receive the basic necessities of food and shelter

   The correct answer is (D). The private enterprise system is based on private ownership of property and the freedom to make private choices. It does not assume that everyone has the basic right to food and shelter; that is an assumption of the communist system.

3. The PQR Corporation is planning to add a new product line to its offerings. To manufacture the product, it will need to build a new factory and expand its headquarters. What source of financing is PQR *most likely* to use?

   (A) A promissory note issued to a supplier
   (B) An unsecured bank loan
   (C) A loan secured by inventory
   (D) The sale of long-term corporate bonds

   The correct answer is (D). The building of a new asset such as a factory requires long-term financing like issuing corporate bonds with maturity dates years in the future. The remaining options are all types of short-term financing.

PRACTICE SET

1. For a firm that has a commitment to quality, the process of setting performance standards by comparing and measuring the firm's performance against those of other companies in the industry, is called

   (A) total quality management
   (B) benchmarking
   (C) reengineering
   (D) continuous process improvement

2. Which of the following is an example of promotion based on demographic segmentation?

   (A) Issuing a press release about a new product that is being offered
   (B) Offering consumers special coupons to a brand name product
   (C) Offering a point of sale discount for quantity purchases
   (D) Running a Spanish-language magazine ad for cosmetics

3. Which of the following is a potential disadvantage of the widespread use of computers to do business?

   (A) Elimination of the human element in customer contact
   (B) Storage of large quantities of information in a small space
   (C) Ability to perform repetitive tasks without tiring
   (D) Fast processing of large amounts of information

4. The Federal Reserve can slow business expansion by

   (A) decreasing the reserve requirement of member banks
   (B) raising the discount rate
   (C) cracking down on fraud in the securities exchanges
   (D) instituting tariffs on interstate commerce

5. Each of the following is one of the five basic management functions EXCEPT

   (A) planning
   (B) directing
   (C) manufacturing
   (D) staffing

6. Which of the following types of organizations has the most difficulty maintaining a high level of entrepreneurship?

   (A) Sole proprietorship
   (B) Partnership
   (C) Corporation
   (D) Franchise

7. In Great Britain, a few major industries, such as health care, are owned and run by the government, but businesses in many other industries are privately owned. Which type of economic system does Great Britain have?

(A) Private enterprise system
(B) Capitalism
(C) Socialism
(D) Mixed economy

8. Allowing a foreign firm to produce and/or distribute a U.S. firm's products in a foreign market is called

(A) exporting
(B) foreign licensing
(C) foreign production
(D) multinational marketing

9. Which of the following is a human resources recruiter most likely to use to do the job effectively?

(A) Job analysis
(B) Job specification
(C) Career development plan
(D) Performance appraisal

10. Which of the following types of insurance is a credit union most likely to have?

(A) Fidelity bonds
(B) Motor vehicle insurance
(C) Transportation insurance
(D) Public insurance

PRACTICE SET ANSWERS

1. **The correct answer is (B).** To benchmark is to set standards of comparison. All of the options are aspects of total quality management, a firm's overall commitment to high quality. Reengineering is remapping a process or procedure to improve quality. Continuous process improvement involves constantly studying and adjusting work activities.

2. **The correct answer is (D).** Running ads in Spanish or other foreign languages is a promotion method that targets a particular demographic market segment. A press release does not target any market segments. Special coupons for brand loyalists and point-of-sale discounts are promotions based on product-related segmentation.

3. **The correct answer is (A).** Customers can be alienated if firms use computers exclusively over human contact in their form letters and telephone answering systems. All the other options are benefits of computer use.

4. **The correct answer is (B).** The Fed can raise the discount rate to member banks, which in turn raise other key interest rates, increasing the cost of borrowing. When the cost of borrowing rises, some firms put off their expansion plans. Decreasing the reserve requirement puts more money into circulation, which has an expansionary effect. Overseeing the securities exchanges and interstate commerce are not functions of the Fed.

5. **The correct answer is (C).** The five basic management functions are planning, organizing, staffing, directing, and controlling.

6. **The correct answer is (C).** Corporations are generally the largest type of business organization, and their size and lines of authority can have a dampening effect on entrepreneurship, which is based on risk and flexibility. Corporations are often more focused on maintaining their current success than on looking for new areas of potential profitability.

7. **The correct answer is (D).** The combination of socialism and capitalism that Great Britain exemplifies is a mixed economy.

8. **The correct answer is (B).** This is a low-cost way for companies to expand their markets overseas, second only to exporting.

9. **The correct answer is (B).** A recruiter's job is to find appropriate applicants for the firm's open positions. A job specification, which lists the skills, abilities, education, and experience needed to do a particular job, is a basic tool of a recruiter.

10. **The correct answer is (A).** This is insurance against theft, forgery, and embezzlement by employees; it is a type of coverage often bought by financial institutions whose employees handle money.

POSTTEST

1. Which of the following organizations was created by Congress in 1953 to assist small businesses?

   (A) Small Business Administration
   (B) Small Business Institute
   (C) Small Business Development Centers
   (D) Active Corps of Small Business Executives

2. Which of the following is NOT an important economic contribution made by small businesses?

   (A) Creating new jobs
   (B) Making technological advances
   (C) Having only a limited potential for failure
   (D) Meeting customers' needs on a personal basis

3. A major advantage of franchising is that franchisees

   (A) receive royalties from franchisers
   (B) can sell to existing clientele
   (C) easily receive venture capital from the Small Business Investment Company (SBIC)
   (D) have the liberty to create business plans

4. Pat wants to open a small business. Pat is granted a license that provides a business name, business plan, and management training. Which of the following best describes Pat's position?

   (A) Franchiser
   (B) Franchisee
   (C) Entrepreneur
   (D) Venture capitalist

5. For any company goal to be effectively undertaken, which of the following groups of employees must reflect the goal's importance in their communication and actions?

   (A) Top management
   (B) Middle management
   (C) Workers
   (D) Supervisors

6. Before management can create a business plan, which of the following must be done first?

   (A) Develop a strategy.
   (B) Identify an opportunity.
   (C) Evaluate the alternatives.
   (D) Analyze the problems.

7. The Tillman Company has instituted a laissez-faire management policy. If an employee wishes to work in a manner other than how the employee was formally trained, which of the following individuals should the employee consult?

   (A) The human resources manager
   (B) An operations manager
   (C) No one
   (D) A financial manager

8. Two employees find that they are at an impasse concerning a difference of opinion. Their manager should refer them to which of the following individuals?

   (A) An operations manager
   (B) A negotiator
   (C) The human resources manager
   (D) A financial manager

9. Terry has excellent motivational skills and usually has the ability to accomplish any task requested. However, Terry has trouble visualizing ideas. Which of the following types of skills does Terry need to improve?

   (A) Diagnostic
   (B) Interpersonal
   (C) Technical
   (D) Conceptual

10. Top management at MegaCorp ascribes to the economic model of social responsibility and has recently discovered that one MegaCorp factory is polluting a local river. Which of the following courses of action can MegaCorp implement in line with its economic model?

    (A) Inform the community of MegaCorp's pollution.
    (B) Stop polluting the river and do nothing else.
    (C) Stop polluting the river and clean the surrounding environment.
    (D) Do nothing unless legally required to act.

11. Chris is the Vice President of human resources for a large Northeastern firm. A position in the firm has opened and one of the candidates for the position is Chris's son, Toby. Because Chris will play a major role in hiring the individual to fill this position, which of the following has occurred?

    (A) Code of ethics
    (B) Conflict of interest
    (C) Nepotism
    (D) Ethical procedure

12. Fran is an African-American applying for a promotion. Fran has the educational requirements and experience for the new position, but is not offered the job. Instead, she learns that her manager's son, who has no work experience, has been hired. To which of the following organizations should Fran bring a complaint?

    (A) National Alliance of Business
    (B) National Association for Advancement of Colored People (NAACP)
    (C) Equal Employment Opportunity Commission (EEOC)
    (D) The judicial system in a trial court

13. Which of the following would best help a company that practices external recruiting to compare candidates' qualifications?

    (A) Structured interviews
    (B) Open-ended interviews
    (C) Job descriptions
    (D) Recommendations

14. The major difference in payment between employees on salary and those paid hourly wages is the

    (A) wage level
    (B) wage structure
    (C) bonuses
    (D) job evaluation procedures

15. A large corporation has found that internal recruiting has provided the company with inferior managers. Which of the following programs does the company need to improve?

    (A) Management development
    (B) Vestibule training
    (C) Orientation
    (D) Attrition

16. Which of the following acts of Congress lists unfair labor practices that unions are forbidden to use?

    (A) Taft-Hartley
    (B) Landrum-Griffen
    (C) National Labor Relations
    (D) Wagner

17. Which of the following is NOT a cause of the declining trend in union membership?

    (A) Additional benefits provided by management
    (B) Cutbacks in major production industries
    (C) Growth in the service industry
    (D) Increasing domestic inflation

18. When applying for a position at Tupalo, Inc., a potential employee is informed that all employees are union members and union membership is a condition of accepting employment at Tupalo. Which of the following types of businesses is Tupalo?

    (A) Agency shop
    (B) Open shop
    (C) Closed shop
    (D) Maintenance shop

19. The Quilting Company makes hand-stitched quilts and uses very few machines for quilt assembly. Which of the following best describes the Quilting Company's business?

    (A) Labor-intensive
    (B) Capital-intensive
    (C) Service industry
    (D) Total quality control

20. Which of the following is the main difference between basic research and applied research?

    (A) Applied research takes longer from start to finish.
    (B) Applied research deals mainly with existing knowledge.
    (C) Basic research deals with putting new knowledge to practical use.
    (D) Basic research is not interested in the potential use of new knowledge.

21. The Kiwi Corporation is a manufacturing firm that takes raw materials and transforms them into a finished product. This process is best described as adding which of the following types of utility?

    (A) Possession
    (B) Place
    (C) Form
    (D) Production

22. Which of the following is NOT a major function of marketing?

    (A) Exchange
    (B) Risk management
    (C) Physical distribution
    (D) Facilitating

23. Many automobile companies offer incentives for customers who own a particular brand of car to remain loyal to that brand. Which of the following types of marketing best describes this strategy?

    (A) Relationship
    (B) Industrial
    (C) Segmentation
    (D) Brand

24. A firm produces only capital goods. In which of the following types of markets does this firm sell?

(A) Producer
(B) Reseller
(C) Institutional
(D) Target

25. Which of the following best describes the marketing strategy used by a company that produces four different carbonated drink products, each with its own unique identity and advertising campaign?

(A) Packaging
(B) Product line
(C) Family branding
(D) Individual branding

26. Which of the following does management NOT expect to accomplish through pricing?

(A) Profit maximization
(B) Return on investment
(C) Modification
(D) Continuity

27. In year 1, a firm had fixed costs of $9,500 and variable costs of $1.70 per unit produced. If the price of one unit sold in year 1 was $4.20, which of the following number of units was the firm's break-even quantity?

(A) 2,262
(B) 3,800
(C) 6,736
(D) 9,500

28. Which of the following types of improvements is NOT a primary function of product modification?

(A) Aesthetics
(B) Quality
(C) Function
(D) Analysis

29. Many brands of antibacterial soap are said to eliminate 99.9 percent of bacteria. Which of the following best describes this form of advertising?

(A) Selective
(B) Institutional
(C) Comparative
(D) Scientific

30. Which of the following is the main difference between selective advertising and primary demand advertising?

(A) Primary demand advertising is designed to enhance a firm's image.

(B) Selective advertising is designed to sell a particular product brand.

(C) Primary demand advertising is designed to sell a particular product brand.

(D) Selective advertising is usually based on a scientific study.

31. Which of the following is NOT an advantage of advertising in a newspaper?

(A) Loyalty

(B) Relative advertising cost

(C) Timeliness

(D) Local coverage

32. A salesman whose company requires the salesman to buy merchandise from the company and then resell it to the public is best described as

(A) an off-price retailer

(B) a manufacturer's agent

(C) a retailer

(D) a merchant wholesaler

33. Which of the following is NOT an advantage to retailers provided by wholesalers?

(A) Reduction of inventory costs

(B) Product analysis

(C) Product promotion

(D) Reduction of credit risk

34. Assuming that rapid economic expansion will cause recessions, while slow expansion will not, which of the following would the Federal Reserve Board elect to do if they detected that the economy was expanding rapidly?

(A) Increase the M1 supply of money

(B) Lower the discount rate

(C) Raise the discount rate

(D) Encourage deposit expansion

35. Which of the following is NOT a primary function of money?

(A) Medium of exchange

(B) Store of value

(C) Source of collateral

(D) Measure of value

36. Chris has an account balance of $347,500 in an FDIC member bank when the bank owner takes all the money from the accounts and flees the country. For which of the following amounts has the FDIC insured Chris's account?

(A) $100,000
(B) $250,000
(C) $340,000
(D) $347,500

37. People from regions of economic uncertainty may want to invest their local currency in U.S. dollars. A reason for doing this is that the U.S. dollar demonstrates which of the following attributes?

(A) Divisibility
(B) Stability
(C) Durability
(D) Independence

38. Which of the following is the major difference between common and preferred stock?

(A) Preferred stock carries voting rights.
(B) Common stock receives interest.
(C) Preferred stock represents ownership.
(D) Common stock shares in capital gains.

39. A potential investor finds that a firm's return on owner's equity is very high. Which of the following financial strategies might the firm be employing?

(A) Financial leverage
(B) Call premium
(C) Secured financing
(D) Equity capital expansion

40. A firm buys a new machine on credit for $17,000 with terms 2/10, n/30. The firm pays for the machine in seven days. Which of the following amounts was the firm was required to pay?

(A) $340
(B) $13,600
(C) $16,660
(D) $17,000

41. Which of the following directly reduces a firm's retained earnings account?

(A) Dividends
(B) Depreciation
(C) Long-term debt
(D) Operating expenses

42. Which of the following is NOT an advantage of investing in a mutual fund?

   (A) Professional management
   (B) Diversification
   (C) Low risk
   (D) High yield

43. An investor places an order to buy 250 shares of stock but is unwilling to pay more than $65 per share. Which of the following best describes this type of order?

   (A) Limit
   (B) Rand
   (C) Market
   (D) Ceiling

44. Which of the following types of market is best described by a market situation that reflects rising prices?

   (A) Bear
   (B) Bull
   (C) Primary
   (D) Liquid

45. A manager has been given raw data and needs to make it usable information. Which of the following activities must the manager undertake?

   (A) Information managing
   (B) Database analysis
   (C) Data processing
   (D) Word processing

46. A large corporation has an interconnected system of computers connected to a mainframe. This configuration is best described as

   (A) the Internet
   (B) an intranet
   (C) a telecommunications model
   (D) a collaborative learning system

47. Amortization applies to which of the following?

   (A) Long-term assets
   (B) Cash
   (C) Goodwill
   (D) Long-term debt

48. Insurance offers protection from which of the following types of risk?

   (A) Pure
   (B) Determined
   (C) Manageable
   (D) Speculative

49. Which of the following are necessary in order to collect insurance on a loss?

   I.   The loss must be under the control of the insured.
   II.   The probability of loss must be predictable.
   III. The loss must be measurable.

   (A) I and II only
   (B) I and III only
   (C) II and III only
   (D) I, II, and III

50. The value of an insured house is $125,000, and the insurance policy includes a 75 percent coinsurance clause. Which of the following is the amount of insurance the homeowner must carry to satisfy the clause?

   (A) $31,250
   (B) $75,000
   (C) $93,750
   (D) $125,000

51. The main difference between robbery and burglary is

   (A) robbery involves a threat of violence
   (B) burglary involves stolen goods
   (C) robbery usually involves forcible entry
   (D) burglary is an uninsurable risk

52. Which of the following types of insurance is legally required in most states?

   (A) Automobile liability
   (B) Uninsured motorists
   (C) Automobile collision
   (D) No-fault automobile

53. In a socialistic society, which of the following best describes the place of goods?

   (A) They are owned by the state.
   (B) They can be purchased and owned by individuals.
   (C) They are distributed by the state.
   (D) They are equally distributed among citizens.

54. Which of the following issues does NOT affect the business system today?

   (A) Inflation
   (B) Government involvement in business
   (C) The United States isolating itself from global markets
   (D) Unemployment

55. A firm may enter the global market through direct investment by doing which of the following?

(A) Establishing a subsidiary in a foreign country
(B) Instituting an embargo
(C) Partaking in a joint venture
(D) Having products exported to the firm's own country

56. Which of the following is a possible benefit of a total quality management (TQM) policy?

(A) Lower levels of customer retention
(B) Higher return on investment
(C) Exceeding customer needs
(D) Lower necessity for employee participation

57. Which of the following is NOT a primary function performed by managers?

(A) Controlling
(B) Planning
(C) Leading
(D) Selling

58. A company which prefers to hire management through promotions and transfers rather than through public advertising is practicing which of the following?

(A) Human resource management
(B) External recruiting
(C) Internal recruiting
(D) Replacement charting

59. Which of the following is the main difference between arbitration and mediation?

(A) Mediation is used to settle disputes.
(B) Mediation takes objective views into consideration.
(C) Arbitration involves a separate third party.
(D) Arbitration is binding.

60. According to the accounting equation, "assets equal liabilities plus . . ." which of the following?

(A) Owner's equity
(B) Debtors' claims against resources
(C) Expenses
(D) Return on equity

POSTTEST ANSWERS

1. **The correct answer is (A).** The Small Business Administration was created by Congress in 1953 to assist small businesses.

2. **The correct answer is (C).** Small businesses have a strong potential for failure.

3. **The correct answer is (B).** An advantage of franchising is that the franchisee can sell to existing clientele.

4. **The correct answer is (B).** A franchisee usually receives a business name, business plan, and management training from a franchiser.

5. **The correct answer is (A).** A company goal can be effective only if top management demonstrates commitment to it.

6. **The correct answer is (B).** Identifying an opportunity for profit is the first step in business planning.

7. **The correct answer is (C).** In a laissez-faire management system, an employee can work using the techniques the employee wishes.

8. **The correct answer is (B).** When two employees have a difference of opinion, they should seek a negotiator.

9. **The correct answer is (D).** Conceptual skills are those that deal with visualizing ideas and putting those ideas into practice.

10. **The correct answer is (D).** The economic model of social responsibility states that social responsibility is not a firm's goal, but rather that it should be left in someone else's hands.

11. **The correct answer is (B).** A conflict of interest often occurs when someone is not able to make an objective decision.

12. **The correct answer is (C).** When an employee has a complaint about an employer's hiring practices, the employee should file a complaint with the EEOC.

13. **The correct answer is (A).** Structured interviews ask the same questions of each candidate. This leads to an easy comparison of potential employees.

14. **The correct answer is (B).** Wage structure determines how an employee is paid.

15. **The correct answer is (A).** A management development program is a method of developing managers inside the company and preparing them for promotions. If internal recruiting has provided the company with poor management, then its management development program is lacking.

16. **The correct answer is (A).** The Taft-Hartley Act lists unfair labor practices that unions are forbidden to use.

17. **The correct answer is (D).** Increasing domestic inflation would not cause a decline in union membership.

18. **The correct answer is (C).** A closed shop is one in which all employees are union members and must join upon being hired.

19. **The correct answer is (A).** A company that produces more with labor than any other factor of production is referred to as labor-intensive.

20. **The correct answer is (D).** Basic research is aimed at discovering knowledge, not its potential uses.

21. **The correct answer is (C).** Form utility is that which is added by transforming raw materials into finished goods.

22. **The correct answer is (B).** Risk management is not a major function of marketing.

23. **The correct answer is (A).** Relationship marketing is a strategy used to encourage brand loyalty.

24. **The correct answer is (A).** Capital goods are those that are purchased to aid in the construction of other goods. A market that sells products used to aid in the construction of other products is referred to as a producer market.

25. **The correct answer is (D).** The marketing strategy of individual branding occurs when a firm produces products and advertises them as separate brands.

26. **The correct answer is (C).** A company does not seek modification through pricing.

27. **The correct answer is (B).** Break even where

$$TR = TC$$
$$TR = P(Q)$$
$$TC = TFC + TVC$$
$$TVC = VC(Q)$$

$$P(Q) = FC + VC(Q)$$
$$4.2Q = 9,500 + 1.7(Q)$$
$$2.5Q = 9,500$$
$$Q = 3,800$$

28. **The correct answer is (D).** The primary functions of product modification are quality, function, and aesthetics.

29. **The correct answer is (C).** Comparative advertising is usually based on information gleaned from a scientific study.

30. **The correct answer is (B).** Selective advertising is designed to sell a particular brand of a product. Primary demand advertising is designed to sell a product but not a particular brand of that product.

31. **The correct answer is (A).** Newspapers do not necessarily demonstrate loyalty to any business advertising in it.

32. **The correct answer is (D).** A merchant wholesaler is a middleman that buys and resells goods.

33. **The correct answer is (B).** Wholesalers are not responsible for any product analysis—their job is sales.

186

34. **The correct answer is (C).** When the Federal Reserve Board raises the discount rate, there is an economic slowdown.

35. **The correct answer is (C).** The primary functions of money are as a store of value, medium of exchange, and measure of value.

36. **The correct answer is (A).** FDIC insurance insures $100,000 per person per bank.

37. **The correct answer is (B).** Stability refers to money's ability to retain value over time. The U.S. dollar is far more stable than dollars from regions of economic uncertainty.

38. **The correct answer is (D).** Common stock does not receive fixed dividends like preferred stock.

39. **The correct answer is (A).** If ROE is high, then the firm is probably getting funds through debt. Financial leverage is a measure of debts to assets.

40. **The correct answer is (C).** 17,000(.98) = 16,660

41. **The correct answer is (A).**

> Retained earnings = undistributed profits
> Dividends = distributed profits
> Profits − dividends = retained earnings

42. **The correct answer is (D).** Mutual funds can be classified as low risk and low yield.

43. **The correct answer is (A).** In a limit order, the broker is requested to buy or sell at a price equal to or better than a specified price.

44. **The correct answer is (B).** A bull market is one that reflects rising prices.

45. **The correct answer is (C).** Data processing is the transformation of data into usable information.

46. **The correct answer is (B).** The intranet is a company's internal network.

47. **The correct answer is (C).** Amortization applies to intangible objects. Goodwill is an intangible object.

48. **The correct answer is (A).** Insurance protects individuals from pure risk.

49. **The correct answer is (D).** Conditions for an insurable loss include that the loss be under the control of the insured, that the probability of the loss be predictable, and that the loss be measurable.

50. **The correct answer is (C).** $125,000(.75) = $93,750

51. **The correct answer is (A).** Robbery involves a threat of violence; burglary does not.

52. **The correct answer is (A).** Auto liability insurance is legally required in most states.

53. **The correct answer is (B).** In a country based on socialism, goods and services are purchased and owned by private individuals.

54. **The correct answer is (C).** U.S. isolation from global markets is not an issue that affects the business system today.

55. **The correct answer is (A).** Establishing a subsidiary in a foreign nation is one method of entering the global market by direct investment.

56. **The correct answer is (B).** Total quality management (TQM) policies normally lead to a higher return on investment.

57. **The correct answer is (D).** The primary functions performed by managers are planning, motivating, and controlling.

58. **The correct answer is (C).** Internal recruiting is the process of hiring employees from inside the company, including through promotions and transfers.

59. **The correct answer is (D).** Arbitration is binding; mediation is not.

60. **The correct answer is (A).**

$$A = L + OE$$
$$OE = \text{creditors' claims against resources}$$
$$A = L + \text{creditors' claims against resources}$$

Organizational Behavior

PRETEST

1. The key elements in organizational behavior are

    (A) people, structure, technology, and environment
    (B) power, leadership, strategy, and goals
    (C) people, management, technology, and production
    (D) knowledge, attitude, ability, and performance

2. The study and application of knowledge about how people act within organizations is known as

    (A) leadership style
    (B) organizational behavior
    (C) human needs
    (D) behavior modification

3. The Mayo-Roethlisberger study in the 1920's and 1930's was the first substantial research

    (A) combining scientific management and organizational theory
    (B) including human needs as a factor in manufacturing
    (C) concerning human behavior and a social system within the work environment
    (D) differentiating between cognitive and emotional factors affecting the workplace

4. Which approach to organizational behavior is characterized by the belief that different situations within organizations require different and appropriate behavioral practices?

    (A) Productivity
    (B) Supportive
    (C) Systems
    (D) Contingency

5. Which of the following correctly describes the one-shot, one group pretest–posttest, and static group comparison designs?

   (A) Quantitative research designs used in experiments to study organizational behavior
   (B) Approaches considered unreliable due to problems in selection and lack of a control group
   (C) Qualitative research designs used in experiments to study organizational behavior
   (D) Approaches that examine human behavior and organizational goals

6. A study in which the researcher conducts interviews with workers, analyzes the history of an organization, and accompanies workers inside the organization to witness their daily routines would be described as an example of

   (A) a traditional research approach
   (B) qualitative research
   (C) individual analysis
   (D) quantitative research

7. Behavioral scientists can gain knowledge and collect data about the functioning of an organization through the use of

   (A) job designs, job descriptions, and job analysis
   (B) selection, ratings, and skills analysis
   (C) case studies, field studies, and experiments
   (D) critical incidents files, performance appraisals, and archives

8. A situation in which a manager considers production quotas to be reasonable and easy to accomplish but an employee regards them as unfair and unreasonable is an example of differences in

   (A) observation
   (B) achievement
   (C) motivation
   (D) perception

9. The term used to refer to the mental state, learned through experiences, that influences how a person responds to people, objects, and situations is

   (A) attitude
   (B) bias
   (C) perception
   (D) belief

10. The concept of selective perception is best illustrated by which of the following statements made by managers about employees?

    (A) "He is too old to learn the new software systems required for this project."

    (B) "I know he is generally cynical and negative, but he performs well under pressure and produces results."

    (C) "I don't have time to review her proposal on this job—it's due by next week."

    (D) "I can't jeopardize the stability of this department by hiring someone with a union background."

11. The theory that the environment or personal characteristics are the causes of behavior and performance is called

    (A) expectancy

    (B) motivation

    (C) attribution

    (D) stimuli

12. An employee who fails repeatedly at a task and believes that the work environment makes success impossible, probably has a low level of

    (A) probability

    (B) cooperation

    (C) awareness

    (D) expectancy

13. Which of the following terms can be used to describe the approach of Carl Rogers who maintained that people are driven by the need to realize their own potential?

    (A) Humanistic

    (B) Freudian

    (C) Psychodynamic

    (D) Characteristics

14. "Promotions are earned through hard work and persistence" would be a statement most likely made by a person with

    (A) an external locus of control

    (B) an internal locus of control

    (C) a low level of expectancy

    (D) an outgoing personality

15. Giving employees time off to work on a problem and allowing them to think about alternative ways to handle situations is an example of an organization trying to encourage

    (A) productivity

    (B) competency

    (C) creativity

    (D) motivation

16. Employee attitudes are chiefly a result of experiences with family, peer groups, society, and

   (A)   previous jobs
   (B)   educational institutions
   (C)   the employee's own behavior
   (D)   the employee's own needs

17. The guidelines and beliefs that a person uses when confronted with a situation in which a choice must be made are known as

   (A)   attitudes
   (B)   values
   (C)   viewpoints
   (D)   opinions

18. The attitude, or set of feelings, with which employees view their work is called job

   (A)   involvement
   (B)   enlargement
   (C)   satisfaction
   (D)   enrichment

19. A manager's leadership style and behavior toward subordinates is greatly affected by the manager's

   (A)   authority
   (B)   job description
   (C)   salary level
   (D)   values

20. All of the following are examples of observational learning in an organizational setting EXCEPT

   (A)   teaching personnel to use office equipment
   (B)   training supervisors to conduct job interviews
   (C)   teaching workers to engage in goal setting
   (D)   training managers to conduct performance appraisals

PRETEST ANSWERS

1. **The correct answer is (A).** The key elements in organizational behavior are people, structure, technology, and environment.

2. **The correct answer is (B).** Organizational behavior is the study and application of knowledge about how people act within organizations.

3. **The correct answer is (C).** The Mayo-Roethlisberger study in the 1920's and 1930's was the first substantial research about human behavior and a social system within the work environment.

4. **The correct answer is (D).** The contingency approach to organizational behavior is characterized by the belief that different situations within organizations require different and appropriate behavioral practices.

5. **The correct answer is (A).** The one-shot, one group pretest–posttest and static group comparison designs are quantitative research designs used in experiments to study organizational behavior.

6. **The correct answer is (B).** Qualitative research involves the interpretation rather than the measurement of data collected through various methods. These methods might include interviews and other types of first-hand participation with research subjects.

7. **The correct answer is (C).** Behavioral scientists can gain knowledge and collect data about the functioning of an organization through three basic research designs: case studies, field studies, and experiments.

8. **The correct answer is (D).** Managers and subordinates often have different perceptions about the same situation because they are affected by different experiences and stimuli.

9. **The correct answer is (A).** Attitude is the mental state, learned through experiences, that influences how a person responds to people, objects, and situations.

10. **The correct answer is (B).** Selective perception occurs when individuals select information that supports their own viewpoints and ignore information that does not. In this case, the manager is selecting the negative features of the employee and rating the employee on the basis of those results.

11. **The correct answer is (C).** Attribution is the theory that the environment or personal characteristics are the causes of behavior and performance.

12. **The correct answer is (D).** Expectancy is the strength of belief that work-related effort will result in the successful completion of a task.

13. **The correct answer is (A).** Humanistic approaches to understanding personality are characterized by an emphasis on the growth and self-actualization of the individual.

14. **The correct answer is (B).** Locus of control determines the degree to which individuals believe that behavior influences what happens to them. Individuals with an internal locus of control tend to think that their actions determine their own success.

15. **The correct answer is (C).** Giving employees time off to work on a problem and allowing them to think about alternative ways to handle situations encourages employees to be more creative.

16. **The correct answer is (A).** Employee attitudes are chiefly a result of experiences with family, peer groups, society, and previous jobs.

17. **The correct answer is (B).** Values are the guidelines and beliefs that a person uses when confronted with a situation in which a choice must be made.

18. **The correct answer is (C).** Job satisfaction is the attitude or set of feelings with which employees view their work.

19. **The correct answer is (D).** Managers tend to adopt a leadership style that reflects their own values and often evaluate subordinates differently depending on whether their values are the same or different.

20. **The correct answer is (A).** Observational learning occurs when an individual observes a model's behavior and tries to duplicate that behavior. Teaching personnel to use office equipment does not involve observational learning.

GENERAL OVERVIEW

OVERVIEW
THE FIELD OF ORGANIZATIONAL BEHAVIOR

Organizational behavior is the study of how people behave in organizations and the application of this knowledge.

UNDERLYING CONCEPTS

Several fundamental concepts underlie the field. They include assumptions about **human nature**:

1. Each individual is unique.

2. In organizations, people function as total human beings.

3. A person's behavior is guided by motivations.

4. Every person has human dignity.

They also include assumptions about the **nature of organizations:** (1) Organizations are social systems governed by social laws as well as the psychological needs of their members. (2) Organizations and their members have mutual interests. Thus, the organization and its people form a system of interrelated interactions.

HISTORY

The field of organizational behavior arose from the industrial revolution. In the 1800s, a few factory owners began to recognize the human factor in manufacturing, providing workers with some training and improved working conditions. In 1911 **Frederick W. Taylor** published *The Principles of Scientific Management*, an influential work that described how human factors influence technical efficiency. In the 1920s and 1930s, the idea that an organization is a social system and that its workers are its most important element took hold. In 1957 **Douglas McGregor** first presented his idea that management actions flow from assumptions about human nature. Those who adhere to **Theory X** take an autocratic approach; and those who adhere to **Theory Y** take a humanistic approach. McGregor's ideas helped clarify the field of organizational behavior in the 1950s and 1960s. Contemporary organization theory focuses on the idea of organizations as systems of interrelated variables.

THE STUDY OF ORGANIZATIONAL BEHAVIOR

Studies of organizational behavior follow the **scientific method**: (1) observe phenomena; (2) formulate an explanation for the phenomena; (3) make a prediction or hypothesis about the phenomena; (4) test the hypothesis; (5) draw conclusions about the hypothesis based on the results. The scientific method is applied using one of several basic research designs:

- **Naturalistic observation** involves watching real-life events.
- In **survey research**, data is collected by means of questionnaires.
- In a **field study**, the researcher studies the relationship between two variables but does not attempt to alter any variables.
- A **field experiment** is similar to a field study, but the researcher manipulates one of the variables to see what effect that has.
- In a **laboratory experiment**, the researcher manipulates a variable in a controlled setting to see its effect.

While naturalistic observation usually yields qualitative data, field studies, field experiments, and laboratory experiments usually yield quantitative data that can be analyzed using statistical methods.

INDIVIDUAL PROCESSES AND CHARACTERISTICS

PERCEPTION

The process of selecting, organizing, and interpreting stimuli is known as **perception**. At any given moment, the environment contains thousands of stimuli competing for our attention. First, we choose what we will attend to, a process called **selective attention**. We then organize or categorize the stimulus, a process called **perceptual organization.** Perceptual organization is influenced by our prior experiences. Finally, we interpret the stimulus and behave accordingly.

SOCIAL PERCEPTION

The process by which we perceive other people is called **social perception**. Our perceptions are influenced by the characteristics of: (1) the person perceived, (2) the situation, and (3) the perceiver. **Barriers** to accurate social perception include:

- **Stereotyping**, or attributing characteristics to a person because of his or her membership in a particular group

- The **halo effect**, allowing knowledge of one trait to influence knowledge of other traits
- **Implicit personality theory**, having a fixed set of biases
- **Selective perception,** limiting our perceptions of others
- **Projection** of our own self-concepts onto the other person

ATTRIBUTIONAL APPROACHES

Attributional approaches to perception and behavior emphasize that behavior is influenced by perception, not actual causes. When a person interprets an event in a particular way, he or she rethinks assumptions about possible causes. Based on the new cognitive structure (way of thinking), the individual makes decisions about behavior. **Locus of control** is an important concept in this approach. An internal locus of control is a feeling that we can personally influence the outcome of events. An external locus of control is a feeling that outcomes are imposed by others.

PERSONALITY
Theories of Personality

A person's characteristic way of thinking, feeling, and acting is his or her **personality**. There are several theories of personality:

- **Psychoanalytic**—Personality is the result of conflicts between pleasure-seeking impulses and social restraints.
- **Trait**—Personality expresses biologically influenced dispositions, such as extroversion.
- **Humanistic**—Personality is the processing of conscious feelings about oneself in light of experiences.
- **Social-cognitive**—Personality is influenced by the interrelationships of people and situations and is colored by perceptions of control.

Traits

Personality is usually described in terms of basic **traits**, or characteristic behaviors. Some psychologists recognize five basic trait dimensions that cover a range of behavior:

Emotional stability ↔ Emotional Instability

Extroversion ↔ Introversion

Openness ↔ Rigidity

Agreeableness ↔ Disagreeableness

Conscientiousness ↔ Carelessness

PERSONALITY AND THE ORGANIZATION

Some theorists believe there is a fundamental conflict between the needs of a person with a mature personality and the needs of a typical organization. Whereas mature, emotionally stable employees want meaningful work that takes advantage of their internal locus of control, flexibility, and openness, many organizations want employees to follow rules, be dependent, and perform repetitive tasks. The strongest conflict occurs when employees are highly mature, the organization is highly structured and formal, and jobs are fragmented and automated.

ATTITUDES

An **attitude** is a tendency to respond in a favorable or unfavorable way to stimuli in the environment. There are three components to attitudes: (1) beliefs and ideas about a person or object, (2) feelings toward the person or object, and (3) behavioral intentions toward the person or object. **Beliefs** are perceived relationships between people, objects, and events. They differ from values in that they have a basis in fact, or at least in what the person holding the belief thinks is fact. **Values**, on the other hand, are closely held norms. They are standards of idealized behavior.

ATTITUDE FORMATION AND CHANGE

There are four major influences on attitude formation: (1) cultural influences, (2) group membership, (3) family, and (4) prior experience. Since attitudes are learned, they can be modified or altered by providing new information that changes beliefs, by arousing and reducing fear, creating cognitive dissonance (an inconsistency between beliefs and behaviors), and by participation in decision making.

ATTITUDES AND WORK

From the organization's point of view, attitudes relating to job satisfaction are the most important. **Job satisfaction** is a positive emotional state that develops as a result of appraising one's job experience. Job satisfaction differs from employee to employee because it results from comparing what an individual expects of a job to what he or she actually experiences. Job satisfaction affects turnover, absenteeism, and organizational effectiveness.

LEARNING

Learning is a relatively permanent change in a person's behavior as the result of experience. There are several models of learning:

- In **classical conditioning**, we learn to associate two stimuli; for example, that a bell ringing indicates the end of a shift.

- In **operant conditioning**, we learn to associate a response and its consequence; for example, that high output results in a bonus.

- In **observational learning**, we learn by watching and imitating the behavior of others; for example, that there are standards of dress.

Learning effectiveness depends on a person's motivation to learn, feedback on performance, prior learning of similar tasks or concepts, whether or not the material to be learned is presented in whole or in part, and if the learning is done in concentrated or distributed sessions. However, the greatest influence on learning is reinforcement.

REINFORCEMENT

Anything that causes a behavior to be repeated is called **reinforcement**. **Positive reinforcement** consists of giving someone a reward following a desired behavior. For example, if an employee exceeds her sales quota, her boss gives her a bonus. **Negative reinforcement** consists of removing something unpleasant following a desired behavior. For example, an employee who completes a task promptly no longer has to listen to his supervisor's reminders. In contrast, **punishment** is an unpleasant response that reduces or stops a behavior.

The frequency and timing of reinforcement affects learning. With **continuous reinforcement,** learning occurs rapidly, but when the reinforcement is stopped, the desired behavior stops, a process called **extinction**. With **partial reinforcement schedules,** the effect on learning varies, and extinction is harder to achieve.

MOTIVATION
Theories of Motivation

Motivation is that which energizes, directs, and sustains human behavior. There are both process and content theories of motivation.

One cyclical model of the **basic motivational process** includes the following sequence: an inner state of disequilibrium involving needs, desires, and/or expectations; behavior; incentives or goals; feedback; reassessment; and modification if necessary.

The best-known content theory of motivation is **Abraham Maslow's hierarchy of needs**. According to Maslow, people are motivated by five basic needs arranged in a hierarchy. Maslow proposed that people generally satisfy their needs in the following sequence: physiological needs, security, belongingness, respect, and self-actualization (self-fulfillment).

A modification of Maslow's hierarchy was proposed by Clayton Alderfer. Known as **ERG theory**, it reformulated needs into three levels: *existence* needs, *relatedness* needs, and *growth* needs. In ERG theory, people both progress and regress as they attempt to satisfy their needs. In addition, more than one need may be activated at a time.

David McClelland developed the idea of the **need for achievement**, one of four important needs in organizational settings. (The others are affiliation, autonomy, and power.) According to McClelland, the need for achievement is characterized by the assumption of personal responsibility for solving problems, a tendency to set moderately difficult goals, a desire for feedback, and a preoccupation with task and task achievement. The need for achievement is an important motive for entrepreneurs.

Applications

Very basically, motivation theories suggest that managers should create a work climate that satisfies employee needs. Using the process model, managers can try to change behavior by influencing the motivation of employees at the goal-setting and feedback stages. Jobs can be designed to provide opportunities for personal growth and high achievement.

Implications for Managers

McClelland suggests that the best managers do not have a high need for achievement or affiliation. Achievement-oriented managers tend to be too task-oriented; affiliation-oriented managers tend to be indecisive and avoid conflict. In contrast, managers with a high need for institutional power tend to have the most productive and most satisfied work groups.

Stress

Stress is the psychological and physical reaction to stimuli in the environment that are perceived as threatening. It is the result of a poor fit between individual capabilities and the demands of a situation.

ORGANIZATIONAL INFLUENCES ON STRESS

Organizational influences on stress include occupational differences (for example, air traffic controllers experience more stress than college professors); role ambiguity, or uncertainty about the job; role conflict; overwork, underwork, or inappropriate work; responsibility for people; and lack of participation. Personal influences include having a Type A personality (impatient, restless, aggressive), locus of control, life-changing events, and abilities and needs.

RESULTS OF STRESS

Under conditions of no stress, job performance is likely to remain at the status quo. Under low stress, job performance improves acting as a stimulus that increases motivation. Under high stress, job performance deteriorates because the stress consumes the worker's attention. For an individual, chronic stress can lead to psychological or physical damage, including anxiety, fatigue, and high blood pressure. From the organization's point of view, prolonged stress leads to high turnover, absenteeism, substance abuse, and aggression.

COPING WITH STRESS

Individual strategies for coping with stress include increased self-awareness, outside activities and hobbies, regular exercise, and leaving the organization. Organizational strategies include better selection and placement of employees to improve fit between person and job, skills training, job enrichment when appropriate, job rotation, fitness programs, counseling programs, increased employee participation in decision making, increased group cohesiveness, and better communication.

INTERPERSONAL AND GROUP PROCESSES AND CHARACTERISTICS
GROUP DYNAMICS

A **group** is two or more people who share a set of norms, play different roles, and interact to pursue common goals.

TYPES OF GROUPS

There are two basic types of groups: formal and informal. **Formal groups** are work units, such as the accounts payable section of the accounting department, that are set up by the organization. Formal groups are set up by management to accomplish specific tasks; people are assigned roles and many behaviors are prescribed through policies and procedures. **Informal groups** arise naturally as people with common interests, mutual friendship, or similar social needs band together. Informal groups develop norms, roles, and unwritten rules of behavior. People join formal and informal groups for many reasons: a feeling of security, the need for social interaction, the need for self-esteem, economic rewards, and a chance to achieve goals.

GROUP DEVELOPMENT

There are several stages in group development:

1. **Testing and dependence**—In the first stage, members try to intuit which behaviors are acceptable and which are unacceptable.

2. **Conflict**—During the early stages of group formation, there is much conflict as members attempt to find their places in the group and to influence the development of norms and roles.

3. **Group cohesion**—After a while, the group comes to accept its members and develops a sense of unity and common purpose.

4. **Performance**—Once the group has a common purpose, members take on specific roles to help achieve group goals.

CHARACTERISTICS OF GROUPS

All groups have norms, roles, and a degree of cohesiveness. A group **norm** is a standard that members agree upon and that regulates their behavior. The social pressure to conform to group norms is very powerful, and members often do so even against their best interest or better judgment. Within the group, work activities are specialized, and each member takes on a **role**, an expected pattern of behavior assigned to a particular position. The third characteristic of groups is **cohesiveness**, the degree to which members of a group are motivated to perform as a group.

GROUP BEHAVIOR AND CONFLICT

Types and Levels of Conflict

Groups may have conflicts about goals, thoughts and opinions, feelings and emotions, and behavior. Conflict can be found on several levels as well. There may be intrapersonal conflict within a single individual, interpersonal conflict between two people, intragroup conflict within the group, and intergroup conflict with other groups in the organization.

Functional and Dysfunctional Conflict

Functional conflict can lead to new ideas, procedures, innovation, and change for the group as well as personal growth and development for members. On the other hand, dysfunctional conflict diverts people's energies from job performance and goal achievement. It can negatively affect the psychological well-being of group members, causing stress. Eventually dysfunctional conflict can destroy group cohesiveness.

Conflict Management

Conflict in organizational groups can be resolved in several ways.

- **Problem solving**—The most straightforward way to resolve conflict is to determine its cause and come up with a solution that is acceptable to everyone.

- **Persuasion**—One person attempts to convince another to change his or her opinion about the conflict and/or its solution.

- **Politics**—A person who has accumulated political power in the group or organization uses influence to resolve the problem.

- **Bargaining**—Parties involved in the conflict give something up and gain something, so no clear winner emerges.

LEADERSHIP

Leadership is the ability to get others to do something, not because it is required or that it will result in punishment, but because they want to do it. The leadership process involves three elements: the leader, the followers, and the situation. Successful leadership requires behavior that stimulates followers to behave certain ways in specific situations. Leaders provide task and psychological support to followers and also provide a role model of behavior. To do this, they draw on technical, human relations, and conceptual skills.

Theories of Leadership

Theories of leadership fall into three broad categories: the trait approach, the behavioral or functional view, and the situational or contingency perspective.

Early approaches to leadership were **trait theories**, which focused on the physical characteristics, personality traits, and cultural background thought to characterize leaders. Although theorists posited traits that characterized leaders, research failed to show any significant relationship between these traits and effective leadership.

Another approach to leadership is to focus on **behavioral or functional patterns or styles** used by leaders. Leaders with an **autocratic style** keep power and decision making to themselves. They focus on tasks, taking full authority and responsibility. Leaders with the **democratic style** lead through group input and decision making. Leaders with the **laissez-faire style** play a minor role in the group, allowing the group almost total freedom.

This research was extended into the behavioral aspects of leadership. Two **dimensions of leadership** were proposed: Leaders high on the dimension of **initiating structure** tended to tell employees what to do; and leaders high on **consideration** for others focused on their workers' satisfaction. In the 1960s, two attitudinal/behavioral dimensions were combined on the **Managerial or Leadership Grid**, which is the concern for people and production. Another approach was to see the role of the manager as two-fold: leader of one group and subordinate in another. This theory, called the **linking pin theory**, views effective leadership behavior as working upward as well as downward.

Contingency theories of leadership emphasize that there is no single best way to lead; rather, the most effective style of leadership is contingent or dependent upon the situation. Situational (or contingency) leaders are able to adapt their leadership style to both the group and to the situation. **Fred Fiedler** proposed one of the classic contingency theories; that effective leadership is based on the degree of fit between a leader's style and the extent to which the situation enables him or her to use it. In this view, three factors influence the favorableness of a situation for a leader: leader-member relations; task structure; and leader's position power. Another contingency theory, **path-goal theory**, is based on expectancy theory and motivation. A leader's effectiveness is based on the ability to clarify the path to an outcome when tasks are ambiguous but to refrain from interfering when tasks are routine. A recent contingency theory is called **situational leadership**, and it attempts to integrate what is known about leadership into a comprehensive model. It focuses on the amount of direction a leader gives, the amount of socio-emotional support he or she provides, and the readiness of group members to perform appropriately.

Implications for Managers

Even though organizations are highly structured with clear lines of authority and stated objectives, leadership is required to manage effectively. Leaders have a great impact on group performance. Understanding the various theories of leadership and using the appropriate style or behavior in particular situations can improve managerial effectiveness.

POWER AND POLITICS

Power is a person's ability to influence people and events. Power differs from authority because authority is given by higher management, whereas power is earned on the basis of an individual's personality and behavior. **Politics** refers to the ways in which a person earns, gains, or uses power to control events. It may involve compromise, negotiation, trade-offs, conciliation, and many other activities. People who are capable but lack political skills usually do not rise to the top of their organizations.

Interpersonal Sources of Power

In some cases a person acquires power through the force of his or her personality. This type of power, called **referent power**, the **power of personality**, or **charisma**, is an innate quality of an individual. The person has personal attractiveness, self-confidence, and a belief in objectives that others find appealing. People submit to this type of power willingly. Note that a person with this type of power may exist at any level of the organization, in a formal or informal group.

Political power is another type of interpersonal power. It develops as a result of a person's ability to work with people and social systems to gain their support.

Structural and Situational Sources of Power

In most cases a person acquires power as a result of his or her position in an organization. Called **legitimate power**, it arises from the cultural assumption that power can be delegated from higher to lower authorities. Legitimate power gives leaders the ability to direct, reward, and punish others. People accept it because it imposes order on what would otherwise be chaos.

Through **expert power,** people exert influence in situations in which specialized learning is required. Known as the authority of knowledge, it develops as the result of a person's having specialized and extensive skills or information that other people need.

POLITICAL BEHAVIOR IN ORGANIZATIONS

There are many types of political behavior that people use to achieve their goals in organizations. Managers use trade-offs to get something they want in return. Managers form alliances with others to work together toward common goals. They form relationships with people higher up in the organization so that some of the power "rubs off" on them. Managers control the flow of information, withholding information from those who do not cooperate with them. Managers are more helpful to those who in turn help them. They use office space, furniture, and other perks as status symbols. Some managers make power plays, taking power away from others, although this tactic is risky because it invites retaliation.

COMMUNICATION

Communication is the transfer of meaning from one person to another. In order for communication to occur, a **communicator** must encode and send a **message** to a **receiver**, who decodes it and responds. Two-way communication occurs when the receiver sends feedback to the communicator. One-way communication occurs when the receiver decodes the message but does not respond.

In organizations, social factors affect what is said, who can say it, to whom it is said, and how it is said. Perceptual processes influence how messages are decoded. In addition, the structure of an organization influences communication. When messages pass through the levels of a hierarchy, there are many opportunities for distortion.

Communication Styles

Communication is influenced by culture, gender, age, and personality. There are many differences in the way people communicate. One way to identify communication styles is to evaluate the degree of responsiveness to others and the assertiveness that a person displays. People with high degrees of both responsiveness and assertiveness are good, forceful communicators. Those with high responsiveness and low assertiveness may be better listeners than speakers. People with low responsiveness and high assertiveness tend to be autocratic in their dealings with others. Finally, people with low responsiveness and low assertiveness are guarded with others and uncomfortable communicating openly.

Communication Networks

There are several communication network patterns in groups. In the chain, a message is passed from one person to the next, often following the chain of command. The Y pattern is similar to the chain, but it branches. In the wheel, the person at the hub communicates with all of the people on the spokes. In the all-channel pattern, all members of the group communicate with each other. In the circle, a message is passed around until it returns to the original sender.

Barriers to Effective Organizational Communication

In organizations, several problems may arise that interfere with effective communication. Distortion may occur as a message is passed from one person to another. Omission occurs when part of an intended message is left out, whether intentionally or not. Overload occurs when too much information is communicated and the receiver cannot distinguish between what is important and what is not. Some messages are communicated too soon and are forgotten; others are communicated too late to be acted upon effectively. Refusal to accept a message occurs when the sender doesn't have the authority and/or credibility to send it.

Nonverbal Communication

Nonverbal communication often imparts as much information as verbal communication, especially about emotions and attitudes. Body language, gestures, facial expressions, eye contact, smiling, and the use of personal space all convey meaning. Miscommunication sometimes occurs when there are cultural or gender differences in interpreting the meaning of nonverbal cues.

ORGANIZATIONAL PROCESSES AND CHARACTERISTICS
ORGANIZATIONAL DECISION MAKING

Decision making is the process of choosing one out of many alternatives. There are three stages in the process: (1) recognize and understand the nature of the problem, and look for causes and solutions; (2) formulate and assess alternative strategies to solve the problem; and (3) select the most appropriate alternative.

Models of the Decision-Making Process

There are several models of the decision-making process, all making different assumptions about how individuals and organizations make decisions.

The **econological model** is based on the assumption that people are economically rational and that they try to maximize outcomes in an orderly way. Thus, people will gather all relevant information and choose the alternative that has the greatest benefit. The strength of this model is that it shows how decisions should be made; the weakness is that people do not behave entirely rationally, and so it does not show how decisions are actually made.

The **bounded rationality model** assumes that people will try to find the best solution, but they will settle for much less because the decisions they make require more information and thought than they are capable of. In this model, people consider alternatives in sequence, they use heuristics (mental shortcuts) to limit the search for solutions, and they settle for an acceptable, although not necessarily the best, solution.

The **implicit favorite model** assumes that people arrive at a choice intuitively and then distort their assessments of other alternatives in order to justify their initial choice. This model may reflect how unstructured, one-of-a-kind (nonprogrammed) decisions are made, but it does not reflect how repetitive, routine (programmed) decisions are made.

Individual Versus Group Decision Making

Whereas the decision-making process may be similar in individuals and groups, the outcomes differ. Groups are usually better than individuals at establishing objectives and evaluating alternatives, because groups have more knowledge and points of view than do individuals. In identifying alternatives and implementing the decision, individuals perform better than groups where responsibility is diffuse. Finally, in choosing an alternative, a group decision has greater acceptance than an individual decision.

ORGANIZATION STRUCTURE

Organization structure refers to the way in which organizations arrange their human resources in order to accomplish their objectives.

Dimensions of Organization Structure

There are several dimensions in which structure can be understood.

- **Decentralization**—The extent to which power and authority are extended throughout the organization
- **Specialization**—The number of divisions in an organization and the number of specialized sections within each division
- **Formalization**—The degree to which employee job activities are regulated by rules, procedures, policies, and so on
- **Span of control**—The number of employees per supervisor
- **Organization size**—The way in which the size of an organization affects its structure
- **Work unit size**—The way in which the size of a work group affects employee attitudes and behavior

Types of Organization Structure

There are several types of organization structure:

- In a **functional organization**, each group performing related activities reports to a manager responsible for that function.

- In a **line and staff organization,** there are staff departments that advise and support the departments directly involved in producing goods or services, the line departments.

- The **product or divisional organization** is a variation of the line and staff organization, in which each major product line has its own suborganization, or division.

- The **matrix organization** is structured around projects, task-force work, or other one-of-a-kind programs.

Responsibility and Authority

In large part, organization structure determines the authority associated with given positions. Managers must have **authority**, that is, the power to make decisions and take action in order to carry out their **responsibilities**, the tasks, and outcomes for which they are held accountable. Even though managers may carry out their responsibilities through delegation, they remain accountable for getting the job done.

ORGANIZATION DESIGN

There are classical and contingency approaches to organizational design.

Classical Organization Theory

In the classical approach, work is divided by function, level of authority, and level of responsibility (scalar process). Work is communicated and assigned to people by means of delegation. This results in a high degree of specialization. The benefits of specialization are technical and economic, leading to great productivity, and its drawbacks are essentially psychological, especially when specialization is extremely narrow.

In classical theory, span of control determines whether an organization is tall or flat. In a **tall organization**, the span of control is small and managers and supervisors work with few people. Thus, there are many levels in the organization. The tall organization is hierarchical; it permits close contact with employees and close control of work. Communication tends to be vertical, in the chain pattern, providing many opportunities for miscommunication.

In a **flat organization** the span of control is much greater and there are few levels of management. Because each manager has so many people to direct, the time that can be spent with a single employee is very limited. Thus, employees have more control over their own work. In general, employees in flat organizations have less stress, greater job satisfaction, and better productivity than those in tall organizations.

Contingency Organizational Design

The more modern approach to organizations is to be flexible in terms of systems and structure, changing them according to a contingency relationship with the environment. The hallmark of this approach is that the structure that may work best in one environment may not work well in another.

Contingency design distinguishes between mechanistic and organic organizations. In a **mechanistic organization**, control and authority are centralized, tasks are specialized, and lines of communication are vertical, flowing along the lines of the hierarchy. Work is carefully scheduled and apportioned to employees whose roles are strictly defined.

In an **organic organization**, there is decentralization of control and authority, task interdependence, and horizontal lines of communication. Tasks and roles are less rigidly defined, allowing people to adjust to changing conditions. Communication occurs in all directions and consists more of information and advice than rules and instructions. Decision making is more decentralized, and the organization is more open to the environment.

In certain environments, the mechanistic structure is very effective. If tasks are stable, changing little over time, and workers prefer stability, then the mechanistic structure is productive. In addition, if changes in technology, the market, and other environmental factors are minimal, the mechanistic structure works well. On the other hand, organic structures tend to be more effective in dynamic environments, which are typical of modern life. When the environment changes constantly and rapidly, the organic structure provides the flexibility for quick adjustments. When tasks are not well-defined and employees prefer autonomy, variety, and opportunity, the organic structure provides flexibility. Within a single organization, some departments may be organized according to mechanistic principles and others according to organic principles.

CHANGE AND DEVELOPMENT
BASIC PROCESSES AND CONCEPTS

Sources of Change

Management initiates a good deal of the changes that organizations experience. However, management is often not the original source of change. Many changes originate in the external environment. Changes in laws and regulations, technology, markets, customers, labor unions, and so on all result in organizational change. The more dynamic the environment, the more change an organization undergoes.

The Change Process

Instituting a change involves three steps:

1. **Unfreezing**—Old ideas, procedures, and structures must be gotten rid of.

2. **Changing**—New ideas and practices are implemented so that employees can do their jobs in new ways.

3. **Refreezing**—The changes that have been made are integrated into the organization's structure and practices.

Individual and Group Change

People are affected in different ways by change. Some have personality traits that allow them to adjust relatively painlessly to new things; others have more rigid personalities. In many cases, change affects employees differently because their roles in the organization differ; some may benefit and others may lose. When an employee has a great deal of trouble adjusting, stress may affect his or her health.

If a group is cohesive, it becomes an instrument of change as long as its social system is not disrupted. Participation with others in change makes the adjustment easier.

Resistance to Change

In instituting change, management tries to restore the individual and group equilibrium that existed before the changes were made. However, this effort often meets **resistance**, or opposition, among both managers and workers. There are three types of resistance to change: logical, based on reasoning; psychological, rooted in emotions and attitudes; and sociological, based on group interests and values.

Organizational Culture

An organization's **culture** is its shared pattern of beliefs, assumptions, and expectations held by its members; their characteristic perceptions of the organization and its environment; and the norms, roles, and values that characterized the organization. An organization's culture affects individual and group behavior, often in subtle ways. Although culture creates social order and has many benefits, it can also discourage change by constraining members to work within the existing framework of beliefs and values.

Organizational Development

Organizational development is a strategy designed to bring about planned change. It uses group processes to focus on the culture of the entire organization, and it views the organization as an operating system. The process of organizational development is time-consuming, and to be successful it must have the support of top management.

A typical organizational development program has many steps, including diagnosis, data collection, feedback, confrontation, action planning, team building, intergroup development, and follow-up.

Some organizational development programs focus on organizational structure and others on employee consideration; still others blend the two approaches of institutional change and take a socio-technical approach. There are several programs that have been used extensively, including the managerial grid, systems one through four, 3-D management, and enriched sociotechnical work systems.

SAMPLE QUESTIONS

1. A type of learning in which one learns to associate a response with a consequence is called

   (A) observational learning
   (B) classical conditioning
   (C) operant conditioning
   (D) selective attention

   The correct answer is (C). Associating a response and a consequence is characteristic of operant conditioning. Observational learning involves watching and imitating, and classical conditioning is learning to associate two stimuli. Selective attention is a perceptual, not a learning, process.

2. An internal locus of control is likely to be more prevalent among low-level employees in which of the following types of organizations?

   (A) A tall organization
   (B) A flat organization
   (C) A hierarchical organization
   (D) A line and staff organization

   The correct answer is (B). In a flat organization, a manager has a large span of control and little time to spend with individual employees. Thus, more responsibility and decision making are delegated to employees, which results in an internal locus of control, a feeling that one influences the outcome of events. Tall, hierarchical, and line and staff organizations are all characterized by centralized authority, which is more likely to be associated with an external locus of control except at the top levels.

3. A top manager called a subordinate into her office. When he arrived, she did not make eye contact or speak but continued to work on some papers on her desk. What form of communication was the manager using?

   (A) Network communication
   (B) Horizontal communication
   (C) Two-way communication
   (D) Nonverbal communication

   The correct answer is (D). Without using words, the manager was communicating the privileges of rank and perhaps indicating displeasure. Network and horizontal communication refer to organization-wide communication patterns. Two-way communicating is not occurring because the subordinate has not responded to the message.

PRACTICE SET

1. When a change is introduced into a work unit, at what point does effectiveness decline?

    (A) When the change is first explained
    (B) When the change is introduced
    (C) During the period of adaptation following the change
    (D) After the change is fully integrated

2. Which of the following is an example of a fixed-ratio reinforcement schedule?

    (A) Paying a bonus after every sixth car is sold
    (B) Using a lottery to reduce absenteeism
    (C) Inspecting a department four times a year at random intervals
    (D) Paying employees every other Friday

3. The pattern of actions expected of a person acting as part of a group is called the person's

    (A) groupthink
    (B) status
    (C) norm
    (D) role

4. Why do labor unions often oppose management programs for employee participation?

    (A) They fear that employees will influence decisions and actions before they occur.
    (B) They fear that employees' loyalties will shift from the union to management.
    (C) They are opposed to the higher quality of output that is likely to result.
    (D) They think it will lead to increased conflict between employees and management.

5. Which of the following is characteristic of downward communication in an organization?

    (A) The flow is from the chief executive to the organization.
    (B) The flow is from higher to lower levels of authority.
    (C) The flow is within the management group.
    (D) The flow is between line and staff work units.

6. Who undertook the industrial experiments at Western Electric's Hawthorne plant that led to the basic understanding that work organizations are social systems whose most important element is people?

    (A) Frederick W. Taylor
    (B) Douglas McGregor
    (C) Elton Mayo and F. J. Roethlisberger
    (D) Clayton P. Alderfer and Henry A. Murray

7. What do the contingency model of leadership and the contingency model of organization design have in common?

   (A) Adaptability to the situation or environment
   (B) Centralized control and authority
   (C) Consideration approach to all problems
   (D) Large span of control

8. All of the following are incentive measures that link pay with performance EXCEPT

   (A) amount of output
   (B) quality of output
   (C) success in reaching goals
   (D) seniority

9. Which of the following attempts to modify the entire organization so that it can better respond to change?

   (A) Employee training programs
   (B) Organizational development
   (C) The "X" chart model
   (D) Organizational behavior system

10. The extent to which the results of a study can be generalized to apply to other organizations or situations is referred to as

   (A) external validity
   (B) internal consistency
   (C) level of rigor
   (D) qualitative measures

PRACTICE SET ANSWERS

1. **The correct answer is (C).** Employees need time to adapt to change, and during the period of adaptation they must get rid of old work habits, adopt new ones, and solve problems of procedure and communication, all of which reduces effectiveness.

2. **The correct answer is (A).** A fixed-ratio reinforcement schedule is one in which there is reinforcement after a certain number of correct responses. The remaining choices are examples of variable-ratio, variable-interval, and fixed-interval reinforcement schedules.

3. **The correct answer is (D).** A role is the part a person plays in a group. Groupthink refers to the tendency of individual performance to level off to the group average. Status refers to social rank. A norm is a standard.

4. **The correct answer is (B).** Unions are jealous of any forces that may weaken the ties between members and the union. The other options all involve potential results for the organization, which would affect the union only indirectly, if at all.

5. **The correct answer is (B).** Downward communication goes down the chain of command, from higher to lower levels of the organization. The other possible option, from the CEO to the organization, is too specific.

6. **The correct answer is (C).** These Harvard researchers conducted their influential studies during the 1920s and 1930s. Taylor's work focused on technical efficiency. McGregor formulated Theory X and Theory Y. Alderfer and Murray did work on motivation.

7. **The correct answer is (A).** The key characteristic of both models is flexibility, the ability to act or change in accordance with the situation or the external environment.

8. **The correct answer is (D).** Of all the options, seniority is the only one that links pay with length of service rather than performance.

9. **The correct answer is (B).** These are organization-wide programs to increase adaptability and effectiveness. Employee training programs are too piecemeal to affect the entire organization. The "X" chart model refers to influences on employee attitudes. The organizational behavior system reflects the organization's climate; it is not a model of change.

10. **The correct answer is (A).** External validity makes results more useful because they can be applied to other organizations and situations. Internal consistency is a characteristic of a good theory. Level of rigor refers to the entirety of the research design's quality. Qualitative measures are descriptive rather than quantitative.

POSTTEST

1. Experiential learning means that participants learn by experiencing
   - (A) the types of real problems they would face on the job
   - (B) both interpersonal and intergroup problems
   - (C) problems that require them to be flexible and pragmatic
   - (D) the effects of peer group pressure

2. Praise from a supervisor, a merit increase in pay, and a transfer to a desirable job are all examples of
   - (A) experiential learning
   - (B) classic conditioning
   - (C) positive reinforcement
   - (D) fair labor practices

3. Giving sales employees a bonus after every fifth car sold is an example of an organization using which of the following types of reinforcement schedules?
   - (A) Partial
   - (B) Continuous
   - (C) Variable interval
   - (D) Fixed-ratio

4. A behavior accompanied by the removal of an unfavorable consequence is known as
   - (A) negative reinforcement
   - (B) empathy
   - (C) punishment
   - (D) compensation

5. A limitation or disadvantage of punishment as a tool for affecting employee behavior is that it
   - (A) decreases employee involvement
   - (B) does not encourage any kind of desirable behavior
   - (C) is effective only for teaching simple tasks
   - (D) is in conflict with performance appraisal standards

6. When an employee is productive and the organization recognizes and rewards the performance, this results in satisfaction of the employee's needs and drives. This statement points out the importance of which of the following factors in organizational behavior?
   - (A) Employee motivation
   - (B) Employee commitment
   - (C) Managerial leadership
   - (D) Worker competence

7. A manager works 12 hours per day for a week in order to complete a budget on time so that the manager will receive a day off with pay the following week. This behavior is consistent with which of the following theories of motivation?

(A) Equity
(B) Goal setting
(C) Reinforcement
(D) Expectancy

8. The process by which managers decide and specify job depth, range, and relationships in order to satisfy both organizational requirements and the needs of workers is called job

(A) design
(B) rotation
(C) enrichment
(D) content

9. Profit sharing, wage incentives, banking time-off, and bonuses are all examples of

(A) benefits
(B) compensation
(C) motivators
(D) reward systems

10. Herzberg's two-factor theory of motivation has value for managers who are trying to understand job satisfaction because

(A) it analyzes how employee behavior is directed and sustained
(B) it provides models for interpreting and comparing both physiological and psychological needs
(C) prior to Herzberg's research, managers focused their attention only on external (maintenance) factors
(D) "fear of success" is not addressed by other major researchers

11. Which of the following statements is TRUE about Maslow's hierarchy of needs, Herzberg's theory of motivation/maintenance, and Alderfer's E-R-G model?

(A) The idea of a modified workweek or flextime is supported.
(B) A foundation for the application of behavior modification in the workplace is provided.
(C) Self-esteem is discounted as a factor in motivation.
(D) Lower-level and higher-level needs are not differentiated.

12. A response that is a result of an external or environmental action, situation, or event that places excessive psychological and/or physical demands on a person is known as

(A) frustration
(B) resistance
(C) stress
(D) motivation

13. Which of the following is an example of an organizational factor that could cause job stress?

(A) Lack of clear company policies
(B) Family illness
(C) Poor relationships with peers
(D) Substance abuse

14. An organizational effect of job stress would be

(A) lower productivity
(B) anxiety
(C) increased blood pressure
(D) poor concentration

15. Job enrichment, role analysis and clarification, counseling, and variable work schedules can all be used by an organization to manage employee

(A) benefits
(B) stress
(C) participation
(D) schedules

16. A popular method of encouraging creative thinking among a group of employees by coming up with ideas first and evaluating them later is called

(A) group dynamics
(B) a task force
(C) brainstorming
(D) deferring judgment

17. A specific type of group in which the members have been delegated authority with regard to a specific problem is generally known as a

(A) constituency
(B) department
(C) unit
(D) committee

18. According to the major theories of organizational behavior, the primary reasons that people form groups in a work environment are

(A) authority, responsibility, support, and pleasure
(B) proximity, attraction, goals, and economics
(C) loyalty, commitment, emotion, and quality of life
(D) technical, psychological, organizational, and physical

19. The performance of a group depends most upon individual learning and

   (A) the clarity of the group's goals
   (B) how well the group members work together
   (C) the style of the group's leadership
   (D) effectively modeling other groups within the organization

20. The social process by which people interact face-to-face in a small group is called

   (A) teamwork
   (B) a relationship
   (C) synergy
   (D) group dynamics

21. The set of expected behaviors associated with a position in the structure of a group constitutes the group member's

   (A) role
   (B) status
   (C) attributes
   (D) performance

22. The production department of an organization wants to purchase new machinery, while the sales department wants to expand its sales force. There are only enough resources to supply the needs of one group. This is an example of

   (A) intergroup conflict
   (B) negotiation
   (C) organizational change
   (D) interpersonal conflict

23. A situation in which an executive fires an ineffective manager and realizes greater employee productivity as a result can be characterized as which of the following types of conflict outcomes?

   (A) Win-win
   (B) Lose-lose
   (C) Win-lose
   (D) Lose-win

24. Facing a conflict and working through it toward a mutually satisfactory resolution is called

   (A) smoothing
   (B) compromising
   (C) goal setting
   (D) confronting

25. Which of the following defines the leader's job in the path-goal leadership process?

   (A) It is to use structure, support, and rewards to create a work environment that helps employees reach the organization's objectives.
   (B) It is to structure the complete work situation for employees in order to achieve a certain outcome.
   (C) It is to act as a consultant within the organization as a whole.
   (D) It is to help all groups within the organization to achieve cooperation and cohesiveness.

26. When one individual attempts to affect the behavior of a group or organization without using coercion or force, the effort can be described as

   (A) role playing
   (B) initiative
   (C) intelligence
   (D) leadership

27. The Vroom and Yetton model of leadership attempts to provide a normative model that a leader can use in

   (A) planning
   (B) strategizing
   (C) decision making
   (D) controlling

28. Although a positive, participative, and considerate leader tends to be more effective in most situations, before choosing a leadership style, a leader should

   (A) consult the most recent research studies concerning models of leadership
   (B) determine whether an autocratic or democratic organizational approach currently exists
   (C) analyze the situation and identify the key factors in the tasks, employees, and organization
   (D) solicit input from the key employees of each constituency or department

29. In order to be effective leaders, managers need to possess which of the following skills?

   (A) Planning, controlling, and directing
   (B) Social, political, and ethical
   (C) Supervisory, management, and executive-level
   (D) Technical, human, and conceptual

30. A research and development manager who intentionally controls new product information needed by a marketing manager is an example of the use of

(A) authority
(B) power
(C) influence
(D) coercion

31. An example of the exercise of reward power would be

(A) a company softball team consisting of employees from all levels of the company
(B) a president's personal assistant making minor decisions for the president
(C) a sales manager giving salespeople a cash bonus or a company car
(D) an alliance forming between two department managers working on a project

32. Which of the following is an example of structural power?

(A) An engineer helping a factory manager get approval for new machinery
(B) A president's personal assistant screening the president's telephone calls and e-mail messages
(C) A manager influencing a vice president to transfer employees from another department to the manager's own department
(D) A CEO allocating resources needed by lower-level managers

33. A purchasing agent who tries to use a friendship to influence the processing of a purchase order is exhibiting which of the following behaviors?

(A) Political
(B) Social
(C) Personal
(D) Organizational

34. The process of communication within an organization generally contains the

(A) sender, technology, receiver, and model
(B) sender, receiver, message, and objective
(C) message, medium, destination, and feedback
(D) sender, message, medium, receiver, and feedback

35. When the communicator of a message is at a lower level in the organization than the receiver, this is called

(A) upward communication
(B) politics
(C) an interchange
(D) downward communication

36. A manager who does not elicit feedback from employees in making decisions is exhibiting an autocratic style of

(A) appraising
(B) selecting
(C) communicating
(D) evaluating

37. Sharing news, information, and ideas with coworkers and members of other departments is an example of

(A) networking
(B) power
(C) involvement
(D) downward communication

38. Which of the following would be considered a barrier to effective communication within an organization?

(A) Filtering
(B) Exposure
(C) Structure
(D) Feedback

39. A manager who leans forward with her arms open when speaking to a subordinate is most likely exhibiting

(A) personal power
(B) a negative attitude
(C) a positive attitude
(D) anger

40. The use of rules, operating procedures, and organizational structure assists companies in making which of the following types of decisions?

(A) Non-programmed
(B) Programmed
(C) Autocratic
(D) Cooperative

41. Which of the following scenarios is NOT an example of a programmed decision-making process within an organization?

(A) A necessary grade point average for admittance to a university
(B) A procedure for processing insurance applications
(C) Periodic reorders of inventory
(D) The purchase of experimental equipment by a hospital

42. Identifying a problem, developing alternatives, evaluating alternatives, choosing an alternative, and implementing a choice are all parts of

(A) choosing a management style
(B) making a decision
(C) using a communication process
(D) setting goals

43. "The situation is that orders have decreased nearly 32 percent compared to last year" is a statement identifying a

(A) cause
(B) symptom
(C) problem
(D) crisis

44. Group decision making can sometimes be negatively affected by which of the following factors?

(A) Lateral communication
(B) The establishment of objectives
(C) A clear meeting agenda
(D) The influence of a dominant personality

45. One of the benefits of group decision making versus individual decision making is

(A) decreased management participation
(B) increased time needed to make decisions
(C) increased interaction among employees
(D) decreased involvement of human resource personnel

46. The structured dimension that refers to the number of distinctly different job titles, or occupational groupings, and the number of different units, or departments, within an organization is known as

(A) centralization
(B) complexity
(C) formalization
(D) span of control

47. A large span of control will generally result in which of the following types of organizational structure?

(A) Tall
(B) Bureaucratic
(C) Organic
(D) Flat

48. The location of decision-making authority in the hierarchy of an organization is called

   (A) power
   (B) tier design
   (C) centralization
   (D) specialization

49. An organizational structure in which one organization structure is overlaid on another resulting in two chains of command directing individual employees can be described as

   (A) matrix
   (B) classical
   (C) neoclassical
   (D) bipolar

50. "The power of a manager to use delegated authority depends on whether or not employees will respond to it." This statement illustrates

   (A) the importance of delegation
   (B) the acceptance theory of authority
   (C) a classical bureaucratic structure
   (D) a classical organizational structure

51. A high level of delegation in an organization generally results in

   (A) higher profits
   (B) increased managerial/professional development
   (C) lower compensation costs
   (D) fewer administrative procedures

52. The classical theory of organizational structure involves which of the following elements?

   (A) Authority, influence, security, and rewards
   (B) Production, division of work, labor force, and management
   (C) Division of labor, delegation, authority, specialization, and links
   (D) Flexibility, communication, influence, rewards, and change

53. Which of the following sets of characteristics best describes an organic approach to organizational structure?

   (A) Multidirectional communication, change, and decentralization
   (B) Hierarchical, scheduled, and centralized
   (C) Multiple roles, project-oriented, and specialized
   (D) Division of labor, delegation, and authority

54. The theory of organizational design that there are different organizational structures and processes required for effectiveness in alternative situations is called

   (A) neoclassical
   (B) contingency
   (C) process-oriented
   (D) traditional

55. Marketplace conditions, technology, and social and political conditions can all be described as which of the following types of forces for organizational change?

(A) Internal
(B) Behavioral
(C) Environmental
(D) Process-oriented

56. Organizational change brought about by management identifying problems and proposing solutions without participation by subordinates is known as

(A) shared
(B) delegated
(C) unilateral
(D) organic

57. A positive outcome of employee resistance to an organizational change initiative would be

(A) decreased social interaction among employees
(B) a chain-reaction effect in organizational behavior
(C) passive resistance
(D) a reexamination of change proposals by management

58. The pervasive system of values, beliefs, and norms that exists in an organization is known as

(A) politics
(B) organizational culture
(C) power
(D) organizational design

59. An intervention strategy that uses group processes to focus on the corporate culture of a company in order to bring about a planned change is called organizational

(A) design
(B) development
(C) research
(D) behavior

60. Participation in the organizational change process can often encourage individual

(A) power
(B) leadership
(C) resistance
(D) commitment

POSTTEST ANSWERS

1. **The correct answer is (A).** Experiential learning means that participants learn by experiencing the types of real problems they would face on the job.

2. **The correct answer is (C).** Praise from a supervisor, a merit increase in pay, and a transfer to a desirable job are all positive rewards that can be administered in order to reinforce an employee's desirable behavior.

3. **The correct answer is (D).** A fixed-ratio reinforcement schedule occurs when there is a reinforcement after a certain number of correct responses or behaviors.

4. **The correct answer is (A).** The removal of negative consequences following a desired behavior is known as negative reinforcement.

5. **The correct answer is (B).** A limitation or disadvantage of punishment as a tool for affecting employee behavior is that punishment does not encourage any kind of desirable behavior.

6. **The correct answer is (A).** Employee motivation, which is affected by rewards and recognition, is instrumental in the success of all organizations.

7. **The correct answer is (D).** The expectancy theory of motivation concerns the individual's belief in the likelihood of a certain outcome as a result of one's own actions or work.

8. **The correct answer is (A).** Job design is the process by which managers decide and specify job depth, range, and relationships in order to satisfy both organizational requirements and the needs of workers.

9. **The correct answer is (D).** A reward system or incentive system is a set of environmental factors established for the purpose of motivating a person.

10. **The correct answer is (C).** Prior to Herzberg's research, managers focused their attention only on external (maintenance) factors. Herzberg's theory considered the impact of internal factors such as self-actualization and self-esteem.

11. **The correct answer is (B).** Maslow's, Herzberg's, and Alderfer's theories of human needs and motivation all provide a foundation for the understanding and application of behavior modification in the workplace.

12. **The correct answer is (C).** A stress is a response resulting from an external or environmental action, situation, or event that places excessive psychological and/or physical demands on a person.

13. **The correct answer is (A).** Choices (B), (C), and (D) are all individual stressors (i.e, internal to an individual), while choice (A) is an external, or organizational, stressor.

14. **The correct answer is (A).** Choices (B), (C), and (D) are personal and physiological effects of job stress. Lower productivity as a consequence of stress affects a person's job and the organization as a whole.

15. **The correct answer is (B).** Job stress often can be reduced or controlled through the use of measures that increase job satisfaction, such as job enrichment, role analysis and clarification, counseling, and variable work schedules.

16. **The correct answer is (C).** Brainstorming is a popular method of encouraging creative thinking among a group of employees by coming up with ideas first and evaluating them later.

17. **The correct answer is (D).** A committee is a type of group in which the members have been delegated authority with regard to a specific problem.

18. **The correct answer is (B).** The primary reasons that people form groups in a work environment are proximity, attraction, goals, and economics.

19. **The correct answer is (B).** The performance of a group depends most upon individual learning and how well the members of the group work together.

20. **The correct answer is (D).** Group dynamics is the social process by which people interact face-to-face in a small group.

21. **The correct answer is (A).** The role of a group member is the set of expected behaviors associated with that member's position in the structure of a group.

22. **The correct answer is (A).** Intergroup conflict is disagreement between departments or groups within an organization about goals or the methods to use to attain goals or utilize resources.

23. **The correct answer is (C).** In this win-lose situation, individual A (the executive) initiated an action that had a positive result for A (viz., greater employee productivity) and a negative result for individual B (the manager who was fired).

24. **The correct answer is (D).** Confronting is facing a conflict and working through it toward a mutually satisfactory resolution.

25. **The correct answer is (A).** In the path-goal leadership process, the leader's job is to use structure, support, and rewards to create a work environment that helps employees reach the organization's objectives.

26. **The correct answer is (D).** Leadership is the effort to affect the behavior of a group or organization without using coercion or force.

27. **The correct answer is (C).** The Vroom and Yetton model of leadership attempts to provide a normative model that a leader can use in decision making.

28. **The correct answer is (C).** Before choosing a leadership style, a leader should first analyze all relevant factors that suggest which approach might be best.

29. **The correct answer is (D).** In order to be effective leaders, managers need to possess technical, human, and conceptual skills.

30. **The correct answer is (B).** Control of information is a common tactic used to gain political power in an organizational setting.

31. **The correct answer is (C).** An example of the exercise of reward power would be a sales manager who gives salespeople a cash bonus or a company car.

32. **The correct answer is (D).** The structure of an organization (i.e., the hierarchy of executives and managers) is often the mechanism that controls decision making. In this situation, the CEO makes decisions regarding the allocation of resources needed by managers.

33. **The correct answer is (A).** When a person behaves outside the normal power system to benefit self or a subunit, that person is engaging in political behavior.

34. **The correct answer is (D).** The process of communication within an organization generally contains the sender, message, medium, receiver, and feedback.

35. **The correct answer is (A).** Upward communication occurs when the communicator of a message is at a lower level in the organization than the receiver.

36. **The correct answer is (C).** One of the traits of an autocratic style of communication is not soliciting feedback from employees in making decisions.

37. **The correct answer is (A).** Networking occurs among a group of people who develop and maintain contact to exchange information informally, usually about a shared interest.

38. **The correct answer is (A).** Filtering refers to the manipulation of information so that the receiver perceives it as positive. This occurrence is a barrier to effective communication.

39. **The correct answer is (C).** Body language, such as leaning forward toward another individual, suggests that the listener is favorably disposed toward the person's message.

40. **The correct answer is (B).** Programmed decisions are those that are repetitive and routine and that depend on a definite procedure for handling situations.

41. **The correct answer is (D).** Programmed decisions are those that are repetitive and routine and that depend on a definite procedure for handling situations. The purchase of experimental equipment by a hospital is a non-programmed decision that depends on new and unknown factors.

42. **The correct answer is (B).** Decision making involves identifying a problem, developing alternatives, evaluating alternatives, choosing an alternative, and implementing a choice.

43. **The correct answer is (B).** The decline in orders is a symptom of a problem. When the problem is identified, the cause of the decline in orders will be found.

44. **The correct answer is (D).** Group decision making can sometimes be negatively affected by the influence of a dominant personality in the group.

45. **The correct answer is (C).** One of the benefits of group decision making vs. individual decision making is increased interaction among employees.

46. **The correct answer is (B).** Complexity is the structured dimension that refers to the number of distinctly different job titles, or occupational groupings, and the number of different units, or departments, within an organization.

47. **The correct answer is (D).** A large span of control in which managers supervise many people generally causes a flat structure with a simpler or shorter chain of communication.

48. **The correct answer is (C).** Centralization is the location of decision-making authority in the hierarchy of an organization.

49. **The correct answer is (A).** A matrix organizational structure is one in which one type of organization is overlaid on another so that there are two chains of command directing individual employees.

50. **The correct answer is (B).** Although authority gives people power to act officially within the scope of their delegation, this power is meaningless unless those affected accept it and respond to it.

51. **The correct answer is (B).** Increased managerial/professional development is one of the results of a high level of delegation.

52. **The correct answer is (C).** The classical theory of organizational structure involves division of labor, delegation, authority, specialization, and links.

53. **The correct answer is (A).** Multidirectional communication, change, and decentralization are some of the characteristics of an organic approach to organizational structure.

54. **The correct answer is (B).** The theory of organizational design that there are different organizational structures and processes required for effectiveness in alternative situations is called contingency.

55. **The correct answer is (C).** Environmental forces for change include marketplace conditions, technology, and social and political conditions.

56. **The correct answer is (C).** The unilateral approach for introducing change does not allow for participation by subordinates. In this approach, management identifies problems and proposes solutions.

57. **The correct answer is (D).** Resistance to change may encourage management to carefully reexamine its change proposals so that it can be more certain the initiatives are appropriate.

58. **The correct answer is (B).** Organizational culture is the pervasive system of values, beliefs, and norms that exist in an organization. Corporate culture can encourage or discourage effectiveness, depending on the nature of the values, beliefs, and norms.

59. **The correct answer is (B).** Organizational development is an intervention strategy that uses group processes to focus on the corporate culture of a company in order to bring about a planned change.

60. **The correct answer is (D).** A fundamental way to build support for change is through employee participation.

Personal Finance

PRETEST

1. A limit order instructs a stockbroker to
   - (A) buy or sell at the best possible price within a specified price range
   - (B) execute an order at the best possible market price
   - (C) sell shares at the market price if a stock declines to or goes below a specified price
   - (D) buy only in lots of 100 shares

2. Investment diversification is best described as the acquisition of a
   - (A) large number of the same stock to eliminate all risk
   - (B) variety of different stocks to eliminate all risk
   - (C) variety of different stocks to reduce risk
   - (D) variety of high-risk stocks to maximize net worth

3. Which of the following is NOT found on a personal balance sheet?
   - (A) Assets
   - (B) Income
   - (C) Liabilities
   - (D) Equity

4. All of the items on a balance sheet should be listed using their
   - (A) fair market value
   - (B) net worth
   - (C) original cost
   - (D) value at maturity date

5. Income statements differ from balance sheets in that
   - (A) income statements include liabilities while balance sheets include expenditures
   - (B) items on income statements are listed using their fair market value while those on balance sheets are listed using their historical cost
   - (C) income statements describe money's motion over time while balance sheets describe net worth at a certain point in time
   - (D) fixed expenditures are not included on income statements

6. Liquidity is an important aspect of financial planning because

   (A) a person should be concerned with the results of planning strategy after taxes
   (B) those who act as agents may be acting in their own self-interest instead of their clients' interests
   (C) a dollar received today is worth more than a dollar received in the future
   (D) a person should have available funds in case something unexpected happens

7. Publicly traded companies are required to periodically report information to which of the following governmental regulatory bodies?

   (A) SEC
   (B) ChFC
   (C) FDIC
   (D) SIPC

8. Which of the following designations requires the applicant to be a certified public accountant (CPA)?

   (A) Certified Financial Planner
   (B) Personal Financial Specialist
   (C) Chartered Financial Consultant
   (D) Professional Financial Planner

9. Savings accounts and Money Market Deposit accounts (MMDA) differ in that

   (A) savings accounts pay interest while MMDAs do not
   (B) an MMDA is issued by the federal government
   (C) the interest rate on an MMDA varies with the current market interest rate
   (D) MMDA investors receive interest rates based on a pool of investments rather than a fixed rate

10. Which of the following is a risk associated with Money Market Mutual Funds (MMMF)?

    (A) MMMFs are invested in a nondiversified portfolio.
    (B) MMMF portfolios include long-term investments in volatile companies.
    (C) MMMFs are not insured by the government.
    (D) MMMFs are often not monitored.

11. According to the Average Daily Balance method, which of the following is the calculated interest payment on a credit card account with an interest rate of 4%, an opening balance of $133.33, and no new purchases over a 30-day period?

    (A) $5.33
    (B) $160.00
    (C) $1,200.00
    (D) $3,333.33

234

12. Using the Previous Balance method, which of the following was the interest charged for the month of July on this credit card?

July	
Monthly Interest Rate	3.5%
Balance as of 6/30/99	$2,000
Payments made	$600

- (A) $1.63
- (B) $2.33
- (C) $4.90
- (D) $7.00

13. Which of the following is the major difference between bank credit cards and travel and entertainment credit cards?

- (A) Travel and entertainment cards do not offer revolving credit.
- (B) Travel and entertainment cards have no grace period.
- (C) Bank cards have no annual fee.
- (D) There is no merchant's discount fee on bank card purchases.

14. An affinity card can best be described as a

- (A) credit card that sends funds to a sponsoring organization
- (B) bank credit card with high limits and additional perks, including emergency medical and legal services
- (C) credit card that can be used only at a specific company
- (D) credit card aimed at business customers

15. A credit bureau's role in credit evaluation can best be described as

- (A) compiling financial data
- (B) scoring a candidate's credit
- (C) figuring credit rates
- (D) recording the "Five C's" of credit

16. One disadvantage of credit scoring is that it may

- (A) discriminate based on race and gender
- (B) determine a candidate's interest rate as well as whether or not the candidate is qualified
- (C) be less efficient than other, non-automated evaluation systems
- (D) involve a lack of common sense

17. If a stolen credit card is used fraudulently before being reported stolen, for which of the following maximum amounts is the cardholder liable?

- (A) $0
- (B) $50
- (C) $100
- (D) The total amount of the fraudulent purchase

18. Which of the following federal laws provides a procedure for correcting billing errors?

    (A) Fair Credit Billing Act
    (B) Fair Debt Collection Practices Act
    (C) Truth in Lending Act
    (D) Fair Lending Charges Act

19. Which of the following types of loan is quite costly and should be avoided?

    (A) Simple interest installment
    (B) Student
    (C) Add-on interest installment
    (D) Early payment

20. Which of the following best states the difference between simple interest and add-on interest installment loans?

    (A) Add-on loans are always secured loans.
    (B) Simple interest loans have an APR equal to a whole number.
    (C) Add-on loan APR's rise throughout the life of the loan.
    (D) Simple interest loans are paid off in a process called loan amortization.

PRETEST ANSWERS

1. **The correct answer is (A).** A limit order is defined as an instruction to the stockbroker to buy or sell at the best possible price within a specified price range.

2. **The correct answer is (C).** Investment diversification is best described as the acquisition of a variety of different stocks to reduce risk.

3. **The correct answer is (B).** Balance sheets record asset, liability, and equity accounts.

4. **The correct answer is (A).** All of the items on a balance sheet should be listed using their fair market value.

5. **The correct answer is (C).** Income statements describe money's motion over time while balance sheets describe net worth at a certain point in time.

6. **The correct answer is (D).** Liquidity is an important aspect of financial planning because a person should have available funds in case something unexpected happens.

7. **The correct answer is (A).** Publicly traded companies are required to periodically report information to the Securities and Exchange Commission (SEC).

8. **The correct answer is (B).** Personal Financial Specialist designation required a CPA certification. Certified Financial Planner and Chartered Financial Planner designations do not require the applicant to be a CPA. Anyone can be a professional financial planner.

9. **The correct answer is (C).** The interest rate on an MMDA varies with the current market interest rate.

10. **The correct answer is (C).** MMMFs are not insured by the government.

11. **The correct answer is (A).** Interest charged = $(4,000/30)(.04) = 5.33$

12. **The correct answer is (D).** Interest charged = $(0.035)(2,000) = 70$

13. **The correct answer is (A).** Unlike bank credit cards, travel and entertainment cards do not offer revolving credit.

14. **The correct answer is (B).** An affinity card is a credit card that sends funds to a sponsoring organization.

15. **The correct answer is (A).** A credit bureau compiles financial data.

16. **The correct answer is (D).** Credit scoring is automated, so it does not involve human consideration and common sense.

17. **The correct answer is (B).** This amount was established by the Truth in Lending Act.

18. **The correct answer is (A).** The Fair Credit Billing Act provides a procedure for correcting billing errors.

19. **The correct answer is (C).** Add-on interest installment loans are quite costly and should be avoided.

20. **The correct answer is (D).** Simple interest loans are paid off in a process called loan amortization. Add-on interest installment loans are not paid off in such a way.

GENERAL OVERVIEW

OVERVIEW

Personal finance is money management for individuals and households. It covers a wide range of activities, from budgeting to paying taxes to buying a house to investing to estate planning. At any given point during a person's life, the relative importance of different aspects of personal finance changes as needs and goals change.

FINANCIAL VALUES AND GOALS

In the United States, great value is placed on material success. For some, financial success is equated with personal self-worth. For others, material well-being is simply a means to achieve personal goals. Values underlie the financial goals people set (or fail to set). They are the foundation of all personal finance decisions.

The types of goals that involve money vary considerably. However, besides an individual's unique goals, most people have goals relating to basic security, indebtedness, home ownership, college education for their children, recreation, and retirement.

NET WORTH

The first step in a money management program is to prepare a financial statement that lists assets and liabilities to arrive at net worth. **Assets** include land, a house or other buildings, furniture, automobiles, checking and savings accounts, stocks, bonds, mutual funds, and retirement accounts. Items that do not have a cash value (like cars or antiques) are appraised at a reasonable selling price. **Liabilities** include everything a person owes: current bills; a mortgage; a home-equity loan; installment loans (car, education, or other bank loans); credit card balances; and any other indebtedness. **Net worth** is figured by subtracting liabilities from assets.

BUDGETING AND CASH FLOW

The purpose of **budgeting** is to devise a plan to keep expenses within income, distribute spending appropriately, and achieve financial goals. **Income** includes salary, alimony, child support, welfare payments, food stamps, social security, disability payments, financial aid, tax refunds, interest, dividends, and capital gains. **Expenses** are either fixed or variable. **Fixed expenses,** such as a mortgage or rent payment, are the same each month, quarter, or year. **Variable expenses**, such as clothing or vacations, change each period.

The first step in making a budget is keeping track of **cash flow**, money coming in and going out, for a period of time, such as two months. At the end of the period, expenses are classified, totaled, and figured as a percentage of gross income. With this process, it is easy to identify expenses on which too much or too little was spent and to incorporate this into a budget.

SOME BASIC ECONOMICS TERMS

bear market—decreasing stock prices over a long period of time

bull market—increasing stock prices over a long period of time

deflation—a general decline in prices

depression—a period of severe economic slowdown characterized by very high unemployment

Federal Reserve Board—the institution that regulates the money supply and interest rates

inflation—a general rise in prices

recession—a period of moderate economic slowdown characterized by high unemployment

INSTITUTIONAL ASPECTS OF FINANCIAL PLANNING

Many organizations play a role in personal finance management. Among them are:

- **Consumer Credit Counseling Service**—An organization that helps consumers pay off debts

- **Federal Deposit Insurance Corporation (FDIC)**—A federal agency that insures savings accounts of member institutions up to $100,000 each

- **Institute of Certified Financial Planners (ICPA)**—An association of financial planners who have passed a certification exam

- **National Association of Securities Dealers (NASD)**—An association of stockbrokers that has licensing information and consumer complaint information
- **Securities and Exchange Commission (SEC)**—Government agency that regulates stocks, bonds, and mutual funds and provides free information about investing

CREDIT AND DEBT
CREDIT CARDS

Credit cards allow the consumer to purchase items or obtain cash advances up to a certain credit limit and to carry most of the debt forward from month to month. However, interest is added to the unpaid balance, sometimes at rates as high as 18 to 20 percent.

Choosing a Credit Card

When choosing a credit card, consumers should check the following:

- **Annual percentage rate (APR)**—The total cost of credit expressed on an annual basis
- **Annual fee**—A fee that ranges from $20 to $100
- **Grace period**—The amount of time finance charges are not assessed if the balance is paid in full before the due date. If a balance is carried on a card, there is usually no grace period for new purchases.
- **Miscellaneous fees**—These may include fees for late payment, exceeding the credit limit, or taking out a cash advance.
- **Minimum payment**—This ranges from 2 to 2.8 percent of the total balance.

Consumers who tend to carry a balance from month to month should look for a card with a low interest rate. Consumers who pay their full balance each month should look for a card with a low annual fee.

INSTALLMENT LOANS

An **installment loan** is a loan that must be paid back in installments over a specific period of time. Interest rates may be either fixed or variable. The most common types of installment loans are car loans, student loans, and personal loans.

Car Loans

Car loans are offered by automotive finance companies, banks, savings and loans, and credit unions. The term of a car loan ranges from two to ten years, although five years is usually the reasonable maximum for the average car. In general, the term of the loan should not exceed the amount of time the consumer anticipates keeping the car.

Car dealers often offer financing for new cars at very low interest rates. These loans usually have conditions: they may be available only on certain models; the consumer must forego a cash rebate; and the low interest rate may be available only with a short-term loan, such as two years, making the monthly payments very large.

Credit unions, banks, and savings and loans also offer car loans. In general, credit unions offer loans at nearly a percentage point less than do banks and savings and loans. Rates for used cars are higher than rates for new cars by one to two percent.

Finally, homeowners often use home equity loans to finance car purchases. Unlike the other types of car loans, a home equity loan is secured by a house rather than a car. Home equity loans have several advantages: rates are usually lower, interest is tax deductible, and the loan can usually be paid off over a very long period of time.

Student Loans

Student loans are used to finance a college education. Many of these loans are subsidized and insured by the federal government. In general, payment is deferred as long as the student attends school more than half-time.

Personal Loans

A personal loan from a credit union, bank, or savings and loan is the most expensive financing after credit card cash advances. It usually has a term of one to five years and a very high interest rate.

INTEREST CALCULATIONS

The two most important factors in evaluating the interest charged on credit is the annual percentage rate, which includes interest, finance charges, and other fees to yield the yearly cost of credit; and (2) whether or not the financing has a **fixed rate** or a **variable rate**. Fixed rate loans have the advantage of having predictable payments. However, variable rate loans may be cheaper in the long run as long as inflation stays in check. Most variable rate loans are adjusted once a year and have a cap on how high the interest can go.

In addition, the way in which credit card issuers compute the account balance makes a difference in the amount of interest paid.

- **Average daily balance (excluding new purchases)—** Interest is charged on the average daily balance during the billing period without counting new purchases. This method results in the lowest interest charges.

- **Average daily balance (including new purchases)—** Interest is charged on the average daily balance, including new purchases.

- **Two-cycle average daily balance (excluding new purchases)**—Interest is charged on the average daily balance for two billing periods, not including new purchases.

- **Two-cycle average daily balance (including new purchases)**—Interest is charged on the average daily balance for two billing periods, including new purchases.

For installment loans, consumers should check whether or not the loan is **front-end-loaded**, meaning that more interest is paid in the early rather than the later months. This costs more than a loan at the same rate with equal interest payments and is disadvantageous if the loan is prepaid.

FEDERAL CREDIT LAWS

If a credit card is lost or stolen and the consumer reports it to the bank before a fraudulent charge is made, the consumer is charged nothing. If the report is made after fraudulent charges are incurred, the consumer is charged a maximum of $50. If fraudulent use is made of the credit card account number and the consumer is still in possession of the card, the consumer pays nothing.

Billing errors and withheld payments for defective merchandise or services are covered under the **Fair Credit Billing Act**. The credit card issuer must be notified in writing and within 60 days of the bill of the nature of the problem. The card issuer has up to 90 days to resolve the problem. In the meantime, the consumer can withhold payment on the disputed item while paying the other charges.

CREDITWORTHINESS, SCORING, AND REPORTING

Lenders have computer models that define **creditworthy** borrowers—those who can be counted on to repay their debts. They assign points for being in a job for a certain amount of time, owning a home, living in a home for a while, having few credit cards, paying bills on time, having a reasonable debt compared to income, and working in a steady field. If a consumer's score is high enough, he or she qualifies for credit.

Credit reporting agencies keep records of consumers' debt payment history and the amount of credit consumers have. They sell this data to potential credit issuers. Consumers can get a copy of their credit reports for free or a nominal charge. If a consumer has been denied credit, the report is free.

BANKRUPTCY

When consumers cannot pay lenders on time, they should inform the lenders of the problem and try to work out alternative payment plans. If this is unsuccessful, help is available from nonprofit **credit counseling** services. A credit counselor reviews the debts and the consumer's ability to pay them, and then sets up a supervised payment plan of two to three years.

If this fails, the consumer may have to file for **bankruptcy**. Bankruptcy protects the consumer from his or her creditors. However, the consumer has to sell most of his or her assets to satisfy the creditors, and a record of the bankruptcy will appear on credit bureau files for up to ten years. Getting a mortgage or a car loan is nearly impossible during this period.

There are two forms of personal bankruptcy. **Chapter 13,** called the wage-earner plan, has a court trustee supervising the full or partial repayment of the consumer's debts, usually over three to five years. **Chapter 7,** called a straight bankruptcy, apportions most of the consumer's assets among his or her creditors but then wipes out the balance of most of the debts.

MAJOR PURCHASES

CARS, FURNITURE, AND APPLIANCES

Research and Shopping

Because big-ticket items like cars, furniture, and appliances have high purchase prices, careful consumers do research before they shop. Publications like *Consumer Reports* review and report on many products. The consumer can learn not only which brands or makes are preferred but the factors to look for when evaluating an item. With this information, comparison shopping becomes easier. During the shopping process consumers can make the final decision on what to buy and where to buy it.

Lease Versus Buy

Leasing a car has become very popular in recent years, primarily because of the relatively low payments and lack of up-front costs. In a typical lease, the consumer makes preset monthly payments over a specific period of time. At the end of the lease period, the consumer has the option of buying the car for a predetermined price. For consumers who trade cars every few years, use their cars for business, drive less than 10,000 miles per year, and don't have cash for a down payment, leasing may be advantageous. In the long run, leasing costs more than buying, so for consumers who plan to own their vehicles for five or more years, buying is preferable.

Warranties and Service Contracts

Major consumer goods that are bought new come with a **warranty** from the manufacturer that guarantees trouble-free use for a period of time. If the item malfunctions during the warranty period, the manufacturer will fix or replace it at no charge. Some products, like cars and major appliances, have accompanying **service contracts** that consumers can purchase at an additional charge, in effect prepaying for repairs that may not be necessary.

Lemon Laws and Consumer Redress

All fifty states have enacted **Lemon Laws** to extend consumers' protection in the event that a new vehicle turns out to be a "lemon." Although the details vary from state to state, in general these laws state that the car dealer/manufacturer must repair problems; if after a certain number of attempted repairs the problem persists, then the consumer gets a replacement car or a refund.

For problems with other products, complaining, usually done in writing, can sometimes net solutions. If negotiating with the retailer or manufacturer is fruitless, consumers can bring their complaints to **small claims court**. Also called the "people's court," this is a forum in which a consumer can pursue a dispute involving less than a certain dollar amount. In Massachusetts, for instance, the amount is $2,000.

HOUSING
Rent Versus Buy

Home ownership has many benefits: a sense of security and satisfaction, a nest egg when the mortgage is paid, deductibility of mortgage interest on federal income taxes, use as collateral, and possible appreciation over the years. On the other hand, renting is advantageous when circumstances are uncertain, as during a divorce, and when there is no money for a down payment on a house.

Financing

There are two basic types of mortgages: **fixed-rate mortgages** that have interest rates that do not change over the life of the loan, usually fifteen to thirty years; and **variable-** or **adjustable-rate mortgages (ARMs)** whose rates can rise or fall along with other interest rates. Most ARMs have fifteen- or thirty- year terms. The interest on an ARM usually cannot rise more than 2 percent in a given year or 6 percent over the life of the loan. The initial interest rate on an ARM is typically 2 percent lower than on a fixed-rate mortgage.

Longer-term loans cost more in the long run, but the monthly payments are smaller and it is easier to qualify for them.

Financing Rules of Thumb

There are a couple of rules of thumb that are used in the real estate business to determine whether or not consumers can afford to buy a particular house. The first is that a consumer can afford to finance a house that costs up to 2.5 times gross income. The second is that the monthly debt payments cannot exceed 36 percent of gross monthly income.

Closing Costs

There are many costs associated with the **closing**, the transfer of title from home seller to buyer. These include the loan origination fee and the loan discount cost (points), a fee for credit reports, an appraisal charge (the evaluation of the house's market value), title insurance, transfer tax, and deed reporting fee. These costs can add up to several thousand dollars.

The Role of Professionals

Several professionals are typically involved in a real estate transaction:

- **Real estate agent**—Sells the house and earns a percentage of the sale price as commission; can be used by buyers also
- **Lawyer**—Helps with the purchase and sale contract and the closing
- **Mortgage broker**—Helps locate the best mortgage
- **Home inspector**—Identifies problems with the house
- **Appraiser**—Assesses market value for the lender

TAXES

The average American household pays about 40 percent of its income in taxes. The taxes include:

- **Federal income tax**—A federal tax on annual income, including wages and salary, self-employment income, interest, dividends, and capital gains
- **Social security**—A payment of a percentage of income to the social security fund; self-employed people pay the full amount, workers pay half and their employers pay the other half
- **State income tax**—An income tax levied by the state in which the consumer resides and the state in which he or she lives
- **Property tax**—A local tax paid on the assessed value of land or real property, such as a house; property taxes are a major source of revenue for localities
- **Excise tax**—A state or local tax on the market value of property such as cars and trucks
- **Sales tax**—A state and/or local tax on the purchase price of (usually) nonfood items
- **Estate tax**—A federal tax on the value of a deceased person's property over a certain amount
- **Gift tax**—A federal tax on gifts over a certain amount

PROGRESSIVE VERSUS REGRESSIVE TAXES

Taxes can be classified as progressive or regressive, depending on their effect on those who pay them. With a **progressive tax**, the more a person earns, the more he or she pays. The federal income tax is the classic example: as income rises, so does the tax rate. With a **regressive tax**, the less a person earns, the more he or she pays *as a percent of income*. Sales tax is the classic example of a regressive tax.

PAYROLL TAXES

To help ensure that citizens pay their taxes, many taxes are withheld from employees' pay and are paid directly to the government(s) by the employer. Amounts are withheld for federal, state, and local (if any) income taxes; social security payments (FICA); and disability taxes. These amounts are deducted from gross pay. When income tax forms for the year are filed, the employee gets a refund if too much has been withheld and pays the balance if too little has been withheld.

TAX PLANNING

The federal tax laws are complex, and over the years many strategies have evolved for minimizing tax liability. These include keeping careful records to back up itemized deductions; shifting income to children, who are likely to be taxed at a lower rate; deferring taxes to later periods; contributing the maximum to a retirement savings plan; investing in tax-exempt securities; selling the most expensive stock, bond, or mutual fund shares first; and using a home equity loan rather than an installment loan for cars and education.

TAX PROFESSIONALS

Two thirds of the nation's taxpayers use professional tax preparers to file their federal income tax return. In general, there are three basic types of preparers: (1) storefront preparers who are employees of large firms such as H&R Block and who usually deal with the most common tax forms; (2) certified public accountants, who have the expertise to deal with all tax matters, from planning to handling audits; and (3) enrolled agents, former Internal Revenue Service (IRS) employees or people who have passed a two-day exam given by the IRS.

THE INTERNAL REVENUE SERVICE

The IRS **audits**, or examines, over a million individual tax returns each year. About 80 percent of taxpayers wind up owing additional tax. In general, the higher the income, the more likely an audit is to take place. Deductions that are larger than the national norm can also trigger an audit. Geographic location can also affect the chances of being audited since IRS regions differ on their audit rate. Simple audits, often involving no more than an arithmetic or transcription error, are usually handled by mail. More complex audits take place at an IRS office.

INSURANCE

The purpose of **insurance** is to protect the insured person and his or her dependents against financial ruin in the event of an unforeseen hazard such as serious illness, accident, theft, fire, or death. The insured person pays periodic **premiums** to the insurance company, which pledges to reimburse claims according to the terms of the **insurance policy**. When purchasing insurance, the consumer needs to balance **risks** against **benefits**. Since the purpose of insurance is to protect against catastrophe, the consumer should only insure against losses that would cause severe financial hardship.

LIFE INSURANCE

A person who has dependents but whose assets would not adequately provide for them in case of his or her death needs life insurance. There are two major types of life insurance.

In **term life insurance**, the premiums go toward the guaranteed death benefit. It is a form of financial protection, such as auto insurance. As the insured person gets older, premiums increase, but until age 70, as long as the premiums are paid, the insurance remains in force. People cancel term life insurance when they have no more dependents or their assets have grown to the point that they can support any remaining dependents.

Cash value insurance is a hybrid financial product. It is life insurance combined with a savings fund. Part of the premium goes toward the death benefit and part goes into a tax-deferred investment account. The balance that builds up in this investment fund is the policy's **cash value**.

PROPERTY AND LIABILITY INSURANCE

Property insurance covers an insured person's losses due to damage or theft of his or her own property. **Liability insurance** protects the insured against claims for injury and property damage brought by others. The most common types of property and liability insurance policies are automobile insurance, homeowner's insurance, and umbrella liability insurance.

Automobile insurance comes with a variety of coverages. Liability protection covers the insured against claims brought by other drivers or property owners who allege that the insured person caused an accident. **Collision** coverage pays for repairs in the event that the car is damaged. **Comprehensive** coverage pays for damages from fire, storm, vandalism, or theft. Both collision and comprehensive coverages have **deductibles**, amounts the insured pays out of pocket before the insurance kicks in.

Homeowner's insurance protects the insured person from losses due to theft and damage from fire and other hazards. It also covers the value of the home. The amount of coverage needed is whatever would be enough to rebuild the house if it were leveled. This can be determined as the **replacement cost** (what rebuilding and refurnishing would cost now) or the cash-value cost (the present value of what was destroyed).

Umbrella liability insurance provides additional liability protection beyond that covered by auto and homeowner's policies. Such a policy covers claims against the insured person and members of his or her household arising from negligence on their part.

HEALTH INSURANCE

Health insurance pays part or most medical costs. In the United States, there are several types of health insurance.

Fee-for-service plans cover visits to any doctor the insured person chooses. For an annual premium, these plans pay about 80 percent of medical expenses after an annual per-person deductible is reached. Generally there is a cap on out-of-pocket yearly expenses.

Managed-care plans restrict the insured person's choice of doctors. With a **health maintenance organization (HMO)**, the insured person must choose from doctors on staff or from a list of network doctors. With a **preferred-provider plan**, the insured person can see a doctor that is not on the network list, but reimbursement will be less. In general, managed-care plans cover preventive care as well as health problems and they do not have a deductible.

MEDICARE AND MEDICAID

Americans aged 65 or older have federal health coverage through **Medicare**. Although it covers both hospital stays and doctor visits, coverage is not adequate for most people. To make up the shortfall, many consumers buy a supplemental policy called Medigap insurance. Low-income people may be eligible for **Medicaid**, another federally subsidized health insurance program.

DISABILITY AND OTHER INSURANCE

Disability insurance is designed to replace income if a person becomes ill or disabled for a long period of time. In general, the policy should cover about 60 percent of gross income during the period of incapacitation. For the severely disabled, social security offers disability payments.

Other types of insurance include malpractice insurance, to protect professionals like doctors against liability claims; renter's insurance, to protect tenants against loss of property and liability claims; and long-term care insurance, to pay for nursing home stays.

INVESTMENTS

Investing is using money to make more money. The basic types of investments are cash investments, bonds, and stocks.

CASH INVESTMENTS

Investing in **liquid assets** means that the investment can easily be converted to cash. Types of liquid assets include:

- **Checking account**—A checking account is used to deposit cash in order to pay bills by writing checks or to obtain cash as needed.

- **Savings account**—A savings account pays a little interest on the deposit.

- **Certificate of deposit**—With a CD, the savings is left on deposit for a predetermined period, from one month to ten years, and penalties are exacted for early withdrawal.

- **Money market funds/deposit accounts**—This is an account invested in short-term government and corporate bonds.

- Most households should have enough liquid assets for an **emergency fund**; the total should be three to six months' living expenses.

BONDS

Bonds are a type of **fixed-income investment**. They represent money lent by investors to government agencies or corporations. The government or corporation pays the bondholder interest for the use of the money for a specified period of time. Bonds are traded, so their face value can fluctuate. Bonds generally provide a steady stream of income and pay more interest than a savings account. There are many types of bonds, including

- **U.S. Treasury bonds**—Payment of face value and interest is guaranteed by the U.S. government, so these are very safe investments. There are a number of these with terms ranging from thirteen weeks to thirty years.
- **Municipal bonds**—These bonds are issued by state and local governments. They are exempt from federal tax.
- **Corporate bonds**—These are issued by businesses; their value depends on the creditworthiness of the issuer. Top-quality corporate bonds are known as investment-grade bonds; lesser-quality bonds from issuers with less credit quality are called junk bonds. Junk bonds typically pay a higher yield than investment-quality or U.S. Treasury bonds because they carry higher risk.

STOCKS

Stocks are **equity**, or ownership, investments; consumers who own shares of stock own part of the equity of a corporation. Over the long term, stocks generally outperform other types of investments. Over the short term, however, they are volatile.

Stock Exchanges

Stocks are traded in **stock exchanges**, such as the New York Stock Exchange (NYSE) and the American Stock Exchange. Stocks traded on the NYSE include the **blue chip** companies, the largest and best corporations, such as Exxon and Procter and Gamble. The thirty stocks that make up the **Dow Jones Industrial Average** and most of the stocks that make up the **Standard & Poor's 500** stock index are traded on the NYSE. Stocks that are not listed on any of the stock exchanges are over-the-counter (OTC) stocks. Several thousand of these are part of the **NASDAQ** Market system, an electronic trading network.

Types of Stock

Corporations can issue two basic types of stock. **Common stock** is the type that most investors buy and sell. It may or may not pay a dividend. In contrast, **preferred stock** pays higher dividends. If the company goes out of business, owners of preferred stock are paid off before owners of common stock.

Stock Analysis

There are two basic types of stock analysis: fundamental analysis and technical analysis. **Fundamental analysis** is the approach used by most investors. It involves analyzing and assessing a company's management, performance, and prospects. The tools of fundamental analysis are a company's financial reports. There are several key ratios that are used in fundamental analysis, including the **price-earnings (P/E) ratio**. This is the price of a share of stock divided by the per-share earnings. In general, the lower a stock's P/E, the better the value it is. **Technical analysis**, on the other hand, involves studying historical trends of the price of the company's, industry's, or market's stocks.

Mutual Funds

Investors can buy individual bonds and shares of stock or they can invest in these by buying shares of mutual funds. A **mutual fund** is a portfolio of stocks, bonds, and money market assets managed by a professional money management firm. Different types of mutual funds trade in different assets or combinations of assets. For example, there are blue chip funds, income funds, and international funds.

Unlike stocks, which are usually sold by a broker charging a commission, many mutual funds are sold directly to investors. Buying and selling may be free of commissions, as in a **no-load fund**, or it may entail paying fees, as in a **load fund**.

OTHER TYPES OF INVESTMENTS

Besides money market, bonds, and stocks, there are other types of investments. **Real estate** includes land, buildings, rental properties, time-shares, real estate mutual funds, real estate investment trusts, and real estate partnerships. **Annuities** are tax-sheltered investments sponsored by an insurance company that pays earnings and a death benefit. Gold and other **precious metals** are regarded by some investors as the ultimate hedge against political and economic chaos. **Commodities** are items such as wheat and orange juice concentrate; investing in commodities involves predicting future price.

ASSET ALLOCATION

Diversifying investments reduces the risk that a poorly performing investment will drag down an entire portfolio. **Diversification** is accomplished by dividing the portfolio of investments among the three major asset types: stocks, bonds, and cash.

The percentage invested in each type of asset depends in part on the investor's appetite for risk and on life cycle considerations. In general, stocks are riskier than bonds and bonds are riskier than cash. An aggressive investor may have a portfolio of 80 percent stocks, 10 percent bonds, and 10 percent cash. A conservative investor might have 50 percent stocks, 20 percent bonds, and 30 percent cash. As people grow older, they tend to shift to more cautious allocations.

SOURCES OF INFORMATION

Information about investing is available from several sources. A company's annual report can be obtained from its shareholder relations office. The *Value Line Investment Survey* and *Standard & Poor's Stock Reports* offer data on thousands of companies. The business press covers developments in companies and markets. Finally, the Internet is a source of endless financial data of value to investors.

RETIREMENT
Pensions

Some people have employer-sponsored retirement plans called **pensions**. Some pensions are **defined-benefit plans**, in which the employer does most of the funding and the payout is a fixed monthly amount. **Vesting**, or eligibility to receive benefits, generally occurs after a certain number of years of service. The amount received in such a pension depends on length of service, average salary, and the ability of the company to keep paying its pension commitments. Another type of pension is the **defined-contribution plan**, such as the **401(K),** in which the employee does most of the funding and takes responsibility for investment decisions.

When a person retires, he or she often must decide whether to take the proceeds of a defined-benefit plan or a 401(K) as a lump sum or an annuity. With a **lump sum**, the retiree gets all the money at once and must manage it. With an **annuity**, the retiree gets a monthly payment for life. Deciding which to choose is complex and usually requires the help of professional financial planners.

Social Security Benefits

In addition to pensions, another source of retirement income is **social security** benefits. The amount of these monthly payments depends on a number of factors, including salary over the years, the age at which a person retires, and whether or not anyone else in the household is receiving benefits.

Personal Investments

A third source of retirement income is personal investments. Those designed specifically for retirement include **Individual Retirement Accounts (IRAs)** and **Keogh plans** for the self-employed. Contributions to retirement accounts are often tax deductible.

ESTATE PLANNING

Estate planning is the process of ensuring the smooth transfer of assets after death. One purpose of estate planning is to make sure each asset goes to the person for whom it is intended. To help accomplish this, a **will** is needed. A second purpose of estate planning is to minimize estate taxes, which can reduce the value of an estate considerably. Estate taxes affect those individuals whose estate is worth $600,000 or more; the amount is set to gradually increase.

OWNERSHIP OF PROPERTY

The disposition of assets after death depends in part on their legal ownership.

- **Fee simple**—A piece of property is individually owned; if the owner is part of a couple, upon death the asset would have to go through **probate**, a lengthy legal process, to determine ownership.
- **Joint ownership or joint tenancy with right of survivorship**—Two people share the title to an asset. Upon the death of one of them, the other automatically becomes the sole owner. If an estate is valued under $600,000, joint ownership is the easiest way to avoid probate (see below).
- **Tenancy in entirety**—A form of joint ownership recognized in about half of the states. It is available only to spouses and stipulates that in order to dispose of his or her share in the asset, the permission of the other spouse is required.
- **Tenancy in common**—Each tenant has a share in the property and can sell or give away the share at any time to whomever the tenant wishes.

- **Community property**—According to the laws of nine states, property acquired by either spouse during a marriage belongs equally to both, regardless of whose name is on it.

PROBATE

Probate is a legal process that proves the validity of a will and that ensures that the deceased's property is passed to the people who are supposed to get it. Probate can be long and complicated, especially if there is no will or a will is disputed, but many estates go through the process easily, especially if a spouse is the only beneficiary.

The three main ways to avoid probate are to (1) put property into joint names; (2) name a beneficiary for a particular piece of property like a bank account or IRA; or (3) put property in trust. **Trusts** are financial devices used to buy, own, transfer, or sell assets. Some types of trusts save on income taxes or estate taxes; others speed up the processing of an estate after the person dies. Depending on the trust, the person may or may not have to give up legal ownership of the assets.

SAMPLE QUESTIONS

1. A person's net worth is figured by
   - (A) multiplying income over years of working life
   - (B) adding assets, then subtracting liabilities
   - (C) adding the value of all owned property
   - (D) calculating the future value of his or her work

   The correct answer is (B). Net worth is the amount a person or household is worth at a particular point in time. To figure net worth, the value of all assets is added. Then the amounts of all liabilities, or obligations, are added. Finally, liabilities are subtracted from assets.

2. "Don't put all your eggs in one basket." This saying summarizes the basic principle underlying
   - (A) umbrella liability insurance policies
   - (B) joint tenancy in the entirety
   - (C) asset allocation in an investment portfolio
   - (D) leasing rather than buying a car

   The correct answer is (C). To minimize the risk of heavy losses in an investment portfolio, people allocate their portfolio over the three basic types of investments: stocks, bonds, and cash. That way if one type is doing poorly, its losses may be offset by the gains of another type. If all assets are in the same type of investment, the portfolio sinks or swims based on its performance.

3. Jay Guilmette, age 36, and Delia Lang, age 35, are married and have two children. They own their own home and two cars. Both of them work full-time. Which of the following types of insurance are they LEAST likely to have?
   - (A) Life insurance
   - (B) Auto insurance
   - (C) Homeowner's insurance
   - (D) Medicare

   The correct answer is (D). Medicare is a federal health insurance program for older citizens. Since Jay and Delia are in their thirties, they do not qualify for it.

PRACTICE SET

1. Which of the following strategies will decrease the cost of insuring a teenage driver?

   (A) Designating the teenager as a part-time driver of one of the household cars
   (B) Assigning the teenager as the principal driver of one of the household cars
   (C) Setting up a carpool with other teenagers for transportation to and from school
   (D) Having the parents teach the teenager to drive

2. Companies may periodically issue a payout to shareholders on each share of common stock. Such a payout is called a(n)

   (A) stock split
   (B) interest payment
   (C) dividend
   (D) bonus

3. Elissa Adams is a conservative, risk-averse investor aged 57. Which of the following portfolio allocations is most suitable for Adams?

   (A) 80 percent stocks; 15 percent bonds; 5 percent cash
   (B) 70 percent stocks; 20 percent bonds; 10 percent cash
   (C) 60 percent stocks; 25 percent bonds; 15 percent cash
   (D) 50 percent stocks; 30 percent bonds; 20 percent cash

4. Which of the following is the best basis for deciding what type and how much insurance to buy?

   (A) Time value of money
   (B) Risk-benefit analysis
   (C) Long-term goals
   (D) Need to avoid probate

5. In which form of personal bankruptcy are a person's assets sold to satisfy creditors, with the balance of the debt being canceled?

   (A) Chapter 4
   (B) Chapter 7
   (C) Chapter 11
   (D) Chapter 13

6. A couple who has just had a child should be considering which of the following short-term goals?

   (A) Establishing a college education fund for the child
   (B) Starting a savings account for a vacation
   (C) Investing their assets in the stock market
   (D) Starting a retirement account

7. Which of the following investments would offer the best federal tax shelter to a person's whose income tax bracket is 31 percent?

   (A) Certificate of deposit
   (B) Treasury bills
   (C) Municipal bonds
   (D) Money market account

8. Marcia and Hiram bought a new Topnotch refrigerator from Appliances Galore. After a few hours, it became apparent that it did not work. Whom should they deal with first in order to get a replacement refrigerator?

   (A) The delivery company
   (B) Appliances Galore
   (C) The Topnotch Corporation
   (D) Small claims court

9. Which of the following describes the usual relationship between the risk and the potential yield of an investment?

   (A) The higher the risk, the higher the yield.
   (B) The higher the risk, the lower the yield.
   (C) The lower the risk, the higher the yield.
   (D) There is no direct relationship between risk and yield.

10. An annual tax on property such as cars is known as a(n)

   (A) real estate tax
   (B) income tax
   (C) sales tax
   (D) excise tax

PRACTICE SET ANSWERS

1. **The correct answer is (A).** Insurance companies discount the cost of a teenage driver if he or she is not the principal driver of one of the household vehicles; in other words, if he or she drives occasionally, not regularly.

2. **The correct answer is (C).** A dividend is a payout on common stock, usually issued by a corporation when it is doing well. Interest is paid on bonds and cash investments, not stock.

3. **The correct answer is (D).** There are two reasons Elissa would want to have a relatively low percentage of stocks: stocks are the most volatile investments in the short term and Elissa is risk-averse, and she is approaching retirement age and needs to protect her assets.

4. **The correct answer is (B).** Since the purpose of insurance is to protect against heavy financial losses caused by certain hazards, consumers have to evaluate their risk of incurring the hazard against the potential payout of the insurance in order to decide whether or not a policy's coverages are right for them.

5. **The correct answer is (B)** . This is a description of Chapter 7 personal bankruptcy. The form of bankruptcy in which the debtor keeps some assets and pays back the debt over a few years is called Chapter 13.

6. **The correct answer is (A).** Because college is so expensive, parents need to start saving as soon as a child is born to maximize the time their investments can grow.

7. **The correct answer is (C).** Since interest on municipal bonds is not subject to federal income tax, they are a tax shelter for someone in that tax bracket. The remaining choices are all subject to federal tax based on the interest they generate.

8. **The correct answer is (B).** The first recourse in such a situation is the retailer. If dealing with the retailer fails, then Marcia and Hiram can move on to deal with the manufacturer.

9. **The correct answer is (A).** Yields on high-risk investments are potentially high; without that incentive, people would not invest in high-risk instruments.

10. **The correct answer is (D).** Tax on the value of property such as a car or boat is called an excise tax. It is levied by a state or municipality.

POSTTEST

1. Which of the following types of bankruptcy is most commonly filed?

   (A) Chapter 7
   (B) Chapter 11
   (C) Chapter 12
   (D) Chapter 13

2. For how long does a Chapter 7 bankruptcy remain on a person's credit history?

   (A) 1 year
   (B) 7 years
   (C) 10 years
   (D) 12 years

3. The purpose of a debt consolidation loan is to

   (A) eliminate all debt
   (B) shorten the term of payments
   (C) lower monthly payments
   (D) change an individual's spending habits

4. Declaring bankruptcy will NOT eliminate which of the following?

   (A) Car payments if the car is retained
   (B) Student loans
   (C) Mortgage payments if the house is retained
   (D) Credit card debt

5. Which of the following organizations is a good place to find a qualified credit counselor?

   (A) Internal Revenue Service
   (B) A local bank
   (C) National Credit Program
   (D) Consumer Credit Counseling Service

6. The "prime rate" is the interest rate that banks charge to

   (A) new customers
   (B) their most creditworthy customers
   (C) customers who have bankruptcy listed on their credit histories
   (D) customers who do not have savings accounts

7. Which of the following aim to assist consumers in research and comparison shopping?

    (I)   *Consumer Reports*
    (II) *Consumer's Resource Handbook*
    (III) *National Automobile Dealer's Association Monthly*
    (IV) Autosite.com

    (A) I and II only
    (B) II and III only
    (C) I, II, and III only
    (D) I, II, and IV only

8. Leasing may NOT be a good idea for a customer in the automobile market if the customer

    (A) drives under 15,000 miles annually
    (B) considers an open-ended lease
    (C) is financially stable and, thus, should buy
    (D) uses the car for business travel only

9. The law requires implied warranties unless the

    (A) seller says that the product is being sold "as is"
    (B) seller offers a service contract
    (C) seller states in writing that there is no implied warranty
    (D) product being sold was pre-owned

10. A consumer purchases a defective appliance and wishes to seek redress. The consumer should first bring the complaint to

    (A) the local business where the purchase was made
    (B) the manufacturer of the item purchased
    (C) a regulatory organization (e.g., the Better Business Bureau)
    (D) a small claims court

11. Advantages of seeking redress in a small claims court include all of the following EXCEPT:

    (A) The cases are local so a court appearance is convenient.
    (B) The court's expense is relatively low.
    (C) The majority of cases are won by the plaintiff.
    (D) A written record of the case is provided.

12. The advantages of buying a house normally outweigh the advantages of renting an apartment for which of the following situations?

    (A) The apartment has a high security deposit.
    (B) The consumer plans on staying in the same location for several years.
    (C) No down payment is required for the apartment.
    (D) The house and the apartment are in similar neighborhoods.

13. Having an adjustable-rate mortgage with a payment cap but no interest rate cap could lead to which of the following?

    (A) A teaser rate
    (B) An assumable mortgage
    (C) A fixed-rate mortgage
    (D) Negative amortization

14. All of the following types of life insurance provide permanent, lifelong protection EXCEPT

    (A) term
    (B) whole
    (C) universal
    (D) variable

15. A couple wants to buy a home. If the lender states their front-end ratio can be no greater than 25 percent and their joint gross annual income is $84,000, which of the following is the maximum amount the couple have for PITI payments?

    (A) $875
    (B) $1,750
    (C) $10,500
    (D) $21,000

16. Which of the following costs associated with home ownership is recurring?

    (A) PITI
    (B) Settlement costs
    (C) Points
    (D) Title search fee

17. Which of the following best describes a fixed-rate mortgage loan?

    (A) An assumable loan
    (B) A loan with a teaser rate
    (C) A loan that has an APR independent of market fluctuations
    (D) A loan with prepayment privileges

18. State sales tax can be categorized as which of the following types of taxes?

    (A) Progressive
    (B) Regressive
    (C) Marginal
    (D) Excise

19. Individuals who practice tax overwithholding on their paychecks do which of the following?

(I) Receive a refund
(II) Give the government an interest-free loan
(III) Are assessed a penalty by the IRS
(IV) Claim no exemptions

(A) I only
(B) I and II only
(C) I and III only
(D) II and IV only

20. Which of the following is a nontaxable form of income?

(A) Proceeds from health insurance policies
(B) Any kind of illegal income
(C) Gambling winnings
(D) Tips earned

21. Subjects for a complete audit by the IRS are selected

(A) randomly
(B) by document matching
(C) through taxpayer error
(D) via anonymous tips

22. How long does the IRS have to audit someone suspected of tax fraud?

(A) 3 years
(B) 6 years
(C) 10 years
(D) No time limit applies

23. The purpose of tax credits is to

(A) have the consumer put money where the government wants it
(B) increase final tax liability
(C) help entrepreneurs create new businesses
(D) create flexible spending accounts

24. Which of the following criteria is necessary to claim someone as a dependent?

(A) The tax filer must provide 100 percent of the dependent's total support.
(B) The tax filer must be a relative of the dependent.
(C) The dependent must be under 24 years old.
(D) The dependent must not file a separate tax return.

25. Which of the following is NOT typically associated with the day of closing on the purchase of a home?

(A) Transfer of title is completed.
(B) Seller is paid in full.
(C) Buyer pays the balance of the down payment.
(D) Closing statement (settlement) is delivered to the buyer.

26. The "marriage tax penalty" refers to which of the following?

(A) There is a state tax on marriage licenses.
(B) Pooled incomes may boost a couple into a higher tax bracket.
(C) "Quickie tax divorces" have become prevalent.
(D) A married couple receives an extra tax exemption.

27. Which of the following is NOT a risk handling mechanism?

(A) Risk elimination
(B) Risk retention
(C) Risk transferal
(D) Loss control

28. Risk management includes identifying and evaluating which of the following types of risk?

(A) Every type
(B) Pure
(C) Speculative
(D) Fortuitous

29. Which of the following is a major difference between term life insurance and cash-value life insurance policies?

(A) Term life insurance covers the insured for the person's entire life.
(B) Term life insurance is referred to as "whole life insurance."
(C) More than the amount of the policy may be paid on cash-value insurance upon the policyholder's death.
(D) Cash-value insurance premiums are always higher than term life policies for the same amount of coverage.

30. Adjustable life insurance allows a policyholder to change all of the following EXCEPT

(A) the premium
(B) the face-amount
(C) whether the policy is term or cash-value
(D) the rate of cash-value accumulation

31. An individual with a moderate to high level of income and net worth may want the additional layer of coverage provided by which of the following types of policies?

    (A) "Umbrella" liability
    (B) Comprehensive personal liability
    (C) Bodily injury liability
    (D) Major medical

32. A type of homeowners insurance that covers losses caused by any peril other than those specifically identified as excluded is referred to as

    (A) a named-perils policy
    (B) an open-perils policy
    (C) no-fault property protection
    (D) general liability protection

33. Which of the following types of automobile insurance coverage is legally required?

    (A) Medical
    (B) Liability
    (C) Protection against uninsured/underinsured motorists
    (D) Physical damage

34. The purpose of Medicaid is to

    (A) provide health care for low-income households
    (B) act as a supplementary medical expense portion of Medicare
    (C) aid families with dependent children
    (D) cover custodial long-term and nursing home care

35. Which of the following is the major difference between Major Medical Expense Insurance and Comprehensive Health Insurance?

    (A) Major Medical does include hospital expenses.
    (B) Major Medical does not include surgical expenses.
    (C) Comprehensive Health is usually written on a group basis.
    (D) Comprehensive Health does not have high policy limits.

36. Which of the following is NOT a well-reputed source of information on insurance companies?

    (A) Best's Life Reports
    (B) Insurance Forum
    (C) The National Insurance Consumer Organization
    (D) The Chartered Life Underwriter

37. Which of the following methods has been adopted by the National Association of Insurance Commissioners as the recommended measure in comparing the cost of life insurance policies?

(A) Premium per $1,000 of coverage
(B) Net cost method
(C) Interest-adjusted cost index
(D) Interest-adjusted net payment index

38. Which of the following is the major difference between savings accounts and checking accounts?

(A) Savings accounts have a minimum deposit.
(B) Checking accounts give a return based on market fluctuations.
(C) Checking accounts require an annual fee.
(D) Savings accounts disallow third-party transfers.

39. Certificate of Deposit (CD) interest rates are generally determined by

(A) market fluctuations
(B) the size of the CD
(C) a third party
(D) the consumer

40. Which of the following types of bonds accounts for nearly half of all bonds issued?

(A) Corporate
(B) Debenture
(C) Mortgage
(D) Agency

41. Zero coupon bonds are unique in that they

(A) are issued by public agencies
(B) carry a high risk of default
(C) pay no interest
(D) have no discount

42. Which of the following amounts is the current yield on a bond with a 10% interest rate, par value of $3,000, and a market price of $2,400?

(A) 8.0%
(B) 12.5%
(C) 16.4%
(D) 25.0%

43. A company's stock is initially traded publicly in which of the following markets?

(A) Primary
(B) Secondary
(C) Initial public offering (IPO)
(D) Over-the-counter

44. The Tiffy Corp. has 2 million outstanding shares of stock. An investor has become interested in purchasing stock in Tiffy because, although Tiffy had a net income of $62 million in 1999, the market price per share of common stock was only $21.50. Which of the following is Tiffy's price-to-earnings (P/E) ratio?

(A) 1.12
(B) 0.75
(C) 0.69
(D) 1.44

45. Owning preferred stock generally results in the stockholder

(A) receiving a fixed amount of dividends and voting rights
(B) receiving an investment with a maturity date and voting rights
(C) sharing in profits without voting rights
(D) receiving a fixed amount of dividends without voting rights

46. Generally, when a person deals directly with a mutual fund investment company, the person purchases which of the following types of funds?

(A) No-load
(B) Load
(C) Back-end load
(D) Front-end load

47. The purpose of dollar cost averaging when investing is to

(A) level price fluctuations in the market
(B) create a budgeted payment plan
(C) take advantage of a bull market
(D) avoid high interest rates

48. Which of the following types of investment is often used as a safeguard against economic uncertainty?

(A) Commodities
(B) Precious metals
(C) Junk bonds
(D) Initial public offerings (IPO)

49. The time value of money is a significant financial concept because

    (A) a dollar invested wisely today will be worth more than a dollar in the future
    (B) inflation causes a dollar to be worth less in the future
    (C) future value is always less than present value
    (D) future value is often impossible to figure

50. Asset allocation is a long-term investment strategy suggesting that different types of securities be invested

    (A) in an escrow account
    (B) in high interest-bearing accounts
    (C) at a fixed ratio
    (D) at zero risk tolerance

51. Qualified pension plans are characterized by

    (A) special tax status
    (B) employer sponsorship
    (C) slowly compounding interest
    (D) increased tax liability

52. Chris is comparing an investment of $4,000 in a tax-sheltered retirement plan and $4,000 in a non-sheltered plan. The interest rate on the tax-sheltered plan is 10 percent, and it is 12 percent on the non-sheltered plan. If Chris is in a 25 percent income tax bracket and neither investment will cause the tax bracket to change, which of the following is the difference in interest income from the two plans being compared?

    (A) $480
    (B) $80
    (C) $400
    (D) $40

53. A company does not guarantee employees any retirement benefits through their first four years of employment but, at the end of five years of employment, employee retirement benefits are fully guaranteed. This employer practices

    (A) graduated vesting
    (B) defined benefit pension planning
    (C) cliff vesting
    (D) early retirement

54. Which of the following best describes how a noncontributory retirement plan is funded?

    (A) The employee must fund the entire plan.
    (B) The employer must fund the entire plan.
    (C) The employer will match whatever funds the employee adds to the account, but the account is not tax-sheltered.
    (D) Monies are set aside by the employee at a predetermined rate.

55. Simplified Employee Pension plans (SEP) are designed for
    (A) the self-employed
    (B) people who are unable to set up IRAs
    (C) large corporations or groups of people
    (D) the unemployed

56. Social Security contributions, unlike private retirement plans, are funded by
    (A) state taxes
    (B) the federal FICA tax
    (C) a government investment in the stock market
    (D) state taxes

57. Eligibility for Social Security benefits is based on
    (A) the number of quarters of coverage earned
    (B) age
    (C) nationality
    (D) length of continuous employment

58. A probate estate is best described as
    (A) holdings that are not controlled by a Will, but rather transferred to survivors by contract or law
    (B) property that is transferred at death according to a Will or under intestate laws
    (C) a small estate in which the court does not involve itself
    (D) the property of a missing person

59. A person who has already written a Will can update it by adding a
    (A) holographic Will amendment
    (B) statute to amend
    (C) codicil
    (D) noncupative memo

60. A durable power of attorney provides
    (A) the ability to act in the place of another
    (B) the selection of an executor
    (C) a letter of last instructions
    (D) an opportunity to avoid probate

POSTTEST ANSWERS

1. **The correct answer is (A).** Chapter 7 bankruptcy is the most commonly filed type of bankruptcy.

2. **The correct answer is (C).** A Chapter 7 bankruptcy remains on a person's credit history for ten years.

3. **The correct answer is (C).** The purpose of a debt consolidation loan is to lower monthly payments.

4. **The correct answer is (B).** Declaring bankruptcy will not eliminate student loans.

5. **The correct answer is (D).** The Consumer Credit Counseling Service is a good place to find a qualified credit counselor.

6. **The correct answer is (B).** The "prime rate" is the interest rate that banks charge to their most creditworthy customers.

7. **The correct answer is (D).** *Consumer Reports,* the *Consumer's Resource Handbook*, and Autosite.com are resources that aim to assist consumers in research and comparison shopping.

8. **The correct answer is (B).** Leasing may not be a good idea for a customer in the automobile market if the customer considers an open-ended lease.

9. **The correct answer is (C).** The law requires implied warranties unless the seller states in writing that there is no implied warranty.

10. **The correct answer is (A).** A consumer seeking redress should first bring the complaint to the local business where the purchase was made.

11. **The correct answer is (D).** A small claims court keeps no written record of the cases it hears.

12. **The correct answer is (B).** Houses have high one-time initial costs but lower periodic and total costs in the long run.

13. **The correct answer is (D).** If the interest accrued per period is greater than the payment cap, then negative amortization will result, i.e., the amount owed will increase.

14. **The correct answer is (A).** Term life insurance provides protection for a specified time period, typically one to twenty years.

15. **The correct answer is (B).** $84,000(.25)/12 = 1,750$

16. **The correct answer is (A).** PITI is the only recurring cost listed. Choices (B), (C), and (D) are one-time costs.

17. **The correct answer is (C).** A fixed-rate mortgage loan is a loan with an APR independent of the market; the rate is fixed and does not change over the life of the loan.

18. **The correct answer is (B).** Regressive taxes charge either higher or the same rate to people with lower incomes than those with higher incomes.

19. **The correct answer is (B).** Overwithholding is withholding more than is necessary. The taxpayer will get a refund of the amount overwithheld, but until the check is received, the taxpayer is giving the government an interest-free loan.

20. **The correct answer is (A).** Choices (B), (C), and (D) are taxable.

21. **The correct answer is (A).** Subjects for a complete audit by the IRS are selected randomly.

22. **The correct answer is (D).** There is no time limit on how long the IRS may take to audit someone of whom they suspect tax fraud.

23. **The correct answer is (A).** The government allows tax credits in order to have consumers invest in programs in which the government wants them to invest.

24. **The correct answer is (D).** Dependents cannot file joint returns with their spouses.

25. **The correct answer is (D).** The closing statement is delivered in advance of the date of closing.

26. **The correct answer is (B).** Income tax is progressive, and when two people marry, they are considered one legal entity. For this reason, two incomes that had been charged at a lower tax rate may now be combined (legally) to one income charged at a higher tax rate.

27. **The correct answer is (A).** There is no such thing as risk elimination.

28. **The correct answer is (B).** Risk management deals only with pure risk, not with every type of risk.

29. **The correct answer is (D).** Cash value premiums are always higher because the policyholder is paying both insurance premiums and a cash value.

30. **The correct answer is (C).** Adjustable life insurance does not allow policyholders to change whether the policy is term or cash-value.

31. **The correct answer is (A).** A person with a high degree of exposure to losing significant assets as a result of a single liability loss may want to buy "umbrella" liability.

32. **The correct answer is (B).** A type of homeowners insurance that covers losses caused by any peril other than those specifically identified as excluded is referred to as an open-perils policy.

33. **The correct answer is (B).** Liability insurance is legally required.

34. **The correct answer is (A).** The purpose of Medicaid is to provide health care for low-income households.

35. **The correct answer is (C).** Comprehensive Health is usually written on a group basis.

36. **The correct answer is (D).** The Charted Life Underwriter is not a well-reputed source of information on insurance companies.

37. **The correct answer is (C).** The interest-adjusted cost index is the method adopted by the NAIC to compare the cost of life insurance policies.

38. **The correct answer is (D).** Savings accounts give a guaranteed return on deposit.

39. **The correct answer is (D).** CD rates are generally determined by the size of the CD.

40. **The correct answer is (A).** Corporate bonds account for nearly half of all bonds issued.

41. **The correct answer is (C).** Zero coupon bonds pay no interest.

42. **The correct answer is (A).** Current yield = (annual interest)/(market price) = .1(3,000)/2,400 = 12.5%

43. **The correct answer is (A).** A primary market is one that makes initial stock trades.

44. **The correct answer is (C).** P/E ratio = market price per share (# shares outstanding)/net income = 21.5(2,000,000)/62,000,000 = .69

45. **The correct answer is (D).** Preferred stockholders receive a fixed amount of dividends; therefore, they do not participate in any capital gains (profit improvement). Furthermore, only common stockholders have the right to vote.

46. **The correct answer is (A).** When dealing directly with an investment company, there is no broker or adviser; therefore, there is no need to charge a load.

47. **The correct answer is (A).** The purpose of dollar cost averaging when investing is to level price fluctuations in the market.

48. **The correct answer is (B).** The value of precious metals does not fluctuate much worldwide, so holding these assets can be more stable than an uncertain currency.

49. **The correct answer is (A).** The time value of money is a significant financial concept because a dollar invested wisely today will be worth more than a dollar in the future.

50. **The correct answer is (C).** Asset allocation is a long-term investment strategy requiring that equities, debts, and cash equivalents be kept at a fixed ratio.

51. **The correct answer is (A).** Qualified retirement plans are characterized by special tax status.

52. **The correct answer is (D).**

$$\text{Sheltered: } 4,000(1.1) = 4,400$$
$$4,400 - 4,360 = 40$$
$$\text{Non-sheltered: } 4,000(.12) = 480$$
$$480(.75) = 360$$
$$4,000 + 360 = 4,360$$
$$4,400 - 4,360 = 40$$

53. **The correct answer is (C).** With cliff vesting (five years), an employee is not vested at all until the end of the fifth year of employment.

54. **The correct answer is (B).** A noncontributory retirement plan is funded entirely by the employer.

55. **The correct answer is (A).** Simplified Employee Pension plans (SEP) are designed for the self-employed.

56. **The correct answer is (B).** Social Security contributions are funded by the federal FICA tax.

57. **The correct answer is (A).** Eligibility for Social Security benefits is based on the number of quarters of coverage earned.

58. **The correct answer is (D).** Probate property is property that the government charges people to legally distribute after the previous owner's death.

59. **The correct answer is (C).** A person who has already written a Will can update it by adding a codicil.

60. **The correct answer is (A).** A durable power of attorney provides the ability to act in the place of another.

Principles of Financial Accounting

PRETEST

1. The current standard-setting board for accounting in the private sector in the United States is the

    (A) Securities and Exchange Commission (SEC)
    (B) Financial Accounting Standards Board (FASB)
    (C) Accounting Principles Board (APB)
    (D) American Accounting Association (AAA)

2. An accounting system includes the procedures and processes used by businesses to do all of the following EXCEPT

    (A) analyze transactions
    (B) structure evaluative information
    (C) perform decision making
    (D) handle bookkeeping tasks

3. Companies are required to follow "generally accepted accounting principles" (GAAP) for which of the following reasons?

    (A) These principles are enforced by the FASB.
    (B) The IRS audits all companies that do not conform to these principles.
    (C) Outsiders need to know and understand the financial assumptions that companies use.
    (D) These principles were passed into law by the International Accounting Standards Committee (IASC).

4. The Securities and Exchange Commission (SEC) was created in order to

    (A) enforce rules set by the FASB
    (B) administer examinations for CPA and CMA certifications
    (C) provide investors with fair information
    (D) regulate state labor laws

5. Financial accounting is best described as the area of accounting most concerned with

    (A) reporting information to external parties
    (B) reporting information internally
    (C) monitoring internal strategic decisions
    (D) regulating cash flow

6. Which of the following is NOT federally required to attain the CPA designation?

   (A) Taking a minimum number of college-level accounting classes
   (B) Achieving a passing grade on the CPA exam, as administered by the AICPA
   (C) Meeting all state requirements
   (D) Working a minimum number of hours as an accountant

7. Which of the following is NOT a key principle of the AICPA's Code of Professional Conduct?

   (A) Loyalty
   (B) Integrity
   (C) Objectivity
   (D) Independence

8. Liquidity is best described as the

   (A) ability of a firm to meet its short-term obligations
   (B) annual revenue growth a firm experiences
   (C) number of shares of common stock a corporation is able to sell
   (D) ratio of dollars borrowed to assets owned

9. A company's price-to-earnings (P/E) ratio does NOT represent the

   (A) amount investors are willing to pay for each dollar of earnings
   (B) company's growth potential
   (C) relationship between market value and current earnings
   (D) profit earned per dollar invested in the company

10. Which of the following is NOT a primary financial statement?

    (A) Balance sheet
    (B) Income statement
    (C) Statement of cash flows
    (D) Statement of retained earnings

11. Which of the following is NOT part of the accounting cycle?

    (A) Analyzing transactions
    (B) Summarizing the effects of transactions
    (C) Recording the effects of transactions
    (D) Choosing the most efficient method of transaction

12. A debit entry in a company's cash account might necessitate a

    (A) credit entry in a liability account
    (B) debit entry in an owner's equity account
    (C) debit entry in an asset account
    (D) decrease in cash on hand

13. Liabilities are best described as

    (A) creditors' claims against resources
    (B) debtors' claims against resources
    (C) long-term debt
    (D) short-term debt

14. An accounting entry that provides an efficient way to categorize transactions is

    (A) an account
    (B) bookkeeping
    (C) a general ledger
    (D) the accounting equation

15. When constructing a journal entry, which of the following entries is entered first?

    (A) Debit
    (B) Credit
    (C) Adjusting
    (D) Closing

16. If, at a specific time, XYZ Corp. has assets worth $15 million and liabilities worth $10 million, which of the following is XYZ Corp. owner's equity?

    (A) $3 million
    (B) $5 million
    (C) $15 million
    (D) $25 million

17. The accounting equation can be rewritten as:

    Resources = Creditor's claims against resources +

    (A) Debtors' claims against resources
    (B) Owners' claims against resources
    (C) Claims against debtors' resources
    (D) Liabilities

18. At the end of an accounting period, which of the following accounts is closed?

    (A) Nominal (temporary)
    (B) Owner's equity
    (C) Retained earnings
    (D) Real

19. The Matching Principle holds that

(A) revenues must be assigned to the period in which the goods they are associated with were sold

(B) expenses must be assigned to the period in which the goods they are associated with were produced

(C) revenues must be assigned to the period in which the goods they are associated with were produced

(D) for each revenue journal entry, there should be a matching expense journal entry

20. Gross profit (gross margin) is equal to

(A) revenues only

(B) revenues minus the cost of goods sold

(C) revenues minus expenses

(D) revenues minus operating expenses

PRETEST ANSWERS

1. **The correct answer is (B).** The current standard-setting board for accounting in the private sector in the United States is the Financial Accounting Standards Board (FASB).

2. **The correct answer is (C).** Accounting systems may serve to analyze and record information, but they do not prescribe any treatments.

3. **The correct answer is (C).** These principles were developed by the FASB so that outsiders could understand assumptions that companies were making and understand their financial reports.

4. **The correct answer is (C).** The Securities and Exchange Commission (SEC) was created in order to provide investors with fair information.

5. **The correct answer is (A).** Internal accounting is the focus of management accounting, not financial accounting, and accounting does not regulate, but rather monitors and reports.

6. **The correct answer is (D).** A person does not need to work a minimum number of hours as an accountant to earn a CPA designation in every state.

7. **The correct answer is (A).** The AICPA's Code of Professional Conduct does not include loyalty.

8. **The correct answer is (A).** Liquidity is a measure of how much cash a company has on hand at any given time and how well a firm is able to meet its short-term obligations (i.e., to pay its bills).

9. **The correct answer is (D).** The profit earned per dollar invested in the company is the return on equity ratio, not the P/E ratio.

10. **The correct answer is (D).** The statement of retained earnings is not a primary financial statement.

11. **The correct answer is (D).** The accounting cycle does not include any decision making.

12. **The correct answer is (A).** A debit entry necessitates an equal credit entry.

13. **The correct answer is (A).** Liabilities are creditors' claims against resources.

14. **The correct answer is (A).** An accounting entry that provides an efficient way to categorize transactions is an account.

15. **The correct answer is (A).** Debit entries are entered in the journal above and, prior to, credit entries. Adjusting entries are entered at the end of an accounting period, as are closing entries.

16. **The correct answer is (B).** The accounting equation reads: Assets = Liabilities + Owner's Equity. Therefore: OE = A − L; $15 million minus $10 million.

17. **The correct answer is (B).** Resources = Assets; Creditor's claims against resources = Liabilities; and Owner's claims against resources = Owner's equity.

18. **The correct answer is (A).** At the end of an accounting period, nominal accounts (e.g., dividends) are closed to retained earnings.

19. **The correct answer is (A).** The Matching Principle holds that revenues must be assigned to the period in which the goods they are associated with were sold.

20. **The correct answer is (B).** Gross profit (gross margin) is equal to revenues minus the cost of goods sold.

GENERAL OVERVIEW

GENERAL CONCEPTS AND PRINCIPLES

WHAT IS ACCOUNTING?

Accounting is the process of identifying, measuring, recording, and communicating the financial activities of an organization. Identifying financial activities involves observing them and selecting events that are evidence of economic activity and relevant to the organization. Measuring economic events, called **transactions**, involves assigning a monetary value to them. Recording, also called **bookkeeping**, provides a history of transactions. And communicating involves the preparation of financial reports to interested users.

People inside and outside the organization use its financial reports. Internal users require financial information to manage the organization and to prepare tax returns. External users have a financial interest in the organization; they may be investors, creditors, labor unions, government agencies, or financial analysts.

THE ACCOUNTING PROFESSION

Accountants work in three major areas: private accounting, public accounting, and government accounting. **Public accountants**, whether self-employed or members of large accounting firms, provide financial services to other organizations. They may audit a firm's finances, prepare tax documents, and provide management consulting. The best public accountants are **certified public accountants (CPAs)**, who earn their licenses through education, experience, and examination. **Private accountants** work for business organizations, performing many financial activities, including preparing the payroll, tracking cash inflow and payments, recording purchases and inventory, and keeping records of property. The top accounting executive of a business is the controller. The **governmental accountant** performs many of the same functions as the private accountant, but for a government entity.

GENERALLY ACCEPTED ACCOUNTING PRINCIPLES

The accounting profession has developed a set of standards, rules, and procedures known as **generally accepted accounting principles (GAAP)**. These describe the basic methods to measure profit and value assets and liabilities. They also prescribe the information that should be disclosed in external financial statements. Their basic purpose is to ensure that financial information is reported consistently from business to business and to establish uniformity in accounting rules and methods.

One important GAAP is that of using cost—the value of something at the time it is bought—to record assets, not market value. Since market value fluctuates, it is not a reliable, objective measure of a held asset.

Two organizations have primary responsibility for these principles: the Financial Accounting Standards Board (FASB) and the Securities and Exchange Commission (SEC). The GAAP rule book is periodically updated as rules are modified or superseded. For reasons of practicality and efficiency, GAAP are generally in agreement with federal income tax accounting rules.

BASIC ASSUMPTIONS

Several assumptions underlie the generally accepted accounting principles. Two of the most important assumptions are the economic entity assumption and the monetary unit assumption.

- The **economic entity assumption** states that economic events can be associated with a specific unit of accountability. Thus the activities of the entity—which can range from a huge corporation to a church organization—are kept separate. Types of business entities include single proprietorships, partnerships, and corporations.
- The **monetary unit assumption** is that only transaction data that can be expressed as money amounts are recorded in the accounting records.

TYPES OF ACCOUNTS

An **account** is an individual accounting record of increases and decreases in a specific asset, liability, or owner's equity item. In its simplest form, an account has three parts: a title, a left or **debit** side, and a right or **credit** side. (This form is referred to as a **T account** because of its shape.) Entering an amount on the left side of an account is called debiting, and entering an amount on the right side of an account is called crediting. When the totals of the two sides of the account are compared, the account will have a debit balance if debits exceed credits and a credit balance if credits exceed debits.

ASSETS

Things with value that are used in the operation of a business or other entity are known as **assets**. The key characteristic of an asset is that it has the capacity to provide future economic benefit to the business, which results in cash inflows. Assets may be tangible, such as trucks, computer systems, or raw materials, or they may be intangible, such as copyrights, patents, franchises, or trademarks. Asset accounts normally have debit balances.

LIABILITIES

Liabilities are the existing debts and obligations of the business. For example, many businesses buy raw materials and supplies on credit; these are accounts payable accounts. Other types of liability accounts include income tax payable, mortgage payable, and wages payable. Liability accounts normally have credit balances.

OWNER'S EQUITY

The claims of its owners on the assets of a business is **owner's equity**. There are several types of owner's equity accounts:

- **Capital**—The investments of owners
- **Drawings**—The owner's withdrawals for personal use
- **Revenues**—The increase in equity that results from the sale of products and services or from property rentals and money lending
- **Expenses**—The costs of assets and/or services used in the process of earning revenue

Owner's equity accounts normally have credit balances.

THE ACCOUNTING EQUATION

The assets of an economic entity are provided by the owners and the creditors. Thus, assets always equal the sum of creditor and owner claims on the business. This relationship among assets, liabilities, and owner's equity is expressed in the **accounting equation**:

$$\text{Assets} = \text{Liabilities} + \text{Owner's Equity}$$

The accounting equation provides the framework for recording and analyzing the transactions of a company. At any given time, the equation must be in balance.

TRANSACTION ANALYSIS

Companies make many transactions, both external and internal. Each of these transactions must be analyzed in terms of its effect on the accounting equation. The analysis indicates the specific items that are affected and the amount by which each changes.

Each transaction has two effects on the accounting equation because its equality must be maintained. For example, if an individual asset is decreased, the assets side of the equation decreases. To keep the equation in balance, there must be (1) an increase in another asset, (2) a decrease in a liability, or (3) a decrease in owner's equity. It is also possible that two or more items could be affected when an asset decreases, as long as the total changes to the accounting equation leave it in balance. Changes in individual liability or owner's equity accounts can be analyzed in a similar manner. Here are a few examples to illustrate the process.

Transaction 1. Investment by Owner

Kayla Bell decides to open a word processing service. She invests $5,000 cash in the business.

Assets	=	Liabilities	+	Owner's Equity
Cash	=			K. Bell, Capital
+$5,000	=			+$5,000 Investment

Transaction 2. Purchase of Equipment for Cash

Bell buys a computer and printer for $3,000 cash.

	Assets			=	Liabilities	+	Owner's Equity
	Cash	+	Equipment	=			K Bell, Capital
Old Bal.	$ 5,000						$5,000
	−3,000		+$3,000				
New Bal.	$ 2,000	+	$3,000	+			$5,000

Transaction 3. Purchase of Supplies on Credit

Bell buys paper and other supplies for $450 using a credit card.

	Assets					=	Liabilities	+	Owner's Equity
	Cash	+	Supplies	+	Equipment	+	Accounts Payable	+	K. Bell, Capital
Old Bal.	$2,000				$3,000				$5,000
			+$450				+$450		
New Bal.	$2,000	+	$450	+	$3,000	+	$450	+	$5,000

THE ACCOUNTING CYCLE

There are several steps in the **accounting cycle**, which begins with an analysis of transactions and ends with a post-closing trial balance.

DAILY ACTIVITIES

1. **Analyze business transactions.** Using source documents such as purchase invoices or salary rosters, decide which accounts are affected and the amount of the change, keeping the accounting equation in balance.

2. **Record entries in the journal.** The whole transaction is first entered into the journal, a chronological record of transactions.

3. **Post entries to ledger accounts.** Each transaction results in at least two entries to the accounts in the ledger, the entire group of accounts maintained by a company.

PERIODIC ACTIVITIES (MONTHLY, QUARTERLY, OR ANNUALLY)

4. **Prepare a trial balance.** A trial balance is a list of accounts and their balances at a given point in time. Accounts are listed in the order in which they appear in the ledger, debit balances in the left column and credit balances in the right column. The totals of the two columns must agree.

5. **Journalize and post adjusting entries to the ledger accounts.** Adjusting entries are made to ensure that revenues are recorded in the period during which they are earned and that expenses are recognized in the period in which they are incurred.

6. **Prepare an adjusted trial balance.** An updated trial balance is prepared. It shows the effects of all financial events during the period.

7. **Prepare financial statements.** The balance sheet, income statement, and owner's equity statement can all be prepared using data from the adjusted trial balance.

ANNUAL ACTIVITIES

8. **Journalize and post closing entries.** The balances in the temporary owner's equity accounts (revenue and expense accounts) are transferred to the permanent owner's equity account (capital). This is done because balances in temporary accounts are not carried forward into the next accounting period, but balances in permanent accounts are.

9. **Prepare a post-closing trial balance.** The purpose of the post-closing trial balance is to prove the equality of the permanent account balances that are carried forward into the next accounting period.

ADJUSTING ENTRIES

A basic assumption of financial accounting is that the economic life of a business can be divided into artificial time periods. However, many transactions affect more than one time period. Thus, accountants must decide what portion of a transaction is relevant to a given time period.

There are two principles that are used to help determine the amount of revenue and expenses to be reported in a given accounting period. According to the **revenue recognition principle**, revenue is recognized during the period in which it is earned, which is not necessarily when payment is made. For example, if a consulting firm does a job for a client during the second quarter, the revenue expected from that job is allocated to the second quarter, even if the firm does not actually receive payment until the third quarter.

According to the **matching principle**, expenses follow revenue and are recognized during the period in which they contribute to the earning of revenue. So, for example, the expense of wages is allocated to the period during which the work takes place, not the period during which the wages are actually paid.

At the end of each accounting period, **adjusting entries** are made to ensure that these two principles are followed and that the resulting financial statements accurately reflect the assets, liabilities, and owner's equity of the business. Adjusting entries may be **deferrals**, or prepayments, or they may be **accruals**.

DEFERRALS (PREPAYMENTS)
Prepaid Expenses

Prepaid expenses are those that will benefit more than one accounting period; they are paid and recorded in an asset account before they are used or consumed. Typical prepaid expenses are rent, insurance, supplies, and advertising. Depreciation, another prepaid expense, is the portion of an asset's total cost reported as an expense during each period of the asset's useful life (see page 000).

Prepaid expenses expire through use and consumption or with the passage of time. However, these expirations are not recorded daily but are recognized at each statement date (at the end of each accounting period). Before the adjusting entries are made, prepaid assets are overstated and expenses are understated. The prepaid expense adjusting entry is an increase (debit) to an expense account and a decrease (credit) to an asset account.

Unearned Revenues

Unearned revenues are those that are received before the accounting period during which they are earned. When unearned revenues are received, they are credited to a liabilities account. Typical unearned revenues are rent, magazine subscriptions, and advanced ticket sales.

Unearned revenues are subsequently earned through providing the service to the customer. As with prepaid expenses, it is customary to defer recognizing the earning of revenues until the end of the accounting period. Before the adjusting entries are made, liabilities are overstated and revenues are understated. The adjusting entries for unearned revenues involve a decrease (debit) to a liability account and an increase (credit) to a revenue account.

ACCRUALS
Accrued Revenues

Revenues that are earned but unrecorded at the end of the accounting period are accrued revenues. They may accrue because of the passing of time, as interest or rent. Or they may accrue as the result of services having been rendered, but neither billed nor collected, as commissions and fees. Before the adjusting entries are made, both assets and revenues are understated. The adjusting entries for accrued revenues involve an increase (debit) to an asset account and an increase (credit) to a revenue account.

Accrued Expenses

Expenses that are incurred but not recorded at the end of the accounting period are called accrued expenses or accrued liabilities. They result from the same causes as accrued expenses and typically involve interest, rent, taxes, and wages. Before the adjustments are made, both liabilities and expenses are understated. The adjusting entries for accrued expenses involve an increase (debit) to an expense account and an increase (credit) to a liability account.

MERCHANDISING TRANSACTIONS

In a merchandising company, most revenues come from the sale of merchandise and are referred to as **sales revenue** or sales. The accounting system also recognizes sales returns, transactions that occur when customers return merchandise, and sales allowances, or deductions from the selling price.

Expenses include the **cost of goods sold** and **operating expenses**. The cost of goods sold is the total cost (to the company) of the goods it sells during an accounting period. This can be determined when each sale occurs if the company is using a perpetual inventory system, or it can be determined at the end of an accounting period if the company uses a periodic inventory system (see page 292).

Sales revenue minus cost of goods sold yields the **gross profit** (gross margin) on sales. After the gross profit has been calculated, the **net income** is calculated by subtracting operating expenses from gross profit.

INTERNAL CONTROL AND CASH

Internal control is an organization's system and procedures for safeguarding its assets from employee theft, robbery, and unauthorized use. A second purpose of internal control is to improve the accuracy and reliability of its accounting system.

INTERNAL CONTROL PRINCIPLES

1. **Assignment of responsibility.** Control is most effective when only one person is responsible for a carrying out a task, authorizing a transaction, or approving a transaction. If an error or fraud occurs, responsibility can easily be determined.

2. **Separation of functions.** When duties are segregated, the work of one employee provides a reliable basis for evaluating the work of another. For example, one person has physical custody of an asset and another keeps the records on the asset.

3.   **Thorough documentation.** Documents provide evidence that transactions and other events have occurred. By having individuals sign off on documents, responsibility for transactions can be traced. Prenumbered documents help prevent a transaction from being recorded twice or not at all.

4.   **Physical, mechanical, and electronic controls.** Physical controls include safes, locked warehouses, and fencing; mechanical and electronic controls include cash registers, gasoline pumps, time clocks, sensors, and error-detection software.

5.   **Independent internal verification.** An employee who is independent of the people responsible for the information reviews and checks its accuracy on a periodic or surprise basis.

INTERNAL CONTROL OF CASH

Applications of internal control principles to **cash receipts** include the following: (1) Only designated employees are permitted to handle cash receipts. (2) The tasks of receiving cash, recording receipts, and holding cash are assigned to different people. (3) Documentation includes cash register tapes, remittances, and deposit slips. (4) Safes, bank vaults, and cash registers are used. (5) Daily cash counts are made by cashier supervisors, and comparisons of receipts and deposits are made by the treasurer.

Applications of internal control principles to **cash disbursements** include the following: (1) Only specified individuals are permitted to sign checks. (2) Approving an item for payment and paying for the item are done by two different departments or individuals. (3) Prenumbered checks are used, and each check is supported by an approved invoice or other document. (4) Blank checks are stored in a safe, and a checkwriter is used to imprint the amount of each check in permanent ink. (5) Each check is compared with the approved invoice before it is issued, and bank balances are reconciled monthly.

CURRENT ASSETS

Current assets are resources that are expected to be cashed in, sold, or consumed in the business within a year. Current assets include cash, marketable securities held as short-term investments, receivables, inventory, and prepaid expenses.

MARKETABLE SECURITIES

Short-term or temporary investments include short-term paper (certificates of deposit, money market certificates, treasury bills, and high quality commercial paper), marketable equity securities (stocks), and marketable debt securities (bonds). Investments are characterized as marketable when they can be sold easily for cash. To be classified as a short-term investment, management must intend to sell within the next year or operating cycle.

In accounting for marketable short-term securities, entries are made when the security is bought, when interest or dividend income is earned, and when it is sold. The loss or gain on the sale is recorded.

During the time that marketable equity securities are held, they may gain or lose market value. On the balance sheet, the value of the securities is reported as the **lower of cost or market value**. Because of this, losses in the value of owned stock are recognized, but gains are not.

RECEIVABLES

Receivables are amounts due in cash from individuals and other companies. There are several types:

- **Accounts receivable** are the most important. These are amounts owed by customers on account. They arise in the normal course of business through the sale of goods or services, and they are expected to be collected within thirty to sixty days.

- **Notes receivable** are claims of formal instruments of credit and are expected to be paid, with interest, in sixty to ninety days or more.

- **Other receivables** include interest receivable, loans to company employees, and income tax refunds.

ACCOUNTS RECEIVABLE

When merchandise is sold on credit, entries are made to the sales revenue and accounts receivable accounts. For financial reporting purposes, accounts receivable are valued at their cash (net) realizable value using the **allowance method**. In order to determine cash (net) realizable value, an estimate must be made of the amount of **uncollectible accounts receivable**. The estimate is usually based on a **percentage of sales** or a **percentage of receivables**. In the percentage of sales basis, management uses past experience and future credit policy to estimate the percentage. To estimate the percentage used in the percentage of receivables method, an **aging schedule** is prepared. Customer accounts are classified according to the length of time they have been unpaid. Then, bad debt percentages based on past history are applied to the totals in each time category to come up with total uncollectibles.

Under the **direct write-off method**, bad debt losses are not estimated and an allowance account is not used. When it is clear that an account is uncollectible, the loss is charged to bad debt expense. In this method, accounts receivable is reported in its gross amount, and the bad debt expense may not be recorded in the same period as the revenue. Thus the write-off method is not acceptable for financial reporting purposes, but it is used for tax purposes.

NOTES RECEIVABLE

A promissory note is a written promise to pay a specified amount of money on demand or at a particular time. The basic accounting issues are the same as accounts receivable: recognizing the notes receivable, setting a value on them, and disposing of them.

INVENTORIES

For merchandising and manufacturing businesses, inventories are often the most significant current asset. The amount of inventory has a large effect in determining the gross profit of a particular period.

In a merchandising operation, inventory consists of many items owned by the company and that are ready for sale. Only one inventory classification, **merchandise inventory**, is needed in this type of company. In a manufacturing company, inventories consist of items ready for sale, called **finished goods**; items still in production, called **work in process**; and items waiting to be used in production, called **raw materials**.

Periodic Inventory System

Inventory quantities are determined by taking a physical inventory or by using a computerized inventory system that tracks items. Items in transit are included in the inventory of the company that has legal title to them according to the bill of sale. After total quantities for each item are found, they are multiplied by unit costs to arrive at the total valuation.

Costing is actually more complicated because the units of a given item may have been purchased at different costs. Some companies use specific identification to match units purchased at each unit cost. Other companies use one of the assumed cost flow methods, based on an evaluation of its effects on the balance sheet, income statement, or income taxes:

- **First-in, first-out (FIFO) method**—Under the FIFO method, the costs of the earliest goods purchased are the first to be recognized as the cost of goods sold. FIFO often parallels what actually happens, because it is good business practice to sell the oldest units first.

- **Last-in, first-out (LIFO) method**—Under the LIFO method, the costs of the latest units purchased are the first to be allocated to the cost of goods sold.

- **Average cost method**—Under the average cost method, the allocation to cost of goods sold is based on a weighted average unit cost.

Perpetual Inventory System

In a perpetual system, there is a continuous record of the quantity and cost of inventory on hand. Perpetual systems are fully computerized. When something is purchased for inventory, its unit and cost data are entered into the computer system. When it is sold, an electronic point of sale terminal updates the perpetual inventory in real time.

PLANT ASSETS

Plant assets, also called fixed assets or property, plant, and equipment, are resources used in the operation of the business and are not available for sale to customers. These assets are expected to last a number of years, over which their value declines, except for land.

They are often divided into four categories: land, land improvements (driveways, sprinkler systems, etc.), buildings, and equipment.

Plant assets are valued at cost, which includes all the expenditures necessary to buy the asset and make it ready for use. Thus the cost of a piece of equipment may include its purchase price, freight, and installation. **Depreciation** is the process of allocating this cost to expense over the asset's useful life, which is an application of the matching principle. There are four depreciation methods:

- **Straight-line method**—The amount of depreciation is the same each period over the life of the asset (an asset valued at $10,000 that is expected to last four years has a depreciation expense of $2,500 per year.)

- **Units of activity method**—In this method, the cost of the asset is divided by the estimated units of production of its service life. The depreciation cost per unit is then multiplied by the number of units during the period to arrive at depreciation expense.

- **Declining balance method**—This is an accelerated depreciation method in which the annual depreciation expense declines over the life of the asset because book value, rather than cost, is used.

- **Sum-of-the-years'-digits method**—This is another accelerated depreciation method. The depreciation rate is based on a fraction, in which the numerator is the years of remaining life and the denominator the sum of the individual years of total life.

Ordinary repairs to assets are charged as revenue expenditures. Additions and improvements are capital expenditures.

CURRENT AND LONG-TERM LIABILITIES

Current liabilities are obligations that are expected to be paid within a year with current assets or by creating other current liabilities. Current liabilities include payroll; accounts payable; and other short-term debts such as notes payable, bank loans payable, taxes payable, and current maturities of long-term obligations. **Long-term liabilities** are obligations that are expected to be paid after one year or from sources other than current assets and current liabilities. Long-term liabilities include mortgages payable, bonds payable, and obligations under employee pension plans.

CURRENT LIABILITIES

For many companies, **payroll** represents the most significant current liability. Payroll includes both **salaries** (the monthly or annual sums paid to managerial, administrative, and sales personnel) and **wages** (the hourly or piecework rate paid to store clerks, factory workers, and manual laborers). Payroll accounting involves paying employees, but it also means maintaining payroll records for each employee, filing and paying payroll taxes, and complying with federal and state regulations regarding compensation. Payroll activities can be divided into four functions: hiring employees, timekeeping, preparing the payroll, and paying the payroll.

Notes payable within a year are classified as current liabilities. When the note is issued and cash is received, the cash account is debited and the notes payable account is credited. During the periods that interest expense accrues, adjusting entries are needed to recognize interest expense and interest payable. When the face value and interest on the note are repaid, the notes payable, interest expense, and interest payable accounts are debited and the cash account is credited.

Sales and the corresponding **sales tax** are rung up separately on the cash register. When the sales account is credited, the sales tax payable account is also credited, and the cash account is debited for the total.

When a company has a long-term debt, part of which is payable in the current year, the amount payable in the current year is reported as a current liability and the balance as a long-term liability. **Current maturities of long-term debt** are often listed on the balance sheet as *long-term debt due within one year*.

LONG-TERM LIABILITIES

To raise large amounts of money, corporations often issue **bonds**. Secured bonds have specific assets pledged as collateral, and unsecured bonds, or debenture bonds, are issued based on the reputation of the borrower. Corporate bonds are traded on securities markets and are purchased by many investors. The present value of a bond is dependent on three factors: the expected dollar amount to be received, the length of time until it is received, and the investor's required rate of return. The process of finding the present value is called **discounting**.

When a corporation issues bonds, the accounting entry debits the cash account and credits the bonds payable account for the face value of the bonds. Over the life of the bonds, entries are required for payment of interest. The bond interest account is debited, and the cash account is credited. At the end of each period, an adjusting entry is required to recognize the interest expense incurred during the period. The bond interest expense is debited, and the bond interest payable is credited. When the final payment of face value and interest is made, bonds payable and bond interest payable are debited and cash is credited.

Long-term notes payable are similar to short-term notes payable except that the term of the note is longer than one year. Mortgage notes payable is a common type of long-term note.

A **lease** allows a renter long-term use of a property for a specified time in return for cash payments. An **operating lease** is for the temporary use of property by the lessee with ownership remaining with the lessor. A **capital lease** is one in which most of the benefits and risks of ownership are transferred to the lessor. The present value of the cash payments for the lease are capitalized and recorded as an asset.

CAPITAL STOCK, RETAINED EARNINGS, AND DIVIDENDS

The ownership of a corporation is divided among those who own transferable units called shares of **capital stock**. In exchange for capital stock, stockholders invest cash and other assets, which are referred to as the corporation's paid-in, or contributed, capital. In contrast, **retained earnings** is the net income that the corporation keeps. It is often called earned capital.

A **cash dividend** is a distribution of cash to stockholders according to the number of shares of stock they own. When a company's board of directors authorizes a cash dividend, an entry is made to debit to retain earnings and credit dividends payable, a current liability account. On the payment date, dividends payable is debited and cash is credited. Dividends may also be paid in the form of stock.

FINANCIAL STATEMENTS

At the end of each accounting period, three financial statements are prepared based on a summary of the accounting data: (1) income statement, (2) owner's equity statement, and (3) balance sheet. The statements are prepared in sequence, as information from the income statement is needed for the owner's equity statement, and information from the owner's equity statement is needed for the balance sheet.

INCOME STATEMENT

An **income statement** shows the revenues and expenses and resulting net income or net loss for the period of time. Its primary focus is on reporting the success or profitability of the company over a specified period of time. The income statement is sometimes referred to as the operating statement because it summarizes the results of operations. Here is Kayla Bell's income statement for the month of September.

BELLDOC

Income Statement
For the Month Ended September 30, 2001

Revenues		
Service revenue		$1,500
Expenses		
Rent expense	$200	
Supplies expense	100	
Advertising expense	75	
Utilities expense	100	
Total expenses		475
Net Income		$1,025

BELLDOC

Owner's Equity Statement
For the Month Ended September 30, 2001

K. Bell, Capital, September 1	$5,000
Add: Net income	1,025
	6,025
Less: Drawings	600
K. Bell, Capital, September 30	$5,425

OWNER'S EQUITY STATEMENT

The owner's equity statement shows changes in owner's equity for the period of time. It presents the beginning balance in the capital account, additions (here, September's net income), and subtractions.

BALANCE SHEET

The **balance sheet** shows the assets, liabilities, and owner's equity of the business at a specific date. Assets are listed first, followed by liabilities and owner's equity. Essentially, the balance sheet is a statement of the business's accounting equation at a specific moment in time. It is sometimes called the statement of financial position.

BELLDOC

Balance Sheet
September 30, 2001

Assets	
Cash	$2,025
Accounts Receivable	500
Supplies	350
Equipment	3,000
Total assets	$5,875

Liabilities and Owner's Equity	
Liabilities	
Accounts Payable	$ 450
Owners Equity	
K. Bell, Capital	5,425
Total liabilities and owner's equity	$5,875

ANALYZING FINANCIAL STATEMENTS

The financial statements of a company allow stakeholders to evaluate the liquidity, profitability, and solvency of a company and to compare the company to its prior performance, to other companies, and to industry averages.

There are several basic tools of financial statement analysis. **Horizontal analysis**, also called trend analysis, is the comparison of data over a period of time to see what the amount and percentage of increase or decrease has been. For example, horizontal analysis can be used to determine whether or not sales increased, decreased, or remained stagnant over a five-year period. **Vertical analysis**, also called common size analysis, expresses items in a financial statement in terms of percentages of a base amount. For example, cost of goods sold can be expressed as a percentage of net sales. This makes the comparison of companies of differing sizes possible. **Ratio analysis** expresses mathematical relationships between two amounts as a percentage, a rate, or a proportion. Liquidity ratios measure the short-term ability of a company to pay its current liabilities. Profitability ratios measure the income or operating success of a company over a period of time. Solvency ratios measure a company's ability to survive. There are many of these ratios, but the best known are as follows: the **current ratio**, which is current assets divided by current liabilities; the **profitability ratio**, which is net income divided by net sales; **earnings per share**, which is net income divided by the weighted average of common shares outstanding; and the **price-earnings ratio**, which is the market price per share of stock divided by earnings per share.

SAMPLE QUESTIONS

1. "Expenses follow revenue and are recognized during the period in which they contribute to the earning of revenue." Of which principle is this a summary?

   (A) Revenue recognition principle
   (B) Matching principle
   (C) Full disclosure principle
   (D) Cost principle

   The correct answer is (B). According to the matching principle, expense recognition is tied to revenue recognition. The revenue recognition principle refers to the fact that revenue should be recognized during the period in which it is earned. The full disclosure principle says that events and circumstances that affect the interpretation of a financial statement should be disclosed. The cost principle says that cost, not market value, is the basis for accounting records.

2. Which of the following is NOT a current liability?

   (A) Salaries payable
   (B) Taxes payable
   (C) Mortgage notes payable
   (D) Current maturities of long-term notes payable

   The correct answer is (C). A mortgage is a type of long-term notes payable because it does not need to be paid in less than a year. The remaining options are all current liabilities.

3. On December 31, 2000, the balance in John Hill, Capital, was $110,000. The following December 31, it was $107,000. During 2001, Hill withdrew $35,000 from his company for personal use and invested an additional $6,000. What was the net income for 2001?

   (A) $26,000
   (B) $29,000
   (C) $75,000
   (D) $81,000

   The correct answer is (A). Start with the first balance in the capital account, $110,000, and subtract the withdrawal of $35,000, which yields $75,000. Then add the additional investment, $6,000, for a total of $81,000. Since the balance in the capital account at the end of 2001 was $107,000, the difference between that amount and $81,000 must be the net income for the year, or $26,000. Review the owner's equity statement if you had trouble with this question.

PRACTICE SET

1. Which of the following is an accepted use of cash basis accounting?
   (A) Preparing financial statements
   (B) Preparing income tax returns
   (C) Preparing adjusting entries
   (D) Posting journal entries to the ledger

2. Why are adjusting entries made at the end of each accounting period?
   (A) To locate errors in the adjusted trial balance
   (B) To ensure the equality of debits and credits posted to the ledger accounts
   (C) To bring the fiscal year and the calendar year into synchrony
   (D) To ensure that the revenue recognition and matching principles are followed

3. How much would you pay for a $1,000 bond with a quoted price of 97?
   (A) $97
   (B) $970
   (C) $1,000
   (D) $1,097

4. Why is internal control over the accounting system most effective when only one person is responsible for a particular task?
   (A) Responsibility for errors and fraud can be easily traced.
   (B) The person can modify the task to suit his or her needs.
   (C) Separating recordkeeping from physical custody improves control.
   (D) The person can check his own work to ensure its accuracy.

5. On November 1, 2000, a company signed a one-year lease on property that became effective immediately. According to the lease, the annual rent of $6,000 is to be paid in two installments of $3,000 each, with the first installment due November 1. On November 1, the accountant debited Prepaid Rent for $3,000 and credited Cash for $3,000 to reflect the rent payment. What adjusting entry should she have made on December 31, 2000?
   (A) debit Cash $2,000; credit Prepaid Rent $2,000
   (B) debit Cash $1,000; credit Prepaid Rent $1,000
   (C) debit Rent Expense $2,000; credit Prepaid Rent $2,000
   (D) debit Rent Expense $1,000; credit Prepaid Rent $1,000

6. Asset, liability, and owner's equity accounts whose balances are brought forward to the next accounting period are called

   (A) T accounts
   (B) permanent (real) accounts
   (C) temporary (nominal) accounts
   (D) ledger accounts

7. Which financial statement represents a detailed presentation of the accounting equation?

   (A) Income statement
   (B) Owner's equity statement
   (C) Balance sheet
   (D) Statement of cash flows

8. Karim Nasar, the owner of a car service, buys a car from First Stop Auto Sales. The purchase price of the car is $14,700. There are make-ready charges of $400, delivery charges of $125, and state sales tax amounting to $1,029. After it is delivered, one of Nasar's drivers offers to buy the car for $16,500. At what cost should this automobile be entered in the accounting records of Nasar's business?

   (A) $14,700
   (B) $15,729
   (C) $16,244
   (D) $16,500

9. Which of the following represents the current ratio?

   (A) Current assets divided by current liabilities
   (B) Net income divided by current liabilities
   (C) Net income divided by current assets
   (D) Current liabilities divided by current assets

10. A piece of equipment has a total cost of $10,000 and a salvage value of $500. The company estimates its service life at 10 years. Using the straight-line method, what is the annual depreciation?

   (A) $10,000
   (B) $9,500
   (C) $1,000
   (D) $950

PRACTICE SET ANSWERS

1. **The correct answer is (B).** The cash basis of accounting does not follow generally accepted accounting principles, but it is acceptable for preparing income taxes (although some very small companies use it on the grounds that they have few receivables and payables).

2. **The correct answer is (D).** Adjusting entries are made to ensure that revenues are recorded in the period that they are earned and expenses are recognized in the period that they are incurred.

3. **The correct answer is (B).** The quoted price of a bond is a percentage of the face value of the bond. In this case, 97 % of $1,000 is $970.

4. **The correct answer is (A).** If two or more people are responsible for the same task, it may be difficult or impossible to trace errors or fraud. Having one person responsible for a particular task is a basic principle of internal control.

5. **The correct answer is (D).** This adjustment recognizes the proper rent expense for the period (two months at $500 per month). It also corrects the asset account, Prepaid Rent, to show the proper balance of $2,000 for the remaining four months. Note that choices (A) and (B) can be eliminated simply on the basis that there is no cash involved in the December 31 transaction.

6. **The correct answer is (B).** This is the definition of a permanent account. Accounts whose balances are transferred to owner's capital at the end of a period are temporary (nominal) accounts.

7. **The correct answer is (C).** The balance sheet shows assets, liabilities, and owner's equity for a particular company on a particular date. If it balances as it should, assets equal liabilities plus owner's equity.

8. **The correct answer is (C).** All of the costs associated with purchasing and making an asset ready for use determine the cost entered on the books. The $16,500 offer for the car is ignored, since cost, rather than market value, is usually used in accounting.

9. **The correct answer is (A).** This is the current ratio, a widely used measure of liquidity.

10. **The correct answer is (D).** The depreciable value of an asset is its cost minus its salvage, or residual value, in this case $9,500. Since the life of the asset is ten years and the straight-line method is being used, the annual depreciation is $9,500 divided by ten years.

POSTTEST

1. Balance sheet for XYZ Corp., in millions:

Cash	$ 5
Accounts Receivable	$10
Property, Plant, and Equipment	$35
Current Liabilities	$12
Long-Term Debt	$25
Owner's Equity	$13

   Which of the following is the correct measurement of XYZ Corp.'s leverage?

   (A) 0.26
   (B) 0.74
   (C) 1.25
   (D) 1.35

2. Accounting assumptions include all of the following EXCEPT

   (A) arm's length transactions
   (B) the (historical) cost principle
   (C) the going-concern assumption
   (D) the market-value rule

3. Which of the following accounts would be increased by a debit entry?

   (A) Revenues
   (B) Accounts payable
   (C) Dividends
   (D) Retained earnings

4. On December 31, 1999, ABC Company's financial statements revealed the following:

Net Sales Revenue	$150,000
Average Accounts Receivable	$ 20,150
Cost of Goods Sold	$ 90,000
Average Inventory	$ 12,000
Net Income	$ 10,500
Total Assets	$940,000

   Given the above information and assuming a 365-day business year, what was ABC Company's average collection period during 2000?

   (A) 41 days
   (B) 49 days
   (C) 53 days
   (D) 56 days

5. The Barber Corp., a calendar year firm, obtained a $15,000, one-year, 10 percent bank loan on October 31, 1999. Interest is payable at the end of the loan term. The adjusting entry needed on December 31, 1999 is a

    (A) debit to interest expense of $1,500 and a credit to cash of $1,500
    (B) debit to interest payable of $1,500 and a credit to interest expense of $1,500
    (C) debit to interest expense of $250 and a credit to interest payable of $250
    (D) debit to interest expense of $250 and a credit to cash of $250

6. On December 31, 1998, the balance in the Retained Earnings account was $18,500. On December 31, 1999, the balance in the Retained Earnings account is $17,100. During 1999, dividends of $4,200 were declared and paid. Net income for 1999 was

    (A) $2,100
    (B) $2,800
    (C) $4,200
    (D) $7,000

7. Which of the following types of accounts is paired with and deducted from a related account?

    (A) Contra
    (B) Deferral
    (C) Accrual
    (D) Carrying

8. Adjusting entries are needed to accurately measure all of the following EXCEPT

    (A) a period's income
    (B) assets
    (C) cash flows associated with depreciation
    (D) expenses

9. At the end of the period when the accountant prepares the financial statements, recording each adjusting entry requires

    (A) a cash transferral
    (B) an entry for one balance sheet account and one income statement account
    (C) an entry for one accrued account and one deferred account
    (D) an unrecorded financial transaction

10. Failure to record which of the following causes net income to be understated?

(A) Revenue earned but not billed
(B) Wages employees have earned but have not been paid
(C) Depreciation expense
(D) Record collection of accounts receivable

11. Accrued revenues are which of the following?

(A) Earned but not yet received in cash
(B) Received before providing a service
(C) Listed in an adjusted trial balance
(D) Signify an error in bookkeeping and must be corrected

12. Common-size financial statements show which of the following?

(A) All items as a percentage of revenue
(B) All items as a percentage of net income
(C) Each financial statement on a similar form
(D) The closing entries at the end of an accounting period

13. The prepaid rent account has an ending balance of $6,400 on December 31, 1999. Rent is paid four months in advance and was last paid on November 1, 1999. The adjusting entry needed would contain a credit entry to

(A) prepaid rent for $6,400
(B) prepaid rent for $3,200
(C) rent expense for $6,400
(D) rent expense for $3,200

14. In a period of inflation, which inventory valuation method would be used for tax purposes?

(A) FIFO
(B) Specific identification method
(C) Average cost method
(D) LIFO

15. Inventory balances for August:

August 1   Inventory 60 @ $6.00
12   Inventory 12 @ $6.50
26   Inventory 32 @ $7.00   Sold 50

Considering a periodic inventory system and the above information, the Cost of Goods Sold for August under a LIFO inventory valuation system would be

(A) $338
(B) $350
(C) $302
(D) $300

16. Which of the following is NOT included in inventory cost?

(A) Goods held with consignee
(B) Inventory purchases
(C) Freight In
(D) Goods sold in transit, FOB shipping point

17. NOT recording some purchases results in the cost of goods sold being

(A) overstated
(B) understated
(C) unaffected
(D) listed accurately

18. A company's internal control structure includes all of the following EXCEPT

(A) a management philosophy
(B) control activities
(C) divisional autonomy
(D) authorization procedures

19. Independent checks on control performance can result from which of the following?

(A) Proper segregation of duties
(B) Physical safeguards
(C) Proper valuation
(D) An audit committee

20. CPAs are required by the Generally Accepted Auditing Standards (GAAS) to

(A) guarantee that financial statements are correct
(B) reasonably assure financial statements are presented fairly
(C) challenge internal accounting systems
(D) report financial statements to the SEC

21. The proper journal entry for establishing a $2,000 petty cash fund would be

(A) Petty cash $2,000
    Cash $2,000
(B) Petty cash $2,000
    Petty cash expense $2,000
(C) Cash $2,000
    Petty Cash expense $2,000
(D) Imprest System $2,000
    Cash $2,000

22. XYZ Corp. is in need of bank reconciliation. The corporation has outstanding checks amounting to $750, a bank service charge of $25, and a NSF check for $2,535. Which of the following amounts is the difference between XYZ Corp.'s balance and the bank's balance?

(A) $1,785
(B) $1,810
(C) $3,260
(D) $3,285

23. On June 30, ABC Company had the following account balances:

Assets	$517,600
Liabilities	$323,400
Owner's Equity	$200,500

Total assets do NOT equal total liabilities plus owner's equity because the following errors were made:

- Supplies of $250 were on hand but not included in assets because all purchases were debited to supplies expense.
- Cash sales of $15,700 were posted to the Sales Revenue account as $17,500. The cash account was posted correctly.
- Equipment purchased on credit for $51,600 was posted to Notes Payable as $56,100. No error was made in the Equipment account.

The correct balances should be:

	Assets	Liabilities	Owner's Equity
(A)	$517,350	$327,900	$189,450
(B)	$517,600	$318,900	$198,700
(C)	$517,850	$318,900	$198,950
(D)	$517,850	$327,900	$189,950

24. The maturity value of a $15,000, 60-day note at 12 percent would be

(A) $300
(B) $13,200
(C) $15,300
(D) $16,800

25. Which of the following amounts would be the discount on a 90-day note with a 10 percent APR and a maturity value of $1,200.

   (A) $30
   (B) $120
   (C) $1,230
   (D) $1,320

26. When the maker of a note does NOT pay the note at maturity, which of the following should the payee do?

   (A) Dishonor the maker.
   (B) Transfer the note on the books to an account receivable.
   (B) Consider the note uncollectible.
   (B) Extend further credit to the maker.

27. Flushing Bowl Company had an accounts receivable balance of $24,500 in its first year of operation. In its second year, Flushing had net sales of $47,000, 60 percent of which were credit sales. Flushing had also received cash payments for $19,200 of accounts receivable in year 2. Which of the following is Flushing's accounts receivable turnover ratio for year 2?

   (A) 1.79
   (B) 2.80
   (C) 4.25
   (D) 8.87

28. Which of the following is the most accurate method of estimating uncollectible accounts?

   (A) Aging accounts receivable
   (B) Percentage of net sales
   (C) Percentage of credit sales
   (D) Allowance for bad debts

29. The Bland Corp. uses the Percentage of Net Sales method to determine the company's uncollectible accounts expense. Bland's average losses from uncollectible accounts amounts to 2.4 percent of net sales, and Bland has the following account balances:

Sales	$9,000,000
Sales Returns and Allowances	$ 123,000
Sales Discounts	$ 42,000

Which of the following is the proper journal entry to record Bland's uncollectible account expense?

(A) Uncollectible Accounts Expense $212,040
       Allowance for Uncollectible
       Accounts $212,040

(B) Uncollectible Accounts Expense $216,000
       Allowance for Uncollectible
       Accounts $216,000

(C) Allowance for Uncollectible
       Accounts $212,040
       Uncollectible Accounts Expense $212,040

(D) Allowance for Uncollectible
       Accounts $216,000
       Uncollectible Accounts Expense $216,000

30. Creating journal entries for the recovery of accounts receivable written off as uncollectible requires two credit entries. One credit entry is to accounts receivable and the other is to which of the following accounts?

(A) Cash
(B) Allowance for uncollectible accounts
(C) Uncollectible accounts expense
(D) Accounts written off

31. As of December 31, 1999, the Brack Corp. had a yearly net sales total of $9,000. The company's average accounts receivable was $2,600. Which of the following is the average number of days it takes Brack Corp. to collect a credit sale?

(A) 70
(B) 85
(C) 92
(D) 105

32. The following information appears in Petty Company's records for the year ended December 31:

Inventory, January 1	$ 325,000
Purchases	$1,150,000
Purchase Returns	$ 40,000
Freight In	$ 30,000
Sales	$1,700,000
Sales Discounts	$ 10,000
Sales Returns	$ 15,000

On December 31, a physical inventory count revealed that the ending inventory was only $210,000. Petty's gross profit on net sales has remained constant at 30 percent in recent years. Petty suspects that some inventory may have been stolen by one of the company's employees. On December 31, which of the following is the estimated cost of missing inventory?

(A) $75,000
(B) $82,500
(C) $210,000
(D) $292,500

33. Microwaves, Inc. sells a microwave on credit for $200 3/10, N/30. A consumer purchases a microwave and pays in cash seven days after the purchase. Which of the following is the dollar amount of the debit entry made to the cash account for this purchase?

(A) $60
(B) $180
(C) $194
(D) $200

34. The direct write-off method of recording uncollectible accounts should NOT be used because

(A) GAAP requirements disallow its use
(B) it violates the Matching Principle
(C) the SEC has declared its use illegal
(D) it involves rough estimates and is inaccurate

35. XYZ Corp. holds common stock in ABC Corp. If ABC Corp. declares and pays dividends, which of the following accounts receives a credit entry in XYZ's journal?

(A) Dividend revenue
(B) Dividends
(C) Dividends paid
(D) Dividend yield

36. If a company finds that the market value of the trading securities it holds is greater than the historical cost, the company must record this difference as

(A) a realized gain
(B) revenue
(C) an unrealized gain
(D) an asset

37. Which of the following best describes the meaning of the term "depreciation"?

(A) The physical deterioration of an asset caused by daily wear and tear
(B) The decrease in market value of an asset over time
(C) The allocation of an asset's cost
(D) A method of valuing an asset

38. Pirates, Inc. buys a new cannon for $700. The cannon has an estimated useful life of fifteen years and will have a salvage value of $25. Pirates, Inc. uses the straight-line method of depreciation. Which of the following is the accumulated depreciation on the cannon after seven years?

(A) $45
(B) $315
(C) $326
(D) $675

39. MegaCorp decides to construct a new building. The building will have a useful life of 40 years and no salvage value. The following are the costs associated with this project:

Materials	$325,000
Labor	$ 78,000
Architects' Fees	$ 20,700
Building Permits	$ 800
Realtors' Fees	$ 5,000

MegaCorp computes the building's depreciation using the double-declining balance method. Which of the following is the depreciation expense for the building in its second year?

(A) $10,347.19
(B) $10,469.06
(C) $20,163.75
(D) $20,401.25

40. The Ridge Corp. bought a machine on January 1, 1999. In purchasing the machine, the company paid $50,000 cash and signed an interest-bearing note for $100,000. The estimated useful life of the machine is 5 years, after which time the salvage value is expected to be $15,000. The machine is expected to produce 67,500 widgets during its useful life. If 10,000 widgets are produced in 2000, and the Ridge Corp. uses the units-of-production method of depreciation, which of the following is the amount of depreciation on the machine that should be recorded in 2000?

(A) $20,000
(B) $22,222
(C) $30,000
(D) $40,000

41. Which of the following is a potential, NOT an existing, liability?

(A) Definitely determinable liabilities
(B) Contingent liabilities
(C) Estimated liabilities
(D) Product warranty liabilities

42. Continental Paper, Inc. makes a ninety-day promissory note for $15,000 with 6 percent interest. If the interest is deducted in advance, which of the following is the amount of the discount?

(A) $225
(B) $900
(C) $14,100
(D) $14,775

43. Tupalo, Inc. made a 120-day promissory note for $12,000 on October 1, 1999 with 8 percent discounted interest stated in the face amount. When Tupalo's accounting period ended on December 31, 1999, after adjusting entries were made, which of the following was the balance in Tupalo's prepaid interest account?

(A) $80 debit
(B) $80 credit
(C) $320 debit
(D) $320 credit

44. Which of the following is most likely to be an estimated liability?

(A) Dividends payable
(B) Income tax
(C) Payroll liabilities
(D) Notes payable

45. An employee worked 40 hours last week and earned $20 per hour. If the employee's federal income tax rate is 22 percent, Federal Unemployment Insurance Tax (FUTA) amounts to $75, and FICA taxes amount to $130, which of the following is the employer's payroll tax liability for the employee?

(A) $205
(B) $251
(C) $381
(D) $829

46. A contingent liability should be entered into the accounting records under which of the following circumstances?

(A) It is probable and can be reasonably estimated.
(B) It is dependent on an unlikely future event.
(C) It liability has a definable cost.
(D) It is possible and could cause great losses to the company.

47. The weekly payroll at the Monday Corp. is $1,255,000. Sixty-nine percent of Monday's employees will receive two weeks of paid vacation over the course of the year. Which of the following is Monday's weekly estimated liability for vacation pay?

(A) $16,652
(B) $132,625
(C) $346,380
(D) $865,950

48. A portion of long-term debt can be considered a current liability when the debt is

(A) paid off
(B) due within the next year and will be paid from current assets
(C) due within the long term and will be paid in cash
(D) under $100,000 and due in the next month

49. Treasury stock is considered to be which of the following accounts?

(A) An asset account
(B) An equity account
(C) A contra-equity account
(D) A liability account

50. Which of the following may increase the retained earnings balance each year?

(A) Decreasing revenues only
(B) Increasing net income
(C) Increasing the dividend payout ratio
(D) Increasing expenses only

51. A company becomes legally required to pay dividends on which of the following dates?

   (A) Declaration date
   (B) Date of registration with the SEC
   (C) Date of record
   (D) Date of payment

52. Which of the following statements best describes dividends in arrears?

   (A) They must be paid to preferred stockholders.
   (B) They do not represent actual liabilities.
   (C) They are included on the balance sheet.
   (D) They are included on the income statement.

53. Revenues, expenses, and earnings per share can be found on which of the following financial statements?

   (A) Statement of retained earnings
   (B) Statement of cash flows
   (C) Income statement
   (D) Balance sheet

54. The statement of cash flows classifies individual items as which of the following?

   (A) Operating, investing, or financing activities
   (B) Operating, interest, or financing activities
   (C) Assets, liabilities, or owner's equity
   (D) Revenues, expenses, or income

55. Which of the following most clearly depicts a company's liquidity?

   (A) Classified balance sheet
   (B) Statement of cash flows
   (C) Comparative balance sheet
   (D) Comparative income statement

56. A company's book value may be less than its market value for which of the following reasons?

   (A) The balance sheet reports items at historical cost.
   (B) Depreciation allocates assets' costs that would otherwise not be changed.
   (C) Inflation deteriorates a company's net worth.
   (D) All economic assets are included in the balance sheet.

57. If a tornado destroys one of a large corporation's buildings, the financial implications should be reported as an extraordinary loss on which of the following financial statements?

(A) Balance sheet
(B) Income statement
(C) Notes to financial statements
(D) The event should NOT be recorded because it is an extraordinary loss.

58. Which of the following is NOT included in the DuPont framework of the return on equity ratio?

(A) Profit margin
(B) Current ratio
(C) Asset turnover
(D) Asset to equity ratio

59. Accrued revenues are

(A) considered a contra account to revenue
(B) based on subjective evidence
(C) regarded as an accumulation of liability
(D) considered an asset account

60. The statement of cash flows includes all of the following EXCEPT

(A) funds from operations
(B) funds from financing activities
(C) funds allocated for depreciation
(D) cash paid for capital expenditures

POSTTEST ANSWERS

1. **The correct answer is (B).** Leverage is measured by the debt ratio = total assets divided by total liabilities: TA/TL = .74

2. **The correct answer is (D).** Choices (A), (B), and (C) are actual accounting assumptions.

3. **The correct answer is (C).** Increases in dividends decrease owner's equity. Owner's equity is decreased by credit entries; therefore, dividends increase with debit entries.

4. **The correct answer is (B).**

   Account receivables turnover = 150,000/20,150 = 7.4442
   Average collection period = 365/7.4442 = approximately 49

5. **The correct answer is (C).**

   Interest = principal(rate)(time)
   Interest = 15,000(.10)(2/12) = 250
   12/31 Interest expense 250
   Interest payable 250

6. **The correct answer is (B).** Beginning retained earnings – dividends + net income = ending retained earnings

   18,500 − 4,200 = 14,300
   17,100 − 14,300 = 2,800

7. **The correct answer is (A).** Contra accounts are paired with and deducted from related accounts.

8. **The correct answer is (C).** Adjusting entries are needed (1) to properly measure the period's income and (2) to bring related asset and liability accounts to correct balances for the financial statements.

9. **The correct answer is (B).** Recording each adjusting entry requires an entry for one balance sheet account and one income statement account.

10. **The correct answer is (A).** Understating revenue leads to an understatement of gross margin, which leads to an understatement of operating income, which leads to an understatement of net income. Choices (B) and (C) overstate net income. Choice (D) does not change net income as accounts receivable and cash are given the same consideration.

11. **The correct answer is (A).** Accrued revenues are those that have been earned but for which no entry has been made.

12. **The correct answer is (A).** Common size financial statements show all items as a percentage of revenue.

13. **The correct answer is (B).**

$$6,400/4 = 1,600$$
$$1,600(2) = 3,200$$

| Rent expense | 3,200 | |
| Prepaid rent | | 3,200 |

Prepaid rent is an asset account. This entry records the loss of half of prepaid rent. As such, prepaid rent is decreasing and, because it is an asset account, is credited.

14. **The correct answer is (D).** In periods of inflation, inventory that is "last in" will have a higher cost. Therefore, using LIFO will lower gross margin and thus lower gross income. A lower gross income leads to lower taxes.

15. **The correct answer is (A).** $(32)(7) + (12)(6.5) + (4)(6) = 338$

16. **The correct answer is (D).** Goods sold in transit, FOB shipping point are the property of those to whom the goods are being shipped.

17. **The correct answer is (B).** Purchases are considered an inventory cost. Therefore, not recording or understating purchases understates inventory. An understatement of inventory cost understates cost of goods sold.

18. **The correct answer is (C).** Divisional autonomy is not considered a part of control structure.

19. **The correct answer is (A).** A proper segregation of duties leads to the necessity of authorization by independent parties who then act as a check on control.

20. **The correct answer is (B).** An audit reasonably assures financial statements are presented fairly. It does not guarantee anything and is not meant to challenge internal systems and structures. CPAs work for companies that are not publicly traded and therefore do not have to report financial statements to the SEC.

21. **The correct answer is (A).** The proper journal entry for establishing a $2,000 petty cash fund includes a debit to "petty cash" and a credit to "cash."

22. **The correct answer is (C).** $2,535 - 25 + 750 = 3,260$

23. **The correct answer is (C).**

Assets: $517,600 + 250 = 517,850$
Liabilities: $323,400 - 4,500 = 318,900$
Owner's equity: $200,500 - 1,800 = 198,950$

24. **The correct answer is (C).** Maturity value = principal + interest

interest = principal (rate)(time)
$$= 15,000(60/360)(.12) = 300$$
$$15,000 + 300 = 15,300$$

25. **The correct answer is (A).** $(1,200)(90/360)(.10) = 30$

26. **The correct answer is (B).** When the maker of a note does not pay the note at maturity, the payee should transfer the note in the books to an account receivable.

27. **The correct answer is (B).** Accounts receivable turnover = sales/avg. accts. Rec. = 47,000/[.5(24,500 + [.6(47,000) − 19,200])]
a.r.t = 2.80

28. **The correct answer is (A).** The most accurate method of estimating uncollectible accounts is the aging accounts receivable method.

29. **The correct answer is (A).** .024(9,000,000 − 123,000 − 42,000) = 212,040. The allowance for uncollectible accounts is a contra-asset account and therefore gets credited.

30. **The correct answer is (B).**

> Accts. Rec. . . .
> > Allowance . . .
> Cash . . .
> > Accts. Rec. . . .

31. **The correct answer is (D).**

$$\text{Avg. collection period} = \frac{365}{\text{A.R. Turnover (A.R.T.)}}$$

$$\text{A.R.T.} = \frac{\text{sales}}{\text{avg. A.R.}} = \frac{9000}{2600} = 3.46$$

$$\text{a.c.p.} = \frac{365}{3.46} = 105 \text{ days}$$

32. **The correct answer is (B).**

> Net sales = sales − returns−discounts
> Net sales = 1,700,000 − 10,000 − 15,000 = 1,675,000
> Gross margin = 1,675,000(.3) = 502,500
> > COGS = net sales − gross margin
> > COGS = 1,675,000 − 502,500 = 1,172,000
> > COGAS = BI + purchases − returns + freight in
> > COGAS = 325,000 + 1,150,000 − 40,000 + 30,000 = 1,465,000
> > > EI = COGAS − COGS = 1,465,000 − 1,172,000 = 292,500
> Stolen amount = EI − physical count
> Stolen amount = 292,500 − 210,000 = 82,500

33. **The correct answer is (C).**

> 200(.97) = 194
> cash   194
> discount   6
> > A.R.   200

34. **The correct answer is (B).** The direct write-off method of recording uncollectible accounts violates the matching principle and therefore should not be used.

35. **The correct answer is (A).** The proper entry for receiving dividend payments is a debit to cash and a credit to dividend revenue.

36. **The correct answer is (C).** Unrealized gains (and losses) indicate that securities have changed in value and are still being held.

37. **The correct answer is (C).** Depreciation is a method of allocating an asset's cost over its useful life.

38. **The correct answer is (B).** Annual straight line depreciation: (cost − residual value)/useful life

$$(700 - 25)/15 = 45$$
$$45(7) = 315$$

39. **The correct answer is (C).** Depreciation percent $= 2/40 = .05$

$325,000 + 78,000 + 20,700 + 800 = 424, 500$ (Realtors' fees should not be included as building cost, but rather as land cost.)

Depreciation schedule:

Year	Yearly Depreciation	Carrying Value
1	21,225.00	403,275
2	20,163.75	

40. **The correct answer is (A).**

$$(150,000 - 15,000)/67,500 = 2 \text{ (per unit depreciation)}$$
$$(10,000 \text{ units})(2) = \$20,000 \text{ depreciation expense}$$

41. **The correct answer is (B).** Contingent liabilities are potential liabilities (i.e., they're dependent on future events).

42. **The correct answer is (A).**

$$\text{Interest} = \text{principle(rate)(time)} = 15,000(.06)(90/360) = 225$$

The amount discounted when interest is deducted in advance is the interest expense.

43. **The correct answer is (A).**

$$I = P \times R \times T = 12,000(.08)(120/360) = 320$$
$$320(.25) = 80$$

One fourth of the prepaid interest remains. Prepaid interest is an asset account, so this is a debit entry.

44. **The correct answer is (B).** Income tax is dependent on results of operations over the course of the year. These figures are often not known until after the end of the accounting period.

45. **The correct answer is (A).** The employer matches the employee's FICA and pays all of FUTA. $130 + 75 = 205$. The employer does not pay 22 percent of the employee's taxes.

46. **The correct answer is (A).** The FASB has established the two requirements for entering a contingent liability into the accounting records as the liability being probable and reasonably estimated.

47. **The correct answer is (C).** 1,255,000(2/50)(.69) = 346,380

48. **The correct answer is (B).** A portion of long-term debt can be considered a current liability when it is due within the next year and will be paid from current assets.

49. **The correct answer is (C).** Buying one's own shares back reduces one's equity.

50. **The correct answer is (B).**

51. **The correct answer is (A).** A company becomes legally required to pay dividends on the declaration date.

52. **The correct answer is (B).** Dividends in arrears must not necessarily be paid (dependent on whether or not the company decides to pay dividends); thus, they're not actual liabilities.

53. **The correct answer is (C).** Revenues, expenses, and EPS can be found on the income statement.

54. **The correct answer is (A).** The statement of cash flows classifies individual items as operating, investing, or financing activities.

55. **The correct answer is (A).** Classified balance sheets distinguish between current and long-term assets.

56. **The correct answer is (A).** Historical cost can be less than market value, so the market price per share is higher than the initial cost per share.

57. **The correct answer is (B).** Extraordinary gains and losses are recorded on the income statement.

58. **The correct answer is (B).** DuPont framework: ROE = profit margin(asset turnover)(asset to equity ratio)

59. **The correct answer is (D).** Accrued revenues are considered an asset account.

60. **The correct answer is (C).** Depreciation is a non-cash expense.

Principles of Supervision

PRETEST

1. Which of the following illustrates the key difference between supervisors and upper management?

    (A) Supervisors work directly with employees to accomplish goals and objectives on a daily basis.

    (B) Upper management has sole concern for budgetary concerns.

    (C) Supervisors are responsible for staffing and training.

    (D) Upper management is more at risk when companies downsize.

2. All of the following are involved in the duties of supervisors EXCEPT

    (A) decision making

    (B) strategic development

    (C) staffing

    (D) communicating

3. All of the following statements describe the roles and responsibilities of supervisors EXCEPT:

    (A) Supervisors spend more time directing and coordinating whereas upper management spends time planning and organizing.

    (B) Supervisors have little concern for identifying goals and objectives and motivating employees to meet them.

    (C) Supervisors are involved in action and results rather than theory and hypothesis.

    (D) Supervisors enable a company to function as a single entity, connecting workers with other departments in the entire organization.

4. All of the following are steps in the decision-making process EXCEPT

    (A) determining who is responsible for the problem occurring

    (B) determining and identifying the problem

    (C) evaluating facts and collecting information

    (D) identifying a range of alternatives for solving the problem

5. A decision tree is used to

   (A) aid in determining future profits and controlling expenses

   (B) perform a detailed cost-benefit analysis

   (C) provide a graphical illustration of how different alternatives result in various outcomes

   (D) illustrate the flow of work through various stages of the production process

6. An example of an authoritative leadership style would be a supervisor who

   (A) motivates through rewards and recognition

   (B) delegates tasks whenever appropriate

   (C) maintains a high degree of control

   (D) makes decisions by involving employees

7. Being held responsible for employee performance without being able to evaluate and correct mistakes is most likely a situation of inadequate

   (A) authority

   (B) leadership

   (C) communication

   (D) planning

8. Which of the following is NOT a key function in the supervisory process?

   (A) Staffing

   (B) Organizing

   (C) Outplacement

   (D) Directing

9. The process of determining which goals should be achieved and developing a scheme for achieving those goals is known as

   (A) organizing

   (B) scheduling

   (C) controlling

   (D) planning

10. Which of the following steps occurs first in the sequential phases of supervisory planning?

   (A) Developing standards for monitoring performance

   (B) Identifying and selecting an action plan

   (C) Selecting the objectives to be achieved

   (D) Preparing a budget and cost outline

11. A clear understanding of organizational goals will most likely allow a supervisor to
    (A) achieve production goals according to a specified time-table and budget
    (B) determine whether a short-term or long-term strategy is required to meet the company's goals
    (C) obtain input from employees who want to be involved in the planning process
    (D) create departmental plans that are consistent with a company's overall objectives and mission statement

12. A supervisor is utilizing a long-term planning approach when
    (A) determining whether or not to include requests for additional staffing in an annual budget proposal
    (B) hiring a replacement through a temporary agency when a worker is on vacation
    (C) requesting an extension of a weekly production deadline due to worker illness
    (D) revising a monthly work schedule in order to meet sales quotas

13. Planning differs from controlling in that
    (A) planning is dependent on information supplied by management and controlling is implemented only on the supervisory level
    (B) controlling is task-oriented and time-oriented, whereas planning usually considers a long-term strategy
    (C) planning considers the goals to be accomplished and controlling evaluates whether they are being achieved
    (D) planning does not require employee involvement or input, whereas controlling requires a supervisor to involve employees

14. Which of the following is essential to a supervisor's development of a good departmental plan?
    (A) Having adequate training and employee development programs
    (B) Understanding the company's overall strategy and goals
    (C) Establishing clear standards for employee performance
    (D) Performing a cost-benefit analysis before finishing the plan

15. Involving workers in the planning process typically results in which of the following?
    (A) A decrease in productivity
    (B) A decrease in absenteeism
    (C) An increase in worker commitment
    (D) An increase in labor expenses

16. The management function of assigning tasks and authority to organizational personnel is referred to as

    (A) delegating
    (B) recruiting
    (C) staffing
    (D) assessing

17. A company that has a decentralized structure most likely promotes a

    (A) low degree of empowerment
    (B) high degree of delegation
    (C) low degree of involvement
    (D) high degree of control

18. All of the following are examples of line managers EXCEPT

    (A) a sales and marketing manager who reports to the vice president of marketing
    (B) a corporate lawyer who reports directly to the president or CEO
    (C) an accounting department supervisor who reports to the vice president of finance
    (D) a production supervisor who reports to the production manager

19. A disadvantage of having numerous units within an organization would be

    (A) a high level of organizational complexity and bureaucracy
    (B) a simple organizational structure
    (C) unclear lines of authority
    (D) a focus on solving problems

20. "Decisions should be made at the lowest level possible" is most likely the philosophy of an organization that

    (A) operates autocratically
    (B) operates as a subsidiary
    (C) is centralized
    (D) is decentralized

PRETEST ANSWERS

1. **The correct answer is (A).** Unlike upper-management employees, supervisors work directly with their workers on a daily basis to accomplish tasks, goals, and objectives.

2. **The correct answer is (B).** Strategic development, determining the appropriate long-term direction of an organization, is typically the responsibility of upper-management personnel such as vice presidents, division managers, presidents, and CEO's.

3. **The correct answer is (B).** Supervisors play a key role in identifying goals and objectives for their units or departments and providing subordinates with the support needed to meet those goals.

4. **The correct answer is (A).** Determining who is responsible for a problem is not part of the decision-making process that is involved in attempting to solve a problem.

5. **The correct answer is (C).** A decision tree is a visual tool used to illustrate the probable change that will result from following various courses of action.

6. **The correct answer is (C).** One of the traits of an authoritative or autocratic leader is the maintenance of a high degree of control instead of allowing subordinates to control aspects of their own jobs.

7. **The correct answer is (A).** Adequate authority allows supervisors to evaluate and correct their employees' mistakes and accomplish job goals.

8. **The correct answer is (C).** The key functions in the supervisory process are planning, organizing, staffing, directing, and controlling.

9. **The correct answer is (D).** Planning is the process of determining which goals should be achieved and how to develop a scheme for achieving them.

10. **The correct answer is (C).** Selecting the objectives to be achieved is the first step in the sequential phases of supervisory planning.

11. **The correct answer is (D).** A supervisor must have a clear understanding of organizational goals in order to create departmental plans that are consistent with a company's overall objectives and mission statement.

12. **The correct answer is (A).** A long-term decision is usually one that will affect a future unspecified duration of time and is made in advance. Short-term decisions are usually measured in terms of short periods of time.

13. **The correct answer is (C).** Planning considers the goals to be accomplished and controlling evaluates whether they are being achieved.

14. **The correct answer is (B).** Supervisory planning at the departmental level must be consistent with overall company objectives in order to be successful.

15. **The correct answer is (C).** When a supervisor solicits the input of employees, it often results in an increase in their commitment.

16. **The correct answer is (A).** Delegation is the function of assigning tasks and authority to organizational personnel.

17. **The correct answer is (B).** One of the characteristics of a decentralized organization is that decision making and participation are distributed throughout levels of management.

18. **The correct answer is (B).** A corporate lawyer reporting directly to the president or CEO is an example of a staff function that is supportive and relieves line personnel of tasks related to legal issues affecting the organization.

19. **The correct answer is (A).** Line organizations with numerous units typically have a simpler structure, more clarity in regards to lines of authority, and more focus on solving problems. One disadvantage of line organizations is their higher degree of bureaucracy.

20. **The correct answer is (D).** One of the characteristics of a decentralized organization is that decisions are made at the lowest level possible.

GENERAL OVERVIEW

THE SUPERVISOR'S ROLES AND RESPONSIBILITIES

Achieving the goals of an organization requires that the organization's resources be managed. **Managers** deploy human, information, and physical resources to meet the objectives of the organization. In most organizations, a major distinction between managers and employees is that managers direct the work that employees perform.

However, all managers are not alike. At the top of an organization are the **executives**, managers responsible for establishing the broad objectives, plans, and policies of the organization. Executives are in charge of the **middle managers**, who plan and carry out programs that help achieve the larger objectives set by the executives. In turn, middle managers direct the work of other managers and supervisors who report to them.

WHAT IS A SUPERVISOR?

Under the guidance of a middle manager, a **supervisor** plans, directs, and controls the work done by a group of employees. The actual tasks performed by supervisors may vary considerably, because supervisors are found in all types of organizations, such as retail, manufacturing, services, and government offices. However, the common thread that binds all supervisors is that they are expected to work with and through employees to achieve the goals of their work units. Rather than doing the hands-on work themselves, they are expected to direct and motivate their workers to perform the work.

Skills Needed by Supervisors

To be a successful supervisor, a person needs skills in three areas:

1. **Technical skills**—These are the skills required to perform the jobs done by the hands-on workers. They are extremely important because a supervisor needs to know how to perform the tasks that he or she is training others to do. Technical skills are also required when monitoring the work of others. For example, a supervisor in charge of a group of airline mechanics must be able to maintain and repair airplanes.

2. **Human relations skills**—The ability to get along with others—both individuals and groupsùis essential for a supervisor. Much supervisory work involves motivating, communicating, and negotiating, both with workers and with management.

3. **Administrative skills**—A supervisor must be able to plan and control the work of a group of people as well as his or her own work. To do this, he or she must understand the organization and its systems and must use or devise systems to manage the work of the group.

The technical skills of supervisors are so various that they are not taught in courses on supervision. Instead, supervision courses focus on the human relations and administrative skills common to all supervisors.

The Many Roles of a Supervisor

Supervisors have a pivotal position in organizations because they provide the interface between management and workers. As such, they play many roles in their daily interactions. They lead, negotiate, facilitate, manage, and communicate in many ways.

- **As employees**—Supervisors report to middle managers, carry out the objectives of their managers, and are responsible for representing their work groups to management.

- **As bosses**—In turn, they manage the work of their employees, providing guidance, training, monitoring of workflow, and work conditions. They help head off problems and solve them as they arise.

- **As peers**—In the course of working in an organization, supervisors draw on the skills and expertise of staff specialists to help them achieve the goals of their work units. In addition, they cooperate with other supervisors in the organization, fostering teamwork across work units.

- **As labor relations specialists**—Many supervisors oversee a unionized work force, and they are responsible for balancing the objectives of the organization as well as the welfare of its employees.

PROBLEM SOLVING AND DECISION MAKING

Problem solving and decision making are major components of a supervisor's job. **Problems** are disruptive occurrences or unsettled matters that must be solved if the organization is to function properly. Some problems have already arisen or are occurring in the present, such as a cost overrun. And other problems are expected to happen in the future, but they can be forestalled or minimized through good planning now.

Supervisors solve problems by thoroughly reviewing relevant information to find the causes of problems and then by applying their knowledge and skills to devise potential solutions. At each step of the way, **decision making** is involved. For example, what information is relevant to solving the problem, and what information is irrelevant? Which solution is best? Whenever there is a choice of more than one way to proceed, a decision is required.

Values and Ethics

The **values** that people bring to their work vary. Some people value work in and of itself; others value their paycheck and little else. Some value their individuality; others value group harmony. A supervisor should understand his or her own values, the organization's values, and individual employees' values in order to develop an understanding of human behavior and organizational culture.

Ethics involves the proper behavior expected of an individual or a profession. Ethics usually involves issues of right and wrong. Supervisors should behave and treat employees ethically.

Responsibility and Authority

Supervisors have many **responsibilities**—the tasks and outcomes they are held accountable for, whether they perform them personally or delegate them to others. For example, controlling costs and meeting deadlines are supervisory responsibilities. In order to carry out their responsibilities, supervisors must have **authority**, that is, the power to make decisions and take action. Ideally, a supervisor has the authority necessary to carry out his or her responsibilities.

MANAGEMENT FUNCTIONS

Like other managers, supervisors carry out their responsibilities by using the basic management functions. These are five broad processes: planning, organizing, staffing, directing, and controlling.

PLANNING

Planning is the process of establishing guidelines for achieving objectives. The outcome of the planning process is a **plan**, or a road map for achieving goals.

Types of Plans—There are several types of plans in organizations.

- **Long-range plans** are usually prepared by higher management. These plans generally focus from one to five years into the future.

- **Short-range plans** are usually the responsibility of supervisors. Short-range plans may involve operations that last a day, a month, a quarter, or a year.

- **Standing plans** involve activities that go on all the time without much change. Standing plans cover matters such as employee discipline, general employment practices, and purchasing procedures.

- **Single-use plans** are drawn up for unique projects and tasks. Designing a new computer game or preparing a departmental budget are examples of activities that require single-use plans.

The Planning Process

The first step in the planning process is to set **objectives**—targets toward which the work unit is expected to move. Some of a supervisor's objectives are set by upper management. Other objectives may be set by the supervisor. Objectives may be very broad, such as making a higher profit each year, or they may be very specific, such as producing 20,000 widgets per week. Whether they are broad or specific, they should be stated as explicitly as possible, explaining both the outcome and the time frame. For example, an objective may be to complete 95 percent of all jobs within budget (the outcome) during the next year (the time frame).

Once objectives are set, then plans can be developed to achieve them. A plan outlines how the objective will be achieved. A plan may include **schedules**, which tell what tasks must be done, who will do them, and when they must be started and finished; and **procedures**, which explain the methods that will be used in step-by-step detail.

Because planning involves looking into the future and making decisions based on what is known today, plans are often based on incomplete information. Conditions may change in the future, so good plans are flexible, allowing for alternate courses of action.

Part of planning involves scheduling the time of employees. In general, a department should not be scheduled to 100 percent of capacity because that leaves no time for the unexpected, which always occurs. On the other hand, underscheduling has its pitfalls, too. It leaves people stretching tasks to fill the time available. One way to avoid this situation is to have secondary back-up projects to do when regular assignments have been completed.

Time Management and Delegation

How does a supervisor plan his or her own time? In general, a supervisor has two types of time: time under his or her control, and time not under his or her control. The time not under the supervisor's control—for example, a meeting with the boss or an emergency with a customer—cannot be planned. The remaining time can be planned, usually by using **time management** techniques such as setting priorities, using a desk calendar, and preparing a daily "to do" list.

One advantage supervisors have in accomplishing all their work is the ability to **delegate** tasks. In general, supervisors benefit when they delegate work that is below their capabilities, leaving themselves time to focus on the big jobs involving management skills. However, delegation is a skill that must be learned. Many supervisors, especially those new to the job, are uncomfortable with delegating tasks to subordinates, feeling that they themselves could do the job better. Unfortunately, this approach leaves supervisors with an overwhelming workload.

ORGANIZING

Organizing is a natural outgrowth of planning. At its most fundamental, **organizing** involves a division of labor. For instance, there are thousands of tasks that need to be done in order to accomplish an organization's objectives. These tasks can be divided up among various people, each of whom will have a job to do. People with related jobs, such as production jobs or marketing jobs, can be grouped together into departments. Establishing work relationships among the departments allows all the people in the organization to function effectively.

Types of Organizational Structures

There are several ways that organizations can be set up.

- **Functional organization**—In a functional organization, each group of people performing related activities reports to a functional manager. For example, in a retail organization all the people involved in stocking storerooms, shelves, and displays are in a single department reporting to a single manager. This is the simplest type of organization.

- **Line and staff organization**—A line and staff organization is a functional organization with additional departments, called staff departments, that give advice and support to the departments directly involved in producing the goods or services, the line departments. For example, in a hotel chain, the line departments may be those involved in operating a particular hotel, and the staff departments may be those providing advertising, computer systems, and legal services.

- **Product or divisional organization**—The product or divisional organization is a variation of the line and staff organization in which each major product line has its own suborganization or division. This is the typical organization for automobile companies such as General Motors, which has Saturn, Chevrolet, and other divisions.

- **Matrix organization**—The matrix structure is suited for organizations that are structured around projects, task-force work, or other one-of-a-kind programs. In this type of structure, a project manager calls together a team of specialists from various parts of the organization to work together on a project. When the project is complete, the people go back to their home units until reassigned. The matrix structure is often used in research and development firms, consulting organizations, and engineering companies.

- **Centralized versus decentralized organization**—In a centralized organization, authority tends to be concentrated at the top. There are many levels of management, facilities tend to be in one location, and functions such as computer systems are provided from a single internal source. In contrast, a decentralized organization consists of smaller, more autonomous units centered on product lines, geographic location, or marketing targets. In decentralized organizations, much authority rests with people at lower levels of the organization, such as supervisors.

SPAN OF CONTROL

The number of workers a supervisor must work with is referred to as **span of control**. There is no ideal span of control. If workers perform jobs that are relatively similar and that do not involve many differing tasks, then a supervisor can supervise more workers—up to fifty or so. On the other hand, if the workers perform complex jobs with diverse tasks, the supervisor's span of control is less—perhaps half a dozen people. The key to span of control is the amount of communicating the supervisor must do with each employee. The more interaction that is required, the fewer employees the supervisor can effectively supervise.

Chain of Command

In an organization, just as in the military, there is a chain of command. In general, this means that responsibility, authority, orders, and information start at the top and then proceed downward from one management level to the next without skipping levels or crossing over to another chain of command. Information and requests going upward would follow the same path.

In general, it makes sense to follow the chain of command in a particular organization in order to get things done. However, in emergencies or special situations that may not be possible. In some organizations it is difficult to follow the chain of command because it has not been clearly defined. For example, two people may have overlapping job responsibilities yet report to two different supervisors. Or one person is asked to report to two people. In line and staff and matrix organizations, the chain of command can become blurred when people from different departments collaborate on special projects. In those situations, the chain of command is often worked out through trial and error and experience.

Staffing

Supervisors usually have more people reporting directly to them than do upper-level managers. In addition, they work directly with their staffs to get the work done, whereas middle managers tend to work more with information than with people. Thus, effective staffing is crucial to a supervisor's success on the job.

There are several aspects to staffing. The **staffing process** begins with the organization's structure—the kinds of jobs and workers needed to meet the organization's objectives. The supervisor has little responsibility for this aspect of staffing because it is beyond the scope of his or her work unit. Within the work unit, however, the supervisor is responsible for forecasting how many and what type of employees are needed to accomplish the unit's goals and recruiting, interviewing, and selecting potential candidates, bearing in mind the legal considerations that affect the employment process. Once workers are on staff, the supervisor must orient and train them.

Forecasting Needs

To determine the number of workers needed to accomplish the work unit's goals, the supervisor takes into account typical workloads, schedules, vacations, and absenteeism. In some large organizations, information such as time studies or labor standards is available to help supervisors make more accurate estimates. This information is not necessary, however.

The basic procedure is to figure out what the work unit is expected to produce for the next period. Then the supervisor calculates how many and what type of workers are required to do the work during the time period. This can be done by checking times for previous similar jobs or by breaking down each job into activities and making time estimates for each activity. If the jobs are dependent on machine speed, the estimate is based on that. Allowances are then made for vacations and other absences.

Recruiting, Interviewing, and Selecting

The supervisor's role in recruiting, interviewing, and selecting varies. In a small organization, the supervisor may do everything with the help of a receptionist or secretary. In a large organization, the human resources department may take over the recruitment function and do the preliminary interviews. The selection of a candidate is usually the supervisor's responsibility, although his or her manager may also play a role.

The purpose of **recruitment** is to develop a large pool of applicants, increasing the chance that a suitable person can be found. Word-of-mouth, newspaper classified ads, Internet postings, and government agencies are all ways in which potential workers are found.

The application form, brief preliminary interview, and in some cases, performance test, physical exam, and references weed out unqualified people from the pool of applicants. Applicants who pass these steps are then interviewed by the supervisor. The purpose of this **interview** is to determine whether the applicant is a good match for the job, both in terms of technical skills and in terms of personal characteristics. To do this, the supervisor gives information about the job, the organization, and the expectations he or she has and elicits information about the candidate's experiences and plans. The subject matter of the interview is limited by law, as described below.

When **selecting** a job candidate, supervisors try to pick the best-qualified person for the job at hand. They sift through all the information, looking for a good match in terms of skills, values, and personality.

LEGAL CONSIDERATIONS IN THE EMPLOYMENT PROCESS

According to equal employment opportunity laws, potential employees cannot be asked about their race, color, religion, national origin, sex, age, and marital status. Questions about other matters, such as disabilities and physical capabilities, are limited to seeking information directly relevant to the candidate's ability to perform the job for which he or she is being interviewed. Questions about education and experience are generally unrestricted. The important point is that all questions must be relevant to the job in question. In legal terms, questions must be about **bona fide occupational qualifications**.

Tests administered in the employment screening process must also meet several legal standards. Personality, intelligence, or career interest tests must be statistically valid and reliable. Tests of general aptitude are often open to legal challenge by applicants. In general, tests must be directly related to the job's content and must not discriminate unfairly against the person taking them.

ORIENTING AND TRAINING

Orienting new employees to the organization and work unit is done by the human resources department and the supervisor in large organizations and by the supervisor alone in small organizations. Topics include pay information, hours, lunch periods, time reporting systems, benefits, calling in sick or late, and safety rules. In addition, the supervisor gives the employee a tour and introduces him or her to coworkers.

Training workers is the supervisor's responsibility. **On-the-job training** involves four steps: (1) preparing a worker to learn by explaining the job's larger context and why it is important; (2) demonstrating and explaining the job one step at a time; (3) letting the worker perform each step under supervision; and (4) gradually withdrawing in order to let the employee work on his or her own. In addition to on-the-job training, there are other training methods, including lectures, vestibule training (similar to on-the-job training but done away from the workstation), apprenticeship training, and computer-assisted instruction.

DIRECTING

Directing the work of a group of employees involves several human relations skills and activities. These include leadership, motivation, performance appraisal, working with a diverse work force, maintaining discipline, counseling employees, and developing employees.

LEADING

In order to lead, a supervisor must have the ability to get workers to do what he or she wants them to do. **Leadership** involves the ability to persuade people, to influence their actions through the power and authority of the supervisory position as well as through one's personal power and authority, and to create an atmosphere of rapport in which people are willing to cooperate.

There are several styles of leadership:

- **Autocratic leadership**—The supervisor is the boss; he or she makes the decisions and gives orders.

- **Democratic leadership**—The supervisor consults with employees before making decisions that promotes involvement and teamwork.

- **Participative leadership**—The supervisor is a dispenser of information, exercising little control and depending on the employees' good sense to do things properly. This approach works only with mature, experienced workers.

- **Results-centered leadership**—The supervisor emphasizes the job to be done and minimizes the personalities involved.

- **Situational leadership**—The supervisor chooses a leadership style based on rapport with workers and their personalities, the nature of the situation, and the amount of real authority that he or she possesses. For example, in an emergency, the autocratic leadership style would be appropriate to get quick, effective action.

MOTIVATING

Motivation is the process that makes a person behave in a certain way. According to **Abraham H. Maslow's hierarchy of needs**, an individual may be motivated by the need for survival, security, companionship, respect, and self-actualization (achievement, power, growth, and a sense of personal worth). A good supervisor can help an individual realize these needs in the context of work, promoting job satisfaction and ensuring productivity.

A good deal of motivation comes from the work itself. When jobs are designed with people in mind, job satisfaction and performance improve. Factors that tend to improve workers' motivation include doing a whole job rather than parts of it; having regular contact with users or customers; using a variety of tasks and skills; directing one's own work; getting feedback from work results rather than from others; and having an opportunity for self-development.

APPRAISING PERFORMANCE

Supervisors observe and evaluate their workers' performance informally on a daily basis and usually conduct formal **performance appraisals** once or twice a year, meeting with each worker. In many organizations, the outcome of formal performance appraisals directly influences the employment status of workers, affecting terminations, transfers, demotions, promotions, and raises, although in some organizations seniority or union rules prevail over performance appraisals. Equally important, performance appraisals provide supervisors with a means to improve workers' job performance.

Organizations that conduct formal appraisals usually have very specific guidelines that the supervisor must follow. The format of the appraisal, the job descriptions, and the standards to which employees will be held are all described in detail. There are several basic formats:

- **Behavioral format**—In this format, performance is evaluated in terms of a range of behaviors expected in given job-related situations. Its weakness is that it focuses on behavior rather than results. Still, it is generally considered an effective form of appraisal.
- **Trait format**—This type of appraisal focuses on personality traits such as initiative; its weakness is that it is very subjective.

- **Results-oriented format**—When employees have stated and agreed-upon goals, performance appraisals focus on evaluating whether these goals have been attained. This type of appraisal is not appropriate for line workers whose activities are closely controlled by their supervisors; however, it may be used to evaluate the supervisor's performance.

Like the employment interview, the performance appraisal is subject to legal considerations. Legal issues include equal pay for equal work; discrimination on the basis of age, sex, religion, color, or national origin; accommodation of the disabled and veterans; and equal employment opportunity. To head off legal challenges, supervisors must (1) be sure the appraisal is based on what the job actually requires, (2) be objective in their judgments, (3) base the appraisal on documented facts, and (4) avoid saying anything discriminatory, whether positive or negative.

WORKING WITH DIVERSE EMPLOYEES

Today's workforce consists of men, women, the young, the old, the disabled, and people of various races and ethnic backgrounds. Although there are laws intended to protect individuals against discrimination in employment, and many organizations set up human resources systems to minimize problems, supervisors must interact on a daily basis with people of all types. Human relations and communication skills are essential to ensure the smooth working of groups of diverse people. Supervisors need to strike a balance between supervising everyone according to the same basic principles and allowing for the individuality of each worker.

In addition to dealing fairly with people of diverse backgrounds, supervisors must also cope with troubled employees. Many employees bring personal problems, such as emotional disturbances and substance abuse, to work. Others react to personal difficulties with a high rate of absenteeism. The personal problems of an employee are not the concern of the supervisor unless his or her performance on the job is adversely affected. The challenge for the supervisor is to differentiate between an employee whose troubles are temporary and minor and one whose problems are deep seated and serious. Those in the latter category are beyond the type of help a supervisor can offer; they need professional intervention.

COUNSELING EMPLOYEES

A supervisor may be able to offer limited help in the form of counseling to an employee whose personal difficulties are interfering with job performance. There are three major signs indicating that an employee needs counseling: (1) normal behavior taken to extremes; (2) a high level of anxiety; or (3) inability to cope, resulting in a breakdown.

The focus of employee counseling is problem solving: helping the employee release the internal pressures that are interfering with job performance. During a counseling session, which should take place in private, the supervisor listens and facilitates the discussion. Supervisors should not control the direction of the session, offer diagnoses, opinions, or moral judgments, and criticize and argue. The supervisor should talk only about job performance problems, solutions, and avenues of help.

Counseling rarely has immediate results, so supervisors must be patient. However, if no results are seen after two counseling sessions, the supervisor should report the case, in confidence, to the organization's health professionals.

MAINTAINING DISCIPLINE

Most employees have a good measure of self-discipline. They are willing to behave according to reasonable rules and standards on the job. A supervisor can foster this innate self-discipline by creating a positive motivational climate for employees and creating a cohesive group of workers who will exert considerable peer pressure on possible dissenters.

Despite a positive approach to discipline, from time to time supervisors will encounter people who do not behave acceptably. They may break rules concerning work schedules, safety standards, punctuality, workmanship, and treatment of coworkers, or they may behave in an insubordinate manner, refusing to carry out reasonable work-related instructions. If the behavior is caused by personal problems, it is dealt with first through counseling, as discussed above. If the performance problem persists or is the behavior of a chronic rule-breaker, then disciplinary action is necessary.

Effective discipline requires that disciplinary rules are clearly understood by everyone at the outset. When a rule is broken, disciplinary action should be taken as soon as possible and not delayed. Supervisors must be impartial, consistent, and fair in disciplining employees. And after an employee is disciplined, the supervisor must follow up to ensure that the problem has been solved.

Many organizations follow a system of progressive discipline in which the penalties are appropriate to the violation or to the accumulation of violations. Steps in such a system may include informal talks, oral warnings, written warnings, disciplinary layoff, demotion, and termination. At each step the supervisor tries to help the employee improve his or her performance.

DEVELOPING EMPLOYEES

Supervisors are responsible for training and developing their employees. To do this effectively, they keep records for each worker indicating what tasks the worker performs effectively, what tasks the worker needs to be trained to do, and how and when the worker will be trained.

In addition to training employees to do the work expected of them, supervisors can develop the skills of employees who seem to have the potential to take on more responsibility, whether in the context of the existing job or through transfer or promotion. Often this is done by delegating supervisory tasks to the employee or by nominating them for extra training or education to improve their qualifications and prospects for promotion.

CONTROLLING

The purpose of an organization's **control process** is to ensure that plans are being carried out and objectives are being reached. From the supervisor's point of view, this means ensuring that the work unit is attaining production goals and meeting quality standards.

The supervisor's role in the control process is twofold. In one role, the supervisor observes the activities of his or her work unit to see whether tasks are being performed properly, work conditions are appropriate, and results are being achieved as expected. In the supervisor's second role, he or she focuses on problem solving and decision making. He or she identifies the source of the problem, comes up with solutions, and decides which solution to implement.

Steps in the Control Process

There are four steps in the control process.

1. **Establish performance standards**. Establishing standards is actually part of the planning process. Standards of quantity, quality, and time are established during planning as objectives. Also established at that time are tolerances, amounts by which a standard may fall short.

2. **Collect information in order to measure performance.** Many of an organization's systems produce control data, such as time cards or production tallies. In addition, the supervisor collects information through observation.

3. **Compare actual performance to the performance standards.** The supervisor compares the control data to the standards, and if they are within the tolerance limits, the supervisor takes no further action. If there is a gap between the actual performance and the performance standard, then the supervisor must take action.

4. **Take corrective action.** The supervisor first finds the cause of the gap in performance and then takes steps to remove or minimize the cause, bringing performance back up to standard. It is also possible, if the cause cannot be dealt with, that the plan or standard may need to be changed.

Budgetary Controls

A **budget** is a plan for the expenses incurred in the operation of a work unit during a specific period of time. Some work units have flexible budgets that account for variations in expenses based on expected variations in output. A supervisor may or may not develop the work unit's budget, but he or she is responsible for meeting it. Thus a work unit budget is a major control document for a supervisor.

If there is a deviation from the budget, the supervisor is expected to determine the cause of the deviation and take corrective action. However, since budgets are estimates of future revenues and costs, they are sometimes inaccurate. Changes in economic conditions, costs of materials, or costs of supplies can make a budget inaccurate. Thus, a supervisor should monitor expense costs on a regular basis (weekly, monthly, or quarterly) so that deviations can be controlled or the budget revised.

OTHER TOPICS OF CONCERN TO SUPERVISORS
LEGAL ISSUES

The law plays a role in several areas that affect a supervisor's work. These include, but are by no means limited to, equal employment opportunity laws and occupational health and safety regulations.

Equal Employment Opportunity (EEO) Laws

These laws are an outgrowth of the civil rights movement, and they cover many aspects of employment. Among other things, the laws require equal pay for equal work; prohibit job discrimination in all employment practices on the basis of race, color, sex, religion, or national origin; institute affirmative action programs to redress past discrimination; prohibit discrimination against disabled workers and workers over 40 years of age unless bona fide occupational qualification can be demonstrated; prohibit discrimination against Vietnam veterans by federal contractors; and forbid sexual harassment.

Occupational Safety and Health Act (OSHA)

With the establishment of the Occupational Safety and Health Administration in 1971, the federal government assumed a large role in regulating the health and safety of workers. The standards set by the government provide minimum specifications for exits, environmental controls, noise, radiation, hazardous materials, sanitation, fire protection, and electrical installations, to name just a few items. Organizations are expected to train employees in safety procedures, both general procedures such as fire drills and procedures specific to the industry such as welding. In addition, OSHA requires extensive recordkeeping about accidents. A great deal of responsibility for the implementation of OSHA regulations falls on supervisors.

UNIONS

In a nonunion environment, supervisors must work within the law and the policies of their companies. When supervisors work with employees who are members of a **labor union**, they must also take into account the impact of the labor contract on policies, practices, and procedures. Supervisors are considered the legal representatives of their companies. Their employers are responsible for any actions supervisors take when dealing with employees and unions.

The basic labor-management law is the **National Labor Relations Act (Wagner Act)** as amended by the **Taft-Hartley Act**. These laws guarantee employees the right to act in a group, if they wish, to bargain for wages, working conditions, and hours. They also prohibit certain unfair practices on the part of management and impose controls on the activities of unions.

If employees are represented by a union, they negotiate with management over the terms of their labor contract, a process called **collective bargaining**. Although supervisors are rarely involved in collective bargaining, their actions over the preceding period influence the terms of the contract. In addition, supervisors are responsible for abiding by the terms of the contract once it has been agreed upon.

INCREASING PRODUCTIVITY

Productivity is a measure of the output created by a set of inputs. In other words, it is a measure of efficiency. It is usually expressed as a ratio: productivity equals output value divided by input costs.

Supervisors can help improve productivity by improving technical factors. They can simplify product or service design, maintain equipment properly, mechanize and computerize operations, improve work area layouts, and improve the condition of materials and supplies. They can also improve productivity by focusing on human factors. Well-trained, highly motivated workers are far more productive than poorly trained, unmotivated workers.

QUALITY CONCERNS

Quality is a measure of the degree to which a product, service, or process conforms to the standards that have been set for it. Although quality is a shared responsibility involving design, materials, purchasing, manufacturing or operations, and inspection, the supervisor is in a unique position to influence the quality of the work produced under his or her guidance. In some organizations there is a formal inspection and quality control function; in others that responsibility falls to the supervisor. Various techniques are used to improve quality, including:

- **Statistical quality control**—This is a technical method that uses frequency-distribution charts, quality control charts, and sampling tables to monitor quality levels. It is often administered by a separate quality control department.

- **Zero Defects**—In this system, responsibility for quality rests with employees. Everyone in the organization is taught to care about accuracy, completeness, attention to detail, and good work habits. In this system, workers aim for consistently high quality output by eliminating errors in planning and implementation.

- **Quality Circles**—As in Zero Defects, Quality Circles accept high quality as a starting point. People directly involved in a particular procedure, system, operating unit, or product will meet (usually voluntarily) to examine and suggest solutions to common problems of quality.

Another aspect of quality that a supervisor influences is **quality of work life**. This is the idea that work must be psychologically and spiritually rewarding in addition to being monetarily rewarding. Supervisors can improve the quality of work life for employees by being flexible, accepting individual differences in motivation, encouraging feedback, and facilitating work rather than giving orders.

STRESS MANAGEMENT

By its nature, the job of a supervisor is stressful. Poor time management, problems with interpersonal relationships, poor working conditions, uncertainty about responsibilities, inadequate resources, and conflicting demands contribute to the normal stress that supervisors are subject to.

The main goal of stress management is to eliminate or minimize the causes of stress. For a supervisor, this may mean delegating some work and being assertive about problems as well as negotiating solutions with superiors, peers, and subordinates. Another way to reduce stress is more personal: supervisors can take a break, get more exercise, pursue an enjoyable activity or hobby, and, in general, look outward for some perspective.

SAMPLE QUESTIONS

1. A manager who is responsible for establishing the goals, plans, and policies of an organization as a whole is referred to as a(n)

   (A) executive
   (B) middle manager
   (C) supervisor
   (D) line worker

   The correct answer is (A). The highest level managers, responsible for the organization as a whole, are called executives. Middle managers plan and carry out the objectives set by executives, and supervisors plan, direct, and control the activities of line workers, the "hands on" employees.

2. What is the ideal relationship between a supervisor's responsibilities and his or her authority?

   (A) A supervisor has more responsibilities than authority.
   (B) A supervisor has more authority than responsibilities.
   (C) A supervisor has the authority necessary to carry out responsibilities.
   (D) A supervisor has responsibilities but no authority.

   The correct answer is (C). Responsibilities are the tasks and outcomes for which a supervisor is held accountable. In order to get these done, whether personally or by delegating, a supervisor must have the appropriate authority, or power, to make decisions and take action. A supervisor's ability to do his or her job properly is hampered if there is less authority than responsibility or no authority at all. Having more authority than needed is not ideal, either, as it means that the supervisor is not working up to capacity.

3. Every month supervisor Sam Jackson represents his work unit at a production meeting. There, he describes the status of his projects, identifies problems in preproduction, production, quality, and schedule, and proposes solutions. In which of the following management functions is Jackson participating?

   (A) Planning
   (B) Organizing
   (C) Directing
   (D) Controlling

   The correct answer is (D). Jackson is taking part in the control process, comparing progress to objectives and proposing corrective solutions. Planning involves devising ways to meet objectives; organizing involves the deployment of the work force; and directing involves getting workers to do the work necessary to meet objectives. None of these major functions is the focus of the planning meeting.

PRACTICE SET

1. In a factory, which of the following is a staff employee?
   (A) A production supervisor
   (B) A machinist
   (C) A lathe operator
   (D) An accountant

2. According to Abraham H. Maslow, which of the following is the highest level need of human beings?
   (A) Respect
   (B) Companionship
   (C) Self-actualization
   (D) Security

3. How does a supervisor usually influence the collective bargaining of a labor contract?
   (A) By attending collective bargaining sessions
   (B) By his or her actions in the preceding time period
   (C) By encouraging workers not to strike
   (D) By proposing contract provisions

4. A graphic technique for planning a project in which a great number of tasks must be coordinated is called a
   (A) schedule
   (B) PERT chart
   (C) table of organization
   (D) work distribution chart

5. To demonstrate just cause for a disciplinary action, one legal requirement is that employees have been notified in advance of the types of performance or behavior that can lead to disciplinary action. What is the second legal requirement?
   (A) The availability of arbitrators to negotiate disputed actions
   (B) Written records of unacceptable performance or behavior
   (C) The unacceptable behavior or performance must affect other employees
   (D) Prior notification of the penalties for unacceptable performance or behavior

6. Which of the following is NOT an assumption underlying Theory Y of management?
   (A) The average person dislikes work and will avoid it if possible.
   (B) The effort involved in work is as natural as playing or resting.
   (C) Most people are able to solve work-related problems.
   (D) People try to achieve goals to which they are committed.

7. A supervisor who facilitates the work of employees

   (A) does the work of employees to meet deadlines
   (B) provides them with on-the-job training
   (C) assists and guides them when necessary
   (D) gives detailed orders on every job

8. For what purpose should a supervisor use the company grapevine?

   (A) To get information about company policies
   (B) To get clues about what is happening in the company
   (C) To communicate changes in rules to employees
   (D) To communicate opportunities for advancement

9. Keisha Durelle supervises an arcade. Game players accumulate tokens that workers must count by hand so players can exchange them for prizes. When the arcade is crowded, this process becomes a bottleneck. Durelle proposes that workers use a machine to count tokens, saving time. In fact, she thinks she can reduce her staff by one person with this method. Which would be the most effective way for Durelle to implement this change without affecting morale?

   (A) Buy the machine and reduce the staff by attrition
   (B) Buy the machine and ask the staff who should be laid off
   (C) Buy the machine and lay off one worker
   (D) Drop the idea completely since it means reducing the staff

10. A company that takes on one-of-a-kind projects is most likely to be structured as a(n)

   (A) functional organization
   (B) centralized organization
   (C) line and staff organization
   (D) matrix organization

PRACTICE SET ANSWERS

1. **The correct answer is (D).** Only an accountant would be a staff employee in a factory. The remaining people all have jobs involved with the production of goods; thus, they are line employees.

2. **The correct answer is (C).** According to Maslow's hierarchy of needs, the highest-level human need is self-actualization (achievement, power, personal growth, and a feeling of worth).

3. **The correct answer is (B).** A supervisor's influence on collective bargaining is indirect; he or she influences the context in which talks take place. Supervisors do not participate in collective bargaining or in proposing contract provisions and should maintain a neutral stance regarding legitimate union activities.

4. **The correct answer is (B).** A PERT (performance evaluation and review technique) chart is a graphic tool used for planning the sequence, coordination, and time frames of various tasks that must be done to complete a project. Schedules and work distribution charts are also planning tools, but they are not ideal for coordinating project tasks. A table of organization shows an organization's reporting relationships.

5. **The correct answer is (D).** Forewarning, both of behaviors and penalties, is legally required in order to demonstrate just cause for disciplinary action.

6. **The correct answer is (A).** This is a negative assumption about human nature, and it underlies Theory X of management, not Theory Y. Theory Y takes a positive view of people's attitudes toward and abilities to do work.

7. **The correct answer is (C).** A supervisor who facilitates tries to help employees accomplish their work without being directive all the time. Facilitating does not mean pitching in to meet deadlines or training employees.

8. **The correct answer is (B).** The grapevine, the conduit of gossip, is good for getting a rough idea about what is going on (or what people think is going on), but it is not a good source of definitive information (like policies). It is not a good means for communicating rule changes or advancement opportunities.

9. **The correct answer is (A).** This is the best option for Durelle because it improves productivity and does not affect morale adversely.

10. **The correct answer is (D).** A matrix organization is flexible, so it is suitable for a company that forms and reforms project teams. The remaining forms of organization are all more formal with more concentrated authority. They are less suited to project teams.

POSTTEST

1. A temporary corporate task force studying the feasibility of outsourcing some in-house functions versus increasing staff is an example of which of the following types of organizations?

   (A) Decentralized
   (B) Hybrid
   (C) Matrix
   (D) Line/staff

2. A departmental supervisor who participates in a special project team in a matrix organization might

   (A) have trouble prioritizing the workload while reporting to two different managers
   (B) see little difference between the new responsibilities and the previous supervisory role
   (C) be able to make more decisions than the supervisor is used to
   (D) have more time to focus on the supervisor's original line functions

3. The number of subordinates that an individual supervises in an organization is commonly referred to as

   (A) authority
   (B) influence
   (C) span of control
   (D) degree of power

4. Additional staff support is ordinarily needed when a supervisor or manager must

   (A) increase productivity and efficiency
   (B) accept a wider span of control
   (C) increase job satisfaction and loyalty
   (D) maintain a narrow span of control

5. Which of the following questions would NOT be legally acceptable during a job interview or on a job application?

   (A) "Are you over 18 years of age?"
   (B) "What was the highest grade that you completed in school?"
   (C) "Do you have any physical condition that would limit your ability to perform the job?"
   (D) "Are you a member of any church or synagogue?"

6. A supervisor most commonly uses a job description to do which of the following?

   (A) Determine the minimum qualifications for the position and provide a benchmark for assessing both applicants and current employees

   (B) Keep employees informed of their responsibilities and solicit feedback from a performance review

   (C) Maintain accurate records of skills and education levels on a departmental level

   (D) Provide performance assessments for annual reviews

7. The portion of a job description that provides a brief description of the purpose, nature, and primary duties of a particular job position is typically referred to as the

   (A) qualifications

   (B) job summary

   (C) position description

   (D) responsibilities

8. If an employee reports to more than one supervisor, confusion and conflict may result. This statement illustrates the importance of the management principle called

   (A) division of labor

   (B) unity of direction

   (C) unity of command

   (D) chain of command

9. Unity of direction concerns an organization's

   (A) goals and objectives

   (B) division of departments

   (C) management style

   (D) entire plan and strategy

10. An appropriate question to ask a former employer when checking a job applicant's references would be

   (A) "How many overtime hours did the person generally work?"

   (B) "Did the person have many personal conversations with coworkers?"

   (C) "Does the person have any problematic physical or medical conditions?"

   (D) "Would you consider rehiring the person if given the opportunity to do so?"

11. Effective training programs for current employees and new hires most often benefit companies by increasing

   (A) profits

   (B) security

   (C) productivity

   (D) control

12. New employee orientation is probably best accomplished by using which of the following training methods?

   (A) Employee manuals
   (B) Adult education courses
   (C) Computer-aided learning
   (D) Classroom teaching

13. Acquainting new employees with their job environment, coworkers, company policies, and procedures is called

   (A) induction
   (B) orientation
   (C) retention
   (D) selection

14. An example of an exploratory question during a job interview would be

   (A) "What was your major in college?"
   (B) "Was your first job full-time or part-time?"
   (C) "What do you enjoy most about work?"
   (D) "Are you involved in any civic organizations?"

15. The ability to direct employees and motivate them toward accomplishing company goals and objectives is commonly referred to as

   (A) responsibility
   (B) delegation
   (C) vision
   (D) leadership

16. An important trait of a good corporate leader is the ability to

   (A) follow a good decision-making process
   (B) implement a corporate-wide advocacy policy
   (C) create cross-department communication channels
   (D) execute an internal training program

17. Which of the following characteristics would a supervisor NOT want to possess if aspiring to be a democratic leader?

   (A) Intelligence
   (B) Rigidity
   (C) Trust
   (D) Modesty

18. If a supervisor observes an employee regularly wasting time and engaging in personal conversations, the supervisor may have to address which of the following employee problems?

   (A) Recognition
   (B) Self-esteem
   (C) Motivation
   (D) Advancement

19. Giving thanks to subordinates for a job well done and praising them when they improve their performance is an example of

  (A) participative management
  (B) democratic leadership
  (C) minimizing frustration
  (D) positive reinforcement

20. Which of the following general statements is consistent with all of the major theories on motivating employees?

  (A) Employees are motivated to achieve a goal if they can derive a sense of personal satisfaction from their work.
  (B) Employees are de-motivated when they are unable to participate in the evaluation process.
  (C) Employees are motivated primarily by tangible economic benefits.
  (D) Employees are de-motivated when changes are made in their work surroundings and environment.

21. Which of the following is a tool used by most supervisors to list and compare the performance characteristics of their employees according to a set of categories or factors?

  (A) Spreadsheet
  (B) Graphic rating scale
  (C) Job description
  (D) Organizational chart

22. The most common business practice is to evaluate the performance of employees

  (A) before an orientation
  (B) every three months
  (C) at least once a year
  (D) twice a year

23. Shortages of materials, future retirements, requests for leave of absence, and changes in market conditions may all affect how a supervisor determines future

  (A) staffing needs
  (B) job descriptions
  (C) recruiting programs
  (D) training programs

24. A systematic approach to gather, evaluate, and organize information about a particular job is referred to as a job

  (A) title
  (B) analysis
  (C) description
  (D) summary

25. Which of the following comments is the best example of a supervisor being specific and concrete rather than abstract and general during a performance review with an employee?

(A) "Your work is better this year—keep it up."

(B) "You're the best worker in the customer service department—you know that."

(C) "People in the marketing department have been complaining about your attitude."

(D) "The additional hours that you spent on the Smith account helped us to increase sales last quarter."

26. All of the following are positive ways of taking disciplinary action with employees EXCEPT

(A) discussing the employee's action at a weekly departmental meeting

(B) being firm but fair with the employee

(C) reprimanding the employee for a specific action in a particular situation

(D) discussing the offense as soon as possible after it occurs

27. All of the following methods would most likely help in providing effective employee development and training programs EXCEPT

(A) programmed instruction

(B) skill reduction

(C) case studies

(D) videotape instruction

28. A good on-the-job trainer would probably start a training workshop by doing which of the following?

(A) Setting clear limits in regard to the time of practice workshop exercises

(B) Asking employees if they have any questions

(C) Finding out what employees already know about the job or task

(D) Distributing programmed instruction materials and review them

29. Written notices of misconduct or poor performance should be given to an employee and placed in the employee's personnel file before a supervisor recommends

(A) probation

(B) dismissal

(C) a warning

(D) a reprimand

30. If a supervisor has failed to give an employee feedback on how to improve his past work and the employee's performance fails to improve, the supervisor should

(A) discuss stern measures and disciplinary action with the employee immediately

(B) relocate the employee to another department or discuss a demotion

(C) give the employee oral and written warnings and monitor performance for a specified period of time

(D) recommend a demotion for the employee and find lower-level tasks for the employee to perform

31. Which of the following terms is officially used to describe unwelcome sexual remarks in the workplace?

(A) Sexual harassment

(B) Profanity

(C) Sexism

(D) Obscene language

32. A supervisor witnesses a worker in the department using abusive language when speaking to a minority coworker whose English-speaking skills are poor. The supervisor's first step should be to

(A) speak directly to the minority coworker and give assurance of the supervisor's support

(B) consult with management about the company's policy concerning using such language on the job and then take appropriate disciplinary action

(C) issue a written warning to the abusive worker for using such abusive language

(D) allow the two coworkers to discuss the incident privately and act as a mediator during the meeting

33. A team leader in a department tells the supervisor that an employee has missed team meetings three times in two weeks, causing delays and confusion in the project. After further discussion, it is learned that the cause of the absences and delays in reporting to the team was due to caring for an elderly parent. Which of the following actions should the supervisor take immediately?

(A) Suggest a meeting of the entire team to discuss the employee's problem and possible solutions.

(B) Talk to the employee directly and give assurance that the supervisor is available to discuss any problem.

(C) Meet with the team leader and the employee to discuss ways to keep the project on track while the employee tries to solve the problem.

(D) Contact Human Resources and inquire about social service agencies that might assist the employee with locating elder-care services.

34. When using the behavioral or nondirective method of counseling, a supervisor should FIRST

(A) evaluate

(B) empathize

(C) communicate

(D) listen

35. All of the following help to enhance the effectiveness of employee counseling EXCEPT

(A) offering direction

(B) listening

(C) being honest

(D) extending empathy

36. Within the supervisory process, an activity involved in the controlling function in an organization would be

(A) analyzing job applications

(B) evaluating employee performance

(C) delegating specific work tasks

(D) writing an action plan

37. Which of the following steps occurs FIRST when a supervisor wants to determine whether goals and objectives are being achieved?

(A) Gather the necessary data regarding employee performance.

(B) Implement corrective action according to an action plan.

(C) Determine which factors should be evaluated in order to make an assessment.

(D) Compare and evaluate the information gathered regarding performance.

38. Weekly status reports, management by objectives (MBO), rating scales, and critical incidence files are all tools used by a supervisor when

(A) planning
(B) motivating
(C) scheduling
(D) controlling

39. When a supervisor monitors the substandard work of an employee with normally satisfactory performance, the supervisor is

(A) evaluating and gathering data
(B) directing and managing
(C) analyzing and researching
(D) reviewing and testing

40. A budget illustrates the economic outcome of a specific management or supervisory plan by showing

(A) the estimated cost of materials tied to a particular project or product
(B) a detailed list of true expenses associated with a specific course of action
(C) a timetable with periodic intervals for gauging whether a project is on schedule
(D) the percentage of profit realized after all production cost factors have been accounted

41. A production supervisor in a graphics design firm has been researching the cost of new software and computer upgrades that will be needed for the upcoming year. Increasing software prices and higher costs for computer repairs will most likely cause the supervisor to revise the estimated

(A) personnel
(B) output
(C) budget
(D) timetable

42. The most important and popular use of a budget in most organizations is to provide a plan for

(A) allocating operating funds for a specified period of time
(B) identifying time, material, and labor needs
(C) comparing actual expenses to allocated expenses
(D) allowing supervisors to give feedback to upper management regarding staffing and materials

43. The chief purpose of the Occupational Safety and Health Administration (OSHA) is to

(A) perform environmental inspections and recommend necessary changes

(B) regulate and monitor safe working conditions on a national basis

(C) investigate personal injury claims in an ad hoc fashion

(D) mediate or arbitrate between employers and unions concerning safety issues

44. The federal organization responsible for creating standards for fair hiring practices and regulations concerning workforce diversity is called the

(A) Federal Mediation and Conciliation Service

(B) American Arbitration Association

(C) Equal Employment Opportunity Commission

(D) Supreme Court of the United States

45. All of the following are common issues negotiated in the collective bargaining process EXCEPT

(A) performance appraisals

(B) disciplinary policies

(C) seniority clauses

(D) grievance procedures

46. Establishing realistic goals, delegating tasks when possible, and constantly reassessing priorities are all helpful guidelines to follow if a supervisor wants to

(A) increase turnover

(B) control on-the-job stress

(C) decrease absenteeism

(D) eliminate anger and frustration

47. "I always try to follow a schedule. However, if a situation calls for me to be flexible, I try to come up with a new action plan." This statement would most likely be made by a supervisor with which of the following types of personality or leadership style?

(A) Type A

(B) Autocratic

(C) Type B

(D) Negative

48. When a company encourages groups of workers to meet regularly to discuss work problems, how to improve the workplace, and how to solve problems they have identified, the company is utilizing which of the following?

(A) Cross-training

(B) Empowerment

(C) Participative analysis

(D) Quality circles

49. A plastics manufacturing company has altered its production processes by implementing changes identified through quality circles. In addition to improved product quality, the changes might also result in

(A) increased production
(B) higher costs
(C) longer production cycles
(D) better supervision

50. The primary responsibility of a supervisor is to

(A) provide status reports to upper management
(B) direct the work of employees
(C) create and maintain work schedules
(D) evaluate the appropriateness of job descriptions

51. A supervisor who communicates in a multidirectional fashion

(A) provides monthly reports to upper management only
(B) utilizes different technologies to deliver information to subordinates
(C) maintains upward, downward, lateral, and diagonal lines of communication
(D) interfaces directly with other departmental supervisors and employees

52. Essential to good decision making is a supervisor's ability to

(A) display courage and initiative
(B) utilize prior supervisory experience
(C) analyze and evaluate alternatives in an in-depth manner
(D) take complete responsibility for solving employee problems

53. Equal Employment Opportunity (EEO) regulations require employers to adhere to which of the following practices in hiring and interviewing?

(A) Exclude a job applicant only on the basis of previous salary level.
(B) Disregard physical capability differences between male and female job applicants.
(C) Include a diverse mix of job applicants in regard to race, nationality, gender, and age.
(D) Create a balanced workforce according to federally-mandated diversity requirements.

54. A supervisor who follows the same written list of interview questions when interviewing a group of job applicants would be

   (A) providing a fair and consistent basis for comparing all the applicants
   (B) avoiding possible lawsuits against the company and the supervisor
   (C) creating an information file that could be evaluated by using special software programs
   (D) eliminating biases and preconceptions from the evaluation process

55. The fundamental purpose of employee orientation programs is to inform new employees of company

   (A) policies, benefits, facilities, and procedures
   (B) history, culture, and regulations
   (C) strategies, goals, and objectives
   (D) organization, departments, and special projects

56. Which of the following actions would a supervisor most likely NOT take to improve the productivity of a work group?

   (A) Analyze the overall output of the group to identify results of lesser value.
   (B) Decrease employee time spent in orientation sessions and new trainee workshops.
   (C) Examine the effectiveness of administrative procedures and modify as needed.
   (D) Update the technology of the operation to improve efficiency.

57. Which of the following methods of recruiting allows a company to recruit the most prospective job applicants with the highest level of confidentiality?

   (A) Using college, trade school, and business school placement services
   (B) Reviewing past applications on file and contacting individuals previously interviewed
   (C) Placing an advertisement in newspapers and trade publications that includes a box number rather than a company name and address
   (D) Recruiting through Internet job sites

58. A supervisor has asked an experienced, skilled worker to provide guidance to a new trainee. This training technique is known as

   (A) job rotation
   (B) cross-training
   (C) modeling
   (D) on-the-job training

59. Detailed information on labor costs, operating expenses, material costs, and overhead for a specified period of time or related to a specific product can be found in a

(A) work schedule
(B) PERT flow chart
(C) production plan
(D) budget

60. A union is attempting to organize workers in a company. A supervisor is concerned about the possible affects that it may have on workers and the department's productivity and calls a meeting with workers to ask about their intentions to vote for or against the union. In this situation, the supervisor's actions would legally be regarded as

(A) an attempt to arbitrate
(B) a management procedure
(C) a collective bargaining process
(D) an unfair labor practice

POSTTEST ANSWERS

1. **The correct answer is (C).** A matrix organizational structure combines the traditional functional chain of command with special horizontal project arrangements such as teams, task forces, or temporary departments.

2. **The correct answer is (A).** A departmental supervisor who participates in a special project team in a matrix organization might experience overload due to new responsibilities in addition to the supervisor's original function.

3. **The correct answer is (C).** The number of subordinates that an individual supervises in an organization is commonly referred to as span of control.

4. **The correct answer is (B).** A wider span of control is usually characterized by greater or increased numbers of personnel within the hierarchy of an organization.

5. **The correct answer is (D).** Asking questions in regard to an applicant's religious affiliation is an unacceptable preemployment inquiry.

6. **The correct answer is (A).** A job description is used to determine the minimum qualifications for a position and provide a benchmark for assessing both applicants and current employees.

7. **The correct answer is (B).** The portion of a job description that provides a brief description of the purpose, nature, and primary duties of a particular job position is typically referred to as the job summary.

8. **The correct answer is (C).** Unity of command is the principle that organizational unity is best achieved when each individual reports to a single superior.

9. **The correct answer is (D).** Unity of direction concerns an organization's entire plan and long-term strategy.

10. **The correct answer is (D).** The most pertinent, appropriate, and essential question to ask a former employer is whether the employer would consider rehiring the candidate.

11. **The correct answer is (C).** Increased productivity is one of the most tangible benefits seen as a result of a company investing in training programs.

12. **The correct answer is (D).** A classroom environment in which supervisors discuss company policies, procedures, and job duties are usually the best means of presenting orientation information to new hires in a personal and focused fashion.

13. **The correct answer is (B).** Acquainting new employees with their job environment, coworkers, company policies, and procedures is called orientation.

14. **The correct answer is (C).** "What do you enjoy most about work?" is an open-ended or exploratory question intended to reveal the candidate's feelings and ideas to the fullest extent.

15. **The correct answer is (D).** Leadership is the ability to direct employees and motivate them toward accomplishing company goals and objectives.

16. **The correct answer is (A).** The ability to follow a good decision-making process is one of the most important traits of a good leader.

17. **The correct answer is (B).** Rigidity is a characteristic trait of autocratic or authoritative leaders rather than democratic leaders.

18. **The correct answer is (C).** Managers must understand how to motivate employees in order to get them to work toward organizational objectives.

19. **The correct answer is (D).** Positive reinforcement is given to employees when a supervisor or manager offers praise and gratitude for good performance. By doing so, the positive behavior of the employee is reinforced and is likely to be repeated.

20. **The correct answer is (A).** The major theorists on human motivation, Herzberg, Maslow, and McClelland, concluded that individuals are motivated to achieve a goal if they can derive a sense of personal satisfaction from their efforts.

21. **The correct answer is (B).** A graphic rating scale is a popular appraisal tool that is used to list and compare the performance characteristics of employees according to a set of categories or factors.

22. **The correct answer is (C).** Although policies vary from organization to organization, the most common practice is an annual performance appraisal or review.

23. **The correct answer is (A).** Shortages of materials, future retirements, requests for leave of absence, and changes in market conditions are all factors that a supervisor must consider when making long-term decisions regarding staffing needs.

24. **The correct answer is (B).** A job analysis is a systematic approach to gather, evaluate, and organize information about a particular job.

25. **The correct answer is (D).** Citing facts, events, and performance indicators are some of the ways that a supervisor can be specific and concrete during a performance appraisal. This is illustrated by choice (D).

26. **The correct answer is (A).** In general, reprimands and disciplinary discussions should be handled privately rather than in a group setting.

27. **The correct answer is (B).** Skill reduction is not a method for delivering employee development and training programs.

28. **The correct answer is (C).** A good trainer does not make assumptions about an employee's knowledge or understanding but rather asks questions to accurately make this determination at the beginning of a training session.

29. **The correct answer is (B).** The four stages of disciplinary action prior to dismissal or demotion are usually oral warnings, a written warning, and, in some cases, a disciplinary layoff.

30. **The correct answer is (C).** If an employee's performance justifies possible dismissal or demotion, a supervisor should be fair by providing ample warning before such action is taken. Performance reviews should always include specific actions that an employee should take in order to perform the job responsibilities in a satisfactory manner.

31. **The correct answer is (A).** Sexual harassment is the legal term used to designate any unwelcome sexual conduct, language, or gestures.

32. **The correct answer is (B).** It is the responsibility of every supervisor and manager to promote a diverse and just work environment. Supervisors need to be sensitive in handling work situations regarding discrimination and prejudice according to federal laws and company policies.

33. **The correct answer is (C).** When counseling employees with personal problems, supervisors should focus on listening rather than taking action for the employee, keep their situation confidential, suggest alternative actions that the employee might consider in order to maintain acceptable job performance, and offer support rather than advice.

34. **The correct answer is (D).** The behavioral or nondirective approach to counseling assumes that the employee can best solve the problem. The supervisor listens, allows the employee to express the problem, and offers possible solutions only if asked.

35. **The correct answer is (A).** Counseling is most effective when a supervisor or manager is sincerely concerned, honest, and willing to listen. Offering advice and direction is less helpful.

36. **The correct answer is (B).** Evaluating employee performance is part of the controlling function of the supervisory process.

37. **The correct answer is (C).** Before evaluating performance and taking corrective action to improve performance, a supervisor must first determine what factors must be evaluated. The factors to be evaluated generally include people, time, tasks, and money.

38. **The correct answer is (D).** Weekly status reports, management by objectives (MBO), rating scales, and critical incidence files are tools used for evaluating performance, which is part of the controlling function of the supervisory process.

39. **The correct answer is (A).** When a supervisor monitors the substandard work of an employee with normally satisfactory performance, the supervisor is evaluating and gathering data.

40. **The correct answer is (B).** A budget shows a detailed list of true expenses associated with a specific product, project, or course of action.

41. **The correct answer is (C).** A budget shows a detailed list of true expenses associated with a specific product, project, or course of action. The supervisor's research revealed information regarding software and computer expenses that will directly affect the figures in the budget.

42. The correct answer is (A). The most important and popular use of a budget in most organizations is to provide a plan for allocating operating funds for a specified period of time.

43. The correct answer is (B). The chief purpose of the Occupational Safety and Health Administration (OSHA) is to regulate and monitor safe working conditions on a national basis.

44. The correct answer is (C). The federal organization responsible for creating standards for fair hiring practices and regulations concerning workforce diversity is called the Equal Employment Opportunity Commission.

45. The correct answer is (A). Specific employee performance appraisals are not included in the issues generally negotiated in the collective bargaining process.

46. The correct answer is (B). On-the-job stress can be controlled on both an individual and organizational basis by addressing the sources of stress. These sources may include, among other factors, unrealistic and burdensome goals, an overwhelming number of tasks that might be delegated, and juggling priorities.

47. The correct answer is (C). Type B personalities have a tendency to be flexible and relaxed and to operate under a slower and more controlled pace. As a result, Type B individuals are more likely to take a realistic approach to work schedules.

48. The correct answer is (D). Quality circles are groups of employees who meet on a regular basis to identify, analyze, and solve problems in their area of interest and expertise, with the objective of improving quality and productivity.

49. The correct answer is (A). The results of the quality circle process usually include reduced errors, improved product quality, cost reductions, safety awareness, increased production, problem prevention, and better decisions.

50. The correct answer is (B). Although a supervisor's job may include a variety of duties, the primary responsibility of a supervisor is to direct the work of employees.

51. The correct answer is (C). One of the roles of a supervisor is to connect upper management and staff personnel. This requires communicating information between these two groups. Lateral or horizontal communication also helps supervisors promote unity within the organization.

52. The correct answer is (C). Effective decision making requires analyzing problems and situations and choosing between two or more alternative solutions. Although decision making also requires courage, risk taking, and initiative, careful analysis of alternative actions is the basis of all good decisions.

53. The correct answer is (C). Equal Employment Opportunity regulations require employers to include a diverse mix of job applicants in regard to race, nationality, gender, and age.

54. **The correct answer is (A).** If the same questions are asked of all candidates, a fair and consistent basis for evaluating interviewees will most likely result. However, questions included may be illegal and/or biased.

55. **The correct answer is (A).** The main purpose of orientation programs is generally to inform new employees of company policies, benefits, facilities, and procedures.

56. **The correct answer is (B).** Worker productivity is generally increased through the use of effective orientation and training programs.

57. **The correct answer is (C).** Placing a blind advertisement in newspapers and trade publications that includes a box number rather than a company name and address typically allows a company to recruit the most prospective job applicants with the highest level of confidentiality.

58. **The correct answer is (D).** On-the-job training allows workers to learn by trial and error, on the job, under actual working conditions.

59. **The correct answer is (D).** A budget contains detailed information on labor costs, operating expenses, material costs, and overhead for a specified period of time or related to a specific product.

60. **The correct answer is (D).** According to federal law, questioning employees about union affairs or how they plan to vote in a union election is an unfair labor practice.

Dantes Subject Standardized Tests

FACT SHEETS/STUDY GUIDES

A Fact Sheet/Study Guide is available for each test. It offers information about the topics that are covered on the exam, books that will help you prepare for it, and the number of credits that the ACE Commission on Educational Credit and Credentials recommends be awarded for a passing score. You should also check with your school to learn about its requirements for earning credit because some schools set higher standards than the ACE minimum recommendation.

The Fact Sheet/Study Guides also contain sample text questions that will provide you with an idea of how the test is structured. The list of recommended books are textbooks that were used in college courses of the same or similar title when the test was developed, but you need not limit yourself to the textbooks listed in the fact sheet. In fact, it is recommended that you review more than one textbook when you prepare for your exam. You should check the table of contents for each book that you are considering using against the content outline that appears on the first page of the fact sheet before you decide to study with a particular textbook.

DANTES
Subject Standardized Tests

Fact Sheet
Study Guide

BUSINESS MATHEMATICS

TEST INFORMATION

This test was developed to enable schools to award credit to students for knowledge equivalent to that which is learned by students taking the course. The school may choose to award college credit to the student based on the achievement of a passing score. The passing score for each examination is determined by the school based on recommendations from the American Council on Education (ACE). This minimum credit-awarding score is equal to the mean score of students in the norming sample who received a grade of C in the course. Some schools set their own standards for awarding credit and may require a higher score than the ACE recommendation. Students should obtain this information from the institution where they expect to receive credit.

The use of non-programmable calculators is permitted during the test. Scratch paper for computations should be provided.

CONTENT

The following topics, which are commonly taught in courses on this subject, are covered by this examination.

	Approximate Percent
I. Number Sense	9%
A. Place value	
B. Percentage	
C. Reasonableness of answers	
II. Algebraic Concepts	17%
A. Linear equations and inequalities	
B. Simultaneous linear equations	

	Approximate Percent
C. Solving for the unknown	
D. Quadratic equations and functions	
E. Evaluating a function at a certain point	
F. Extrapolation and interpolation	
III. Statistics	12%
A. Central tendency (mean, median, mode)	
B. Weighted averages	
C. Percentiles	
IV. Business Applications	40%
A. Interest	
B. Depreciation/salvage value	
C. Discounts and credit terms	
D. Installment purchases	
E. Markup/markdown	
F. Taxes	
G. Inventory (turns/turnovers)	
H. Payroll	
I. Breakeven analysis	
J. Financial ratio analysis	
K. Promissory notes and other loans	
L. Interpretation of graphical representations (and misuse of data)	
M. Unit conversions	
N. Investment performance measures (e.g., p/e ratios, yield factors, rates of return)	
V. Financial Mathematics	22%
A. Annuities and present value	
B. Amortization and future value	

Copyright © 2000 by The Chauncey Group International in trust for the United States Department of Defense.
Unlimited reproduction of this fact sheet is allowed.

Dantes/DSST Program

Questions on the test require candidates to demonstrate the following abilities. Some questions may require more than one of the abilities.

- Knowledge of basic facts and terms
(about 20-25% of the examination)

- Understanding of concepts and principles, including the meanings of operations
(about 55-60% of the examination)

- Ability to apply knowledge to specific cases or issues, including the ability to compute figures and to read and interpret charts, graphs, and tables
(about 20-25% of the examination)

SAMPLE QUESTIONS

1. If the general term of a sequence is given by

$$S_n = \frac{(-1)^{n+1} \bullet n}{n+1}$$

and for a certain k the term S_k is negative, which of the following statements is true?

(A) S_{k+1} and S_{k+3} are both negative.
(B) S_{k+2} and S_{k+6} are both negative.
(C) If n is odd, then S_n must be negative.
(D) If n is a multiple of 3, then S_n must be negative.

2. During one month, Jane works 42 hours during the first week and 40 hours during the second week. Her regular pay is $7.50 per hour for 35 hours per week, and she is paid time and one-half for each hour worked in excess of 35 hours. Her FICA deduction is 6.25 percent and her federal income tax is deducted at a rate of 25 percent. If she pays no other taxes, what is her net pay for the first two weeks of the month?

(A) $422.81
(B) $453.75
(C) $461.25
(D) $576.56

3. In Year 1, a company used 120,000 gallons of fuel oil at a cost of $0.75 per gallon. In Year 2, the company used 150,000 gallons at a cost of $0.80 per gallon. By what percentage did the company's total fuel cost increase in Year 2 over Year 1?

(A) -25.0%
(B) 6.7%
(C) 25.0%
(D) 33.3%

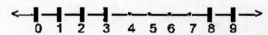

4. If X is the coordinate of one of the points indicated by on the number line above, which of the following statements is true?

(A) X is any whole number greater than 3 and less than 7.
(B) X is any whole number between 3 and 8.
(C) X is any whole number between 3 and 7.
(D) X is any whole number greater than 4 and less than 7.

5. A jewelry store wants to sell five diamonds for $1,200 per carat. If the weights of the diamonds are 1/4, 5/6, 3/7, 1/3, and 1/2 carats, what is their total value?

(A) $2,400
(B) $2,750
(C) $2,800
(D) $2,814

6. What is the current yield of a 3 percent bond with a face (par) value of $1,000 if it is quoted at a deep discount price of 6½ percent?

(A) 3.5%
(B) 9.5%
(C) 19.5%
(D) 46.2%

2

7. A company has five employees and reports its salary averages as a median. If the salary range is $29,000 and the average salary is $20,000, which of the following salary listings could represent the company?

    (A) $12,000, $14,000, $20,000, $25,000, $29,000
    (B) $15,000, $19,000, $20,000, $23,000, $29,000
    (C) $18,000, $19,000, $20,000, $29,000, $47,000
    (D) $20,000, $20,000, $20,000, $23,000, $29,000

8. A new car is going to cost the buyer $12,345.67. The buyer intends to make a down payment and finance the balance with equal payments of $400 at the end of each of the next 30 months. If the loan interest is 12 percent, compounded monthly, what is the amount of the down payment?

    (A) $256
    (B) $1,568
    (C) $2,022
    (D) $2,680

STUDYING FOR THE EXAMINATION

The following is a list of reference publications that were being used as textbooks in college courses of the same or similar title at the time the test was developed. Appropriate textbooks for study are not limited to those listed below. If you wish to obtain study resources to prepare for the examination, you may reference either the current edition of the following titles **or** textbooks currently used at a local college or university for the same class title. It is recommended that you reference **more than one textbook** on the topics outlined in this fact sheet. You should **begin by checking textbook content against the content outline** included on the front page of this Fact Sheet/Study Guide **before** selecting textbooks that cover the test content from which to study. Textbooks may be found at the campus bookstore of a local college or university offering a course on the subject.

Sources for study material suggested but not limited to the following:

Brooks, Lloyd D. *Business Math*. St. Paul, MN: EMC Paradigm Publishing Co., current edition.

Busche, Don, and Flora Locke. *College Mathematics for Business*. New York: John Wiley & Sons, current edition.

Gossage, Loyce C. *Business Mathematics: A College Course*. Cincinnati, OH: South-Western Publishing Co., current edition.

Kelley, J. Roland, Jimmy C. McKenzie, and Alton W. Evans. *Business Mathematics*. Boston: Houghton Mifflin Co., current edition.

McCready, Richard R. *Business Mathematics*. Boston: PWS-Kent Publishing Co., current edition.

Roueche, Nelda W., and Virginia H. Graves. *Business Mathematics: A Collegiate Approach*. Upper Saddle River, NJ: Prentice-Hall, current edition.

Slater, Jeffrey. *Practical Business Math Procedures*. Burr Ridge, IL: Irwin Publishing Co., current edition.

Snyder, Llewellyn R., and William F. Jackson. *Essential Business Mathematics*. New York: McGraw Hill, current edition.

Current textbook used by a local college or university for a course on the subject.

CREDIT RECOMMENDATIONS

The Center for Adult Learning and Educational Credentials of the American Council on Education (ACE) has reviewed and evaluated the DANTES examination development process. ACE has made the following recommendations:

Area or Course Equivalent:	Business Mathematics
Level:	Lower-level baccalaureate
Amount of Credit:	Three (3) semester hours
Source:	ACE Commission on Educational Credit and Credentials

3

INFORMATION

Colleges and universities that would like to review copies of tests, have additional information about the national norming, or assistance in local norming or score validation studies should write to: DANTES Program, Mail Stop 11-P, The Chauncey Group International, 664 Rosedale Road, Princeton, New Jersey 08540.

It is advisable that schools develop a consistent policy about awarding credit based on scores from this test and that the policy be reviewed periodically. The Chauncey Group will be happy to help schools in this effort.

Correct Responses to sample questions: 1.B; 2.B; 3.D; 4.B; 5.D; 6.D; 7.C; 8.C.

I.N. D204283

4

DANTES

Subject Standardized Tests

Fact Sheet
Study Guide

ETHICS IN AMERICA

TEST INFORMATION

This test was developed to enable schools to award credit to students for knowledge equivalent to that which is learned by students taking the course. The school may choose to award college credit to the student based on the achievement of a passing score. The passing score for each examination is determined by the school based on recommendations from the American Council on Education (ACE). This minimum credit-awarding score is equal to the mean score of students in the norming sample who received a grade of C in the course. Some schools set their own standards for awarding credit and may require a higher score than the ACE recommendation. Students should obtain this information from the institution where they expect to receive credit.

The essay will ask the examinee to analyze a morally problematic situation in terms of issues relevant to a decision and arguments for alternative positions; it will require the examinee to reach his or her own reasoned conclusion.

The essay section will not be scored by The Chauncey Group. It will be forwarded to colleges and universities for their use in determining the award of credit.

CONTENT

The following topics, which are commonly taught in courses on this subject, are covered by this examination.

Approximate Percent

I. Ethical traditions   **29%**
  A. Greek views: Thucydides, Socrates, Plato, Aristotle
    1. Relationship of morality to community

2. Duty to obey the law
3. Relationship between self-interest and virtue
4. Relationship between virtue and happiness
5. Conceptions of justice
6. Justice as the interest of the stronger
7. Justice as playing the proper role
8. Equity as proper ratio of benefits
9. Virtue and human nature
10. Nature and kinds of virtue
11. Virtue as excellence
12. Virtue, habit, and character
13. Voluntary action
14. Doctrine of the mean
15. The best human life

  B. Biblical traditions: books of the law, prophets, gospels, writings of Paul
    1. Relationship between law and morality
    2. Role of the covenant
    3. Role of the prophets in denouncing evil
    4. Conceptions of justice in punishment and in the distribution of wealth
    5. Relationship between morality and community
    6. Place of mercy and love
    7. Apparent paradoxes in the traditions

Dantes/DSST Program

C. Moral law: Epictetus, Aquinas, Hobbes, Locke, Jefferson, Kant, Rawls, King, Rousseau, and others
   1. Views of human nature
   2. Basis of natural law
   3. Natural rights and duties
   4. Relationship of natural law to religious belief
   5. Source of political authority
   6. Social contract
   7. Relationship of natural law and human law
   8. Justifiability of revolution or civil disobedience
   9. Equality and liberty
   10. Deontological vs. consequential moral frameworks
   11. Hypothetical and categorical imperatives
   12. Good will and duty for its own sake
   13. Persons as ends in themselves, not as means only
   14. Loyalty and virtue
   15. Relationship of morality to self-interest and happiness
   16. Conceptions of justice
   17. Fairness and distributive justice
D. Consequential ethics: Epicurus, Bentham, Mill
   1. Consequential vs. deontological moral frameworks
   2. Hedonism and kinds of pleasure
   3. Self-interest or prudence and the common good
   4. Principle of utility or greatest happiness principle
   5. Felicific (or hedonic) calculus
   6. Conscience and external sanctions of morality
   7. Self-regarding and other-regarding conduct
   8. Individual liberty and the limits of the state's authority
E. Feminist ethics
   1. Critique of standard ethics
   2. Alternative visions - care ethic and ethic of trust

Approximate Percent

II. Ethical analysis of issues arising in interpersonal and personal-societal relationships and in professional and occupational roles (such as law, government, medicine, business military service, journalism). Issues such as, but not limited to: **35%**

   A. Doing good, not doing harm, and preventing harm
   B. Obligations to strangers
   C. Special moral relationships (such as parenthood)
   D. Conflict of duties
   E. Autonomy and privacy
   F. Fidelity, accountability, and trustworthiness
   G. Veracity
   H. Right to information
   I. Confidentiality
   J. Informed consent
   K. Institutional responsibilities
   L. Professional code of ethics
   M. Paternalism
   N. Retributive and distributive justice
   O. Balancing harms

III. Relationships between ethical traditions and the ethical analysis of situations   **36%**

2

SAMPLE QUESTIONS

1. Which of the following thinkers evaluates the morality of actions in terms of the amount of pleasure and pain they produce?

   (A) Aristotle
   (B) Kant
   (C) Bentham
   (D) King

2. According to which of the following philosophers is it immoral to commit suicide?

   (A) The hedonist Epicurus, because suicide decreases one's pleasure
   (B) The Stoic Epictetus, because suicide is contrary to nature
   (C) Kant, because persons who commit suicide treat themselves as a means only
   (D) Mill, because suicide never maximizes utility

3. For a utilitarian, the ethical evaluation of a decision to tell a lie will NOT depend on whether the

   (A) person to whom the lie is told will benefit from the lie
   (B) person telling the lie would mind someone else lying to him or her
   (C) person telling the lie will suffer if the truth is told
   (D) lie will cause suffering to third parties

Directions: The following questions are based on fictional situations and are in a different format from that of other questions in this test. Moral relevance and the moral reasons are to be understood in terms of the theories presented in the course materials. Judge a consideration to be morally relevant if at least one of those views would allow its relevance.

Preceding each group of numbered phrases or statements is a question that can be answered "Yes" or "No." Answer this question separately for each phrase or statement in the group by marking lettered space A on your answer sheet for "Yes" or lettered space B for "No" next to the number for each phrase or statement. Do not assume that there are more "Yes" answers or more "No" answers.

Questions 4-10 are based on the following situation.

Dr. DePaolo, chief of psychiatry at University Hospital, submitted a research plan to the hospital's Institutional Review Board to use patients in the hospital to test the effectiveness of a new type of drug for treatment of severe depression. The doctor proposed a "double-blind" design in which subjects would be randomly assigned to one of three groups: one group to receive the experimental drug, a second group to receive a standard agent for treatment of depression, and a third group to receive a placebo (a harmless inert substance). Dr. DePaolo as the experimenter was not to know which subjects were assigned to each group. The plan was approved. A third of the way through the experimental trials, one of the subjects complained to Dr. DePaolo, saying,"Doctor, since I have been taking this medication, I have been feeling much more depressed and have been thinking again about committing suicide."

3

Dantes/DSST Program

Is the following an issue that would have been relevant for a member of the Institutional Review Board to raise in judging the plan from the point of view of the ethics of research on human subjects?

4. Whether the patients were depressed to a degree that would impair their judgment in agreeing to participate in the trial

5. What information was to be given to the subjects about the possible risks and benefits of the trial to them

6. Whether the hospital would incur unreimbursed costs by participating in the trial

Is the following an appropriate course of action for Dr. DePaolo to follow concerning the depressed subject if Dr. DePaolo applies the principle, "First, do not harm"?

7. Record the comment as data for the experimental trial and continue the trial

8. Wait until the end of the trial to treat the subject with the drug that has been found to be most effective for that subject

9. Remove the subject from the experimental trial and resume treatment with an approved drug suitable for that subject

10. Unseal the trial records to determine which experimental group the subject is in before deciding whether to continue the trial for that subject

ESSAY QUESTION

Choose one of the following situations to analyze.

Situation: While off duty, Timmons, a police officer, finds a package containing $1,000 on the floor of a supermarket. The package and its contents give no indication of its owner's name. In the package, however, is a betting ticket for a legal lottery which the owner of the package could use to identify the package if it is reported found. Timmons needs cash in order to make a down payment on a new house. Without new housing, Timmons's children will continue to be exposed to high levels of radon, a dangerous gas emanating from the granite underneath Timmons's present house. Radon exposure, if prolonged, can cause cancer.

Decision: Should Timmons keep the package and its contents without reporting it to the store or the local authorities?

Part 1.   List the most significant moral principles or issues and the most significant facts, including any undecided factual issues, that have a bearing on making the decision, and describe the alternatives available.

Part 2.   Then, using this analysis, take an ethical position about what decision should be made, and support your position with the best ethical arguments you can make.

Part 3.   Then, in the most reasonable way that you can, state a view that is strongly opposed to your position in the most reasonable way that you can, and make the best ethical arguments you can for this opposing view.

Part 4.   Then reconsider your position, and say whether and why it should be changed or modified in view of the opposing arguments you have made.

Write one and no more than two paragraphs on each part.

Allocate your time equally among the four parts.

4

STUDYING FOR THE EXAMINATION

The following is a list of reference publications that were being used as textbooks in college courses of the same or similar title at the time the test was developed. Appropriate textbooks for study are not limited to those listed below. If you wish to obtain study resources to prepare for the examination, you may reference either the current edition of the following titles **or** textbooks currently used at a local college or university for the same class title. It is recommended that you reference **more than one textbook** on the topics outlined in this fact sheet. You should **begin by checking textbook content against the content outline** included on the front page of this Fact Sheet/Study Guide **before** selecting textbooks that cover the test content from which to study. Textbooks may be found at the campus bookstore of a local college or university offering a course on the subject.

Sources for study material suggested but not limited to the following:

Barcalow, Emmett. *Moral Philosophy Theory and Issues.* Belmont, CA: Wadsworth, current edition. An interpretive analysis without primary source references.

Goldberg, David T. *Ethical Theory & Social Issues: Historical Texts & Contemporary Readings.* Orlando, FL: Holt, Rinehart, and Winston, current edition. Anthology of classical readings in ethics. Articles on affirmative action; censorship and pornography; sexual morality and AIDS; and other applied ethics topics.

Newton, Lisa H., ed. *Ethics in America Source Reader.* Englewood Cliffs, NJ: Prentice-Hall, Inc., current edition.

Sommers, Christina, and Fred Sommers. *Vice & Virtue in Everyday Life.* Fort Worth, TX: Harcourt Brace College, current edition. Short selections, both historical and contemporary, in ethical theory and its applications.

White, James E., ed. *Contemporary Moral Problems.* Minneapolis/St. Paul, MN: West Publishing, current edition. Anthology of readings on contemporary moral issues with an opening section covering ethical theory. Includes feminist theory and selections from feminist writers.

Current textbook used by a local college or university for a course on the subject.

CREDIT RECOMMENDATIONS

The Center for Adult Learning and Educational Credentials of the American Council on Education (ACE) has reviewed and evaluated the DANTES examination development process and has made the following recommendations:

Area or Course
Equivalent: Ethics in America
Level: Lower level Baccalaureate
Amount of Credit: Three (3) semester hours
Source: ACE Commission on
                     Educational Credit
                     and Credentials

INFORMATION

Colleges and universities that would like to review copies of tests, have additional information about the national norming, or assistance in local norming or score validation studies should write to: DANTES Program, Mail Stop 11-P, The Chauncey Group International, 664 Rosedale Road, Princeton, New Jersey 08540.

It is advisable that schools develop a consistent policy about awarding credit based on scores from this test and that the policy be reviewed periodically. The Chauncey Group will be happy to help schools in this effort.

Correct responses to sample questions: 1.C; 2.C; 3.B; PART II: 4.A; 5.A; 6.B; 7.B; 8.B; 9.A; 10.B.

5

DANTES

Subject Standardized Tests

Fact Sheet
Study Guide

HUMAN RESOURCE MANAGEMENT

TEST INFORMATION

This test was developed to enable schools to award credit to students for knowledge equivalent to that which is learned by students taking the course. The school may choose to award college credit to the student based on the achievement of a passing score. The passing score for each examination is determined by the school based on recommendations from the American Council on Education (ACE). This minimum credit-awarding score is equal to the mean score of students in the norming sample who received a grade of C in the course. Some schools set their own standards for awarding credit and may require a higher score than the ACE recommendation. Students should obtain this information from the institution where they expect to receive credit.

CONTENT

The following topics, which are commonly taught in courses on this subject, are covered by this examination.

	Approximate Percent
I. An Overview of the Personnel Field	2%

    A. Historical development
    B. Personnel functions
    C. The personnel manager

II. General Employment Issues	17%

    A. Human resource planning
    B. Recruiting
    C. Selection
    D. Orientation
    E. Promotions and transfers
    F. Layoffs and outplacement

	Approximate Percent
III. Job Analysis	3%
IV. Training and Development	12%

    A. Career planning
    B. Training programs
    C. Retraining
    D. Development programs
    E. Principles of learning

V. Performance Appraisals	11%

    A. Reasons for performance evaluation
    B. Techniques
    C. Problems

VI. Motivation, Communication, and Leadership Styles	4%
VII. Compensation Issues	18%

    A. Job evaluation
    B. Wage and salary administration
    C. Incentive systems
    D. Benefits
    E. Nonfinancial compensation

VIII. Security Issues	5%

    A. Safety and health
    B. Discipline
    C. Unsatisfactory work performance

	Approximate Percent
IX. Personnel Legislation and Regulation	15%

    A. Social insurance
    B. Minimum wage legislation
       (Fair Labor Standards Act)
    C. Equal employment opportunity
       legislation and affirmative
       action regulations
    D. ERISA
    E. OSHA

X. Labor Relations	11%

    A. Unions
    B. Collective bargaining

XI. Current Issues	2%

    A. Comparable worth
    B. Employee participation groups
    C. Flex-time

Questions on the test require candidates to demonstrate the following abilities. Some questions may require more than one of the abilities.

- Knowledge of basic facts and terms
    (about 30-35% of the examination)

- Understanding of concepts and principles
    (about 30-35% of the examination)

- Ability to apply knowledge to specific problems and situations
    (about 25-30% of the examination)

SAMPLE QUESTIONS

1. Specific standardized questions are used primarily in which of the following types of interviews?

    (A) Patterned or structured
    (B) Nondirective
    (C) Group or board
    (D) Stress

2. Organizational or companywide incentive plans include all of the following EXCEPT

    (A) employee stock ownership plans (ESOP's)
    (B) Scanlon plans
    (C) profit-sharing plans
    (D) standard-hour plans

3. Which of the following theories of employee motivation distinguishes between "satisfiers" and "dissatisfiers"?

    (A) Herzberg's Maintenance Theory
    (B) Maslow's Need Hierarchy
    (C) McClelland's Achievement Theory
    (D) McGregor's Theory X and Theory Y

4. A full-time employee of a local union is generally known as a
    (A) shop steward
    (B) national representative
    (C) business agent
    (D) union organizer

5. Which of the following programs frequently uses simulation to train employees?

    (A) Apprenticeship training
    (B) On-the-job training
    (C) Job instruction training
    (D) Vestibule training

6. Which of the following statements is NOT true about exempt employees?

    (A) They are subject to the overtime provisions of the Fair Labor Standards Act.
    (B) They are permitted to bargain collectively under the provisions of the Tart-Hartley Act.
    (C) They are permitted to have flexible work schedules.
    (D) They are paid hourly wage rates.

2

7. A job specification is usually a written document that

(A) specifies how a job is to be done
(B) outlines the specific duties of a job
(C) lists the employee characteristics required to perform a job
(D) describes the process used to obtain specific job information

8. Which of the following performance appraisal methods does NOT require the supervisor to compare the performances of subordinate employees in the unit?

(A) The forced-choice method
(B) The forced-distribution method
(C) The paired-comparison method
(D) The ranking method

9. The Hay Plan is best known as

(A) an incentive plan
(B) a job evaluation plan
(C) a pension plan
(D) a performance evaluation plan

STUDYING FOR THE EXAMINATION

The following is a list of reference publications that were being used as textbooks in college courses of the same or similar title at the time the test was developed. Appropriate textbooks for study are not limited to those listed below. If you wish to obtain study resources to prepare for the examination, you may reference either the current edition of the following titles **or** textbooks currently used at a local college or university for the same class title. It is recommended that you reference **more than one textbook** on the topics outlined in this fact sheet. You should **begin by checking textbook content against the content outline** included on the front page of this Fact Sheet/Study Guide **before** selecting textbooks that cover the test content from which to study. Textbooks may be found at the campus bookstore of a local college or university offering a course on the subject.

Sources for study material suggested but not limited to the following:

Carrell, Michael R., Frank D. Kuzmits, and Norbert S. Elbert. *Personnel: Human Resource Management.* Columbus, OH: Charles E. Merrill Publishing Co., current edition.

Cascio, Wayne F. *Managing Human Resources.* New York: McGraw-Hill, current edition.

French, Wendell L. *Human Resource Management.* Boston: Houghton Mifflin, current edition.

Heneman, Herbert G. et al. *Personnel/Human Resource Management.* Homewood, IL: Richard D. Irwin, Inc., current edition.

Ivancevich, John M., and William F. Gluech. *Foundations of Personnel/Human Resource Management.* Homewood, IL: BPI/Irwin, current edition.

Leap, Terry L., and Michael D. Crino. *Personnel/Human Resource Management.* New York: MacMillan, current edition.

Mathis, Robert L., and John H. Jackson, *Personnel.* Anaheim, CA: West Publishing Co., current edition.

Mondy, R. Wayne, and Robert M. Noe. *Personnel: The Management of Human Resources.* Needham Heights, MA: Allyn and Bacon, current edition.

Schuler, Randall J., and Vandra L. Huber. *Personnel and Human Resource Management.* Anaheim, CA: West Publishing Co., current edition.

Sherman, Arthur H., George W. Bohlander, and Herbert J. Chruden. *Managing Human Resources.* Cincinnati, OH: South-Western Publishing Co., current edition.

Werther, William B., Jr., and Keith Davis. *Human Resource and Personnel Management.* New York: McGraw-Hill, current edition.

Current textbook used by a local college or university for a course on the subject.

3

CREDIT RECOMMENDATIONS

The Center For Adult Learning and Educational Credentials of the American Council on Education (ACE) has reviewed and evaluated the DANTES examination development process. ACE has made the following recommendations:

Area or Course
  Equivalent: Human Resource
                       Management
Level: Lower level baccalaureate
Amount of Credit: Three (3) semester hours
Source: ACE Commission on
                       Educational Credit
                       and Credentials

INFORMATION

Colleges and universities that would like to review copies of tests, have additional information about the national norming, or assistance in local norming or score validation studies should write to: DANTES Program, Mail Stop 11-P, The Chauncey Group International, 664 Rosedale Road, Princeton, New Jersey 08540.

It is advisable that schools develop a consistent policy about awarding credit based on scores from this test and that the policy be reviewed periodically. The Chauncey Group will be happy to help schools in this effort.

Correct Responses to sample questions: 1A; 2D; 3A; 4C; 5D; 6A; 7C; 8A; 9B.

I.N. D204307

DANTES

Subject Standardized Tests

Fact Sheet

Study Guide

INTRODUCTION TO BUSINESS

TEST INFORMATION

This test was developed to enable schools to award credit to students for knowledge equivalent to that which is learned by students taking the course. The school may choose to award college credit to the student based on the achievement of a passing score. The passing score for each examination is determined by the school based on recommendations from the American Council on Education (ACE). This minimum credit-awarding score is equal to the mean score of students in the norming sample who received a grade of C in the course. Some schools set their own standards for awarding credit and may require a higher score than the ACE recommendation. Students should obtain this information from the institution where they expect to receive credit.

CONTENT

The following topics, which are commonly taught in courses on this subject, are covered by this examination.

	Approximate Percent
I. Economic Issues Affecting Business	14%
A. Private enterprise	
B. Socialistic societies	
C. Today's business and its challenges	
II. International Business	7%
III. Government and Business	5%
IV. Forms of Business Ownership	7%

	Approximate Percent
V. Small Business, Entrepreneurship, and Franchise	5%
VI. Management Process	12%
A. Management functions and decision making	
B. Organizational strategies	
C. Human relations	
D. Business ethics, social responsibility, and the legal system	
VII. Human Resource Management	10%
A. Human resource strategies	
B. Labor relations	
VIII. Production and Operations	2%
IX. Marketing Management	16%
A. Marketing strategies	
B. Marketing mix	
1. Product	
2. Price	
3. Promotion	
4. Placement/distribution	
X. Financial Management	14%
A. Money, banking, and financial institutions	
B. Financial strategies	
C. Securities market	
XI. Risk Management and Insurance	3%
XII. Management and Information Systems	5%
A. Accounting	
B. Computers	

Questions on the test require candidates to demonstrate the following abilities. Some questions may require more than one of the abilities.

- Knowledge of basic facts and terms (about 25-30% of the examination)

- Understanding of concepts and principles (about 30-35% of the examination)

- Ability to apply knowledge to specific case problems (about 35-40% of the examination)

SAMPLE QUESTIONS

1. Assets are defined as

    (A) everything a company owns
    (B) everything a company owes
    (C) a company's profits
    (D) the total of a company's equity capital

2. All of the following are necessary features of capitalism EXCEPT

    (A) profit
    (B) corporations
    (C) private ownership
    (D) competition

3. Business people who support involvement in social problems for humanitarian reasons usually believe that business

    (A) is responsible for most of society's problems
    (B) fulfills its social obligation by supplying jobs to millions of people
    (C) must follow the example of Andrew Carnegie
    (D) must put something back into the society from which it profits

4. All of the following are functions of management EXCEPT

    (A) controlling
    (B) selling
    (C) planning
    (D) organizing

5. Which of the following is a true statement about a job specification?

    (A) It describes the qualifications required of a worker.
    (B) It details the job's objectives.
    (C) It sets forth the relationship of the job to other jobs being performed within the firm.
    (D) It describes the working environment of the job.

6. All employees are required to join the union and pay dues in which of the following types of shop?

    (A) An open shop
    (B) A union shop
    (C) An agency shop
    (D) A closed shop

7. Since both drive up the cost of imported goods, there is little difference between import quotas and

    (A) embargoes
    (B) sanctions
    (C) tariffs
    (D) dumping

8. Which of the following are considered part of the marketing mix?

    I. Price
    II. Promotion
    III. Labor
    IV. Product

    (A) I and II only
    (B) III and IV only
    (C) I, II, and IV only
    (D) I, II, III, and IV

9. In order to cover risk, an insurance company must have a sufficient number of policyholders to do which of the following?

    (A) Examine the risk
    (B) Estimate probable loss
    (C) Construct actuarial tables
    (D) Average out the risk

2

10. Demand deposits are also know as

(A) credit cards
(B) charge accounts
(C) savings accounts
(D) checking accounts

11. The interest rate that banks charge their best corporate customers is the

(A) prime rate
(B) discount rate
(C) credit rate
(D) commercial rate

STUDYING FOR THE EXAMINATION

The following is a list of reference publications that were being used as textbooks in college courses of the same or similar title at the time the test was developed. Appropriate textbooks for study are not limited to those listed below. If you wish to obtain study resources to prepare for the examination, you may reference either the current edition of the following titles **or** textbooks currently used at a local college or university for the same class title. It is recommended that you reference **more than one textbook** on the topics outlined in this fact sheet. You should **begin by checking textbook content against the content outline** included on the front page of this Fact Sheet/Study Guide **before** selecting textbooks that cover the test content from which to study. Textbooks may be found at the campus bookstore of a local college or university offering a course on the subject.

Sources for study material suggested but not limited to the following:

Boone, Louis E., and David L. Kurtz. *Contemporary Business*. Fort Worth, TX: The Dryden Press, current edition.

Jackson, John H., and Vernon A. Musselman, *Business – Contemporary Concepts and Practices*. Englewood Cliffs, NJ: Prentice-Hall, Inc., current edition.

Nickels, William G., James McHugh, and Susan M. McHugh. *Understanding Business*. Chicago, IL: Irwin, current edition.

Pride, William M., Robert J. Hughes, and Jack R. Kapoor. *Business*. Boston, MA: Houghton Mifflin, current edition.

Rachman, David J. *Business Today*. New York, NY: McGraw Hill, current edition.

Reinecke, John A., Gary Dessler, and William F. Schoell. *Introduction to Business*. Boston, MA: Allyn and Bacon, current edition.

Current textbook used by a local college or university for a course on the subject.

CREDIT RECOMMENDATIONS

The Center for Adult Learning and Educational Credentials of the American Council on Education (ACE) has reviewed and evaluated the DANTES examination development process and has made the following recommendations:

Area or Course Equivalent:	Introduction to Business
Level:	Lower-level baccalaureate
Amount of Credit:	Three (3) semester hours
Source:	ACE Commission on Educational Credit and Credentials

INFORMATION

Colleges and universities that would like to have review copies of tests, additional information about the national norming, or assistance in local norming or score validation studies should write to: DANTES Program, Mail Stop 11-P, The Chauncey Group International, 664 Rosedale Road, Princeton, New Jersey 08540.

It is advisable that schools develop a consistent policy about awarding credit based on scores from this test and that the policy be reviewed periodically. The Chauncey Group will be happy to help schools in this effort.

Correct Responses: 1.A; 2.B; 3.D; 4.B; 5.A; 6.B; 7.C; 8.C; 9.D; 10.D; 11.A

3

DANTES

Subject Standardized Tests

Fact Sheet
Study Guide

ORGANIZATIONAL BEHAVIOR

TEST INFORMATION

This test was developed to enable schools to award credit to students for knowledge equivalent to that which is learned by students taking the course. The school may choose to award college credit to the student based on the achievement of a passing score. The passing score for each examination is determined by the school based on recommendations from the American Council on Education (ACE). This minimum credit-awarding score is equal to the mean score of students in the norming sample who received a grade of C in the course. Some schools set their own standards for awarding credit and may require a higher score than the ACE recommendation. Students should obtain this information from the institution where they expect to receive credit.

CONTENT

The following topics, which are commonly taught in courses on this subject, are covered by this examination.

Approximate
Percent

I. Organizational Behavior   **6%**
    Overview
    A. The field of organizational
       behavior
       1. Definition and framework
       2. Fundamental concepts
       3. History
    B. The study of organizational
       behavior
       1. Scientific approaches
       2. Research designs
       3. Data collection methods

Approximate
Percent

II. Individual Processes and   **36%**
    Characteristics
    A. Perpetual processes
       1. Characteristics of the
          perceptual process
       2. Barriers to accurate
          perception of others
       3. Attributional approaches to
          perception and behavior
    B. Personality
       1. Theories of personality
       2. Personality traits and
          characteristics
       3. Influence of personality on
          work behavior
    C. Attitudes
       1. Attitude formation
       2. Attitude and values
       3. Key employee attitudes
    D. Learning processes
       1. Basic models of learning
       2. Major influences on the
          learning process
       3. Reinforcement theory
          a. Nature of punishment
          b. Types of reinforcement
          c. Schedules of
             reinforcement
    E. Motivation
       1. Role of motivation in
          organizations
       2. Theories of motivation
          a. Process theories
             (e.g., expectancy,
             equity, goal-setting)

Dantes/DSST Program

<table>
<tr><td></td><td style="text-align:center">Approximate
<u>Percent</u></td></tr>
</table>

b. Content theories (e.g., Maslow's theory of hierarchy of needs, Herzberg's two-factor theory, Alderfer's ERG-existence, relatedness, and growth-theory, McClelland's achievement theory)

3. Application in organizations
   a. Behavior modification
   b. Job design
   c. Reward systems
4. Evaluation of theories and models of motivation
5. Implications for managers

F. Work stress and the individual
   1. Nature of stress
   2. Causes and consequences of stress
   3. Coping with stress--individual and organizational approaches

III. Interpersonal and Group Processes and Characteristics   **32%**
   A. Group dynamics
      1. Types of groups
      2. Reasons for group formation
      3. Stages of group development
      4. Characteristics of groups
   B. Group behavior and conflict
      1. Levels of conflict
      2. Consequences of functional and dysfunctional conflict
      3. Conflict management
   C. Leadership
      1. Nature of the leadership process
      2. Models of leadership
      3. Evaluation of models of leadership
      4. Implications for managers

<table>
<tr><td></td><td style="text-align:center">Approximate
<u>Percent</u></td></tr>
</table>

D. Power and politics
   1. Power and influence
   2. Interpersonal sources of power
   3. Structural and situational sources of power
   4. Political behavior in organizations
E. Communication processes
   1. The communication process
   2. Models of interpersonal communication styles
   3. Communication networks
   4. Barriers to effective communication within organizations
   5. Nonverbal communication

IV. Organizational Processes and   **19%**
   Characteristics
   A. Organizational decision-making
      1. Classification and definition of decisions
      2. Models of the decision-making process
      3. Individual vs. group decision-making
   B. Organization structure
      1. Dimensions of organization structure
      2. Types of organization structure
      3. Responsibility and authority
   C. Organization design
      1. Classic approaches
      2. Contingency approaches

V. Change and Development Processes   **7%**
   A. Basic processes and concepts of change
      1. Pressures for change
      2. Models and processes for planned organizational change
      3. Resistance to organizational change
      4. Corporate culture

   B. Applications and techniques of change and development
      1. Overview of organization development
      2. Group and individual change
      3. Sociotechnological approaches to change
      4. Structural approaches to change

2

Questions on the test require candidates to demonstrate the following abilities. Some questions may require more than one of the abilities.

- Knowledge of basic facts and terms (about 50-55% of the examination)

- Understanding of concepts and principles (about 30-35% of the examination)

- Ability to apply knowledge to specific problems and situations (about 10-15% of the examination)

SAMPLE QUESTIONS

1. An employee who bases his or her job-evaluation rating on an unfair rating form may be

    (A) stereotyping supervisory personnel
    (B) engaging in perceptual defense
    (C) making a causal attribution
    (D) learning about job tasks

2. Which of the following accurately lists needs in Maslow's hierarchy?

    (A) Physiological, power, growth, and esteem
    (B) Security, esteem, power, and self-actualization
    (C) Security, belonging, mastery, psychological, and self-esteem
    (D) Physiological, security, belonging, esteem and self-actualization

3. Operant conditioning is primarily concerned with

    (A) physiological causes of behavior
    (B) cognition of behavior
    (C) consequences of behavior
    (D) punishment of behavior

4. Which of the following is one reason why Herzberg's two-factor theory is viewed as controversial?

    (A) It states that job satisfaction and dissatisfaction do not exist on a single continuum.
    (B) It does not explain why people desire to achieve.
    (C) It states that organizational policies have too strong an impact on intrinsic rewards.
    (D) It does not explain why people choose particular behaviors to accomplish work-related goals.

5. Standing close to another individual to communicate a sense of power is an example of

    (A) an authority stance
    (B) a stereotype
    (C) a nonverbal cue
    (D) a leadership behavior

6. From the organization's perspective, which of the following is an example of a positive norm?

    (A) The appearance of working hard, regardless of results
    (B) The use of group sanctions against the person who exceeds productivity levels
    (C) A general practice of arriving to work on time
    (D) A supervisor's public criticism of a subordinate's poor performance

3

7. Which of the following statements best describes the path-goal theory of leadership?

   (A) It focuses on goals to achievement.
   (B) It measures the philosophical assumptions behind a leader's style.
   (C) It looks at leader behaviors, subordinate characteristics, and environmental pressures.
   (D) It emphasizes personality traits critical for effective leadership.

8. George Bacon is considered one of the leading surgeons in the field of artificial heart transplants. Even though he is not associated with Western Memorial Hospital, he exerts much influence over many of the surgeons there. Such influence is best termed

   (A) legitimate power
   (B) coercive power
   (C) reward power
   (D) expert power

9. Which of the following is a major feature of a matrix organization?

   (A) Provision for horizontal communication
   (B) Establishment of profit centers
   (C) Presence of employees with two supervisors
   (D) Increased separation of line and staff responsibilities

10. Which of the following statements is NOT true about organizational development (OD)?

   (A) It is a system-wide change effort.
   (B) It frequently leads to new organizational structures.
   (C) It is characterized by participatory methods of change.
   (D) It emphasizes short-term rather than long-term methods of change.

STUDYING FOR THE EXAMINATION

The following is a list of reference publications that were being used as textbooks in college courses of the same or similar title at the time the test was developed. Appropriate textbooks for study are not limited to those listed below. If you wish to obtain study resources to prepare for the examination, you may reference either the current edition of the following titles **or** textbooks currently used at a local college or university for the same class title. It is recommended that you reference **more than one textbook** on the topics outlined in this fact sheet. You should **begin by checking textbook content against the content outline** included on the front page of this Fact Sheet/Study Guide **before** selecting textbooks that cover the test content from which to study. Textbooks may be found at the campus bookstore of a local college or university offering a course on the subject.

Sources for study material suggested but not limited to the following:

Davis, Keith A., and John W. Newstrom. *Human Behavior at Work: Organizational Behavior*. New York: McGraw-Hill, current edition.

Gibson, James L., John M. Ivancevich, and James H. Donnelly, Jr. *Organizations: Behavior, Structure, Processes*. Chicago, IL: Irwin, current edition.

Gordon, Judith R. *A Diagnostic Approach to Organizational Behavior*. Upper Saddle River, NJ: Prentice Hall, current edition.

Hellriegel, Don, John W. Slocum, and Richard W. Woodman. *Organizational Behavior*. Cincinnati, OH: South-Western College Publishing, current edition.

Luthans, Fred. *Organizational Behavior*. New York: McGraw-Hill, current edition.

Moorhead, Gregory, and Ricky W. Griffin. *Organizational Behavior: Managing People and Organizations*. Boston: Houghton-Mifflin, current edition.

4

Newstrom, John W., and Keith Davis. *Organizational Behavior: Human Behavior at Work*. New York: McGraw Hill, current edition.

Organ, Dennis W., and Thomas S. Bateman. *Organizational Behavior*: Homewood, IL: Irwin, current edition. (Note: this is a slightly advanced-level text).

Robbins, Stephen P. *Organizational Behavior*: *Concepts, Controversies, Applications*. Upper Saddle River, NJ: Prentice Hall International, current edition.

Robbins, Stephen P. *Essentials of Organizational Behavior*. Upper Saddle River, NJ: Prentice Hall International, current edition.

Schermerhorn Jr., John R., James G. Hunt, and Richard N. Osborn. *Organizational Behavior*. New York: Wiley, current edition.

Current textbook used by a local college or university for a course on the subject.

CREDIT RECOMMENDATIONS

The Center For Adult Learning and Educational Credentials of the American Council on Education (ACE) has reviewed and evaluated the DANTES examination development process. ACE has made the following recommendations:

Area or Course
  Equivalent: Organizational Behavior
Level: Lower level Baccalaureate
Amount of Credit: Three (3) semester hours
Source: ACE Commission on
                   Educational Credit
                   and Credentials

INFORMATION

Colleges and universities that would like to review copies of tests, have additional information about the national norming, or assistance in local norming or score validation studies should write to: DANTES Program, Mail Stop 11-P, The Chauncey Group International, 664 Rosedale Road, Princeton, New Jersey 08540.

It is advisable that schools develop a consistent policy about awarding credit based on scores from this test and that the policy be reviewed periodically. The Chauncey Group will be happy to help schools in this effort.

Correct Responses: 1.B; 2.D; 3.C; 4.A; 5.C; 6.C; 7.C; 8.D; 9.C; 10.D.

5

DANTES

Subject Standardized Tests

Fact Sheet

Study Guide

PERSONAL FINANCE

TEST INFORMATION

This test was developed to enable schools to award credit to students for knowledge equivalent to that which is learned by students taking the course. The school may choose to award college credit to the student based on the achievement of a passing score. The passing score for each examination is determined by the school based on recommendations from the American Council on Education (ACE). This minimum credit-awarding score is equal to the mean score of students in the norming sample who received a grade of C in the course. Some schools set their own standards for awarding credit and may require a higher score than the ACE recommendation. Students should obtain this information from the institution where they expect to receive credit.

CONTENT

The following topics, which are commonly taught in courses on this subject, are covered by this examination.

	Approximate Percent
I. Overview	12%

  A. Financial goals and values
  B. Budgeting (spending plan) and financial statements
  C. Cash management
  D. Economic terminology (recession, depression, etc.)
  E. Institutional aspects of financial planning (e.g., CFP, CHFC, FDIC, NASD, SEC)

	Approximate Percent
II. Credit and Debt	20%

  A. Credit cards
  B. Installment loans
  C. Interest calculations
  D. Federal credit laws
  E. Creditworthiness, credit scoring and reporting
  F. Bankruptcy
    1. Various chapters
    2. Alternatives
    3. Advantages and disadvantages

III. Major Purchases	14%

  A. Auto, furniture, appliances
    1. Preshopping research/comparison shopping
    2. Lease vs. buy
    3. Warranties/service contracts
    4. Lemon laws and redress
      a. Effective complaining
      b. Small claims court
  B. Housing
    1. Rent vs. buy
    2. Financing
      a. Adjustable Rate Mortgages (ARMs)
      b. Fixed-rate mortgages
      c. Closing costs
      d. PITI
    3. Rules of thumb (ratios)
    4. Roles of professionals (real estate agents, inspectors, appraisers, lawyers)

	Approximate Percent
IV. Taxes	**11%**

IV. Taxes   **11%**
A. Payroll
B. Income
C. IRS and audits
D. Estate and gift
E. Tax planning/estimating
F. Progressive vs. regressive
G. Other (excise, property, state income)
H. Tax professionals

V. Insurance   **14%**
A. Risk management
B. Life policies
1. Term vs. cash value
2. Policy terminology
C. Property and liability policies
1. Personal and family auto
2. Homeowners
3. Umbrella coverage
4. Terminology
D. Health and Disability policies
1. Major medical
2. HMOs
3. Medicare and Medicaid
4. Terms and concepts
E. Specialty insurance (e.g., professional, malpractice, antiques)
F. Insurance analysis and sources of information

VI. Investments   **17%**
A. Liquid assets
1. Savings accounts
2. Certificates of Deposit (CDs)
3. Money market funds/Money market deposit accounts
4. Emergency funds
B. Fixed income/Bonds (e.g., Treasury, municipal, deep discount, corporate, junk, zero-coupon, Ginnie Mae)

C. Equities   **Approximate Percent**
1. Stock exchanges
2. Over-the-counter stocks
3. Primary vs. secondary markets
4. Common vs. preferred stocks
5. P/E ratio
6. Stock analysis techniques

D. Mutual funds
1. Dollar-cost averaging
2. Load vs. no-load
3. Fee structures
E. Other (e.g., commodities, precious metals, real estate, options)
F. Sources of information (e.g., professionals, Moody's, S&P, *Morning Star, Barrons, Value Line*, prospectuses, audited annual financial reports)
G. Time value of money
H. Asset/Portfolio allocation

VII. Retirement and Estate   **12%**
Planning
A. Qualified retirement accounts (roll-overs) (e.g., IRA, SEP, Keogh, 401(k), 403(b)
B. Terminology (vesting, maturity)
C. Social Security benefits
D. Wills and trusts
E. Tax-deferred annuities
F. Estate planning (e.g., probate vs. non-probate)

Questions on the test require candidates to demonstrate the following abilities. Some questions may require more than one of the abilities.

- Knowledge of basic facts and terms (about 45 - 50% of the examination)

- Understanding of concepts and principles (about 30 -35% of the examination)

- Ability to apply knowledge to specific problems and situations (about 15 - 20% of the examination)

-2-

SAMPLE QUESTIONS

1. Which of the following resources could be used to evaluate the financial strength of an insurance company?

    (A) Morningstar
    (B) Best's
    (C) Dun & Bradstreet
    (D) Standard and Poor's

2. Joe and Betty are both recent college graduates in their mid-twenties and are working at junior executive positions in medium-size firms. They plan to get married in two months and hope to have a baby within the next three years. Which of the following short-term goals should they be considering now?

    (A) Accumulating a savings fund for their honeymoon
    (B) Establishing a retirement plan for themselves
    (C) Establishing a college tuition fund for their child
    (D) Accumulating a down payment for a house

3. The federal income tax is considered a progressive tax because as a person's income rises the person's tax rate

    (A) remains the same
    (B) increases
    (C) decreases
    (D) fluctuates

4. Which of the following types of bankruptcy is designed for debtors with regular incomes who must attempt to repay as much of the debt as possible within a certain time period?

    (A) Chapter 5
    (B) Chapter 7
    (C) Chapter 11
    (D) Chapter 13

5. A lender is offering a fixed-rate loan with two points. If a family plans to purchase an $80,000 house by putting 20% down and borrowing $64,000, how much will the two points cost?

    (A) $1,600
    (B) $1,280
    (C) $2,000
    (D) $1,400

6. Which of the following types of insurance provides an individual with a percentage of lost income due to physical or mental incapacity?

    (A) Health
    (B) Major medical
    (C) Disability
    (D) Umbrella

7. A 65-year-old retiree with a 50-year-old spouse is considering various annuity payout options. Which of the following payout options would provide the retiree with the largest annual payment?

    (A) Straight life
    (B) Joint life
    (C) 20-year-certain
    (D) Refund

8. A blue chip company is generally defined as a

    (A) new company whose stock trades over-the-counter
    (B) well-established company whose stock trades on the NYSE
    (C) 20-year-old limited partnership that is sold by stockbrokers
    (D) 3-year-old mutual fund whose stock trades on the NYSE

9. An increase in the consumer price index (CPI) is generally an indication of

    (A) increased unemployment
    (B) increased inflation
    (C) continued recession
    (D) reduced trade deficit

-3-

STUDYING FOR THE EXAMINATION

The following is a list of reference publications that were being used as textbooks in college courses of the same or similar title at the time the test was developed. Appropriate textbooks for study are not limited to those listed below. If you wish to obtain study resources to prepare for the examination, you may reference either the current edition of the following titles **or** textbooks currently used at a local college or university for the same class title. It is recommended that you reference **more than one textbook** on the topics outlined in this fact sheet. You should **begin by checking textbook content against the content outline** included on the front page of this Fact Sheet/Study Guide **before** selecting textbooks that cover the test content from which to study. Textbooks may be found at the campus bookstore of a local college or university offering a course on the subject.

Sources for study material suggested but not limited to the following:

Garman, E. Thomas and Raymond E. Forgue. *Personal Finance*. Boston: Houghton Mifflin Company, current edition.

Gitman, Lawrence J. and Michael D. Joehnk. *Personal Financial Planning*. Chicago: The Dryden Press, current edition.

Hallman, G. Victor and Jerry S. Rosenbloom. *Personal Financial Planning*. New York: McGraw-Hill, Inc. current edition.

Kapoor, Jack R., Les R. Dlabay, and Robert J. Hughes. *Personal Finance*. Homewood, IL: Richard D. Irwin, Inc., current edition.

Lang, Larry R. *Strategy for Personal Finance*. New York: McGraw-Hill, Inc., current edition.

Quinn, Jane Bryant. *Making the Most of Your Money: Smart Ways to Create Wealth and Plan Your Finances in the '90s*. New York: Simon & Schuster, current edition.

Rosefsky, Robert S. *Personal Finance*. New York: John Wiley & Sons, Inc. current edition.

Winger, Bernard J. and Ralph R. Frasca. *Personal Finance: An Integrated Planning Approach*. New York: Macmillan Publishing Company, current edition.

Current textbook used by a local college or university for a course on the subject.

CREDIT RECOMMENDATIONS

The Center for Adult Learning and Educational Credentials of the American Council on Education (ACE) has reviewed and evaluated the DANTES examination development process. The American Council on Education has made the following recommendations:

Area or Course	
Equivalent:	Personal Finance
Level:	Lower-level baccalaureate
Amount of Credit:	Three (3) semester hours
Source:	ACE Commission on Educational Credit and Credentials

INFORMATION

Colleges and universities that would like to review copies of tests, have additional information about the national norming, or assistance in local norming or score validation studies should write to: DANTES Program, Mail Stop 11-P, The Chauncey Group International, 664 Rosedale Road, Princeton, New Jersey 08540.

It is advisable that schools develop a consistent policy about awarding credit based on scores from this test and that the policy be reviewed periodically. The Chauncey Group will be happy to help schools in this effort.

Correct responses to sample questions: 1.B; 2.D; 3.B; 4.D; 5.B; 6.C; 7.A; 8.B; 9.B.

I.N. D204306

-4-

DANTES
Subject Standardized Tests

Fact Sheet
Study Guide

PRINCIPLES OF FINANCIAL ACCOUNTING

TEST INFORMATION

This test was developed to enable schools to award credit to students for knowledge equivalent to that which is learned by students taking the course. The school may choose to award college credit to the student based on the achievement of a passing score. The passing score for each examination is determined by the school based on recommendations from the American Council on Education (ACE). This minimum credit-awarding score is equal to the mean score of students in the norming sample who received a grade of C in the course. Some schools set their own standards for awarding credit and may require a higher score than the ACE recommendation. Students should obtain this information from the institution where they expect to receive credit.

The use of non-programmable calculators is permitted during the test. Scratch paper for computations should be provided.

CONTENT

The following topics, which are commonly taught in courses on this subject, are covered by this examination:

	Approximate Percent
General concepts and principles	12%
Accounting cycle and account classification	7%
Transaction analysis and accounting equation	11%
Adjusting entries; accruals and deferrals	11%
Merchandising transactions	4%
Cash and internal control	7%
Current accounts - marketable securities, receivables and inventories	17%
Property, plant, and equipment	4%
Long- and short-term liabilities and interest calculations	11%
Capital stock, retained earnings, and dividends	4%
Financial statements - their components and interpretation	12%

Questions on the test require candidates to demonstrate the following abilities. Some may require more than one of the abilities.

- Knowledge of basic facts and terms (about 25-35 percent of the examination)

- Understanding of concepts and principles (about 25-35 percent of the examination)

- Ability to apply knowledge to specific problems and situations (about 35-45 percent of the examination)

SAMPLE QUESTIONS

1. All of the following are considered asset accounts EXCEPT

    (A) short-term investments
    (B) capital stock
    (C) cash
    (D) land

2. On January 2, XYZ Company pays salaries previously accrued as of December 31. As a result of this transaction, the effect on the accounting equation is

    (A) an increase in assets, an increase in liabilities
    (B) a decrease in assets, a decrease in owners' equity
    (C) a decrease in assets, a decrease in liabilities
    (D) a decrease in assets, an increase in liabilities

Copyright © 2000 by The Chauncey Group International in trust for the United States Department of Defense.
Unlimited reproduction of this fact sheet is allowed.

3. Cam Company sends a check for $12,000 to Ray Realtors on December 15 for next year's rent on a warehouse building. CAM Company will initially classify this payment as

(A) an operating expense
(B) an intangible asset
(C) a prepaid asset
(D) a prepaid expense

4. XYZ Company, which uses the periodic inventory method, has the following record for a particular inventory item.

	Beginning	
Jan 1	Balance	100 units @ $3.00
Feb 15	Purchase	400 units @ $3.10
June 7	Purchase	500 units @ $3.20
Oct 29	Purchase	400 units @ $3.30

If 200 units remain in the inventory at December 31, what is their LIFO cost?

(A) $610
(B) $630
(C) $650
(D) $660

5. A bank reconciliation is performed in order to

(A) verify the accuracy of a company's recorded cash balance
(B) ensure that all bank loans have been properly accounted for
(C) verify that all cash disbursements are for a legitimate business purpose
(D) verify that only authorized personnel signed the disbursement checks

MACRS Recovery Allowance Percentages
for Personal Property (not Real Estate)

Ownership Year	Class of Investment			
	3-Year	5-Year	7-Year	10-Year
1	33%	20%	14%	10%
2	45	32	25	18
3	15	19	17	14
4	7	12	13	12
5		11	9	9
6		6	9	7
7			9	7
8			4	7
9				7
10				6
11				3
	100%	100%	100%	100%

6. A truck with a salvage value of $2,000 and a class life of 10 years was purchased for $32,000. According to the depreciation expense for the second year under the modified accelerated cost recovery system (MACRS) method is

(A) $2,900
(B) $4,800
(C) $5,120
(D) $6,400

7. RAM Company keeps its records on a calendar-year basis and makes adjusting entries only at the close of each year. The unadjusted trial balance for December 31, Year 1, shows Unearned Revenue of $1,200 for a year's rent collected on October 1, Year 1. The rent is a one-year lease ending September 30, Year 2. The adjusting entry needed on December 31, Year 2, should include a debit to

(A) unearned revenue for $300
(B) unearned revenue for $900
(C) rental revenue for $300
(D) rental revenue for $1,200

2

8. A company receives a $5,000, 60-day, 8 percent note dated May 1, Year 1. What is the total amount of cash to be collected on the due date? (Assume a 360-day year.)

   (A) $5,006.67
   (B) $5,050.00
   (C) $5,066.67
   (D) $5,666.67

9. Which of the following best describes the calculation of the gross profit rate?

   (A) Net income is divided by net sales.
   (B) Net sales is divided by net assets.
   (C) The cost of goods sold is added to operating expenses, and the sum is divided by net sales.
   (D) The cost of goods sold is subtracted from net sales, and the difference is divided by net sales.

10. Bonds with a face value of $100,000 are sold at 97½. This transaction will result in recording

    (A) a discount of $975.00
    (B) a premium of $1,097.50
    (C) a discount of $2,500.00
    (D) an accrued interest of $9,750.00

11. On the date that a company declares a cash dividend, which of the following is true?

    (A) Checks are mailed to the stockholders.
    (B) The company incurs a liability.
    (C) The stockholders' equity is increased.
    (D) The assets of the firm are decreased.

12. Which of the following would be of LEAST value in predicting a company's future net income?

    (A) Extraordinary items of income
    (B) Comparative income statements
    (C) Net income from continuing operations
    (D) An analysis of future changes in tax rates

STUDYING FOR THE EXAMINATION

The following is a list of reference publications that were being used as textbooks in college courses of the same or similar title at the time the test was developed. Appropriate textbooks for study are not limited to those listed below. If you wish to obtain study resources to prepare for the examination, you may reference either the current edition of the following titles **or** textbooks currently used at a local college or university for the same class title. It is recommended that you reference **more than one textbook** on the topics outlined in this fact sheet. You should **begin by checking textbook content against the content outline** included on the front page of this Fact Sheet/Study Guide **before** selecting textbooks that cover the test content from which to study. Textbooks may be found at the campus bookstore of a local college or university offering a course on the subject.

Sources for study material suggested but not limited to the following:

Asman, Mark F., Cowen, Scott S., and Mandell, Steven L. *Accounting Today: Principles and Applications.* St. Paul, Minn: West Publishing Co., current edition.

Diamond, Michael A., Flamholtz, Eric G., and Flamholtz, Diane T. *Financial Accounting.* Boston, MA: PWS-KENT Publishing Co., current edition.

Larson, Kermit D., and Miller, Paul B. W. *Financial Accounting.* Homewood, IL: Richard D. Irwin, Inc., current edition.

Meigs, Walter B., and Meigs, Robert F. *Financial Accounting.* New York: McGraw-Hill Book Co., current edition.

Needles, Belverd E., Jr. *Financial Accounting.* Boston, MA: Houghton Mifflin Co., current edition.

3

Walgenbach, Paul H., Hanson, Ernest I., *Financial Accounting - An Introduction.* San Diego, CA: Harcourt Brace Jovanovich Inc., current edition.

Current textbook used by a local college or university for a course on the subject.

CREDIT RECOMMENDATIONS

The Center For Adult Learning and Educational Credentials of the American Council on Education (ACE) has reviewed and evaluated the DANTES examination development process. The American Council on Education has made the following recommendations:

Area or Course
  Equivalent: Financial Accounting
Level: Lower level baccalaureate
Amount of Credit: Three (3) semester hours
Source: ACE Commission on
                               Educational Credit
                               and Credentials

INFORMATION

Colleges and universities that would like to review copies of tests, have additional information about the national norming, or assistance in local norming or score validation studies should write to: DANTES Program, Mail Stop 11-P, The Chauncey Group International, 664 Rosedale Road, Princeton, New Jersey 08540.

It is advisable that schools develop a consistent policy about awarding credit based on scores from this test and that the policy be reviewed periodically. The Chauncey Group will be happy to help schools in this effort.

Correct responses to sample questions: 1.B; 2.C; 3.D; 4.A; 5.A; 6.C; 7.B; 8.C; 9.D; 10.C; 11.B; 12.A.

I.N. D204310

4

DANTES
Subject Standardized Tests

Fact Sheet
Study Guide

PRINCIPLES OF SUPERVISION

TEST INFORMATION

This test was developed to enable schools to award credit to students for knowledge equivalent to that which is learned by students taking the course. The school may choose to award college credit to the student based on the achievement of a passing score. The passing score for each examination is determined by the school based on recommendations from the American Council on Education (ACE). This minimum credit-awarding score is equal to the mean score of students in the norming sample who received a grade of C in the course. Some schools set their own standards for awarding credit and may require a higher score than the ACE recommendation. Students should obtain this information from the institution where they expect to receive credit.

CONTENT

The following topics, which are commonly taught in courses on this subject, are covered by this examination.

	Approximate Percent
I. Roles and Responsibilities of the Supervisor	16%

    A. Definition of a supervisor
    B. Skill requirements (e.g., technical, communi-cations, human relations)
    C. Multiple supervisory roles (e.g., facilitator, negotiator spokesperson)
    D. Decision making and problem solving
    E. Values and ethics
    F. Authority

	Approximate Percent
II. Management Functions	
A. Planning at the supervisory level	11%

      1. Definition of planning
      2. Types of planning (e.g. long-range, short-range)
      3. Goals and objectives
      4. The planning process
      5. Time management and delegation

	Approximate Percent
B. Organization and staffing at the supervisory level	26%

      1. Organizational principles
        a. Line and staff
        b. Centralized vs. decentralized
        c. Matrix or project organization
        d. Span of control
        e. Unity of command
      2. Staffing principles
        a. Determining needs
        b. Legal considerations
        c. Recruiting and selecting
        d. Orientation and training

	Approximate Percent
C. Directing at the supervisory level	26%

      1. Leadership
      2. Motivation
      3. Performance appraisal
      4. Working with diverse employees (e.g., people with minority status, disabilities, substance abuse problems)
      5. Maintaining discipline
      6. Counseling employees
      7. Employee development

		Approximate Percent
D.	Controlling at the supervisory level	9%

    1. Steps in the controlling process

    2. Budgetary considerations

III. Other Topics   **12%**

    A. Legal issues (e.g., sexual harassment, EEO, OSHA, AIDS)

    B. Stress management

    C. Union/nonunion environments

    D. Increasing productivity

    E. Quality concerns (e.g., quality assurance, quality circles quality of work life)

Questions on the test require candidates to demonstrate the following abilities. Some questions may require more than one of the abilities.

- Knowledge of basic facts and terms (about 20-25% of the examination)

- Understanding of concepts and principles (about 60-65% of the examination)

- Ability to apply knowledge to specific problems and situation (about 15-20% of the examination)

SAMPLE QUESTIONS

1. Which of the following terms is commonly used to refer to each employee's obligation to execute all duties to the best of his or her ability?

    (A) Authority
    (B) Responsibility
    (C) Delegation
    (D) Accountability

2. The planning that supervisors do is directly derived from plans of

    (A) customers
    (B) subordinates
    (C) upper management
    (D) colleagues

3. A supervisor who works in a company that follows the parity principle of delegation would be most likely to say which of the following?

    (A) "I have adequate responsibility but not enough authority."
    (B) "I have adequate authority but not enough responsibility."
    (C) "I have an equal amount of authority and responsibility."
    (D) "I have adequate authority to meet my responsibility."

4. Which of the following is an example of a line employee?

    (A) An industrial engineer
    (B) A salesperson
    (C) A security guard
    (D) A manufacturing department foreman

5. Employee counseling is usually NOT appropriate for addressing an employee's

    (A) marital problems
    (B) substance abuse
    (C) career planning
    (D) preretirement planning

6. When a prospective employee is being interviewed, which of the following questions CANNOT be asked?

    (A) "Do you have any training that qualifies you for this job?"
    (B) "Do you have any relatives working for this company?"
    (C) "What is your marital status?"
    (D) "Are you in this country on a visa that permits you to work?"

7. Which of the following persons developed the theory of a hierarchy of needs?

    (A) Douglas McGregor
    (B) Rensis Likert
    (C) Abraham Maslow
    (D) Kurt Lewin

2

8. Maintenance of departmental discipline in a factory is the function of the

   (A) human relations manager
   (B) supervisor
   (C) president
   (D) shop steward

9. All of the following are steps in the controlling process EXCEPT

   (A) establishing performance standards
   (B) developing employee benefits
   (C) monitoring performance
   (D) taking corrective action

10. Which of the following organizations has the power to enforce basic labor laws?

   (A) National Labor Relations Board
   (B) Federal Mediation and Conciliation Service
   (C) United States Department of Labor
   (D) American Federation of Labor

STUDYING FOR THE EXAMINATION

The following is a list of reference publications that were being used as textbooks in college courses of the same or similar title at the time the test was developed. Appropriate textbooks for study are not limited to those listed below. If you wish to obtain study resources to prepare for the examination, you may reference either the current edition of the following titles **or** textbooks currently used at a local college or university for the same class title. It is recommended that you reference **more than one textbook** on the topics outlined in this fact sheet. You should **begin by checking textbook content against the content outline** included on the front page of this Fact Sheet/Study Guide **before** selecting textbooks that cover the test content from which to study. Textbooks may be found at the campus bookstore of a local college or university offering a course on the subject.

Sources for study material suggested but not limited to the following:

Frunzi, George L., and Patrick E. Savini. *Supervision: The Art of Management*. Upper Saddle River, NJ: Prentice Hall, Inc., current edition.

Hilgert, Raymond L., and Edwin C. Leonard *Supervision: Concepts and Practices of Management*. Cincinnati: South-Western Publishing Co., current edition.

Lowery, Robert C. *Supervisory Management: Guidelines for Application*. Englewood Cliffs, NJ: Prentice Hall, Inc., current edition.

Mosley, Donald C., Leon C. Megginson, and Paul H. Pietri, Jr. *Supervisory Management: The Art of Empowering and Developing People*. Cincinnati: South-Western Publishing Co., current edition.

Plunkett, W. Richard. *Supervision: The Direction of People at Work*. Boston: Allyn and Bacon, Inc., current edition.

Rue, Leslie W., and Lloyd L. Byars. *Supervision: Key Link to Productivity*. Chicago, IL: Irwin, current edition.

Steinmetz, Lawrence L., and Ralph H. Todd, Jr. *Supervision: First-Line Management*. Homewood, IL: Irwin, current edition.

Timm, Paul R. *Supervision*. St. Paul: West Publishing Co., current edition.

Travers, Alfred W. *Supervision: Techniques and New Dimensions*. Englewood Cliffs, NJ: Prentice Hall, Inc. current edition.

Von der Embse, Thomas J. *Supervision: Managerial Skills for a New Era*. New York: Macmillan, current edition.

Current textbook used by a local college or university for a course on the subject.

3

CREDIT RECOMMENDATIONS

The Center For Adult Learning and Educational Credentials of the American Council on Education (ACE) has reviewed and evaluated the DANTES examination development process. ACE has made the following recommendations:

Area or Course
  Equivalent: Principles of Supervision
Level: Lower-level baccalaureate
Amount of Credit: Three (3) semester hours
Source: ACE Commission on
                         Educational Credit
                         and Credentials

INFORMATION

Colleges and universities that would like to review copies of tests, have additional information about the national norming, or assistance in local norming or score validation studies should write to: DANTES Program, Mail Stop 11-P, The Chauncey Group International, 664 Rosedale Road, Princeton, New Jersey 08540.

It is advisable that schools develop a consistent policy about awarding credit based on scores from this test and that the policy be reviewed periodically. The Chauncey Group will be happy to help schools in this effort.

Correct Responses: 1.B; 2.C; 3.D; 4.D; 5.A; 6.C; 7.C; 8.B; 9.B; 10.A.

I.N. D204314

NOTES

NOTES

NOTES

NOTES

NOTES

NOTES

NOTES

NOTES

NOTES

NOTES